INFANTILISED

INFANTILISED

How Our Culture Killed Adulthood

Keith Hayward

CONSTABLE

CONSTABLE

First published in Great Britain in 2024 by Constable

1 3 5 7 9 10 8 6 4 2

A CIP catalogue record for this book is available from the British Library.

Hardback ISBN 978-1-4087-2059-2

Typeset in Minion Pro by Hewer Text UK Ltd, Edinburgh
Printed and bound in Great Britain by Clays Ltd, Elcograf S.p.A

Papers used by Constable are from well-managed forests and other responsible sources.

MIX
Paper | Supporting
responsible forestry
FSC
www.fsc.org   FSC® C104740

Constable
An imprint of
Little, Brown Book Group
Carmelite House
50 Victoria Embankment
London EC4Y 0DZ

An Hachette UK Company
www.hachette.co.uk

www.littlebrown.co.uk

For Mum and Dad. Wonderful parents, exemplary adults.

I need a man. Not a little boy with a Teddy Bear.

Mila Kunis's character Lori
Collins in the 2012 movie *Ted*

Contents

Introduction

Our Infantilised World

Adulthood is not ageing well.

We live in an age debased by a cult of youth, where grown men and women talk and behave as if they've forgotten what it means to be a competent adult and where the vice of immaturity has become a virtue. At the same time, young children talk and behave in ways that suggest a wisdom and knowingness far beyond their years. This book explains how this strange and disquieting role reversal came about, what it means for society, and whether or not there is anything we can do to combat these pathologies and their tightening stranglehold on our culture.

It takes as its starting point the nagging feeling that something has gone fundamentally wrong with adulthood; that wherever you turn, grown-up competencies and adult values are under assault from a contemporary culture driven by infantile preoccupations and let's-pretend distractions. There's every chance you've experienced this feeling as you go about your daily round. Maybe you've felt it while negotiating a world of pointless and condescending health-and-safety signage that tells you how to use a handrail or a flight of stairs, or in the wheedling tone of that Tannoy announcer who reminds you to 'stay hydrated' on a hot day? Perhaps you've sensed it as you resign yourself to the fact you're being watched over at every turn by an all-seeing surveillance apparatus, like a (big) baby trapped in the swivelling camera arc of a (big) baby monitor?[1] Or it could be that you've intuited your diminishing adult autonomy when being talked down to by barely educated politicians or, even worse, told what to think by entirely uneducated celebrities? But whenever and wherever it happens, you're left with a sinking feeling that something's not quite right; that instead of inhabiting a mature, grown-up world of foresight and experience, you've been enrolled, without your consent, into something resembling universalised adult day care.

While you may have sensed society's creeping descent into infantilisation in everything from those irritating 'Be Kind' posters on the Underground to Donald Trump's penchant for bestowing adolescent nicknames on his political opponents, understanding the roots and causes of the phenomenon is not quite so easy. In fact, one of the strange things about our infantilised world is that, despite its transparent and myriad idiocies, hardly anyone stops to consider how this situation came about and what it could potentially mean for the existing liberal order. Perhaps it's just too deranging, making it difficult for us to marshal the necessary clarity and balance to understand its roots. Perhaps, too, it's because we don't want to appear 'uncool' – after all, only a fuddy-duddy criticises youth culture or extols the virtues of adulthood these days. But whatever the reason, infantilisation as a subject of analysis has been almost entirely ignored by mainstream commentators. This book addresses this oversight by making it clear that infantilism is not some niche subject of interest only to psychiatrists or scholars of the life course, but is in fact something relevant to almost everybody, irrespective of age or political persuasion. It captures a story about a cultural phenomenon that is simultaneously everywhere but nowhere, pervasive yet oddly overlooked. It provides answers

2

to many of those questions that may already be troubling you, such as why do so many young (and increasingly not-so-young) people seem only too happy to eschew adulthood in favour of elongated teenagerdom? What will society look like as age-old adult competencies – parenting, emotional self-reliance, the importance of a work ethic, etc. – continue to be assailed by an infantilised culture? And perhaps most importantly, who exactly stands to gain from turning our world into a giant pop-cultural playpen? In short, this book explains how we got ourselves into this mess and what, if anything, we can do to get out of it.

At the centre of the story is *culturally induced infantilisation* – a deep-rooted and deeply corrosive process behind the culture of immaturity that today thrives in almost every sphere of society. It is there at the movie theatre, where Spandex superhero films and tiresome comic-book spin-offs dominate the box office at the expense of more complex human stories. It is there in our universities, in the 'adulting classes', 'safe spaces' and 'crying rooms' that are the inevitable and embarrassing by-products of an education system that mollycoddles students instead of preparing them for the inescapable challenges of adult life. It is there in the way grown men act like hysterical teenage boyband fans when screeching their opinions on forums and in comment threads about which overpriced footballer 'their' club should buy next. It is there on our television screens in the constant parade of emotionally incontinent sports personalities and delusional reality stars, and in a deliberately lulling new form of *adult* programming known as 'second-screen content' or 'ambient TV' – televisual Muzak created to allow viewers to watch programmes while simultaneously scrolling on their phones. And it is there, perhaps most obviously, in society's pathological obsession with social media – the always-available digital pacifier designed specifically to reward infantile dispositions and normalise childish fantasies.

Such developments suggest we have entered a distinct new phase of capitalist modernity – a patronising, anti-adult era characterised by adolescent diversions and pop-cultural infantilisers. For me personally, the feeling that our adult-oriented society was being eclipsed by something more desperate and childish started over a decade ago. At that point, I found myself frustrated and dismayed by a culture that appeared to be constantly spamming me with infantile ephemera. Turn on a screen and it seemed like every other commercial was employing babyish jingles and cutesy cartoon animals in campaigns for adult goods and services. Around the same time, we also entered the era of the over-exposed 'man-boy'. From Jeremy Clarkson to the emasculated Louis C.K. and his masturbatory fantasies, from Russell Brand (who in 2015 was inexplicably voted 'the fourth most significant thinker in the world' by *Prospect* magazine) to Pat McAfee, Michael Irvin and all those other braying American NFL TV hosts, postmodern man-boys were everywhere, their hair-trigger opinions inflated, their politics taken seriously. But it was infantilising developments taking place in my professional life that really clued me in to the fact that society had a serious problem.

I am a criminologist who studies urban crime with a special interest in the seductions and repulsions of deviance, violence and transgression. This is a world away from adulting classes and bloviating man-boys, and so let me offer a few words of authorial explanation as to why I'm researching and writing on this subject. The truth of it is that there was no single moment that catalysed my interest in infantilism. It started with a cumulative apprehension, built up over several years, that the newly arrived eighteen-year-old undergraduates on my criminology courses resembled less mature teenagers on the cusp of adulthood and more fearful schoolchildren adrift in an alien world of adult autonomy. This sense that something odd was happening, something significant and convulsive, crystallised with each passing semester, as the tentacles of infantilism penetrated ever deeper into university culture. I had been teaching a class on terrorism for over a decade, but now I was getting student emails claiming the content was 'too challenging', the images in my lecture slides 'upsetting' and 'disturbing'. If this wasn't bad enough, random parents started popping up on campus, fussing about their child's workload, or acting as crypto-lawyers in plagiarism hearings.

Even the criminals I was studying were behaving like kids. Back in the early-2010s, while researching a book on the commodification of crime in the media, I trawled through hundreds, if not thousands, of caught-on-camera moments of violence that had been uploaded to various streaming sites. Very early in that process it became clear to me that, although these were serious incidents, punctuated by anger, rage, fear and indignation, something else was discernible beyond the broken bones and concussions. Look closely at the faces of the protagonists involved in these incidents – the juvenile-but-serious street fights, the anti-adult velvet-rope nightclub altercations, the customer–retailer interactions gone horribly wrong – and one could see that these moments of violent spectacle were often little more than frenzied temper tantrums. Perpetrated by individuals with an abundance of confidence but a deficit of adult self-control, these videos conveyed a sense of perpetual adolescence – schoolyard bully-boy (and -girl) antics scaled up for the big city. For all their seriousness and criminality, the individuals captured in these grainy videos evoked, for me at least, a profound sense of waning adulthood.

This nascent feeling that parts of society were beating a hasty retreat from adulthood was also evident in the criminal justice system. In the 2010s, prison researchers started documenting increased levels of what they termed 'psychosocial immaturity' in young offenders aged between eighteen and twenty-five.[2] The balance between security and discipline in prisons is always a deli-cate one, and so penologists were understandably worried about what this finding would mean for the future of order maintenance. On the ground, however, the fallout from growing prisoner imma-turity was already apparent. Talking with staff during a prison visit in the mid-2010s, one officer told me that he and his colleagues regularly dealt with inmates who lacked even the most basic adult competencies, including cooking, cleaning and, on more than one occasion, even tying their own shoelaces.

Attuned to infantilising developments, I started seeing exam-ples everywhere. On social media, young men, browbeaten by the vogueish trope of 'toxic masculinity', declared that they no longer had any interest in adult responsibilities like marriage, fatherhood or even saving for the future. In the workplace, things that used to be dismissed as office politics were recast as 'bullying' – a school-yard comparison that felt appropriate given many corporate offices now physically resembled school classrooms, with 'play spaces', kindness aphorisms, and workstations shrunk down to childish dimensions. The mood music of infantilisation could also be heard emanating from our elite institutions, as museum and gallery curators began to slather their holdings with warning labels and expository text informing visitors that they might find certain objects and artworks 'provocative', 'unsettling' or 'prob-lematic'. Even my academic colleagues, who really should have known better, were complaining to me about how the lives and interests of their children had started to merge with their own.

But while infantilisation was taking hold all around us, it was its impact on the political sphere that concerned me the most. Here, my issue was not simply with politicians acting like attention-seeking adolescents on TikTok, or celebrity pundits stupefying the political arena with their ill-informed opinions. Rather, what worried me was the emergence of a new anti-adult form of political expression evident in everything from 'Brexit-derangement syndrome' to the look-at-me hissy fits of middle-class Just Stop Oil protestors. However, it was the toxic fallout that followed in the wake of Donald Trump's election that really brought home the full extent of the new infantocracy.[3] In a society of adults, voters accept the results of democratic elections and move on – or at least they used to. Unable to comprehend the simple fact that, in large swathes of the American hinterland, Hillary Clinton was about as popular as asbestos, coastal Democrats and campus liberals threw their toys, and their dignity, out of the pram. Rather than accept the result, they called for 'resistance'. Instead of using the moment to reflect on their own party's numerous shortcomings, they roiled in adolescent rage. For the American novelist, Bret Easton Ellis, the indignation of the anti-Trump movement was too much to take. With characteristic frankness, he described Clintonite sore losers as 'big fucking babies', commenting that their incessant whinging reminded him 'of the complaints of spoiled children at a birthday party when they didn't win the relay race, and who wanted the race rerun with different rules, while stomping their feet, arms crossed, pinched faces crimson and wet with tears'.[4]

Fast forward four years and it was the turn of Trump supporters to act like unsupervised teenagers at a house party. Cosplaying as revolutionaries, angry, red-faced middle-aged men and women thought that if they screamed loud enough and waved a few hand-made flags about they would eventually get their own way and overturn the result of a democratic election. While millions were rightly enraged by what took place on Capitol Hill on 6 January 2021, few framed it as an expression of an infantilised society – but that's exactly what it was. Indeed, the more I thought about it, the more I came to understand that many of today's antagonistic conflicts and culture-war spats could and should be viewed through the lens of infantilism. Seen in this way, infantilisation represents something far more serious than just the elongation of youthful pursuits. It suggests a new way of viewing the world that's already shaping our history by damaging democracy, destabilising institutions and tearing civilisation apart.

What follows, then, is a story about how the whims, concerns and affectations (cultural, political, pseudo-intellectual) of young people have come to be prioritised over and above those associated with mature adulthood. But let's not get ahead of ourselves. Before we cross over the border into Kidultland, we must start, as any good guidebook should, by defining our primary object of study – *infantilisation*.

Defining infantilisation, introducing 'the Kidult'

Pick up a book on developmental psychology and you'll see the word infant defined as the period of a child's life before it can walk or speak – the Latin origin of the term being *infāns*, meaning 'unable to speak' or 'speechless'. However, the word infant also has another more common-sense application that sees it used as a general synonym for a baby or a young child, thus meaning 'infant' (and the developmental stage, infancy) often covers a slightly longer and less clearly definable period of early life. Things get more interesting when it comes to the adjective 'infantile'. Logically enough, the primary function of this word is to define/describe matters 'of or relating to infants or infancy', but importantly it also has a second, derogatory use, meaning childishness or 'to display or suggest a lack of maturity'. From here, the term is modified into the transitive verb, 'to infantilise', meaning to 'treat (someone) as a child or in a way which denies their maturity in age or experience'. The noun 'infantilisation' adds an active dimension that refers specifically to the '*act of infantilising*, the act of prolonging an infantile state in a person by treating them as an infant'.[5]

Beyond the dictionary, the term 'infantilism' has a specific connotation within psychiatry, where it is used to describe a defence mechanism or psychological regression in which an older child or adult exhibits the cognitive and emotional behaviour of an infant. In the wider academy, a lack of research on infantilisation means scholarly definitions are few and far between. However, the sociologist Simon Gottschalk recently came up with a useful summary of the diminished and childlike behaviour that characterises the infantilised actor: 'An infantile individual is a person who fails to enact the cognitive, affective, and interpersonal qualities that are considered appropriate to his or her age in the life-cycle, and who instead enacts those that s/he acquired in a previous stage of development. The infantile individual is a regressive one.'[6]

The emergence of this 'regressive' or infantilised individual has not, of course, gone unnoticed. As the noise emanating from our pop-cultural crèche grew ever shriller, a series of news articles and editorials started appearing in the first decade of the twenty-first century that tried to make sense of the situation.[7] Very often, these commentaries took as their starting point the phenomenon of the grown-up male, both factual and fictional, who refused to relinquish his pre-adulthood lifestyle; a slacker-striver character memorably described by one critic as the twenty-first century's 'disaffected man-child'. These articles were aided in their efforts by a series of neologisms that began creeping into popular consciousness around the same time, including adultescent, rejuvenile, boy-men and, most memorably, 'Kidult'.[8] The novel nature of these terms afforded journalists the opportunity to attach their own specific concerns to the Kidult figure. As a result, adult immaturity became a convenient vehicle to discuss themes such as the end of masculinity and the demise of the patriarchy, the triumph of popular culture over high art, and the failure of young adults to flee the family nest.[9] Initially, many of these articles used cinematic representations of the regressive, infantilised adult as their critical starting point; representations which were then projected back onto society in an effort to make sense of what some had started to call the long road to adulthood. For example, in his influential 2014 *New York Times* article, 'The death of adulthood in American culture', the columnist A. O. Scott recognised that the on-screen depiction of arrested male development was not simply a Hollywood trope, but a symbolic representation of a much wider problem relating to the life course: '. . . the antics of the comic man-boys were not merely repetitive; in their couch-bound humor we can detect the glimmers of something new, something that helped speed adulthood to its terminal crisis. Unlike the antiheroes of eras past, whose rebellion still accepted the fact of adulthood as its premise, the man-boys simply refused to grow up, and did so proudly.'[10]

Scott was right to point out that what was happening went much deeper than a Hollywood trend. Elsewhere, in the real world, a host of contemporaneous demographic developments were already under way that suggested twenty-somethings were indeed proceeding through life in a markedly different way to their parents and grandparents. In 2016, the Pew Research Center noted that, for the first time in more than 130 years, American eighteen- to thirty-four-year-olds were more likely to be living with their parents than with a spouse or partner in a separate residence. The same organisation also reported that, in 2012, 78 per cent of American men and 67 per cent of American women had never been married by age 25 – up from 28 per cent of men and 13 per cent of women in 1960.[11] Equivalent demographic shifts have also taken place in the UK, where recently the Office for National Statistics (ONS) reported that, for the first time in recorded history, half of all women in England and Wales remained childless by their thirtieth birthday. The ONS also reported that the average (median) age at marriage for opposite-sex couples in 2020 was 35.3 years for men and 33.2 for women – roughly ten years older than the average age at marriage in the early 1960s.[12] Obviously, using marriage as a fixed indicator of adulthood is problematic these days. But even so, as one American commentator has pointed out, if current demographic trends regarding relationships and parenting continue, today's youngsters are 'on track to be the generation with the largest number of single people' and 'the lowest birth rate on record'.[13]

This sense that the transition to adulthood is more convoluted and confused than it was in the twentieth century is further supported when one considers recent developments surrounding the concept of adolescence.[14] Traditionally understood as the physiological phase of development triggered by the onset of puberty,[15] adolescence is now surrounded by such confusion that even the experts appear unclear about where this phenomenon begins and ends. In America, the Society for Research on Adolescence, for example, has historically been 'devoted to research on the "second decade of life"'. However, in the UK, a recent piece in *The Lancet Childhood & Adolescent Health* journal argued that adolescence should be extended from the ages of ten to nineteen years to ten to twenty-four.[16] The US health professionals' association, the Society for Adolescent Health and Medicine, meanwhile has pushed the number back even further, stating some time ago that its remit is to care for persons 'aged 10–26'. And this direction of travel is only going one way. Dr Brenna Hassett, an anthropologist at University College London, recently went so far as to state that today childhood can last up until the age of forty ('Humans tend to have a long, long period of dependency – I'm going with 40 but you know, it could be much longer or much shorter depending on what your parents are willing to tolerate').[17]

Over a decade has passed since both the Pew Research Center data and the clutch of stories about adultescents and rejuveniles that momentarily preoccupied journalists like A. O. Scott. In that time, the cultural and social forces driving infantilisation and its subsequent transformation of our tastes, values and modes of being have only deepened. For example, in previous eras it never occurred to anyone that adulthood should come with an instruction manual. Today, however, go to any bookshop and you'll find a slurry of self-help books offering guidance to young people on how they should manage the self through those 'tricky years' between eighteen and thirty. Likewise, in 2022, when the fast-food giant McDonald's decided that their grown-up customers could no longer exist without the option of ordering a 'Happy Meal for adults', few seemed surprised – let alone concerned. But beyond such cultural expressions of infantilism, it's clear something else is happening, something far more unsettling.

The death of the 'life stage'

Something odd has happened to children's books: they are no longer the preserve of children. Whether it's the despoilation of classic stories by turning them into tawdry horror movies (2023's *Winnie the Pooh: Blood and Honey*, 2020's *Gretel & Hansel: A Grim Fairy Tale*, 2024's *Mickey's Mouse Trap*, etc.), or the recycling of adult obsessions, including sexual and sadistic fantasies, in rebooted kid's comic books, childhood innocence is being subverted to feed the demands of an adult society that seems incapable of growing up. Meanwhile, actual children's books have taken a distinctly adult turn. *Baby's First Book of Banned Books* is an illustrated text written to introduce 'babies and toddlers to key lessons learned through infamously banned books'. It is typical of a new wave of overtly political children's literature that replaces fun and imaginative playfulness with hectoring ideological messaging. Why has this happened? Why is Anglo-American society actively promoting the blurring of long-standing generational borders and conventions?

Historically, in adult societies, individuals have had no difficulty dividing the life course into a series of culturally defined, age-graded roles – a process human development scholars term 'informal age structuring'. In our infantilised world, however, established sequential life categories are fast breaking down, as the concepts of childhood, adolescence and adulthood are battered on all sides by society's fixation with cultural relativism and its inability to exert a semblance of adult authority. Things have even reached the point where certain lobby groups are now promoting a concept known as 'age queering': 'the refusal to conform to the social constructs of age – namely, rejecting the young/old binary, [and] embracing the measurement of time without clinging to the idea that time is linear'.[18] Such extraordinary developments suggest something has gone fundamentally wrong with the way many people are proceeding through the life course. The question, of course, is whether or not it's already too late to do anything about it.

Famously, in the study of human personality, the post-Freudian psychologist Erik Erikson claimed that a person's identity develops over the life span as each individual passes through a fixed sequence of 'eight stages of psychosocial development' – each stage emerging out of and building on the next.[19] Extending Freud's classic account of childhood development into adolescence, adulthood and, ultimately, old age, Erikson asserted that, as individuals proceed though each stage of the life course, they 'face an interaction of opposing attitudes, which leads to a conflict, or *psychosocial crisis*. Resolution of the crisis produces an appropriate *basic strength* and enables a person to move on to the next stage.'[20] Erikson's developmental framework has been the subject of much criticism, but his underlying point that personality development proceeds because of the inherently 'oppositional attitudes' that exist *between* stages of the life cycle is important if we want to understand why life stages have started to feel so indistinct. In this book, I argue that the primary reason infantilisation is so prevalent today is because the innate *opposition* between life stages has largely disappeared. Consequently, rather than being distinct – or oppositional in Erikson's terms – life stages have started to collapse in on each other.

Several years ago, in a bid to make sense of this situation, I developed the concept of representational life stage dissolution, a merging process that makes it increasingly difficult for many young people to differentiate and disassociate themselves from the generation immediately ahead of them – and indeed vice versa.[21] An ongoing development rather than a distinct phase, life stage dissolution is a way of conceptualising the implosion of previously *oppositional* life stages. This book is an attempt to chart life stage dissolution's development to its logical conclusion. I argue that if society continues along its current path, life stage dissolution could result in the end of the established, centuries-old paradigms of childhood and adulthood. In their place will emerge a new behavioural type: a perpetually immature *adult-child amalgam*. Although still in its emergent state, this new hybridised social figure is the inevitable by-product of economic and cultural forces that, under the cover of postmodernism, have undercut the psychosocial distinctions that traditionally differen-tiated and disassociated one generation from another. In other words, life stage dissolution is slowly but surely undermining the concept of a linear or sequential life course and replacing it with something that more closely resembles *generational mulch*.

The fallout of life stage dissolution is all around us, most obvi-ously in the guise of infantilisation, but also in the secondary process of *adultification*. From schoolchildren being given politi-cal platforms at major geopolitical events like COP21, to claims that toddlers as young as three are racist and must be taught to 'reject the "smog" of white privilege', adultification is a conceptual term for thinking about the way children are being treated as the cultural and moral equivalents of adults. By impacting the life course at both ends of the age spectrum, adultification and its obverse cultural pressure, infantilisation, have combined to create a society that exhibits a profound sense of generational confusion. At least two troubling consequences flow from this situation.

First, the bi-directional forces of life stage dissolution mean we now inhabit a topsy-turvy world characterised by all sorts of bizarre generational anomalies. For example, while millions of adults play children's games on their phones, major toy manufacturers develop smart devices and kid's toys with 'adult features' (Mattel's proposed Aristotle device, for example, includes an AI-driven speaker that connects to smart-home features and the internet, the stated goal being to 'simplify parenting', i.e., to relinquish the tasks of parental guidance and supervision to the algorithm). Even governments seem confused about who is a child and who is an adult. It used to be the case that European nations would condemn barbaric terrorist groups like Islamic State and Boko Haram for failing to draw a line between young people and adults when it came to the use of children as soldiers or executioners in combat zones. Yet, in recent years, governments in the West appear equally confused about this issue. In the UK, in the period between 2016 and 2019, more than six hundred children under the age of six were referred to the Home Office's counterterrorism Prevent scheme, including one four-year-old boy whose terrorist boasts turned out to be a reference to the video game *Fortnite*.[22]

Likewise, consider the current situation regarding one of the most important moral issues we have in society: the sexualisation of children. For decades, feminist scholars voiced concerns about the 'mainstreaming of pornography' and its harmful effects on young people. Today, however, having largely ignored this advice, childhood is being threatened by something even worse – a coordinated campaign to erode the barriers designed to protect young people from sexual exploitation. In example after example, from the use of paedophilic symbolism by high-fashion house Balenciaga to the dubious content of Drag Queen Story Hour and *The Family Sex Show* to Netflix series like *Cuties* (2020) and *Sex Unzipped* (2021), it appears that some factions in the upper echelons of the culture industry are extremely confused about where adult sexuality starts and childhood ends. Indeed, such is the confusion about children's place in society that some commentators consider it acceptable to moot the idea of 'porn for children',[23] or even worse to publicly promote the acronym MAP [minor attracted person] as a way of 'destigmatising' (i.e. shamefully excusing) paedophilia.[24] Likewise, transgender activists regularly speak of the so-called 'transexual child', with trans rights lobbyists arguing that physiological interventions like puberty blockers and gender realignment surgery should be made available to children as young as twelve. Unfortunately, we can't even look to policymakers or influential NGOs to draw a red line when it comes to the sexualisation of children. For some time now, the World Health Organisation has been promoting the idea that 'sexuality education' should start 'from birth', including instruction about 'early childhood masturbation' for children aged four and under.[25] In the twenty-first century, by treating children in this manner, as the moral and cultural equivalents of adults, we are essentially annulling the idea of the life course. As a result, we now exist in such a bizarre, upside-down world that a judge presiding in an English court is prepared to accept that an adult teacher who had sex with one of his sixteen-year-old pupils had been groomed *by the student* rather than the other way round.[26]

Second, as life stages blur and the psychosocial experiences of adults and children become more interchangeable, conflicts *between* generations will intensify. This might seem paradoxical, but as the ongoing 'generational war' between Millennials/Gen Zers and Baby Boomers makes clear, as individuals at different stages of the life cycle start to resemble each other (in terms of their mindset, interests and concerns), generational cohorts end up competing against each other for the same cultural and economic resources. This type of inter-generational conflict is, of course, not new. As early as 1992, Lawrence Grossberg documented the growing enmity between Generation X and its Baby Boomer parents. However, at that point, the tension remained cultural, specifically a generational turf war over which group had the right to be considered 'young', as Boomers sought to elongate youth 'by redefining it as an attitude' as much as a physical or biological state.[27]

Three decades on, what started out as a cultural skirmish has escalated into a full-on battle for economic and political supremacy. Two bi-directional strands of resentment are responsible for the emergence of this 'every generation for itself' mindset. On the one hand, Millennials and Gen Zers blame the older generation for the problems of the present day – some even going so far as to question the right of 'ancient Boomers' to even exist (the fabulously contemptuous put-down, 'OK Boomer', nicely epitomises this sort of thinking). On the other hand, Baby Boomers, and my fellow Gen Xers, respond to being maligned in this way by unfairly castigating today's youngsters as a generation of workshy, TikTok-obsessed, trophy kids. With the obvious exception of newspaper columnists, and perhaps Greta Thunberg, it's hard to see who benefits from all this cohort-based negativity. Not only is it counterproductive in terms of establishing any sort of political consensus, but it also masks the real reason for all this pent-up generational tension.

We often forget that for many people young adulthood is a period of considerable economic hardship. (For example, youth unemployment in the US has been about twice the national average since the 1970s). The global downturn has only exacerbated this problem, as over the last fifteen years, the fortunes of young adults have deteriorated faster than any other demographic group.[28] Consequently, to be a young person today often means being hemmed in by a depressing combination of precarious employment, wages that fail to keep up with inflation, mounting student debt and overpriced rent. But it's the overheated real estate market that more than anything has driven a wedge between Baby Boomers and subsequent generations. Only a few decades ago, buying a home was a common landmark on the road to adulthood. Today, however, home ownership is seen by most young people as an unattainable luxury. In the UK, for example, housing experts predict that a third of the Millennial generation will never be able to afford to purchase a house and will thus be trapped in the rental sector – or their parents' house – for ever. For Gen Z, that figure is even higher. In contrast, over half of the Baby Boomer generation owned their own homes by the time they were thirty. Any sane society would do something about this. But instead of government action, or even public sympathy, young people are criticised as if the situation was somehow their fault; that if only they stopped buying expensive coffees and upgrading their iPhones, they would magically be able to afford that bedsit on the Fulham Road.

This nasty politics of reciprocal generational enmity is what happens when life stages collapse, and people start to look and feel the same. As material aspirations and cultural lifestyles align, and individuals of different ages assimilate and develop ideas in the same way, people end up reinterpreting those above and below them in the life course as competing factions in a Hobbesian generational battle of all against all. However, most of this intergenerational strife is actually a phony war, a fabricated opposition based on socially constructed 'generationalism'. What today's generational wars in fact represent is just another twist along the well-trammelled paradox-of-equality axis, i.e., as differentials narrow – in this case between established stages of the life course – differences become all the more noticeable.

Infantilism and the 'culture wars'

Although life stage dissolution is happening all around us, eroding what Jacopo Bernardini calls 'the canonical indicators of adulthood' as distinct categories, it's not something that has generated a great deal of commentary. This is no longer the case, however, when it comes to the more singular phenomenon of infantilisation. Not that long ago, discussions about infantilism were limited largely to psychiatrists, psychologists and the odd cultural theorist. In the last few years, however, the term has broken free of its roots in the 'psych industry' and started to feature more prominently in popular and political discourse. One of the consequences of this more general usage is that infantilisation is now a regularly, if haphazardly, deployed narrative in the twenty-first-century culture wars, with important political and psychological implications.

For example, in contemporary feminist commentary it's now quite common to see the term mobilised in all sorts of different contexts, from critiquing young men who seek out 'MILFs' and so-called 'Mommy Girlfriend' figures to consumer products that supposedly challenge the unfair age stereotyping of middle-aged women. Similarly, on Twitter/X, hardly a day goes by without a debate bubbling up about the 'toxicity' of age-gap relationships, or whether or not it's 'infantilising' for male workers to describe a female colleague as 'brilliant' or 'clever'.[29] Infantilisation has also emerged as something of a concern for gay rights activists in relation to the way certain gay celebrities are coddled and patronised in the media. For example, after the NBA player Jason Collins came out in 2014, Bret Easton Ellis coined the term 'the Gay Man as Magical Elf' to describe how media-approved gay men like Collins are regularly treated as 'over-sensitive babies', or as Ellis put it, 'as some kind of saintly, adorable ET whose sole purpose is to remind us *only* about tolerance and our prejudices'.

If anything, the use of the term infantilisation as a rhetorical device is even more pronounced in contemporary debates about race and ethnicity. As we will see later in the book, one of the features of contemporary culture is the relationship between infantilisation and a preoccupation with victimhood and vulnerability, a dynamic that is amplified when seen through the prism of race. Drawing on themes such as safety, mental health, awareness raising, etc., it has become almost standard practice in certain areas of society to make concessions and remove barriers in an effort to combat racism or address a purported lack of diversity. It is a form of social rebalancing that can take any number of different forms, including removing standardised grammar from English language teaching in an effort to increase 'linguistic justice', suggesting employers give black employees a day off work after high-profile racial killings, and arguing that more needs to be done to make the British countryside less 'intimidating' for BAME communities. But although well intentioned, many view such initiatives as deeply infantilising. In particular, a core group of black writers such as John McWhorter, Coleman Hughes, Adolph Reed and Thomas Sowell have argued that this approach to race relations essentially reinforces the politics of low expectations and in doing so recasts black people as fragile children. For example, in a now infamous article critiquing Robin DiAngelo's tendentious 2018 book, *White Fragility*, McWhorter wrote, 'And I cannot imagine that any Black readers could willingly submit themselves to DiAngelo's ideas while considering themselves adults of ordinary self-regard and strength. Few books about race have more openly infantilized Black people than this supposedly authoritative tome.'[30]

Pull the lens back far enough, and it's clear that infantilising language and comparisons feature right across the contemporary culture wars. Even the concept of Wokeness itself has been criticised for adopting a worldview that childishly divides society up along Manichean lines of good and evil. However, while many 'social justice warriors' are guilty of over-simplifying arguments and sacrificing reason on the altar of identity politics and nebulous theories of 'lived experience', we must also recognise, as astute commentators like McWhorter and Hughes clearly do, that lots of Woke progressives clearly have good intentions. Thus, rather than demonising young people and their ideological concerns, we should instead acknowledge that today's often grating mode of Woke political expression is the product of patterns of behaviour and emotional states that are normalised features of our infantilised age. As a result, much of today's progressive ideology is sadly a form of magical thinking, a set of vague ideas and superstition-like beliefs that float freely from older-order concerns such as class consciousness or the protection of the rights of workers from capitalist exploitation.

In all these examples, it's clear that, whether implicitly or explicitly, infantilisation is now an integral element of the late-modern culture wars, deployed in all sorts of different ways to prop up all sorts of political positions. But it's also much more than that – it's also an essential concept for mapping out core aspects of the world in which we now live. Hence the need to enlarge and refine the term so it's more than just a rhetorical hammer for beating down ideological adversaries, or a pejorative label to delegitimise stuff we don't like. What follows, then, is my attempt to do just that; to expand and, if you like, upgrade infantilisation so that we have a better sense of what it is and how it's transforming society.

My goal in writing this book is to introduce the concept of infantilisation to as large an audience as possible. I have intentionally cast my net wide, both in terms of the examples used to illustrate the phenomenon, and the themes and disciplines mobilised to make my arguments. That said, although I frequently draw on cultural examples and scholarship from an array of different countries and contexts, it's important to be clear from the outset that my observations and criticisms of infantilism refer specifically to developments taking place in the Anglo-American world.[31] This is not to suggest that life stage dissolution and infantilisation are limited only to the United Kingdom and the United States. Far from it. There is mounting evidence that indicates elongated adolescence is being experienced everywhere from Italy to India.[32] Rather it is to point out that, as a by-product of late capitalism, infantilism has reached its most developed state in the US and the UK – the two societies which have most enthusiastically embraced postmodernism and its cultural logics.

It should be obvious by now that this book is an unapologetic critique of infantilisation and the cultural, economic and technological developments that engender it. However, this does not mean that adopting a youthful perspective on life or striving to stave off the depredations of old age is inherently bad. Quite the contrary. As eminent figures like the psychologist Abraham Maslow and the cultural historian Johan Huizinga pointed out decades ago, whether it's the positive traits associated with childlike creativity, or games playing and the playing of games, our lives are more enjoyable when we occasionally give ourselves over to youthful pursuits. For that reason, you shouldn't feel bad about whiling away a few hours playing video games or watching *You, Me and Dupree* – I know I don't.

The problem, of course, comes when mature adults exist entirely in a lifeworld of toddler-like self-indulgence, when all sense of mature responsibility is subsumed by what the philosopher Slavoj Žižek calls 'the injunction to enjoy'. The tragedy is that in a society fixated with puerile pastimes and juvenile distractions, the line between natural moments of intermittent childlike spontaneity and all-encompassing arrested development is getting thinner by the minute.

Whether you choose to gaze at society through a political, cultural, psychological or moral lens, it's clear we are heading for trouble – generational trouble. The gusts of infantilisation blown in by post-modernism and its associated capitalist logics have reshaped contemporary society into something resembling a cross between a Neverland fantasy and a low-risk play area. The evidence for this claim is all around us. Consider, for example, the public sphere. Previously, politics was characterised by reasoned argument and mature critical debate. Today, thanks to the clown world of social media and a TV-marinated commentariat, the vast majority of political argumentation has all the discernment of a baby spitting out food it hasn't even had time to taste. Things are even worse in the realm of popular culture where, instead of being seen as an aspirational state, adulthood is depicted as something either to be avoided entirely or, like an ageing gigolo who continues to ply his trade despite diminishing returns, a past-its-prime irrelevance from a bygone era.

But just because it's no country for old (wo)men out there doesn't mean that young people have it easy. Just as former bastions of adult competence are collapsing all around us, so too are the social dispensations and ring-fenced spaces that used to be reserved exclusively for children. In the same way Hollywood studios have altered the tone and humour of children's movies and rebranded them as 'family films' in a bid to expand their demographic appeal, late-modern capitalism has adultified young

23

people to such an extent that we must now talk about the existence of a *conjoined adult–child life experience*. This blurring of long-standing generational borders and conventions is clearly one of the reasons why today's parents have become so protective of their offspring. But while bourgeois parents frantically coddle and cosset their sprite-sized Caesars and Cleopatras, deep down they already know they're fighting a losing battle against the encroachment of capitalism into the lives of their children. Before long, the contemporary child, thanks in large part to the internet, is lured away from childhood pursuits and carefully repositioned in a pop-cultural world that exists somewhere betwixt and between youth and adulthood. Once there, no amount of 'hothouse' or 'helicopter' parenting can stave off the fantasies and consensual hallucinations promulgated by the increasingly interconnected dreamscapes of social media and lifestyle capitalism.

In a brief discussion of the pathological dimension of infantile narcissism, the French aesthetic philosopher Paul Virilio talks about how consumer capitalism has created what he calls 'false adults' and 'false children' – captured and confused actors hijacked by consumer desire to the extent they have become estranged from the very culture into which they were originally socialised.[33] As late-modern society becomes ever more populated with infant-ilised false adults and adultified false children, it will become increasingly impossible for the established categories associated with human maturation to survive. Already, in almost every sphere of life, a series of subtle yet meaningful changes are under way that are collectively transforming the human condition to such an extent that we currently have no choice but to re-evaluate what we mean when we talk of childhood, adolescence and, most importantly, the traditional paradigm of mature adulthood.

This may not be the world we want, but it's the world we've created, and whether you like it or not, you're living in it.

PART I

RISE OF THE KIDULT

The belief that individuals proceed through a series of distinct life stages has been a feature of human history for centuries. From the 'Wheel of Life' renderings of medieval Europe to Carl Jung's allegory of life as a 'journey of the sun through the sky', life has repeatedly been represented as a developmental odyssey through a series of distinctive, if inconsistent, life phases. Today, however, things are changing. We now exist in an age predicated on the primacy of youth: a state of affairs that makes a mockery of the notion that human maturation takes place via a sequence of widely understood processual life stages. Whether it's people in their twenties, thirties, forties and now even their fifties failing to step over the boundary into the world of grown-ups, or subtler transformations taking place elsewhere in the life course, it's clear that as we proceed deeper into the twenty-first century, the life cycle has started to slip its gears. This slippage, this sense of freewheeling on the road to adult maturity, should concern us all. In almost every sphere of life, a series of changes are under way that collectively are transforming the concept of adulthood from something based on discernment, wisdom and the confidence that comes from hard-won life experience, to something predicated on self-indulgence, playfulness and the childlike exuberance associated with juvenile pursuits.

But the story of our not-so-brave new world of infantilisation and juvenilisation goes much deeper than simply the celebration of immaturity. It also poses a number of important, yet largely unaddressed, questions about what the eroding moral status of adulthood means for other phases of the life cycle. In a bid to answer such questions, Part One also introduces the reader to the problematic flipside of infantilisation – *adultification*. By undermining adulthood as an aspirational life stage, Anglo-American society has been forced to look elsewhere for guidance and worldly insight. This has resulted in the veneration of childhood as a source of wisdom and moral guidance. Numerous consequences flow from this reversal of generational authority, not the least of which being the ongoing eradication of many of the traditional conventions and boundaries associated with childhood and teenagerdom. In such circumstances, the traditional avenues through which adult identity is forged and shaped are severely obstructed, if not blocked altogether. Or to put it differently, when adults stay younger longer (infantilisation), and when children grow older earlier (adultification), the result is a sort of *generational mulch*: a homogeneous, ever-expanding life stage in which shared and interchangeable cultural and psychological experiences become the norm. But to understand how this situation came about, we must begin with infantilisation, and specifically the forms of cultural messaging that have helped create a world full of adults-in-waiting.

Assailed at every turn by a contemporary culture unable to assert any positive images or values not associated with the cult of youth, growing old has today grown, well, old. As a result, many young and not-so-young men and women have sadly concluded that, rather than embracing a sense of adult identity, they will instead make their stand in the ever-expanding redoubt of youth culture. Unfortunately for them, as will become clear throughout this book, it is a defensive position that is shot full of holes and will do nothing to stave off the existential realities – good and bad – that are the unavoidable consequence of growing old.

Chapter 1

Staying Young For Ever: The Infantilisation of Everything

Remember, 50 years ago adults did not dress like children. They did not read – try to read – children's books. They did not enjoy children's diet. The more they have been consulted as consumers of everything, the more they've elected to be fed drivel – the more they've regressed into irreversible infantilism and helpless dependency.

Jonathan Meades[1]

We live in an infantilised age. From colouring-in books for adults to Disney-themed wedding readings, the overriding ethos of Anglo-American culture is one that commands us to embrace immaturity. It is a world where the inner child triumphs over the inner adult, and where any worthwhile sense of grown-up identity is fast being eroded as many individuals embark on what can only be described as a mass exodus from the world of adult responsibility. The cultural fallout from this situation is all around us. It can be seen in the penchant of many young adults to extend their youth via 'instant nostalgia' and other forms of 'synchronic pastiche' (when Hasbro recently launched its new 'Play-Doh for Grown Ups' line, they added what they described as 'Grown Up Scents', including 'Overpriced Latte', 'Dad Sneakers', and 'Spa Day'),

31

and it is evident in the way advertisers use neotenous traits to imbue products with a sense of untrammelled youthful purity. But whatever form it takes, the result is always the same: by constantly promoting and celebrating 'the conscious and unconscious cultivation of immaturity', postmodern consumer societies have come to resemble a giant pop-cultural kindergarten.[2]

So, like an apprehensive parent who has finally plucked up the courage to enter their teenage son's bedroom, it's time to gird your loins, ignore the 'Adults Keep Out' sign hanging askew on the door, and step across the threshold into the decidedly immature world of the twentieth-first-century Kidult. And where better to start this tour of our infantilised world than in the ever-expanding arena of popular culture?

Infantilise this: Contemporary popular culture and the retreat from adulthood

It's no longer just teenagers and students who seem to be running away from real life, it's people in their twenties and thirties, too. People who really should know better, but don't seem to know how to do much else.

Clive Martin, 2014[3]

In 2010 Colombia Pictures released the movie *Grown Ups* with the tagline: 'Just because you grow older doesn't meant mean you have to grow up.' While the film itself was forgettable, the promotional tagline nicely captures the essence of a genre of Hollywood movies that attempt to portray the prolonged period of 'adultesence' that is now an established feature of contemporary society. To some extent, films that perpetuate and celebrate immaturity have been around for a while – obvious examples being the early Tom Hanks comedy *Big* (1988) and the prototype slacker-schlub movie, *Billy*

Madison (1995). But it was in the first decade of the twenty-first century that a discernible genre started to emerge. Two main strands constitute this genre, both of which turn around an avowed and unequivocal rejection of adulthood.

The first strand is that of the unreconstructed man-child. Here, fully fledged adult males refuse to transition to adulthood, preferring instead the more stunted, pop culture-defined world of teenagerdom. Classic examples here include *Ted, Hall Pass, Old School, She's Out of My League, Grandma's Boy, American Loser, Zack and Miri Make a Porno, Wedding Crashers, The 40-Year-Old Virgin, The Promotion, The Tao of Steve, School of Rock, You, Me and Dupree, Our Idiot Brother* (in which lead actor Paul Rudd is repeatedly forced to shout 'I'm a man') and the 2011 remake of *Arthur,* in which the butler from the original film is replaced by a nanny who controls the lead character's cartoon addiction. These 'masters of nothing' man-child movies even have distinct subthemes, such as the now all-too-familiar plot of the adult male who staunchly rejects any attempt to remove him from the parental home (e.g., *Jeff, Who Lives at Home, Step Brothers, Cyrus* and *Failure to Launch*).[4]

Less obvious is a second strand of film that we might call the lost-in-transition movie. In these works, although the central characters are fully cognizant of the fact that youth has long since passed them by, they are wracked with self-doubt about what awaits them when, ultimately, they are forced to embrace adulthood as their master status. In this strand of film, the anxiety is palpable, whether it's an out-and-out comedy (*Knocked Up, Kicking & Screaming*), or something with more reflexive pretentions, such as *The Adults, Greenberg, Momma's Man, Oh Boy, While We're Young* or *The Future*. The last of these films, Miranda July's *The Future*, is especially interesting. Not only does it exemplify existential angst about becoming an adult (the motif used to symbolise adult commitment in *The Future* is the adoption of a rescue cat), but as one half of an underachieving couple, July's character, Sophie, is emblematic of a new type of filmic 'woman-child' – a twist on the 'slacker' persona that previously was solely a male preserve.[5] Putting paid to the idea that the man-child movie was simply a reaction to the rise of feminism and the subsequent erosion of male authority, the 'female slacker' has emerged as an increasingly common sight in both Hollywood and independent cinema (e.g., *Young Adult*, *Tiny Furniture*, *Juliette*, *Laggies*, *Obvious Child*, *Preggoland* and *Lady Bird*). Pre-existing gender stereotypes ensure that the man-child and woman-child are portrayed differently in film, but while disparities exist, what's apparent is that, in movies as in real life, shrugging your shoulders at adulthood is now very much a gender-neutral phenomenon.

The infantilisation of cinema does not end there. Contemporary film has been completely transformed by franchise movies based on cartoons, comic books, video games and young-adult novels. From endless Batman, Superman, Hulk and Spider-Man remakes to the tiresome Iron Man, Avengers and X-Men franchises, a visit to the movies these days feels more like a trip to a toy shop than a meaningful cinematic experience. Green-screened to within a pixel of their lives and characterised by unoriginal, anti-government masculine-fantasy narratives, these over-branded Spandex superhero films are not just a reflection of 'a society that has basically given up',[6] they also illustrate the extent to which infantilisation has taken root in the minds of the cinematically illiterate executives who run today's media conglomerates. Whether it's the umpteenth iteration of the *Fast & Furious* franchise, or yet another spin-off churned out by the *Star Wars* corporate meat grinder, we have reached the point where many studio films now function as reassuring bedtime stories – safe, comforting, familiar fairy tales that can be told over and over again in a bid to lull us off into an untroubled sleep.[7]

Unable to perceive moviegoers as anything other than big children, the corporate infantilisers who run Hollywood are doubling down on stories involving children's toys and action figures. Following the success of *Barbie* (2023), toy manufacturer Mattel has signed up Lena Dunham and J. J. Abrams to develop films based on their top-selling Polly Pocket dolls and Hot Wheels toy cars respectively; Netflix are rebooting the *Masters of the Universe* cartoon as a feature film; Universal Pictures are developing movie versions of Rock 'Em Sock 'Em Robots and a horror franchise based on the Magic 8 Ball toy; and Mattel are looking for partners to develop future film franchises based on the 1970s strongman Big Jim action figures, Barney the purple dinosaur, and their Chatty Cathy doll. If all this wasn't enough, sixty-eight-year-old Tom Hanks is set to star in a new movie about the Major Matt Mason astronaut toy.

But feasting on a sugary diet of children's toy stories comes at a cost. It is a common refrain among film critics that characterisation, plot and dialogue in today's major studio movies have all taken an infantilised turn, or as one online commentator put it, modern movies are 'written by children for children – or rather people with the intelligence, attention span, and emotional maturity of children'. Operating under the pseudonym 'The Critical Drinker', novelist and film critic Will Jordan has amassed 1.33 million subscribers to his YouTube channel. In one of his many online videos entitled 'Why modern movies suck – they're written by children', Jordan contrasts the writing and characterisation of contemporary science-fiction spin-offs with the original versions. Commenting on one of the recent Star Trek retreads, Jordan has this to say about the childlike nature of the lead characters: 'They're like teenagers that have suddenly been put in charge of a star ship with no training or preparation. They are impulsive, hyperactive, emotionally unstable, unprofessional, and generally pretty incompetent. They are practically the last people on earth you'd trust your life to, and unfortunately, they've become kind of the norm in modern film and TV.'

By now, according to demographic data from movie ticket sales, most adults have abandoned the cinema and retreated instead to streaming services where a more diverse palette of programming awaits. But while the TV box set might represent the art form of the age, mainstream terrestrial television, with its incessant emotionality and parade of look-at-me-now celebrities, is becoming more crèche-like with every passing day. Consider the evidence.

For almost two decades now, our TV schedules have been rammed full of ('lost-in-transition') sitcoms and comedy dramas that attempt to represent the ever-expanding liminal period between adolescence and adulthood. Examples here include *Broad City* and *Moone Boy* (both of which feature characters who have an adult alter ego that encourages childlike or spontaneous behaviour); *Badults, Peep Show, A.P. Bio, Two and a Half Men* and *Bored to Death*, which turn around characters engaged in childish male fantasies; and *Silicon Valley, $#*! My Dad Says, Cuckoo, Workaholics, Big Lake, Girls, Difficult People, Teachers, Bad Education* and *Uncle* (tagline: 'One of them is a complete juvenile and the other one is his nephew').

Even more obviously infantilising is a recent style of TV programming that relies on the sort of babyish language and patronising concepts that not so long ago would have been deemed suitable only for pre-teens. Best described as children's TV for adults, examples here include the 'adult cookery show' *Choccywoccydoodah* and its inevitable celebrity spin-off *Choccywoccydoodah: Starstruck*, a one-stop-televisual-shop for 'spellbound wizard cakes' and other 'fantasy baking ideas'; *The Fantastical Factory of Curious Craft*, a perfect glitter-storm of infantile celebrities, dress-up and nursery rhyme-themed activities; *All I Want(ed) for Christmas*, in which adult celebrities 'reminisce about Christmas past and finally get to open the toy they always hoped to get in their childhood stocking'; *Heston's Fantastical Food* and *Heston's Feasts*, the former involving the creation of a one-tonne ice cream and a life-sized sweet shop made of confectionery, and the latter comprising episodes entitled 'Heston's Fairytale Feast' and 'Heston's Chocolate Factory Feast', in which the celebrity chef gets to 'emulate his fictional hero, Willy Wonka'; *Taskmaster*; *One Night In* [*Hamleys, Alton Towers*, etc.]; *The Science of* Home Alone; and *James May's Top Toys* and *James May's Toy Stories*, in which the former *Top Gear* presenter and self-confessed man-child sets out to answer 'questions you asked yourself as a six-year-old child', such as 'If you had enough LEGO bricks, could you build yourself a real house?'

Children's TV for adults also extends to a host of food/travel shows, including *Man V. Food, Kid in a Candy Store, Monster Munchies, Outrageous Food, Carnival Eats* and *Diners, Drive-ins and Dives*, all of which turn around a preoccupation with children's food (doughnuts, burgers, milkshakes, etc.), and promote the idea that more *always* means better.[8] The message of these shows is that unconstrained self-indulgence is a good thing and that, now you're an adult, nobody is allowed to stop the fun. Perhaps this accounts for a third type of infantile programming – the hectoring parental advice show, as exemplified by *Supernanny, Take Home Nanny, Little Angels, Extreme Guide to Parenting, Nanny 911, There Goes the Motherhood* and *America's Supernanny*. In these programmes, the format is always the same: an external figure – a nanny or self-credentialled 'family expert' – is needed to impose control and set boundaries, not just for the spoilt and unruly children but for the adult parents who clearly are no longer capable of thinking for themselves.

But by far the most insidious form of infantilised programming is 'reality TV'. Two decades ago, this format produced some interesting and original fly-on-the-wall documentaries. Today, however, what masquerades as 'real life' programming is largely and very obviously a reality-free contrivance. With their fabricated rivalries, overly dramatic reveals, emotional meltdowns and forced tearing-up, these 'scripted reality' shows (an oxymoron if ever there was one) such as *Keeping Up with the Kardashians*, *Jersey/Geordie Shore*, *The Only Way is Essex*, *Made in Chelsea*, and *The Real Housewives* and *Million Dollar Listing* franchises, offer only a simulacrum of reality, the obvious problem being that both the participants and the viewers are acutely aware of the make-believe nature of the format. In this sense, reality TV is, as the writer Michael Bywater noted, 'just playing at Wendy House . . . it is entirely disengaged from anything to do with the real world, except through an almost impenetrable net of let's pretend'.

Even further estranged from the real world is arguably the most absurd of all the reality genres – paranormal TV. Since this style of programming became popular around the turn of the century, thousands of shows have been transmitted, including long-running series like *Ghost Hunters*, *Ghost Adventures*, *Ghost Nation*, *Most Haunted Live!* and *A Haunting*. Merging a bit of parapsychological hokum with *Scooby Doo*-level detection narratives, these paranormal TV shows are essentially scary ghost stories for grown-up children who want to escape the more challenging world of adult documentaries.

By now it should be clear that reality TV has done much to normalise infantilism on our screens, but there is one final aspect of the format that's worth mentioning. Here, I refer to the 'watched over' nature of reality TV, and how it helped clear the ground for society's uncritical, tacit acceptance of ubiquitous surveillance and other forms of visual social control; an ever-expanding process that ensures that – however you may feel about it – we must all now live a life on camera. Consider the daddy of all reality TV shows, *Big Brother*, the long-running gameshow in which contestants live within the camera arc of a totalising 'scanscape', and where all the material needs of those involved are provided for by unseen agents of situational control. Under these conditions, *Big Brother* provides us with a glimpse of a scalable techno-surveillance future in which infantilism is not just encouraged but normalised.

'Oh my god. It's like being in a house with crazy children. Why do these people have no boundaries?' fumes *RuPaul's Drag Race* judge Michelle Visage during her stay in the *Celebrity Big Brother (CBB)* house. It's a good question. The problem is that at least part of the answer is found in the very programming that brought Visage to prominence in the first place. After twenty years of let's-pretend TV, the protagonists in shows like *Big Brother* – celebrity and civilian – have grown so accustomed to the ersatz nature of reality TV that they effortlessly embrace infantilism as the behavioural default setting. Hence the apparent ease with which grown adults accept being told to go and 'sit on the naughty step' (as was required of the thirty-year-old *Jersey Shore* reality star, The Situation, in *CBB* series eight), to admit to being unable to tie their own shoelaces (Helen Flanagan, *I'm a Celebrity Get Me Out of Here*, series twelve), and to openly confess to wetting the bed (as twenty-three-year-old *Geordie Shore* cast member Charlotte Crosby did on *CBB* series twelve). When reality TV makes forty- and fifty-year-old celebrities dress up as toy cars, children's bears, and dinosaurs (*CBB* series six), or asks rappers, rugby players and radio hosts to pretend to be fairy-tale characters in a fake children's TV show (*CBB* series nine), it is normalising infantilisation by mocking adult autonomy. This may seem superficial, but as elements of reality TV seep deeper into everyday life via live-streaming practices, the tendency to exist in a visual and performative world of perpetual childhood becomes ever more pronounced.

Plate 1:
The *Big Brother* **Kidult-scape:** The clownish infantility of
much contemporary reality TV is epitomised in the design and
sub-adult feel of the *Celebrity Big Brother* house. (Shutterstock)

But the creeping tentacles of infantilisation extend well beyond
film and television. Recently, a paper by researchers at the
Spanish National Research Council used an algorithm to analyse
the tonal, timbral and melodic qualities of nearly half a million
pop songs recorded between 1955–2010.[9] It concluded that pop
music in 2010 was characterised by fewer chord changes, simpler
pitch sequences and a narrower 'timbral palette' than music
recorded in previous decades. Almost immediately, the paper
sparked debate online. On the one hand, YouTubers and Baby
Boomer music bores used the article to substantiate their view
that modern music was homogeneous, bland and uninspiring.
On the other hand, musicologists criticised the study for its
crude analytic categories and its failure to factor in composi-
tional elements like structural context and implied harmonies.
Neither position framed the debate correctly. The bigger issue
here is not about the declining overall quality or tonal complexity of contemporary music, which after all is a massive category.
Nor is it about a lack of talent – at grassroots level, today's

musicians are undoubtedly as skilled and creative as they have ever been. Rather, the problem lies in what constitutes mainstream music today and the type of songs we encounter as we go about our daily round. Here, we need to consider the relationship between infantilisation and two mutually reinforcing developments that over the last two decades have emerged as fundamental features of the music industry.

The first point concerns the late-modern sonic ecology and the spatio-temporal 'stickiness' associated with certain urban 'soundmarks'. If Muzak was an early auditory marker used to brand space and lubricate consumption in shopping malls and other retail spaces, today an altogether more sophisticated form of sonic branding is in operation. From the use of audio-visual screen advertising in toilets, taxis and coach headrests, to the ubiquitous 'rhythmic contemporary' and 'adult-urban' playlist blandcasts that saturate pubs, bars, restaurants and shops, the contemporary urban experience is one marred by digitally compressed, formulaic noise pollution. Make no mistake, *this is by design*. In the same way the saccharine jazz stylings of Muzak defined consumer spaces in the 1970s, in today's city, standardised 'urban' beats and unremarkable 'bounce-wid-me' tracks have become the corporate-approved musical backdrop for today's lifestyle consumers. The twenty-first-century Kidult must be constantly sonically stimulated, if not via socially isolating ear buds or noise-cancelling headphones, then via the aural pacifier of piped-in musical ear wash. Given its role as a consumption emollient, this music must be both uplifting and unchallenging, repetitively stressing positive vibes like happiness ('Because I'm happy, Clap along if you feel like happiness is the truth') and freedom ('Mind, use your power, Spirit, use your wings, Freedom, Freedom, Freedom') to ensure the customer feels relaxed, safe and, most importantly, primed to spend.[10] The important knock-on effect of this colonisation of public space by a thin range of corporately approved musical forms is that these styles have now *become* the mainstream. Hegemonic and harmonically homogeneous, the simpler pitch sequences and diminished timbral style characteristic of the rhythmic contemporary and adult-urban genres have narrowed tastes and expectations, and as a result blocked more diverse forms of music from entering the mainstream.

In 2016, when writing about 'patterning' in contemporary pop, the musicologist Patrick Metzger identified what he termed 'the Millennial Whoop', a musical sequence that alternates between the fifth and third notes of a major scale. According to Metzger, the Millennial Whoop takes the form of a 'wa-oh-wa-oh' pattern that is evident in countless twenty-first-century pop songs. Metzger recognises, however, that, rather than being just another musical hook, the Millennial Whoop symbolises something more significant: the rise of a new genre of comfort music for a generation that seems happy to trade originality for something superficial but reassuringly safe.

> . . . the Millennial Whoop evokes a kind of primordial sense that everything will be alright. You know these notes. You've heard this before. There's nothing out of the ordinary or scary here. You don't need to learn the words or know a particular language or think deeply about meaning. You're safe. In the age of climate change and economic injustice and racial violence, you can take a few moments to forget everything and shout with exuberance at the top of your lungs. Just dance and feel how awesome it is to be alive right now. Wa-oh-wa-oh.[11]

This blanding-down of music to something that resembles what Michael Bywater describes as 'a coarser, harsher simulacrum of the womb', is not limited only to urban forms like hip hop or autotuned Latin trap. Other genres have also been affected by the compulsion to play it safe and target middle-ground taste. Consider folk music. It used to be the case that, behind the gentle guitar picking of the likes of Woody Guthrie, Phil Ochs and Joan Baez lurked a ferocious anti-establishment leftist politics. While a few hardy musicians try to keep the genre alive on the extreme peripheries of the music industry, what passes for folk music today is about as far from political folk as you can get. In fact, as the music critic John Harris argued when reviewing a book on the state of popular culture:

> [today's faux folk acts have done] a 180-degree flip, so that the dominant voices now mirror the values of the powerful. Good examples are the hugely successful Mumford and Sons, privately educated chancers whose banjos, beards and raggedy clothes embody a woeful kind of austerity chic, or the equally posh Noah and the Whale, products of the same affectedly folky milieu whose music sounds like a noncommittal shrug (the embodiment, perhaps, of all that 'Keep Calm and Carry On' paraphernalia).[12]

The progressive homogenisation of musical discourse is further exacerbated by a second development more obviously associated with infantilisation. Once again, the issue is not simply about the diminishing tonal complexity of popular music, but about why certain performers are promoted while other more heterogeneous, and clearly more talented, artists are largely ignored. Previously, record companies adopted a bread-on-the-water approach when it came to signing and promoting new bands. However, as marketing costs skyrocketed, it's now far more cost effective for companies to only push a very limited number of new acts. Given this situation, it makes sense for labels to sign performers that have an established fan base. It is for this reason that charts and music channels are dominated by acts that either started out as children's TV stars, or who were discovered on 'music-by-committee' TV talent shows. It would be too mind-numbing a task to compile a list of the third-rate crooners and human juke-boxes spawned by the latter, but in terms of the former, one thinks immediately of Miley Cyrus, Ariana Grande, Christina Aguilera, Justin Timberlake, Hilary Duff, the Jonas Brothers, Vanessa Hudgens and Britney Spears, many of whom record interchange-able songs churned out with the help of songwriters working to order. In either case, however, these are not musicians so much as glorified children's entertainers, and as such illustrate the infanti-lised state of much contemporary popular music.

Infantilised music and lyrics now encompass everything from babyish ditties like 'We're Just Babies, Man' by hip-hop act Digable Planets to the gummy-bear-and-gingerbread world of Katy Perry's 'California Gurls' video. Perry, soon to enter her forties, is especially interesting in this context because of the way she embodies a prac-tice common among many female celebrities of 'ageing backwards'. With her text-speak song titles, *Teenage Dream* album concept and childish interview pronouncements ('I feel a real connection to fairy tales. And I think that in some ways I live in a fairy tale.'), Perry's entire oeuvre is festooned with symbols of infantilism. At some point, Perry will have no option but to reinvent herself, prob-ably via one of the usual music-industry clichés – the introspective acoustic album, the Annie Leibovitz black-and-white photo shoot. But then again, maybe not. In the video for her 2012 release 'Give Me All Your Luvin'', Madonna was still dressing as a pom-pom-waving teenage cheerleader at fifty-three.

It would be reassuring to think that the forms of infantilisation outlined above were limited only to the popular arts – film, TV, music. Sadly, this is not the case. In recent years the elite modern art market has succumbed to similar tendencies. Just as a fish rots from its head, this development can be traced in large part to two of the world's most expensive living artists. As the high priest of postmodernism, the American artist Jeff Koons has made a career out of reproducing symbols of childhood as high-end sculptures (balloon animals, Easter eggs, puppies and cartoon characters such as Popeye, Olive Oyl and The Hulk). He even turned a mound of multicoloured putty created by his two-year-old son into a three-metre-tall sculpture (*Play-Doh*, 1994–2014). The creative thought process behind these works is nicely summed up in comments Koons made about the sculpture *Balloon Dog* (Orange), which in 2013 was hammered down at Christie's for an eye-watering $58.4 million. When quizzed about the meaning behind *Balloon Dog* (Orange), Koons responded by saying he hoped it recreated and celebrated the experiences that evoke a child's enjoyment of the world.[13] Such thinking is all too common in the rarefied enclaves of modern art. Consider Damien Hirst, one of Koons's main rivals for the tag of the most expensive living artist. As each year passes, Hirst's oeuvre seems to grow more juvenile in orientation. In 2017, for example, his *Treasures from the Wreck of The Unbelievable* exhibition turned around a ludicrous 'the-legends-are-real' premise that mixed comic-book fantasies with 'fossilised cartoon characters'. One art critic, Andrew Goldstein, even commented that Hirst 'has begun to regard his audience not as a friend to be ennobled but as a cupiditous, infantile enemy to be debased'.

Infantilisation is also prevalent lower down the art-world totem pole. For example, in his solo exhibition *The Fairy Godmother*, the Canadian artist Mathieu Malouf included paintings of Cinderella, Gremlins, Miss Piggy (licking Kermit the Frog) and the musician 'Eddie van Halen shredding on a guitar whose neck also happens to be an ejaculating penis'.[14] Or what about Yayoi Kusama's 2016 installation *Guidepost to the New World*? Greenlighted by the

Plate 2: Tate St Ives. After various rooms of art dating from the nineteenth century featuring works that explore themes such as community, work and metaphysics, this is what visitors to Tate St Ives encounter in the final exhibition space as the exemplification of twenty-first-century artistic expression. The accompanying leaflet reads, 'Your imagination and your identity are very real' – perhaps, but in this case, only if you identify as a child and your imagination extends no further than the nearest adult romper room. (© Tate Joe Humphrys & Lucy Dawkins)

Armory Show's director on the strength of something Kusama sketched out on a napkin, what eventually materialised in the Armory space was a juvenile 'polka-dotted playground' installation. For the art critic Julia Halperin, *Guidepost to the New World* exemplified a new type of object 'that is symbolic of an increasingly popular kind of art fair-friendly, mass-produced work. Like cotton candy, it's devoid of nutritional value and it provides no lasting satisfaction – but it looks really good on Instagram.'

Halperin's observation is both damning and insightful. While

Instagram provides a useful digital platform for artists to promote their work, it has also given rise to a new type of comically shallow art often referred to as 'Instagram Art' or 'Influencer Art'. The goal, of course, is to generate 'likes' and click traffic, but in doing so many artists pander to the lowest common aesthetic denominator – and this frequently means resorting to infantilism. Consider the Brooklyn-based Australian artist CJ Hendry. Hendry's initial success came from photorealistic drawings of consumer items like Louboutin trainers and Hermes shopping bags. But as her popularity grew – Hendry now has well over three quarters of a million Instagram followers – so did the adolescent feel of her work. In recent years, Hendry's profound creative moments have included an installation of seven monochrome rooms constructed using giant LEGO-style building blocks, a 50-foot inflatable swimming pool in the desert and a colossal Chuck-E-Cheese-style adult indoor playground. The anti-adult feel of Hendry's oeuvre is not helped by her social media pronouncements. For example, in April 2018, after urging her followers to 'brave the Instagram paparazzi' and come along to her MONOCHROME exhibition, Hendry posted: 'Just jumping into bed for a nap before opening night tonight AYYYOOOO 🎪🛁🌸🧸🤍', alongside a video of herself in the 'hot pink bubble-gum' bedroom diving into a tub filled with pink teddy bears.

Stuffed animals also feature in the work of LA-based art personalities the Kaplan Twins, who in 2016 produced 'Boy Toys', a series of photographs which featured the twins sleeping with various children's playthings. It's possible that the Kaplan Twins are saying something profound here, but given that a second series, #SatOnYourFace, involved the sisters painting each other's bottoms and then sitting on illustrations of Donald Trump, Dr Phil, and (art cliché klaxon) Marcel Duchamp, it seems rather unlikely. Instead, as the critic Ben Davis observed, the Kaplan

Twins' teenage oeuvre adds up to little more than a 'a pile-up of charmless dumbassery'.

Perhaps we shouldn't be too surprised that tranches of contemporary art end up resembling doodles on the inside of a teenager's exercise book. After all, although the popular assumption is that life follows art, in reality society gets the art it deserves. Consider graffiti artist Banksy, whose sixth-form-style radicalism is so lionised by latte liberals and bourgeois tastemakers that in 2019 he was voted 'Britain's favourite artist of all time', and in 2010 was selected as one of *Time* magazine's '100 most influential people in the world'. As Alexander Andrews has pointed out, despite being middle-aged, Banksy's art has a sophomoric quality to it that at times feels almost childlike: 'Another Banksy trope is irreverent children with paints. For him, children are embodiments of the free spirit of humanity and act as truth-speakers. His children represent hope by undermining authority, disrupting adults' consumerist assumptions and dissolving walls.' Such 'pedestrian homilies' are lapped up as subversive street politics by middle-class pseudo-rebels who can't be bothered to engage in actual critical thinking. Unsurprising, then, that Banksy is the artistic figurehead of our times – a 'cosy culture warrior' whose world view is as clichéd as it is commercial.[15]

But when it comes to the relationship between infantilised art and mindless commercialism masquerading as critique, even Banksy has been surpassed. The Brooklyn artist KAWS (top auction sales price $14.8m), has made a good living from creating paintings, sculptures, and action figures featuring altered cartoon characters from *The Simpsons*, *The Smurfs*, *Sesame Street*, *Peanuts* and *SpongeBob SquarePants*. (KAWS's big critical inversion is to replace the characters' eyes with 'X's). His trademark artform is the character Chum, a toy-like, sub-Koonsian bubble figure that he uses in everything from huge bronze, wood, and even inflatable sculptures to smaller, gift-shop-friendly figurines in glass, metal and plastic. Unchallenging and kitsch, Chum has been described by the critic Hrag Vartanian as having 'less emotional complexity than an emoji or a cereal commercial [and] acting more like an avatar of greed and hubris for those who bring a huge dose of cynicism to contemporary art without any of the needed intro- spection or criticality'.[16] But in today's infantilised art world, uncomplicated sells. KAWS's insipid, soulless toy-art has proven to be a huge success not only with today's celebrity collectors who apparently have no interest in anything outside of the self-referential world of popular culture, but also with corporations like Christian Dior and Comme des Garçons who use KAWS's bland iconography as wallpaper-like backdrops for their own equally juvenile brand ideas. To paraphrase Vartanian, it is art produced for adult-children by an artist who has all 'the sophistication of a high school student' and who is 'unable to provide anything but bromides to an audience of fan boys and hangers-on eager to learn more'.

And this school-ified art is everywhere these days. When I was in primary school, kids who couldn't draw were told by the art teacher to cut pictures out of magazines and make a collage. Back then, everybody involved knew this process was the preserve of the artistically challenged. Today, however, this same technique can result in artistic stardom – as long it ticks the right political boxes. Cold War Steve is one of Britain's best known contemporary artists. His medium: digital photo-collage. His politics: a yawn-inducing blend of left-wing clichés and ad homi- nem satire. He first came to prominence after his work, which typically involves photoshopping images of politicians and celebrities into dystopian-looking urban landscapes, went viral on Twitter. From here, he was quickly lauded by aesthetic illiterates as the artistic prophet of post-Brexit Britain, a sort of postmodern Hogarth whose oeuvre supposedly symbolised the age. Aged twenty-three, Michelangelo carved the *Madonna della Pietà* out of a solid block of marble, a work so awe-inspiring it marked the beginning of the High Renaissance. Who do we get as our *artiste de l'époque*? A graduate of Nuneaton Art College who uses his iPhone to Photoshop a soap-opera character (Phil Mitchell from *EastEnders*) into his artworks and then, fittingly perhaps, bundles them up for sale in the form of a jigsaw or children's annual.

In truth, there's little new about the likes of KAWS, CJ Hendry or Cold War Steve. Since the onset of postmodernism, there have always been individual artists whose work has exemplified the cultural slide into infantilism (a prime example being Cy Twombly's abstract expressionist daubings). However, thanks to the emergence of non-fungible-tokens (NFTs), we now have an entire art form that appears to be predicated on infantilised imagery (Nyan Cats, CryptoPunks, Bored Apes, Pudgy Penguins, etc.). Even when NFTs feature in the most exclusive gallery sales, what rises to the top of the market has a distinctly teenage feel to it. Take the world's most expensive NFT artwork, *Everydays: The First 5,000 Days*. Produced by the Charleston-based digital artist Beeple (aka Mike Winkelmann), *Everydays* is a square image file (21,069 by 21,069 pixels) composed of 5,000 unique digital images that Winkelmann produced at the rate of one per day for a thirteen-year period starting on 1 May 2007. Bought unseen by the Singapore-based programmer Vignesh Sundaresan for $69.3m at Christie's in May 2021, *Everydays: The First 5,000 Days* has been described as the first masterpiece of the NFT art world. In reality, it's little more than a series of gross-out cartoons and futuristic fantasy landscapes dressed up as political satire. As artnet.com's Ben Davis commented after laboriously trawling through all 5,000 digital images, overall, *Everydays* is little more than a collection 'of late-2000s hipster irony-bro culture: cartoons, porno, and the intersection between cartoons and porno'. Even worse, Beeple's often poorly rendered DeviantArt fantasyscapes are not only 'directionless' and 'loutish', but at times the language accompanying the images is both 'racist' ('it's fun to draw black people') and 'misogynistic' ('the Dalai Lama should give some girl the peace symbol then like totally finger fuck her').[17] I suppose it's still possible that NFTs might emerge as an important new frontier for contemporary art, but for that to happen, today's digital artists will need to move beyond cutesy cartoons and adolescent puerility.

Sadly, one can go through almost any sphere of contemporary cultural life and trace similar infantilising tendencies. For example, the publishing industry has been profoundly affected by life stage dissolution. During the nineteenth and twentieth centuries, children's literature existed in what the media scholar Joshua Meyrowitz described as an 'informational ghetto, a self-contained world that was both isolated and isolating'. This distinction, however, no longer exists. Thanks to the rise of 'young adult fiction', 'children's literature for adults', and what Rachel Falconer calls 'the crossover novel', approximately half of books written for adolescents are now bought by adults. Sometimes referred to as the Harry Potter effect, this distinctly twenty-first-century development has ensured that contemporary bestseller lists are regularly dominated by Potter-esque and *Hunger Games*-style titles commissioned specifically to tap into the Millennial (wo)man-child book market. Commenting on this development, the Irish novelist John Banville recently described contemporary literary culture as being characterised by 'a creeping retreat into infantilism'. Banville's concern is with how the infinitely wide world of adult fiction is being eclipsed by childish fantasy stories and other magical narrative tropes – but perhaps there's something even more significant at stake here. According to the anonymous online critic 'Christopher Lasch's Angry Ghost', the fetishisation of youth fiction has ensured that today's children's and young-adult authors have emerged as 'the moral entrepreneurs and bellwethers of the age', the 'simplified good/evil schematics in their books leaking out into the external world' to fuel fantasy and shape the nature of contemporary cultural and political debate.

To make matters even worse, the few bookshops that still populate the high street are piled high with adult colouring-in books, fantasy and magical-realism sections, treasure-hunt and other 'adult activity books' and 'naughty children's parody stories for adults' (*The Very Hungover Caterpillar, Harry Pothead: The Stoned Sorcerer, Everybody Dies: A Children's Book for Grown-ups*). Many publishers have also succumbed to the 'Wunderkind' author phenomenon, the tendency to over-value and over-promote young authors based on media hype. On this issue, however, publishers are not alone. One of the more obvious aspects of our infantilised world is the all-too-familiar inclination to celebrate youthfulness as a marker of success in and of itself. Hence the ever-growing number of lists such as *Time* magazine's 'Most influential teens of the year', the London *Evening Standard*'s '25 future faces 25 and under' and *Teen Vogue*'s '21 and Under List', the latter of which has (since the list's inception in 2017) included an eleven-year-old designer, a thirteen-year-old 'sex education savior', a sixteen-year-old 'future [US] president', and the 'seven-year-old activist' Havana Chapman-Edwards.

The fashion industry has also enthusiastically embraced infantilism. In fact, as the always impeccably turned-out style commentator Peter York documented as far back as 1984, the tastemakers and stylists of the fashion world have been playing around with the idea of children's clothes for adults for decades. Indeed, according to York, the fashion industry has been in thrall to what he termed 'Babytime' since the late 1960s:

> Babytime was, roughly, from 1968 to 1980: a magic time when thousands of adult, sane, bourgeois men and women aspired to Babyhood. The man with the child in his eyes, Kickers on his feet and dungarees round the rest, walked the land, grown women in short socks at his side. They live in a new primary and pastels Babyland, a time where time stood still, and forged a new Babystyle ... The Babytimers weren't, you understand, just like the rest of mankind wanting to hang on to the Sex Prime with facelifts and hair pieces and all that familiar, understandable stuff. They wanted something astonishing – Second Childhood.[18]

In his book *Modern Times*, York identified a clutch of early infantilising fashion trends, including ironic school wear (satchels, prefect badges, goofy spectacles), and the fixation with cartoon-based clothing (Tin-Tin T-shirts, Micky Mouse watches, etc.). However, he was most preoccupied with footwear, which he viewed as the most obvious manifestation of infantilised fashion: 'The shoe's the thing in Babyland – soft shoes, sweet bounce of youth, every kind of soft shoe there ever was' – Kickers (which were originally designed as bootees for children), Clark's daisy sandals, flip-flops, jellies, plimsolls, etc. As ever, York was onto something. Today, the 'sweet bounce of youth' is everywhere. Alongside UGG boots, knit boots, urban slippers and chunky trainers, we also have the spectacle of the 'comically oversized' or 'massive' shoe trend (see Plate 3).

Manufactured by everyone from Adidas to Bottega Veneta, these clownishly large, over-stuffed shoes are designed to be simultaneously futuristic and nostalgic, as psychologist to the fashion business Carolyn Mair explains: 'They remind us of childhood memories, evoking a sense of familiarity and warmth, fun times: splashing in puddles and playing with friends in a carefree world'.[19] If you say so.

Since York penned *Modern Times*, Babytime fashion has sprouted from the ground up to envelop the entire body, resulting in the delusional infantility of contemporary clothing: those too-small 'urchin' suits, the 'onesie', flip-flops and beachwear worn in

Plate 3: '**Sweet bounce of youth**'. Crocs 'Big Yellow Boot'. (Photo by Aruro Holms/Getty Images for NBA 2K24)

urban spaces during winter, faux insouciant leisurewear festooned with branding, and the greatest men's fashion crime of all, those three-quarter length 'man-pri' combat shorts – the perfect symbol if ever there was one of the contemporary male Kidult's predicament: too old for short pants but not sufficiently mature enough to transition into long trousers. Sadly, this same sense of generational confusion is apparent in all sorts of sartorial abominations, including the recent trend of wearing training shoes with a suit and turning up to formal adult functions in replica sports team apparel.

No account of the infantilisation of fashion, or indeed of infantilisation more generally, would be complete, however, without a word about that exemplar of ironic youthful regression: the hipster. Writing about the emptiness of postmodern irony in the *New York Times*, the Princeton University language scholar Christy Wampole offers the following definition of the contemporary hipster:

> The hipster haunts every city street and university town. Manifesting a nostalgia for times he never lived himself, this contemporary urban harlequin appropriates outmoded fashions (the mustache, the tiny shorts), mechanisms (fixed-gear bicycles, portable record players), and hobbies (home brewing, playing trombone). He harvests awkwardness and self-consciousness. Before he makes any choice, he has proceeded through several stages of self-scrutiny. The hipster is a scholar of social forms, a student of cool. He studies relentlessly, foraging for what has yet to be found by the mainstream. He is a walking citation, his clothes refer to much more than themselves. He tries to renegotiate the age-old problem of individuality, not with concepts, but with material things.[20]

Wampole's essay stresses the political vacuum at the heart of hipsterism, but importantly she doesn't stop there. Like Andrew Calcutt's earlier work on the irony-infantilism nexus more generally, Wampole understands that ironic living is just another 'part of a wider process which is pushing adulthood even further off limits . . . sending up adulthood, and confirming the idea that it cannot be taken seriously'.[21] To live ironically, she argues, is 'to hide in public', to exist in an infantilised world of dress-up and psycho-political subterfuge:

> Look at your clothes. What parts of your wardrobe could be described as costume-like, derivative or reminiscent of some specific style archetype (the secretary, the hobo, the flapper, yourself as a child)? In other words, do your clothes refer to something else or only to themselves? . . . The most important question: How would it feel to change yourself quietly, offline, without a public display, from within? . . . People may choose to hide behind the ironic mantle, but this choice equals a surrender to commercial and political entities more than happy to act as parents for a self-infantilizing citizenry. So rather than scoffing at the hipster – a favorite hobby, especially of hipsters – determine whether the ashes of irony have settled on you as well. It takes little effort to dust them away.

Today, the idea that you can use clothing to cling on to adolescence (and thus superficially signal that you are laid back, 'chill', and someone with a laissez-faire attitude towards work and other adult activities), is so prevalent, it even has its own distinct fashion subcategories known as 'Kidcore' and 'Tween'. Described by one commentator as 'adult-size clothes with serious Children's Place overtones', these 'expressive juvenile outfits'[22] are the perfect expression of culturally induced infantilisation. Why choose adulthood when the market offers you prolonged adolescence in a range of adult sizes?

Plate 4: 'Bronies' take it to the streets at BronyCon. (Photo by
Andre Chung for The Washington Post via Getty Images)

By now it should be clear that infantilisation is a ubiquitous
element of contemporary culture. It manifests itself in everyday
vernacular through now-popular childish terms used by adults,
such as 'forever home', 'girly girl', 'ickle', 'bestie', 'yummy', 'crib',
'man cave', 'my bad', 'aah, bless', 'funemployment' and 'X sleeps
until Y'. It is evident in contemporary business culture in juvenile
initiatives like corporate 'sleepovers' and 'rage rooms' (designed
to allow businesspeople to vent pent-up anger). And it is a
consistent feature of many of the new youth subcultures that
society today spawns. It used to be the case in criminology and
sociology that the subfield of subcultural studies traced the relationship between youth subculture and deviance. Today, however,
the talk is of 'post-subcultural theory' and the idea that, rather
than *deviant* subcultures, youth culture is now increasingly associated with *hyper-conformity*. In a bid to capture this important
shift, post-subcultural scholars now study 'neo-tribes', 'lifestyle
groups' and the fast-changing fads, fashions, and foibles

associated with so-called 'urban scenes'. While this research is often interesting, it cannot hide the fact that many contemporary youth subcultures are infantile, inane and distinctly consumerist. Consider, for example, contemporary youth scenes like Potterheads, PLUR Ravers, Haul Girls, LARP (live-action role-play) and fantasy cosplay enthusiasts, Technoshamanists, Steampunks, Kandi Kids, Cutesters (the Hipster's 'cleaner cut little bro'), and perhaps most bizarrely of all, Bronies (adult, predominantly male, fans of the My Little Pony children's toy franchise – see Plate 4).[23] In almost every case, these subcultural clusters turn around the relationship that exists between specialised forms of prosocial consumerism and a deep commitment to escapist teenage fantasy worlds.

This concludes (for now) our brief cultural tour of the infantilised world – but let me end what might be seen by some as a frivolous subject on an important point. The deleterious effects of infantilism now extend well beyond the TV screen, the art gallery and the celebration of glittery-pink children's toys. Infantilisation has burst out from the realm of popular culture to become a fundamental feature of late-modern society, its values and cultural motifs penetrating deep into the collective conscious. For example, later in the book I will show how infantilisation has emerged as one of the most discernible tropes in contemporary lifestyle advertising, where it is used to sell everything from mineral water to mortgages. Likewise, the verb 'to infantilise' is now commonly deployed in important cultural debates and mobilised, often in symbolic form, in all kinds of public and political messaging (e.g., Plate 5). But before we delve deeper into the corrosive effects of Kidult imperialism as infantilisation leeches without impediment from one socio-cultural domain to another, we must take a moment to review the surprisingly few extant theories that have sought to explain how our infantilised world came into existence.

Plate 5: #InfantilizingWomen: The 'silence sucks' billboard and poster campaign was launched by the pharmaceutical company Sage Therapeutics in 2017 to encourage women to speak out about their struggles with postpartum depression. However, the decision to use a series of images of grown women crying and sucking on children's pacifiers was seen by some postpartum depression sufferers as patronising and disturbing. (Sage Therapeutics)

A Grown-Up's Guide to Infantilisation: The Story So Far

Concerns about infantilisation are not new. As early as the mid-twentieth century, prominent figures such as the French anthropologist Claude Lévi-Strauss and the German critical theorist Theodor Adorno were commenting on the infantile nature of American society, especially in relation to advertising and cultural forms like popular music and Hollywood film. Later in the 1960s and early 1970s, infantilisation, or more accurately, the 'infantile state' in adults, emerged as an important theme in the work of a new breed of psychiatrists and pop psychologists. Of central importance in these works were the psychotherapeutic themes of regression (of the personality) and repression (of childhood trauma), both of which served as starting points for a series of eclectic books, including David Jonas and Doris Klein's odd mash-up of psychiatry and evolutionary theory, *Man-child: A Study of the Infantilization of Man*, and more famously Arthur Janov's *The Primal Scream*. However, it was not until the 1980s that the subject of infantilisation started to feature as a subject in popular sociology and psychology, largely as a result of Neil Postman's bestselling 1982 work, *The Disappearance of Childhood*, in which he introduced the concept of 'the adult-child', and Dan Kiley's companion books, *The Peter Pan Syndrome: Men Who Have Never Grown Up* and *The Wendy Dilemma: When Women Stop Mothering Their Men*.

Few, if any, commentators seemed particularly interested in infantilisation during the 1990s. In fact, instead of being concerned about kids failing to grow up, most journalists were busy peddling the alternative view that they were growing up too quickly. Thanks in no small part to the American media's weaponisation of the deeply flawed youth 'super predator' theory,[24] the 1990s was a decade of rampant fearmongering about young people, neatly summarised by one scholar as 'a war on youth, a war against youth'.[25] But although the anxiety fuelling this war was real enough, the target was misconceived. Predicted by almost no one, crime rates generally, and youth crime rates specifically, had started to fall. Instead of youthful super predators, the quotidian battalions of Generation Y were in fact opting for lifeworlds characterised by increased safety and an enhanced sense of personal wellbeing. It was at this precise moment that infantilisation once again became a topic of interest.

Around the turn of the century, a series of books began to appear that explored the subject of infantilisation from various new angles. First out of the blocks were two insightful works by the media commentator Andrew Calcutt (*Arrested Development: Pop Culture and the Erosion of Adulthood*) and the anthropologist Marcel Danesi (*Forever Young: The 'Teen-Aging' of Modern Culture*). Brimming with original ideas and examples, the main concern of these books was how adult status was being undermined by transformations associated with youth culture. Calcutt, in particular, was keen to stress the role of the 1960s counterculture movement in establishing the social and moral conditions that allowed cultural infantilisation to flourish in the 1990s. The shifting cultural landscape also featured in Diane West's 2007 book *The Death of the Grown-Up* and Gary Cross's *Men to Boys: The Making of Modern Immaturity*, published just a few months later. However, in both these works, the critical focus was trained more on a series of moral concerns linked to historical generational transitions.

If Cross and West were both keen to offer moral evaluations of infantilisation based on what they perceived as a growing lack of respect for adult status/rules, two other books published around the same time focused instead on the role played by the market in infantilising adults and corrupting – adultifying – children. In *Born to Buy: The Commercialized Child and the New Consumer Culture*, Juliet Schor essentially updates Neil Postman's work on 'the disappearing child' – only this time the agent of erosion is not television, but the new arsenal of sophisticated marketing techniques being used to target kids at every possible opportunity. This theme also featured in the late Benjamin Barber's more expansive 2007 book *Consumed: How Markets Corrupt Children, Infantilize Adults, and Swallow Citizens Whole*. In Barber's hands, however, the critical lens is widened to encompass 'a global market culture' that is promoting what he called an 'Infantilist ethos' designed explicitly to undermine mature adulthood.

It was around this time that the idea of the infantilised or 'regressive' individual began to creep into popular consciousness, something which inevitably triggered a series of news articles and popular commentary on the subject. Very often this commentary was couched in concerned, even occasionally morally outraged, tones, as evidenced in the subtitle of Diana West's book *The Death of the Grown-Up: How America's Arrested Development is Bringing Down Western Civilization.* Other times, it was underpinned by very specific generational concerns and anxieties. For example, much ink was spilt – on behalf of Baby Boomers – about the increasing financial burden of supporting so-called 'boomerang kids', 'parasite singles', 'quarterlifers', 'thresholders' and other extended adolescents who either refuse or fail to leave the familial nest.[26] Finally, feminist columnists also penned a series of articles about the inability or unwillingness of male 'twentysomethings' to commit to the traditional sacrifices and duties associated with adulthood, and how this made it more difficult for women of that age to find mature life partners.[27]

Media interest in infantilisation continued to grow throughout the 2010s (see Table 1), even if at this point there was still a great

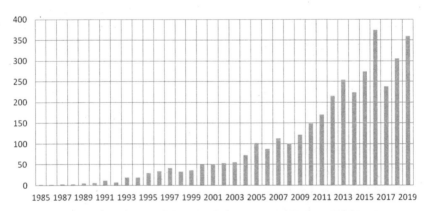

Table 1: Citations of the words 'infantilize/infantilise' and 'infantilization/infantilisation' in British newspapers (1985–2019)

deal of confusion about what exactly it was and how best to explain it. No surprise, then, that around this time a second clutch of books emerged that attempted to explain if not infantilism itself then some of its main consequences. Greg Lukianoff and Jonathan Haidt's *The Coddling of the American Mind*, Jordan Peterson's *12*

Rules for Life, Julie Lythcott-Haims's *How to Raise an Adult*, Steven Mintz's *The Prime of Life*, Susan Neiman's *Why Grow Up?* and Ben Sasse's *The Vanishing American Adult*, were all published within a four-year span and all achieved notable success, some even making the bestseller list. The fact these books have been so successful – Peterson's *12 Rules for Life* recorded global sales of over 5 million – says much about the public's interest in what Mintz calls 'the tangled transition to adulthood'. But while each book has much to say about the prolongation of youth, none of them specifically addresses the issue of culturally induced infantilisation, and the words 'infantilisation', 'infantilism' and 'infantilise' do not even feature in any of the six indexes. In fact, rather than confront infantilism in any direct way, they are all focused instead on combatting its effects. This being the case, the best way to think of these titles is as *de-infantilisation* books – attempts by authors from across the political spectrum to reaffirm and, in most cases, re-traditionalise adulthood.

Collectively, these works gave the study of adulthood a much-needed shot in the arm, especially in the way they brought the subject to the public's attention. But while each attempted to deal with issues relating to extended adolescence, they all left important questions about infantilism unanswered. Consider Lukianoff and Haidt's *The Coddling of the American Mind*, Lythcott-Haims's *How to Raise an Adult* and Peterson's *12 Rules for Life*. In their own way each of these books is concerned with the cosseted and infantilised lifestyles of many (middle-class) young people today, and how a lack of independence and responsibility often results in emotional fragility, anxiety and depression. Yet while these 'de-infantilization brokers' are strong on how to remedy the situation – for Lukianoff, Haidt and Lythcott-Haims, the solution lies in a combination of educational reform and more relaxed, less paranoid, styles of parenting; for Peterson, the answer is to be found in self-reflection and a series of moral or stoic life lessons – their analysis of infantilisation is partial at best and often entirely lacking. In Peterson's case, this absence is especially odd given that, since emerging in 2016 as one of the key figures in the contemporary culture wars, he has used his high-profile status to critique and undermine new forms of 'Woke' infantilism.

It's a slightly different story with Neiman's *Why Grow Up?* and Sasse's *The Vanishing American Adult*, which both place more emphasis on infantilisation as an intensifying cultural phenomenon. Sasse includes a lengthy chapter entitled 'Stranded in Neverland', which offers a thoughtful analysis of why many young people are choosing to delay the transition to adulthood. Likewise, Neiman's book provides an insightful philosophical account of human development which is then mobilised to confront what she describes as 'a culture of rampant immaturity'. However, this is where the similarity ends. As a former Republican junior state senator for Nebraska and now university president, Sasse is worried about the impact 'perpetual adolescence' is having on democracy, and thus most of his book is taken up with what is best described as a conservative action plan for rebuilding (American) adulthood. Sasse's pull-yourself-up-by-the-bootstraps prescription for overcoming the 'passivity' of today's young people is a familiar mix of Peterson-esque 'character-building habits' (reading, work before play, rejecting consumerism, etc.) and a revanchist sense of parental authority. In contrast, Neiman's de-infantilisation narrative is one forged from the classical philosophical liberalism of Immanuel Kant and Jean-Jacques Rousseau. As a result, there's much talk of exercising the mind, of the virtues of travel, and of abstention (from the internet) – but almost nothing about the cultural and economic forces that produce infantilism in the first place.

In terms of contextualising infantilisation, the most significant book of the six is Mintz's comprehensive *The Prime of Life: A*

History of Modern Adulthood. Mintz's goal is not to criticise today's 'prolonged transition' to adulthood, but to point out that the decade stretching from the late teens to the late twenties has always been 'a period of uncertainty, hesitation and indecision'. His underlying argument is one well known to historians and sociologists of the life course, i.e., that:

> [F]ar from being etched in stone, the life course is a historical artifact, a trajectory shaped by contingent, historically specific circumstances. Only an apprehension of these circumstances can allow us to truly understand the factors that shaped the arc of adult lives in the past and that are transforming the course of life today.

From here, he advances the argument that the long road to adult maturity currently being taken by young people is only perceived as drawn out and uncertain because we measure it against a paradigm of adulthood forged in the 1950s, a period of rising prosperity and relative social stability. Mintz argues that, in contrast to the mid-twentieth century, 'the overwhelming majority of young people in the past did not enter adulthood at a very young age'. Instead, marriage was delayed until debts were cleared, or inheritances received, while participation in the workplace was often just as uneven and non-linear as it is for many Millennials today. In short, according to Mintz's wide-ranging history of American adulthood, growing up is, and always has been, a difficult thing to realise.[28]

Whether intentionally or not, by making this point Mintz is lending historical heft to what is currently the most popular and influential explanation of twenty-first-century arrested development. I refer here to the work of the developmental psychologist Jeffrey Jensen Arnett and his extensive writings on the concept of 'emerging adulthood'.[29] According to Arnett, emerging adulthood is a new and distinct 'life stage' that applies to the years eighteen to twenty-nine, a period that he suggests is 'neither adolescence nor young adulthood but is theoretically and empirically distinct from both'. In a series of influential publications, Arnett asserts that, following the radical transformations in technology, gender and youth culture that took place during the 1960s and 1970s, young people today are developing and maturing in different ways than previous generations. Specifically, they are delaying the arrival of fully fledged adulthood by pursuing 'longer and more wide-spread education', 'entering into marriage and parenthood later in life' and 'experiencing a longer transition to stable employment'. Based initially on a survey of three hundred non-random interviews with Americans aged eighteen to twenty-nine, Arnett identified what he termed a 'distinct subjectivity' associated with this period of the life cycle. As his work developed, he then outlined five key features that he claimed defined emerging adulthood: identity exploration; a sense of instability (of residence, employment and romantic partnerships); self-focus; optimism associated with this concurrent 'age of possibilities'; and a sense of feeling 'in between' adolescence and adulthood. According to Arnett, such beliefs are functioning to delay the traditional transition to adulthood, resulting in an elongated period of 'identity formation' associated with the pursuit of higher education, self-exploration and the search for a future linked to personal goals not associated with the preparation for adult roles.

At around the same time Arnett was developing emerging adulthood, other research emerged that lent considerable evidential weight to his putative new life stage. First was demographic research undertaken by University of Pennsylvania sociologist Frank Furstenberg. Furstenberg and his colleagues compared the 1960 and 2000 US censuses, identifying 'a large decline [men down 34%; women down 31%] in the percentage of young adults who, by age 30, have completed all the traditionally defined major adult transitions (leaving home; finishing school; becoming financially independent; getting married; and having a child).'[30] In a subsequent volume, which is seen by many as the definitive overview of the transition into adulthood in the United States at the end of the twentieth century, Furstenberg concluded, 'Adolescence has become a prolonged affair. Entry into adulthood has become more ambiguous, and generally occurs in a gradual, complex, and less uniform fashion.'[31]

Second, neuroscientific data produced by the US National Institute of Mental Health discovered that the prefrontal cortex and cerebellum – the part of the human brain responsible for emotional control – is not stable at the age of eighteen as previously assumed, but rather continues developing well into the early twenties.[32] This second finding was important. Since the mid-1990s, Arnett had been interested in how concepts such as 'cognitive self-sufficiency', 'emotional self-reliance' and 'behavioral self-control' were key elements in the passage from adolescence to young adulthood. Later, when developing the concept of emerging adulthood, he described it as 'a critical stage for the emergence of complex forms of thinking required in complex societies'. The neurological evidence, it seemed, was catching up with him.

This combination of demographic data, neuroscience and media-friendly psychology proved irresistible to many journalists. Before long a battery of articles started to appear heralding the discovery of an entirely new developmental life stage, very often accompanied by headline-friendly neologisms such as 'middle youth', 'adultescence', 'twixters' and 'Peter-Pan-Syndrome'. The emerging adulthood bandwagon had started to roll, but while media commentators, with few exceptions, wholeheartedly embraced Arnett's formulation, others were less convinced.[33]

For nearly two decades, scholars working in the field of youth studies had expressed their concern about the lengthening time it was taking for young people to transition to adulthood. In 2005, one leading group of UK youth studies scholars commented that the traditional youth stage has become 'fragmented and extended', with the transition to adulthood now characterised by 'unpredictability, backwards steps and false starts'.[34] However, in contrast to Arnett's primarily psycho-cultural interpretation, youth scholars focused instead on structural and economic factors, including the contraction of traditional post-school employment opportunities, labour market deregulation, corporate restructuring, changing income and employment patterns and, perhaps most significantly, the extended educational demands required by information-based economies.[35] From this position, a number of important critiques of emerging adulthood have been developed. For example, in his work on the 'missing middle' of youth studies, the sociologist Steve Roberts claims that, far from being a universal period of 'self-focus' and lifestyle-based 'identity-exploration', emerging adulthood is little more than a middle-class construction. Lower down the social structure, many young people are failing to transition to adulthood not because they are enjoying a carefree 'age of possibilities', but because they are fundamentally trapped by a lack of employment opportunities.

By drawing attention to what has since become known as 'the long road to adulthood', Arnett has clearly identified something of considerable importance. However, by over-emphasising the liberating potential of emerging adulthood as a creative space for young adults to find themselves and shape the future direction of their lives, he has essentially psychologised something that is ultimately determined by socio-economic factors.

The issue of emerging adulthood's universality is equally problematic within Arnett's home field of developmental psychology, where key figures have been keen to point out the not inconsiderable evolutionary leap of faith required to subscribe to the concept's neuroscientific hypothesis. Consider the following quote by one of the world's leading developmental psychologists, the late Richard Lerner:

> To qualify as a developmental stage, emerging adulthood must be both universal and essential. If you don't develop a skill at the right stage, you'll be working the rest of your life to develop it when you should be moving on . . . The rest of your development will be unfavorably altered. The fact that Arnett can be so casual about the heterogeneity of emerging adulthood and its existence in some cultures but not in others – indeed, even in some people but not in their neighbors or friends – is what undermines, for many scholars, his insistence that it's a new life stage.[36]

The Canadian identity-formation specialist James Côté goes even further, dismissing emerging adulthood as a 'dangerous myth' that, if taken on board by institutions, could result in serious policy missteps.[37] Côté's robust and measured critique is important because it casts doubt on the methodological and evidential basis of Arnett's developmental theory. It is a point worth developing regarding the way demographic data have often been used – if not by Arnett himself, then certainly by his supporters in the media – to promote the existence of a new 'pre-adulthood' life stage.

Essentially, the problem here is a simple one: the failure to situate demographic shifts within their correct historical and cultural context. While it's undeniably the case that the Furstenberg data from 1960–2000 highlights something of real significance, it does not mean that what we are experiencing is historically without precedent. Indeed, entirely overlooked by the commentators who moved to use Furstenberg's research as evidence of emerging adulthood is the fact that, as Furstenberg himself has stated, the current demographic transformations are not entirely new: 'A century or more ago, the transition into adulthood was also a protracted affair. In an agriculture-based economy, it took many young adults some time to gain the wherewithal to leave home and form a family.'[38] Similarly, class-sensitive demographic analysis of the age of marriage for men for the period 1830–1870 would likely reveal that many men married much later than they did, say, in 1945. Moreover, from a feminist perspective, the underlying assumption that, in the twenty-first century, marriage can be used as a stable sign of adulthood is rather strange given that contraception, cohabitation and shifting gender dynamics have all eroded the notion of marriage as a solid indicator of anything. Such critiques highlight the importance of distinguishing between socio-cultural transformations that are the product of specific historic conditions and something *intrinsic to the generation itself,* as advocates of emerging adulthood's temporal relationship to late modernity appear to be suggesting.

It is a distinction that has already been famously articulated in the literature on the history of childhood.[39] What is perhaps less familiar is the large body of work produced in the field of generation studies and more recently by exponents of what has become known as life-course theory. Extending the argument beyond stating simply that life stages such as adolescence are socially constructed and thus mutable over time, many scholars now propose the idea that generations themselves can have 'agency'.[40] Augmenting sociological analysis with insights from demographics, anthropology, psychology and social history, proponents of life-course theory attempt to understand 'how chronological age, relationships, common life transitions, and social change shape people's lives from birth to death'.[41]

The key figure here is the very appropriately named Glen Elder

Jnr., whose research documented the impact of the Great Depression on individual and family pathways. Elder's work paved the way for subsequent cohort analyses of the relationship between individual life trajectory and wider historical/socioeconomic factors (including geopolitical events, economic cycles, and technological advancements such as the onset of digitised communication). However, within sociology, the assertion that generations themselves have collective and active agency is problematic, and in part explains why the specific category 'generation' has never really gained wide sociological currency. Instead, sociologists have tended to focus on how generational *relations* – normally adult–child relations – are affected and shaped by the particular historic conditions in which they occur. For example, in the mid-1990s and early 2000s, a group of sociologists and historians working under the banner of 'the new childhood studies' paid considerable attention to how relationships are constituted *between* parent and child. It is this focus on the social interactions between generations that is crucial for understanding infantilisation and its associated cultural practices. In other words, rather than expend time and energy trying to identify new stages of the life cycle, à la Arnett, we should focus attention instead on the growing *intergenerational confusion* caused by society's inability to differentiate between established ones.

This, of course, brings us back to Erik Erikson and his theory of human personality development discussed in the Introduction. Erikson's goal was to provide young people with a positive model of what it means to be a grown-up person, and in this sense his work remains essential for anyone interested in understanding infantilism. But in positing a fixed sequence of 'eight stages of psychosocial development', Erikson was as guilty then as Arnett is today of viewing the life course predominantly through the lens of his own categorical and sequential order. But the specific characteristics and related 'personality crises' that underpin Erikson's

71

eight stages are not what should concern us here. Rather, what's important about the Erikson model is his belief that our sense of identity emerges over time as a result of the inherently 'oppositional attitudes' that differentiate each stage of the life cycle; say, for example, between childhood and adolescence, or mid- and late adulthood.

Half a century on from Erikson, one glance at our infantilised world tells us that this inherent opposition *between* developmental phases is fast eroding. The importance of this erosion process cannot be overstated as it is key to understanding not just infantilisation, but also why other recognised phases of the life course have started to blur to the point of indistinguishability.

Chapter 2

Generational Mulch: How Society 'Middled' Itself

In the guesthouse behind one of the many multimillion-dollar homes that dot the beautiful tree-lined valleys and winding hill roads of Marin County, California, a very familiar West Coast scene is taking place. Amid empty beer and wine bottles, amplifier stacks and an atmosphere thick with the aroma of Humboldt County's finest agricultural product, four musicians are midway through their weekly band practice. The music is decent, and I find myself nodding along and enjoying the laid-back ambience. Before long it's time for a break, and whether it's the solid playing or the indica kicking in, the band members are in a reflective mood. 'Friday night was great, the kids really seemed to enjoy it,' says the drummer as he hands me a cold beer. 'Yeah, makes such a big difference when they're into it,' replies one of the band members. 'Just the fact they took time out from their schedules to come up here and hang out, and to really listen to the new songs means a lot, you know? Makes it seem like we're not just wasting our time here.' Nothing unusual about any of this you might think, just another fledgling band finding themselves through their music. But this was no college band or high-school combo. The musicians in question are old friends of mine from back when I lived in the US in the early 1990s. They, like me, have turned fifty. Meanwhile, the 'kids' supposedly enjoying the band's new songs were not peers or fans of the band but *actual* kids, specifically the drummer's ten-year-old daughter and thirteen-year-old son, both of whom had indeed taken 'time out from their schedules' to check out their dad's band's new songs.

Things were not always like this. In 1968, the psychiatrist Arthur Chapman wrote a now largely forgotten book about what he described as the different age-related 'maneuvers' and 'stratagems' employed by people to achieve various interpersonal objectives. When discussing how juveniles differentiated themselves from adults, he articulated the concept of the 'Different Breed of Cat':

> In the stratagem of Different Breed of Cat, the teenager seeks to establish his independence and individuality [from adults] by developing customs, standards and behaviour which are strikingly different from those of his parents . . . The boys let their hair grow long and the girls wear their skirts very short. Adolescents carry out mild varieties of Different Breed of Cat in clothing, grooming, speech idioms and the way they entertain themselves.[1]

Today, however, the behavioural similarities and overlapping cultural concerns that exist between young people and adults suggest Chapman's 'Different Breed of Cat' is an endangered species. Instead of 'maneuvers' and 'stratagems' being used to discern one age group from another, what's more common in contemporary society is a dedifferentiation process, or what I call *representational life stage dissolution*. Evident across the life course, life stage dissolution involves the merging of differential qualities and characteristics associated with previously established age/generation demarcations so that what remains is a sort of generational mulch in which mutual interests and shared cultural

74

experiences become the norm. As we've seen, this tendency is most pronounced in the infantilising practices currently eroding the differences between the social group 'teenagers' and the social group 'adults'. However, the rising level of generational mulch is also affecting social interactions at other points in the life cycle. To illustrate this, let's start by exploring how the blurring associated with life stage dissolution is undermining the concept of childhood as it has come to be understood since the start of the twentieth century.

Adultification: The elevation of the child in contemporary society

Veteran British broadcaster Noel Edmonds grins at the camera and poses the studio audience a question: 'Are you smarter than a ten-year-old?' It is the opening sequence of the Anglo-American TV game show of the same name in which adults pit their wits against a panel of eager schoolchildren. A few decades ago, all but the least confident of adults would have responded with a resounding 'yes'. Today, however, like the confused and embarrassed adult contestants on *Are You Smarter than a 10 Year Old?*, many individuals might just need a moment or two to mull the question over. Although anecdotal, the transfer of cerebral and emotional power relations that drives *Are You Smarter than a 10 Year Old?* and a slew of similarly conceived TV shows that play with and actively reverse child and adult roles (e.g. *What Do Kids Know?*; *Boys and Girls Alone*; *Born to Shine*; *Tarrant Lets the Kids Loose*; and *Hotter Than My Daughter*, in which mothers competed against their daughters in the fashion stakes) is interesting in the way it further evidences the erosion of life stages in contemporary society. This time, however, rather than undermining adulthood by elongating youth, life stage dissolution is functioning to chip away at the psychological and moral boundaries which conventionally have distinguished children from adults – a process we might term *adultification*.

From the eclipse of childhood associated with the mass-medicalisation of juvenile disorders, to the sexualisation of younger and younger girls (the so called 'Lil' Britney effect'), adultification is a conceptual term for thinking about the way children are now treated as the cultural and moral equivalents of adults. Like its corollary, infantilisation, adultification is the product of two closely intertwined cultural dynamics: the undermining of adult authority and the over-valorisation of youth. By devaluing and deriding the moral status traditionally associated with adulthood, society has hamstrung recent generations by failing to provide them with an aspirational model of what it means to be a grown-up person. Likewise, intergenerational confusion is further exacerbated by our ongoing fixation with youth culture; a process that has resulted in the perverse situation wherein the figure of the child is now thought of not simply as the equal of the adult but very often her superior.[2]

In Beth Harpaz's book, *13 is the New 18: And Other Things My Children Taught Me While I Was Having a Nervous Breakdown Being Their Mother*, the joke is how the generation gap will have vanished by the time the author's kids become teenagers. Yet a trawl of popular culture today shows that in many ways it already has. In TV shows like *Junior Apprentice, Project Runway Junior, The Voice Kids, Chopped Junior* or *Junior Masterchef*, it's not simply a case of swapping out grown-ups for children, but of encouraging children to replicate adult attitudes and ape their emotional psychodramas. Other shows go even further than just situating children in adult scenarios. In *Little Big Shots, Blinging Up Baby, Toddlers & Tiaras* and *The 12-Year-Old Shopaholic and Other Big Spending Kids*, the goal is to superimpose adult pathologies on to what are often extremely young children. Even more adultifying are TV formats that move beyond replication into instruction. Here one thinks of *Born to Shine*, in which moderately talented kids function as sagacious role models for hapless adult celebrities, or the late-night UK sketch show *School of Comedy*, in which 'school-aged performers' offered a 'satirical take on adult life'. From a comedic perspective, *School of Comedy* was an unmitigated failure. Yet, in terms of adultification it was groundbreaking in that, even though all the roles were played by schoolchildren, the show's content was deemed mature enough that it could only be broadcast *after* the watershed.

It used to be the case that when films featuring youngsters in dark adult scenarios such as *Kids* (1995) and *Thirteen* (2003) were released they were quickly met with condemnation. Today, however, such content is the stuff of primetime TV, with soap operas and other early-evening drama series regularly featuring storylines in which children are forced to deal with issues that previously were the preserve of adults. This tendency is also pronounced in televisual programming that specifically targets younger audiences. Tea-time 'teen dramas' like *The O.C.*, *Ackley Bridge*, *One Tree Hill*, *Sugar Rush* and the long-running UK soap *Hollyoaks* frequently feature plotlines about stalking, suicide, incest, murder, etc. If anything, the practice of televisual adultification starts even earlier in the United States. Social psychologists Jean Twenge and Keith Campbell noted as early as 2009 that very young children were watching TV shows like *Hannah Montana* and *High School Musical* that originally had been conceived for a much older demographic: 'Even though these shows are about teens, their biggest fans are elementary school and even preschool kids as young as three. Girls are now exposed to the culture of "tweens" – a label applied to ages 9 to 12 – at age 4, eschewing *Sesame Street* and *Dora the Explorer* for *Hannah Montana*, *The*

Suite Life of Zack & Cody, and other preteen shows.' No surprise, then, that 55 per cent of six- to nine-year-old girls now regularly use lip gloss and lipstick, a new make-up sales demographic that cosmetic industry insiders refer to as 'the starter market'.[3]

Stories that transpose the traumas and crises of the adult world onto teenagers and children are equally common in contemporary film, with at least two adultifying tropes discernible. First, generation-destabilising stories like *Licorice Pizza*, *Little Miss Sunshine*, *Leave No Trace*, *Beautiful Girls*, *Juno* and *Captain Fantastic*, which turn around the idea that adults should learn life lessons from children rather than the other way round; and second, films such as *Brick*, *The Bling Ring*, *The Land*, *Aoi Hauru*, *Alpha Dog* and *Kidulthood*, in which teenagers wrestle with serious adult/criminal problems, while the actual adult world is marginalised to the point of insignificance.

This notion that children and young people can exist independently of adults is not limited to movie plots. Today, we are constantly being informed about supposedly important teen bloggers, schoolgirl influencers and child prodigies, all of whom seem to function entirely detached from, and often in opposition to, the adult world with all its boring old prerequisites of education, responsibility and practical life experience. The same dynamic is evident in the contemporary art market, which should be concerned with works that represent the zenith of aesthetic human achievement, but too often embraces adultification by hyping child art prodigies and supposedly influential art wunderkind. For example, the Australian abstract artist, Aelita Andre, had her first solo art show when she was only twenty-two months old. Since then, she has been the subject of exhibitions and museum shows in New York City, China and Russia. Her 'unique' approach to painting and sculpture has been called by some 'magical abstraction', although to the untrained eye it looks uncannily like a small child emptying pots of paint on the floor and then covering the mess with glitter. Be that as it may, Andre is feted in the art world ('Is Aelita the next Jackson Pollock?' was the title of one *New York Times* op ed by the art historian Noah Horowitz), with her works regularly selling for prices in excess of $10,000. But is the glitter on Andre's career star beginning to fade? Andre is now in her late teens, but the photographs on her website depict someone much younger. But, of course, that's the thing about adultification – essentially, it's a young person's game.

Such was the publicity surrounding Kieron Williamson, the so-called 'mini Monet', that by age ten, his average-looking impressionist renderings had generated more than £1.5 million in gallery sales. It was a similar story with the Las Vegas-based art prodigy, Autumn de Forest. Touted on the Discovery Channel as 'an artistic genius' when she was just eight years old, Forest amassed sales of over $7m for her paintings by the time she was seventeen. But the best example, not just of adultification in the art world, but of life stage dissolution more generally, is the accidental collaboration of the artist Mica Angela Hendricks and her four-year-old daughter, Layla. Apparently, one day, entirely unprompted, Layla grabbed a pen and started to scribble all over one of her mother's unfinished drawings. The finished images look precisely how you might imagine – crude and childlike. Social media commentators, however, thought differently, and before long, this heartwarming tale of 'mother–daughter collaboration' had spawned an 'amazing' collection of works that were subsequently published in a book entitled *Share With Me*.

In *The Anthropology of Childhood: Cherubs, Chattel, Changelings*, the veteran American anthropologist David Lancy provides a fascinating account of the way children are raised and valued in different cultures around the globe. Challenging the ethnocentricity of much classic anthropological research into childhood development, Lancy goes to great lengths to make the obvious but nonetheless important point that a 'child's worth varies widely across cultures, across social classes, even within a single family'. Early in the book, he introduces the concept of 'the neontocracy' – any society in which young children are highly valued, despite their relatively low social utility in objective terms. According to Lancy, modern neontocracies such as the US and the UK are the exact opposite of what most societies have looked like throughout human history, which, typically, 'have been dominated by attention to the oldest members – the classic model in which elders are esteemed'.[4] You don't need to conduct any anthropological fieldwork to recognise that, whether you like it or not, you're now living in a neontocratic world – just take a quick glance around.

For example, paediatricians and childhood experts now regularly discuss the phenomenon of so-called 'baby-led parenting': a child-rearing strategy that inverts the established idea of parents guiding and conditioning their offspring and instead urges them to let their babies 'take the lead' when it comes to setting behavioural patterns. Hence a glut of recent articles on everything from 'baby-led walking' to 'baby-led potty training' to 'baby-led sleeping'.[5] But for some commentators, even putting babies in charge of their own upbringing isn't enough. Because of the supposed power inequality associated with something called 'adultism' – the engrained cultural assumption 'that adults are better than young people, and entitled to act upon young people without agreement' – many now subscribe to the bizarre belief that one shouldn't even pick up a baby or place it in its crib without first receiving the infant's 'affirmative consent'.

How did we arrive at this point? How did we create neontocratic societies so obsessed with children that the role of parent is fast being replaced by something that more closely resembles a subservient caregiver? These are complex questions, answers to which exceed the remit of this work. However, what we can say given what we've already seen is that the cultural and psycho-social processes associated with infantilisation and adultification are part of the same concerning development, i.e., the general drift towards the over-valorisation of youth and the corresponding depreciation of the moral status historically associated with adulthood.

In Western nations, such has been the erosion of adult wisdom and forms of authority connected with experiential expertise, that the bearing of the moral compass is now regularly set according to the supposed sagacity and insight of the young. This reversal of roles associated with the idealisation and adultification of youth is perhaps most evident in the figure of the celebrated climate-change activist Greta Thunberg. Since rising to prominence in 2018, Thunberg has been nominated for the Nobel Peace Prize by Norwegian politicians, voted *Time* magazine's 2019 Person of the Year, and been lionised by everybody from the Archbishop of Canterbury to Barack Obama. In June 2020, a former mayor in Sweden even proposed that a monument to one of the nation's most significant monarchs, King Charles XII (Carolus Rex), be torn down and replaced with a new statue honouring Thunberg. Her meteoric rise is even more remarkable when one considers that she possesses no scientific expertise and has said nothing original whatsoever about climate issues. So how did an unqualified (sometime) schoolgirl manage to become the moral conscience of the green movement? The answer is simple. Thunberg embodies a role reversal in which young people are increasingly assigned the intellectual gravitas and cultural authority to educate adults and correct their supposedly errant thinking. In Thunberg's case it is a dynamic fuelled by emotionality – she is never far from the type of fire-and-brimstone divination that used to characterise apocalyptic millenarianists. But more importantly, what drives this generational inversion is the perceived sense that the ills of the adult world need correcting, a point Thunberg made abundantly clear in her address to the United Nations: 'Since our leaders are behaving like children, we will have to take the responsibility they should have taken long ago . . . We have to understand what the older generation has dealt to us, what mess they have created that we have to clean up and live with.' It is the same logic that drove the 2019 school strike movement, which saw mostly middle-class kids seize the chance to skip school and protest what they perceive to be the radical cause of environmentalism. At the root of this process is not simply a concern with climate change but a deep resentment about the way adults seem to be mismanaging the situation. Slogans such as 'You'll Die of Old Age, We'll Die of Climate Change' and 'Adults Ruin Everything' make it clear that the school strike and the cult of Thunberg that triggered it represent a new type of generational activism that only serves to further erode the parameters of adult responsibility.

Rather than acknowledge they are listening to the political views of a child, politicians and civic leaders take every possible opportunity to genuflect before Thunberg and her emotive mode of reasoning. One particularly perverse moment came in April 2019, when Thunberg addressed a group of British parliamentarians. 'I speak on behalf of future generations,' thundered Thunberg in her opening statement. But instead of questioning what right someone who had yet to finish school had to speak on behalf of such a broad constituency, the assembled group, that included cabinet ministers, instead fawned over her like penitents seeking absolution from a spiritual guru. And if all this wasn't bad enough, the scope of Ms Thunberg's apparent expertise seems only to be expanding. From Coronavirus epidemiology to the complex geopolitics of the Middle East, few subjects these days are beyond the purview of this worked-up Swedish doomsayer.

Thanks to Thunberg's promotion to environmental demigod, it's now become quite common for institutions to virtue signal about the importance of hearing 'the voice of youth' prior to making policy decisions. Writing in the *Independent*, Rosie Lockwood and Serena Kelly argued that today's policymakers must prioritise the thoughts of this 'energetic, diverse, passionate generation' of young people. They base this claim on the fact that 'thousands of children and young people have taken to the streets to call for climate action', and that 'they have the motivation and ideas we need to win the race to net zero'.[6] Motivated they may be, but when it comes to *actual* ideas to tackle climate change, my money is on the older generation of equally motivated scientists who are currently developing nanotube and graphene technologies, mass-desalination equipment, fourth-generation nuclear plants, etc., rather than phalanxes of self-righteous five-foot student radicals.

That said, youthful climate activists do have at least one idea they're running with – lawyering up. Egged on by a 2023 United Nations report which stated that children have more moral authority than adults when it comes to issues of the environment, young people around the world have started the process of bringing lawsuits against their own countries for failing to tackle climate change. But while adultifying developments such as these continue to elevate the status of childhood to levels unprecedented in human history, elsewhere other problems are emerging.

We've already discussed how adultification has eroded some of the established norms and conventions associated with adulthood, but perhaps even more worrying is how growing older younger is fundamentally changing what it means to be a child. For some time now, there has been unease in society about the growing sexualisation of children, especially girls. As early as the 1990s, teenage magazines such as *More!*, *Just Seventeen*, *Sugar* and *Nineteen* were courting controversy for their advanced sexual content. By the 2000s, fears about the premature sexualisation of girls had taken the form of news stories about inappropriate clothing being sold to pre-teens. British retailer Primark came under fire for designing padded bikini tops for seven-year-old girls, while UK companies Next and New Look were also assailed in the press for selling high-heeled shoes to girls as young as six.[7] Such was the level of concern in Australia, one controversial report even went so far as to coin the term 'corporate paedophilia' to describe the way this type of clothing was potentially portraying young girls as sexual objects.[8] By the decade's end, institutions involved in the care and protection of young people had also started to express unease. In 2010, The Children's Society's Penny Nicholls stated: 'There is a big distinction between children dressing up for fun and retailers producing items of clothing that target children and encourage premature sexualisation . . . Retailers and adults have a responsibility to ensure children and young people grow up valuing the right things in themselves and other people.'[9] The teaching profession was similarly worried, demanding more guidance from the government about how schools should tackle the over-sexualised nature of youth culture.[10]

Such criticism, however, did little if anything to stem the tide. Over the last decade, the adultification and sexualisation of young girls has continued apace. In 2012, the French manufacturer Jours Apres Lunes released a 'loungerie' line for three- to thirty-six-month-old girls, while in Colorado, shoppers were shocked to find crotchless panties on sale at a 'Kids N Teen' store. For many feminist commentators, the growth of such inappropriate clothing is what happens when the sexualisation of children is folded into celebrity culture.[11] In 2009, when a then seventeen-year-old Miley Cyrus performed a fairly innocuous pole dance at the Teen Choice Awards she was immediately mired in controversy for being a poor role model to her impressionable young fans. Today, this performance would barely raise an eyebrow. In 2021, Cyrus, whose estimated net worth is $207 million, urged her fans to 'ask Daddy' to buy them her new line of suggestive merchandise, including a $35 'I ♡ dick', muscle T-shirt with semen droplets on it. In the contemporary celebrityscape, it's now entirely normal for Kim Kardashian – whose fame is inextricably bound up with the release of a sex tape – to be held up as a role model for teenage girls, or for showbiz tabloids to pry into the romantic relations of fourteen-year-old *Stranger Things* star Millie Bobby Brown. Indeed, when singer Jessica Simpson sparked controversy for posting pictures of her four-month-old daughter wearing a bikini, her fans immediately sprang to her defence, dismissing the critics as 'mommy shamers'.

The premature sexualisation of childhood is exemplified in the 2020 Netflix offering *Cuties*, a French film about eleven-year-old girls in a twerking dance group. Defended by some as a commentary on the sexualisation of children, it's hard to see how scenes involving pre-teen girls performing slut drops and bump-and-grind simulated sex moves as anything but gratuitous exhibitionism, a point made by the commentator and former UK government advisor Katharine Birbalsingh:

> Apart from the last few minutes, the film glorifies and endorses the hyper-sexualised behaviour of children . . . *Cuties* does an excellent job of ticking off men's fetishes with the girls. Porn directors try to do this but they are at a disadvantage: they aren't allowed to use real children. Porn directors have to make do with 20-year-old porn actresses and then they try to dress them in such a way to make them look younger. But *Cuties* isn't restricted like this and is free to use children as young as 11 because this is 'art'. The fetish 'spotty girl' makes shy and girly faces. The fetish plump girl satisfies any man who likes them a 'little big'. The girl with abnormally big glasses satisfies the awkward and goofy fetish. No real edgy 11-year-old would wear ugly oversized glasses. The film departs from an accurate portrayal of reality in

order to make the girl look a certain way to satisfy an adult male audience.[12]

Birbalsingh's words are especially powerful as she is also the headmistress of the Michaela Community School in north-west London, and as such is deeply concerned about how films like *Cuties* and other cultural developments – in 2023, the city of Berlin released a book titled *Rosie Needs Money* (*Rosi sucht Geld*) which aimed to explain prostitution (using extremely graphic illustrations) to youths 'aged six to twelve years old' – are functioning to normalise hyper-sexualised behaviour among the young children in her care.

The sexualisation of children's spaces is perhaps most evident in the recent trend of 'Drag Queen Story Hour', where drag artists teach gender identity, sometimes by engaging in striptease, other times by giving twerking lessons to preschool kids in libraries and other municipal settings. Often welcomed by liberal parents as a way of challenging 'cisnormativity', this type of queer performativity is just another form of adultification in which very young children are exposed to adult sexuality.[13] Giving preschool children access to sexualised content, even if done under the guise of equality or trans activism, can never be a good thing. It raises questions in children's minds that should only be posed later in the life course and in doing so unravels the delicate structure that is childhood innocence.

The problem, of course, is that elsewhere in society adultified culture is already dismantling childhood innocence in several other troubling ways. Psychologists and childhood studies experts, for example, have all expressed concern over what they call 'the pornification of childhood'.[14] As Gail Dines, an expert on the developmental impact of pornography on children explains, the concern here is twofold. First, in relation to young boys, the porn industry has 'hijacked' the adolescent brain, which is 'primed for novelty and risk-taking', making it harder for young males to form meaningful intimate relationships later in the life course. Second, in terms of young girls, although 'not the major consumers of pornography, they suffer the consequences because they engage in sexual relationships with boys and men who have had their sexual templates shaped by mainstream online violent pornography'.[15] Although there remains much debate about the damaging nature of sexualised imagery on minors, some things are already very clear: levels of depression, low self-esteem and eating disorders are all markedly higher in girls who have internalised porn culture. In fields like digital sociology, researchers have identified that the social practice of producing, using and sharing digital sexual images is increasingly integral to the everyday lives of young people – both as a mode of consensual flirting ('sexting'), but more worryingly as a form of non-consensual pornography. There is, of course, much more one could say about the damage caused to childhood by exposure to all kinds of sexualised practices ushered in by the digital age, but for now suffice it to say that sexting and the sharing of digital sexual images is also interesting in terms of how it highlights one of the most serious ambiguities associated with our adultified society: the profound confusion that exists within the criminal justice system about exactly who is an adult and, conversely, who is a child?

Around the turn of the century, in the United States alone, an estimated 250,000 kids were being tried, sentenced, or incarcerated as adults each year. At that time, on any given day in America, hundreds, and most likely thousands, of kids were doing time not alongside their peers in juvenile detention facilities but in adult jails and prisons. You don't need to be a professional criminologist to understand and appreciate the damage this does to young people.[16] Youth offenders incarcerated in US adult prisons are thirty-six times more likely to commit suicide than youngsters held in juvenile facilities, as well as being at a far greater risk of ending up in solitary confinement. They are also much more likely to become victims of serious sexual abuse and less likely to receive the supportive therapies needed if they are to become productive members of society later in the life course. Thankfully, because of the hard work of youth advocacy groups, the number of youth offenders held in US adult jails and prisons has declined since its high point of around 10,000 in the early 2000s. Yet while the practice of dumping kids in the dark recesses of the adult prison system may finally be waning, elsewhere the adultifying tendencies of the criminal justice system have only intensified.

One of the most troubling examples of adultification is how young people of school age – especially those from already racialised communities – are being harshly punished for minor disciplinary infractions that previously would not have warranted criminal sanction. Typically, the result of a combination of poor police training and constipated zero tolerance crime policies, American childhood is being de-legitimated by a society that cannot distinguish youthful excess from serious offending. Consider the following incidents: Oakland County, Michigan, a fifteen-year-old schoolgirl was incarcerated for failing to do her online homework; Albuquerque, New Mexico, a thirteen-year-old schoolboy was arrested for burping in gym class; Forest Hills, New York, a twelve-year-old girl was handcuffed and taken out of school for doodling 'I love my friends' on a school desk; Cincinnati, Ohio, a cop uses a Taser on an eleven-year-old girl suspected of shoplifting; Austin, Texas, Sarah Bustamantes, twelve, was arrested and cited for spraying perfume on her neck after classmates teased her about body odour; Jefferson Parish, Louisiana, an eighth-grader was dragged from class in handcuffs and spent six days in a juvenile detention facility for throwing Skittles on a school bus; and in Lee County, Florida, police were called out by the assistant principal of an elementary school after a little girl kissed a boy during gym class. In these and countless other stories from across America, what we are seeing is a form of police-state madness where every misbehaviour, no matter how trivial, is a matter for the police or the authorities.[17] Two decades ago, disrupting class or messing around on a school bus would result in a visit to the principal's office, detention, or at worst a short period of suspension. Today, because of an inability to recognise that schoolchildren should and must be treated differently from adults, American schools have opened their gates to the criminal justice system, exposing children in their care to criminal sanctions that in many cases will last a lifetime.

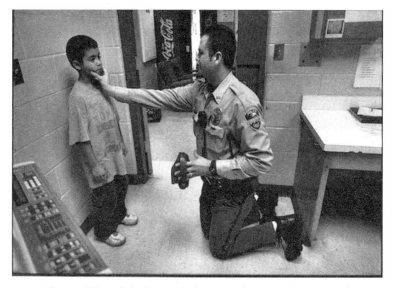

Plate 6: The adultification of criminal justice. (Steve Liss)

Something else that no doubt will last a lifetime are the developmental side effects and mental health problems caused by Anglo-American society's unending eagerness to drug its children. It should be clear by now that the process of adultification takes many forms, but without doubt its most perverse manifestation has been the medicalisation of childhood that has taken place during the twenty-first century. Under the guise of addressing a supposed crisis in children's mental health, the ever-expanding therapeutic community and the profiteers of the pharmaceutical industry have conspired to produce the most medicalised generation of young people in history. It is a misdiagnosis scandal of epic proportions. In 1997, only 3 per cent of American children were diagnosed with ADHD. Just over two decades later, and a staggering 20 per cent of all boys under eighteen in the US are now said to have the condition. In two thirds of these cases, the prescribed treatment is a combination of stimulants like amphetamine-dextroamphetamine and methylphenidate. And these repeat prescriptions add up. In 2016, following an 89 per cent spike in sales in just four years, the ADHD drug market was estimated to be worth $14 billion annually (in the UK, NHS prescriptions for ADHD rose by over 50 per cent from 2007 to 2013).[18] It's a similar story with antidepressants. Figures released by the NHS in August 2021 revealed that prescriptions for antidepressants given to children aged five to sixteen had risen by 22 per cent in the previous five years (in 2020, a record 231,791 prescriptions were written, compared with 189,457 in 2016). Worryingly, this tendency to solve all behavioural problems with prescription drugs is now routinely extended to preschool children, where equally alarming rises in prescriptions have been documented – despite clear medical guidelines by the UK's National Institute for Health and Clinical Excellence that restrict the use of potent methylphenidate-based drugs for children under six.

In previous generations, children's unruly behaviour was seen and largely dismissed as part of the chaos of growing up. Today, that same behaviour is re-categorised as a neurological condition so serious it necessitates the administration of adult stimulants and mood-altering chemicals to primary-school children. This mass drugging of kids provides a vivid illustration of how many parents, therapists, counsellors and clinicians have completely lost their way when it comes to understanding the distinction between children and adults.

Plate 7: If I knew you were going to be diagnosed with a neurodevelopmental disorder, I would have baked a cake. In 2018, in the Danish version of the TV cookery show *Bake Off* (*Den Store Bagedyst*), one of the aspiring confectioners, Marianne Bjerring, baked a 'brain' cake as a tribute to her son and his ADHD diagnosis. It's no surprise that *Bake Off* would offer a space for the celebration of childhood mental health disorders. Over the years, it has proven itself a veritable case study in infantilisation. Hardly a week goes by without somebody bursting into tears over an over-egged pudding or collapsed soufflé. In the UK, the show was previously fronted by fifty-year-old Matt Lucas, a self-confessed man-boy who came to prominence dressed literally as a 'big baby' (on the game show *Shooting Stars*). Lucas happily admits to having 'the [food] tastes of a nine-year-old', and once hosted a TV chat show in which he had his mother sit next to him as he opined on subjects such as 'the most irritating children's TV character'. (DR Archive)

Sadly, the ADHD/antidepressant prescription drug crisis is only one way in which childhood is being degraded by a neo-therapeutic community whose future sustainability depends on constantly inventing new medical health problems. So unchecked has been the growth of the psych industry that there is almost no area or stage of human development that is not subject to some sort of psycho-therapeutic intervention.[19] Consider, for example, the nursery. Once seen as a site of fun and learning, it is now viewed by many psychologists as a hotbed of 'preschool stress'. 'Starting day care can be a stressful time, for both babies and parents alike,' claims Cindy Hovington, PhD, the founder of the website Curious Neuron, in what could almost be an advertising strapline for life stage dissolution. How should we deal with this? According to Michael Lamb, professor of psychology at Cambridge University, the solution is to 'de-stress children before and after nursery'. But no matter how much de-stressing kids do, it will never be enough. If we believe the experts, stress will inevitably re-emerge at every stage of their young lives, like dry rot in an untreated house.

School examinations especially are a lightning rod for all manner of psychobabble. One childhood expert recently claimed that 'thanks to groundbreaking discoveries in developmental science', the 'pressure' of sitting GCSE exams is now 'damaging' the sixteen-year-old brain.[20] The plain fact of the matter is that the more we have psychologised childhood, the more we have created young adults who are anxious and susceptible to mental health disorders later in life. Today's teenagers already report significantly higher levels of anxiety, stress and emotional vulnerability than their parents did at the same age. This in itself should worry us, but lurking on the horizon is something even worse. If it is the case, as the psychologists also tell us, that anxious parents make anxious kids, then what awaits us in a single generation's time will no longer simply be a 'crisis of childhood' but likely the death of the entire concept.

As I hope has been illustrated, the generational blurring associated with adultification is now a common feature of the Anglo-American cultural script. Its effects are still unfolding, but it has already generated a profound sense of confusion among many adults about how best to guide and protect children, and even about when children should be listened to and when they should be ignored. But adultification's greatest impact is on the children themselves. Often empowered beyond their years, and frequently confronted with issues that should not concern them, they are now being treated not as children but as mini-adults, and as such often struggle with the extra responsibility that comes from carrying such a heavy existential load.

And one final irony. Despite what they may think, when adultified children 'adult blame', or when teenagers condemn the older generation for its poor stewardship of the future, they are themselves contributing to the process of infantilisation. For as kids hurtle at full speed towards adulthood, what awaits them when they get there will be the very same childlike state they seem so keen to leave behind.

Life stage dissolution: Swimming in a tank full of half-adults

> *People don't bother to grow up, and we are all fish swimming in a tank of half-adults. The rule is: Where repression was before, fantasy will be now ... Adults regress towards adolescence; and adolescents – seeing that – have no desire to become adults. Few are able to imagine any genuine life coming from the vertical plane – tradition, religion, devotion.*
>
> Robert Bly, 1996[21]

Up to this point we have concentrated on how the bi-directional dynamics of adultification and infantilisation have diminished the conventional distinctions between children and adults – a process I call *life stage dissolution*. But it is important to recognise that life stage dissolution is also occurring elsewhere in the developmental sequence. Consider, for example, the so-called 'generation wars' currently taking place at the other end of the life course.

One of the livelier debates of the 2010s concerned the 'Baby Boomer' generation, and how their lifestyle, politics and economic heft is supposedly depriving younger generations of the opportunities and resources required to create their own prosperous lives. 'Boomer blaming' involves the practice of accusing the demographic cohort of people born between 1946 and 1962 (dates can vary) for all the flaws and problems of the present day. To get a sense of the nature of this argument, one need look no further than the title of some of the key books on the subject. Whether it's in David Willetts's *The Pinch: How the Baby Boomers Took Their Children's Future – and Why They Should Give it Back*, Francis Beckett's *What Did the Baby Boomers Ever Do for Us: Why the Children of the Sixties Lived the Dream and Failed the Future*, or Ed Howker and Shiv Malik's *Jihad Generation: How Britain Has Bankrupted its Youth*, Boomers are deemed to be guilty of failing to protect the interests of future generations. Typically, this critique takes two forms.

First, at the economic level, Baby Boomers are said to be problematic because, on the one hand, they are characterised by affluence, self-interest and a monopolisation of economic resources; and on the other, because their 'excess longevity' is creating a series of 'time bombs' in pensions, health and social care. Second, at the cultural level, Boomers are often depicted as self-absorbed, greedy and trapped in a world of permanent nostalgia. It is also claimed by writers like Joe Queenan that Boomers are obsessed with staying young and as a result have 'never devised an exit strategy from their youth'. It is in relation to the second issue, their prevailing cultural values and mindset, that Boomers have received more criticism than perhaps any generation in history.[22] Clearly, there is much to deride about Boomer culture: the unnecessary intellectualisation of popular music; the idolisation of political hypocrites like Jerry Rubin, Jane Fonda and (later) the Clintons; the culture of 'self-help'; the fashion sense. (And let's not forget that the penchant for virtue signalling common among today's Wokerati stems from 'the Boomer habit of annexing another person's suffering and then adorning it with some ludicrous personal iconography').[23] However, my concern is not with the debates that surround 'Boomergeddon culture', but rather with the generational tension that exists *between* Baby Boomers and the age cohorts that followed them – and how this tension perfectly exemplifies life stage dissolution.

One of the central arguments of this chapter is that, when adults stay younger longer (infantilisation) and when children grow older quicker (adultification), the inevitable result is a sort of generational mulch where shared and interchangeable cultural and psychological experiences become the norm. Today's generational squabbles between supposedly avaricious Boomers and virtuous Millennials nicely illustrate this phenomenon.[24] In this case, generational mulch is produced via a two-step process. First, since 2010, we have witnessed what Jennie Bristow in her book *Baby Boomers and Generational Conflict* calls 'a reversal of the normal pattern of generational continuity and conflict'.[25] In other words, rather than the older generation being conscientious custodians of the future, Boomers are socially constructed as an irresponsible cohort who, by clinging to their youthful values, are endangering succeeding generations. As a result, younger people are being tasked with 'restoring order to chaos'. It is a logic that often finds expression though the metaphor of an out-of-control 'party', as typified in this passage from David Willetts's bestselling book *The Pinch: How the Baby Boomers Took Their Children's Futures*:

We all know the story. The parents return home from a night away to find a teenage party had got out of hand and the house has been trashed. Every few months a particularly dramatic episode gets into the media – with distraught parents tidying up a mess left by a swarm of young people summoned on Facebook. It plays to a deep-seated fear that younger people will not appreciate and protect what has been achieved by the older generation. This is the eternal anxiety of each generation about what comes after. But what if, when it comes to many of the big things that matter for our future, it is the other way round? What if it's actually the older generation, the baby boomers, who have been throwing a party and leaving behind a mess for the next generation to sort out.[26]

Once the normal pattern of life has been reversed, the second element of generational mulch is inevitable. Here I refer to the destabilisation of adult identity that is the inescapable consequence of the generational-wars narrative. With the elder generation's authority traduced, the young are forced into a position of moral superiority. Or, as Bristow suggests in a later article, 'the "voice of youth" is increasingly presented, not as something politicians should listen to, but as something they should take a lead from'. Hence Greta Thunberg, hence Havana Chapman-Edwards (the 'seven-year-old activist') – and hence *generational mulch*, as both Millennials and Baby Boomers end up looking and sounding more like each other as each year passes. Both feel undervalued and underappreciated, both are only too happy to deploy the victim card, and, most importantly, both blame each other for their own problems and failings. In gambling terms, it's as if the protagonists in the generation war have been *middled*, i.e., their original bet, and the subsequent hedge they made against that bet, *both* lost when the points spread shifted against them, turning both positions into losses. And this is where we currently find ourselves. The life cycle has well and truly stalled, and as a result we are stuck flailing around in an increasingly inhospitable middle ground of our own making. Once again, Bristow nails it by pointing out that, while generational mulch causes all kinds of developmental problems, the real tragedy here is the slow death of adult authority: 'Both sides of the rhetorical "generation war" seek to dissolve the creativity and optimism of youth in an acid bath of existential bitterness, in which the kids are expected to sink or swim. And in doing so, both sides express the problem at the core of the "generation wars" narrative: an abject disregard for the responsibility that adults have in shaping their world, and bringing the younger generations into it.'[27]

Looking beyond the Boomer debate, it's clear that life stage dissolution and the generational mulch it inevitably produces are all around us. It's evident in the way parents and children play the same games together (LEGO recently released a 'Let's Build Together' range 'for people of all ages', while video game companies barely bother to disaggregate their games by age group these days), listen to the same music, watch the same films (I've lost count of the number of adults, including academic colleagues, who tell me their favourite film is something produced by Disney, Pixar or Aardman Animations – pathetic when you think about it) and even dress alike. It's there in TV shows that purport to reflect the changing nature of the contemporary American family like *Modern Family* (in which hapless dad Phil Dunphy describes what he does as 'peeranting' as opposed to parenting), *Weeds* (where, over the course of eight seasons, single mum Nancy Botwin and her youngest son, Shane, essentially swap roles as carer and cared, before ultimately meeting somewhere in the middle), and *Ozark* (in which an entire family, including two high-school-aged kids, are involved in an international money-laundering operation). And it's there in those adultifying, supposedly ironic, bib and T-shirt slogans – 'chick magnet', 'shot caller', 'future supermodel', 'I'm the boss', etc. – that parents buy for their children (see Plate 8). Clearly, in and of themselves, these things are not especially problematic; indeed, a case could be made that such practices bring families closer together and make it easier for children to relate to their parents. The problem is that the deleterious effects of generational mulch have penetrated much deeper into the core of Anglo-American society.

Plate 8: 'What happens at day care stays at day care.' (Author's own)

Today, a profound sense of confusion surrounds growing up. By venerating children and simultaneously depreciating adulthood, society is now incapable of asserting any positive vision of what it means to be grown-up. Instead, a thick fog of uncertainty has settled over the life course. This confused state of affairs is exacerbated by the almost boundless hypocrisy that commonly surrounds generational mulch. Consider, for example, the contrasting treatment of two young people of the same age who figured prominently in the 2019 news cycle. We have already discussed how society celebrated the schoolgirl activist Greta Thunberg as an all-knowing sage. Yet, the very same liberal commentators that talked endlessly about the wisdom and autonomy of a sixteen-year-old then turned around – often in the same newspaper – and loudly condemned the British government for its decision not to allow Shamima Begum, the British-born teenager who appeared to leave London willingly for the Islamic State, to return to the UK. In this instance, despite being the exact same age as Thunberg, Begum was presented as a duped child, someone far too young and naive to know her own mind, and therefore not responsible for her subsequent actions – which, lest we forget, reportedly included playing an active role in IS's brutal 'morality police', defending the rape and slavery of Yazidis, and allegedly helping to stitch suicide bombers into their explosive vests. When society acts in such a hypocritical fashion, adultifying on the one hand and infantilising on the other, it is playing a dangerous and duplicitous game. No good comes from keeping two sets of books, and thus it should come as little surprise that a great many young people are today deeply conflicted about which path they should follow as they begin their ascent towards adulthood.

But this is not the only mixed message that surrounds the contemporary life course. One of the most pervasive themes our culture instantiates in young people is that the route to success and fulfilment lies not in hard work and delayed gratification but in fun, hedonism and self-expression. Correspondingly, everywhere they turn, young people are bombarded with pop-culture messages that stress the need to 'live the dream' or 'go big or go home'. This promotion and celebration of self-indulgence and playful transgression is seen as a key component of contemporary identity formation; a way of unlocking the door to a new kind of adulthood that is less about maturation and more about maintaining a sense of stasis wherein the individual is always situated on the cusp of (traditional) adulthood.

Earlier, I mentioned LEGO's new 'Let's Build Together' sets as an example of generational mulch, but in many ways the cultural imagination that has grown up around LEGO also illustrates my point about how life stage dissolution is reshaping the nature of adulthood. Here one thinks of how the Danish toy manufacturer has made a lucrative business out of its LEGO Serious Play division, which offers corporations a 'generative toolkit' for business modelling. Recently, an academic friend of mine took part in a 'PlayAhead: Creative Winning Strategies LEGO Serious Play Day' (I probably would have slipped out the door before that title had even been read out), in which he was asked to imagine and then use LEGO blocks to build the university culture/department he wished to work in. This at the very moment his actual university building – a beautiful nineteenth-century lakeside structure – was being sold off to cover debts incurred after his university massively overspent on a building project elsewhere in the city. Today's supposedly progressive corporations and universities are full of such 'tradition challenging' and 're-imagining' initiatives. But while ideation 'sandboxes' and 'adult playgrounds' might help the bottom line, they also reinforce the idea that what matters most in society is youthful play as opposed to a generational detachment from immaturity. And while we're on the subject of LEGO, let's consider one final example that perfectly illustrates the way creative playfulness is feted in contemporary society. Sean Kenney is a LEGO Certified Pro, a forty-something man whose job is making large-scale LEGO sculptures. As the following passage from the type of puff piece that can be found in lifestyle magazines the world over suggests, Kenney's message to others is a beguilingly simple one: why bother growing up when you can use your favourite toy or youthful pursuit as a maturity repellent.

Kenney is a personal hero for every schlub who's grinding out a living while humming 'Take this job and shove it' under his breath. His old career was good while it lasted but, ultimately, it was about as satisfying as a light beer when compared to playing every day in his own personal LEGOLAND. 'In my head, I was thinking it was nuts to leave a six-figure job,' he says. 'But I just wanted to go home and play with LEGOs, and it turned out to be the right decision. Every kid dreams they're going to do what they want to do for a living,' he adds. 'For me, it was the natural progression of things . . . I just followed my gut. As an adult, I still played with LEGOs for fun after work, and then someone paid me to do a project. Then a few people paid me. Now I do it for a living.'[28]

Good luck to Sean Kenney and his ilk, but in truth the sense of perpetual teenagerdom that these playful late-modern careers embody is an unattainable fiction for all but a very select few in these economically depressed times.

Far away from the adult ball pits and the LEGO play areas of the corporate world, a very different festival of play and boundary breaking has been under way for some time. In the urban enclaves, student wastelands and down-on-the-their-luck commuter suburbs of Britain and America, large numbers of young people have also decided, whether by choice or more likely because of a lack of meaningful employment opportunities, that they too will dedicate their lives to fun and self-expression. The problem is that, bereft of the cultural capital and all-important contacts needed to make it as a creative imagineer or a LEGO Certified Pro, they must find an alternate vector through which to 'live the dream'. That vector is, of course, the bars, night clubs, casinos, eateries and lap-dancing venues that constitute the contemporary night-time economy (NTE). In these highly commercialised spaces of inebriation and intoxication, playfulness and excess are also very much to the fore – the difference being that, within the NTE, expressive, liminal moments are not so much celebrated as they are captured by consumer markets adept at exploiting pleasure and marketing experience.[29] Loved by some, loathed by others, whatever one's particular view of the NTE, one thing is absolutely clear: millions of people are using its party spaces and lagervilles as the primary site of identity creation and self-expression. However, as the criminologist Oliver Smith points out, what appears initially to be an alluring world of VIP club nights and roped-off luxury lounges is ultimately a dissatisfying experience – an over-priced cocktail sugar-high that wears off before you even make it to the taxi rank.

> What these consumers desire is to distance themselves from artifice and wholeheartedly embrace a world free from normative social control . . . a world that stands in contrast to the mundane, the workaday monotony of work under late-modern capitalism . . . Excessive alcohol consumption within the NTE provides the most simple, legal and accessible route into something that looks like where they want to be, even though they know, in a barely conscious way, that real 'liberation' is not on offer and that they are being carried along [on] an experiential conveyor belt only to find that at the end of their journey their pockets are empty and they didn't really enjoy the experience quite as they thought they would.[30]

Smith's particular take on the NTE stands out because rather than morally condemning the boozers and users who populate these spaces, he recognises something of far greater significance. In his detailed research, Smith concentrates on how 'adulthood is being worked on' in the drink-and-drugs-based NTE and, more specifically, how many people in their thirties and forties are so deeply attached to a youthful culture of excess and transgression they are trapped by the lifestyle:

> While one might expect that individuals discard these leisure activities as they head towards middle age, the data seems to suggest that a commitment to hedonism and intoxication is retained until much later in the life course and can inform the construction of a significant part of the properly 'adult' identity . . . these individuals are essentially 'captured' by processes associated with the consumer economy and display the cultural characteristics of infantilisation, individualisation and myriad anxieties and pressures that make adherence to what might be considered a more traditional life course hard to imagine.[31]

What's interesting about these quotes is how they hint at something deeper than the 'binge and brawl' culture that is often spun into moral panics by a hypocritical media. As Smith suggests, there is a tangible sadness discernible behind all the 2 a.m. shouting and stumbling, a sadness born of the fact that many young people have lost sight of what it means to be an adult and have opted instead to hold fast in the ever-expanding terrain of middle youth that is the inevitable by-product of life stage dissolution. In an Anglo-American society almost incapable of asserting any positive images of adulthood, and where traditional cultures associated with responsibility and hard work have been beaten back by the imperialistic encroachment of playfulness and 'look-at-me' self-expression, you don't have to search too hard to see that, behind all the overt displays of youthful hedonism, there exists a disquieting sense of unease, even anxiety. It is a truly sad state of affairs. A retreat from adulthood that has resulted in millions of young people being trapped in what the *Vice* columnist Clive Martin once nicely described as 'an Escher maze of immaturity'.

Life stage dissolution and its various attendant processes are wreaking havoc across the life course. Adultification has ensured that childhood is now surrounded by confusion and ambiguity, while many young people are so unprepared for the world of adulthood that they have decided the natural process of 'moving on' is simply not for them. By dismantling many of the social and cultural norms that surround growing up, we have succeeded in creating entire generations who appear uncertain about their status and what is expected of them as they advance (or not) through the life course.

At various points in this book, I have discussed the psycho-dynamic theorist Erik Erikson, and I return to his work here by way of conclusion. Erikson asserted that, if the transition from adolescence to adulthood was marked by an 'identity crisis' (his term) whereby people become too absorbed in themselves, too narcissistic, then the 'generational cycle of productivity and crea-tivity' would no longer function. As much an anthropologist as a psychologist, Erikson used cultural and historical sources to make his case that, from a psychic perspective, 'each person is a product of his or her time' as much as they are of their familial environ-ment.[32] By negating the fact that people today are the product of an infantilised culture that actively seeks to undermine the life cycle and unnecessarily complicate the transition to adulthood, society has some very hard lessons to learn.

Just before kick-off at Manchester United's Old Trafford stadium during the 2015/16 season, an excited fan leans across a dividing wall in search of an autograph. It's a familiar pre-match scene that has been going on at football grounds around the world for over a century. On this occasion, however, there's something unusual about the generational dynamic between fan and the object of their adulation. Instead of a wide-eyed schoolkid seeking the signature of an aspirational adult athlete, the request was being made by a middle-aged woman of a five-year-old boy named Kai, the son of the then Manchester United captain, Wayne Rooney. Even if we afford the woman the benefit of the doubt and say the autograph is for one of her children, she really should know better. Not only is she fuelling the unwarranted celebrification of kids, but by venerating a five-year-old she's also placing herself in the role of an adult supplicant, a grown-up looking to a child for guidance about what one is supposed to be or become.

As we have seen, late-modern society is awash with such allegories of adultification and infantilisation, but despite their increasing frequency, few have stopped to consider what's actually behind these moments of intergenerational confusion. In this chapter, I offered my own explanation. It's my contention that we are witnessing the onset and instantiation of *representational life stage dissolution* – a blurring, or more accurately, a merging process that takes several psychosocial and cultural forms and is operational at all stages of the life course. This erosion of the inherent opposition between established life stages is most easily identified in popular culture, but as later chapters will make clear, it's already bleeding, unstaunched, into other areas of social and political life, with far graver consequences.

Having taken the time to introduce this phenomenon, our task now must be to identify its origins. One of the features of the twenty-first century is how children, teenagers and adults increasingly share and enjoy the same cultural and behavioural experiences – experiences that are very often based on the mindset, values and sensibilities of Anglo-American youth culture. To understand how this situation came about we need to chart the ascendance of youth that occurred during the second half of the twentieth century.

For the infantilised actor, 'doing history' is often viewed as a chore, an unwanted distraction from the personalised, always-on world of consumer stimulation and digital diversion. Adults, on the other hand, understand that to make sense of the present you must know something of the past, and so, dear adult reader, it's time to take a brief historical detour. The story that unfolds next begins in the 1950s, with the emergence of the capacious new consumer markets that triggered the explosion of youth culture as a mainstream mode of self-expression. It then continues by tracing the blast pattern left by the lift-off of 'lifestyle' consumerism, a new form of commodity-based identity creation that occurred alongside the flawed countercultural convulsions of the 1960s. It's fairly well known that the 'teen-aging' of Western culture which took place during these two decades spawned a new type of youthful actor – one who was only too happy to stand in defiance of the conventional, 'square' world. However, in contrast to the usual liberal hagiography about radicals and rebelliousness, I will argue instead that the real legacy of the Sixties was not its transformative politics but its sustained, self-interested assault on the moral status of *adult* authority.

Chapter 3

The Ascendance of Youth

We ain't never gonna grow up! We're going to be adolescents forever.

Jerry Rubin[1]

The desire to stay young is an old story. From Gilgamesh's Babylonian quest for life-preserving powers to Ponce de León's search for the fountain of youth, history abounds with parables and folk tales about man's pursuit of immortality. No doubt the genealogical roots of twenty-first-century infantilism can be traced – at least in part – to this age-old quest to unlock the secrets of eternal youth. In this chapter, however, I want to offer an altogether more recent historical account that turns around a related but specific question: when did infantilisation first emerge and what cultural conditions enabled it to flourish? In other words, it's time to situate the Kidult within its historical context.

It should be clear by now that the social and cultural landscape has been thoroughly recontoured by infantilisation. Numerous consequences flow from this, but the most far-reaching is the ongoing depreciation of the moral status historically associated with adulthood. By fetishising youth culture and looking to children for inspiration and answers, postmodern society has created a perverse situation in which a growing number of adults now view infantilism as a *good* thing, something to lean into, celebrate even. For such individuals, self-infantilisation does not mark the death of personal growth, but is instead perceived as liberating, a way of freeing oneself from the chore of having to make difficult life choices. But how did this situation come about? What caused society to embrace infantilisation to such an extent that today many institutions actually grant all sorts of rewards – sympathy, care, visibility – to those who choose to self-infantilise? To answer these questions, we need to travel back in time to the United States of the 1950s, a place characterised by rising prosperity and a commensurate sense of optimism. Historians use the word 'boom' to describe a plethora of things that mushroomed during the 1950s and 60s – suburbs, babies, car ownership, the market for consumer goods – but here I will focus on a different but related convulsion: the unchecked rise of youth culture and its effect on intergenerational relations. What follows, then, is a story about how jouissance and playful hedonism won out over adult autonomy, rationality and the ability to make collective progress a reality. But supporting that narrative, of course, is the related, subliminal story about our ongoing obsession with the age-old quest for perpetual youth – only this time as refracted through the pseudo emancipatory fictions and fantasies that reside at the heart of the modern cult of youth.[2]

Rebel sell: Teen culture in the 1950s

Every now and then a line of movie dialogue comes to stand as cultural shorthand for an entire decade. In the 1980s, it was Gordon Gekko's paean to capital accumulation – 'Greed, for lack of a better word, is good' – in Oliver Stone's 1987 film *Wall Street*. For many observers of the 1950s, the equivalent decade-defining line was the one delivered by Marlon Brando in the iconic 1953 movie *The Wild One*. Asked by one of the good-time girls at Bleeker's bar what he's rebelling against, Brando's character, the brooding biker-gang leader Johnny Strabler, famously responds, 'Whadda you got?' But while Gekko's aphorism was an apposite synopsis of 1980s materialism and the triumph of the capitalist value system, Brando's line is a somewhat misleading characterisation of 1950s rebel culture. Yes, this was the decade when the 'troubled', 'rebellious' teen came of age, but what sort of rebellion was it?

In the first part of this chapter, I will argue that youth culture in the 1950s had as much to do with market conformity as it did with provoking and defying all-comers, Johnny Strabler style. At first sight, this might appear an odd thing to stress when tracing the genealogy of infantilisation, but, as will become clear later when we discuss contemporary politics and popular forms of pseudo-rebellion, the co-optation of resistance by consumerism is key to understanding the mindset of today's Kidult. Perhaps then, another line from *The Wild One* would be a more appropriate epitaph for 1950s rebel culture? Shortly after Brando's Black Rebel motorcycle gang screech into town, entrepreneurial bar owner Frank Bleeker upbraids the town's gas-station attendant for not stepping to it and meeting the gang's demands for fuel. 'Business before pleasure,' he declares matter-of-factly, before opening the cash register and quietly instructing his bartender to put some more beers on ice for the bikers. Bleeker realises that, if handled correctly, there's money to be made from these young rebels. In essence, his position is no different from that of the film's producer, Stanley Kramer, or countless other 1950s entrepreneurs – teenage rebellion was ultimately a business opportunity ripe for commercial exploitation.

The explosion of the American teen market in the 1950s was an economic expedient. Consumer demand had slowed after an initial spike in the post-World War II years, and if over-production was to be avoided, US manufacturers needed something to kickstart it. But there was a problem: a sluggish Depression-era birth rate meant there was a diminished cohort of newly married couples setting up home to sell wares to. Marketing executives were forced to look elsewhere for sales and quickly latched onto the fact that the American teenager had cash on the hip. Not only had their allowances benefited from the trickle-down effect of a rise in real personal income, but many of them also had their own jobs. What's more, unlike in previous eras, this generation of teens was not forced to kick into the family coffers. Instead, most of them were free to spend their money how they liked. It was a situation that some had predicted, most notably the pioneering market researcher Eugene Gilbert. Drawing on data from his substantial network of teenage pollsters, Gilbert convinced corporate America of the size of the teen market, estimating it at approximately $10 billion a year, more than the annual sales of General Motors. Before long a huge array of teen-specific products hit the shops, including everything from bedroom extension phones and portable record players to cheerleader uniforms and 'French-style' cosmetics. Demand for such products, along with other teen-specific developments like 3D movies and afternoon 'teen dance party' TV shows, was easily and effectively stimulated thanks to the advertising power of youth periodicals like the million-selling *Seventeen* magazine. However, the real catalyst for the explosion of the teen market was the emergence of rock 'n' roll music in the mid-1950s.

Rock 'n' roll served to solidify the teen age as a separate and economically important section of society, distinct from both childhood and adulthood.[3] Unlike previous musical crazes such as swing, Dixie or jazz, which appealed to all age groups, rock 'n' roll music (at this point) played almost exclusively to the young. Consequently, it marked the end of an 'adult-directed adolescent culture', and its replacement with one that 'turned the concept of adolescent culture on its adult-approved head: In the rock 'n' roll world of teenage rebels, the future was now and the culture was age-exclusive, defiant, and reckless to boot'.[4] And it was this recklessness, allied to the music's inherent sexuality, that sold – and has continued to sell ever since.

The selling of rock 'n' roll cemented the concept of teen culture in the popular imagination, and not just in America. Whatever country it reached, though, the response was always the same – part teen hysteria, part adult condemnation. Consequently, it marked the start of a period of unprecedented generational tension between teenagers and adults. Fifty years on from G. Stanley Hall's 'Sturm and Drang' and adolescence had its soundtrack. But although the threatening allure of rock 'n' roll and its attendant teenage anti-authoritarianism were sources of great agitation for censors, clergy and politicians, it is important not to lose sight of the fact that undergirding the phenomenon was a commercial imperative that musical rebellion, and indeed rebellion generally, sold incredibly well. But what was it about the 1950s that made commodified rebellion so popular?

While educated beat poets and tenured intellectuals like Herbert Marcuse, William Foote Whyte and David Riesman might have been troubled by the sterile, well-laundered mass culture of postwar America, for most young people it was an era alive with a sense of optimism and fun. Unlike their parents, who had memories of Depression and World War, the 1950s teens came of age in an era of relative affluence. All sections of society were benefiting from this flush of prosperity, but none more so than teenagers, whose comfortable lifestyles included huge servings of television, film and popular music. It was a culture that demanded participation through consumption, and so it's unsurprising that the cultural concept of the teenager that emerged in the 1950s was at its core a self-indulgent construct. The music may have been loud, fast and provocative, and the films full of rebellious sentiment and restless emotion, but in truth the disaffection and frustration that coursed through the more high-profile cultural products of the era were more often than not directed inwards rather than outwards. Like the introverted anxieties and inchoate protests of Brando and Dean, 1950s-style rebellion had a distinctly self-conscious, existential feel to it. On reflection, even Brando's famous 'Whadda you got?' line now seems more like an admission of confused uncertainty than a *cri de coeur* against a specific oppressor.

If young people in the 1950s were not kicking against society, why all the agitation and rebellious posturing – what sociologists would later call 'youthful alienation'? The answer can be found in the concept of the teenager itself, or more specifically its cultural separation from other stages of the life course, specifically adulthood. This was the first generation raised on a mass media that spoke directly to *them*. It told them they were distinct, a new breed, as unique and unprecedented as their cherished rock 'n' roll music. Most significantly, it opened a generational cleavage that subsequently has never been bridged. This experiential divide, a product of 1950s affluence as much as anything else, marked the moment when teenage culture started to vanquish more mature tastes, when cool rebelliousness won out over grown-up interests. Modern Western society's enduring infatuation with youth culture, what the Italian semiotician Marcel Danesi calls 'the forever young syndrome', begins here.

Consider one of the less commented upon features of the rise of the teen age – the emergence in the 1950s of faux *rites de passage* ceremonies. As the market continued its march into every aspect of social life, new benchmark events such as 'Sweet Sixteen' parties, high-school proms and graduation celebrations were sold to the American public. What's interesting here is not that these teen-driven events were highly commercialised, but that what they represented was a fabricated and largely meaningless 'coming of age' experience. Instead of using these supposedly momentous milestones to jettison youthfulness and embrace adulthood, this cohort of teenagers clung on to and continued to celebrate teenage interests and influences. This had two important consequences that are still being felt today. First, and most obviously, this valorisation and elongation of youth inevitably slowed the onset of adult maturity. Second, by extending their love affair with teen culture, and especially rock 'n' roll music, the younger generation now existed in a more generationally self-contained world in which adults and their values were not only outmoded but increasingly ridiculed. In Danesi's words, 'By the end of the decade, it was clear that musicians and the media had taken over the role of "village elders"'.[5]

By the end of the 1950s, the new self-oriented teen had successfully gathered together the economic and cultural resources required to expand its domain and construct a sprawling empire that would go on to dominate large swathes of the life course. At root, for all its rebellious pretentions, this would be an empire defined as much by self-indulgence and conformity as fatalism or anti-authoritarianism. There is an established cultural and sociological account which claims that, as the 1950s gave way to the 1960s, this dynamic was dramatically reversed as conformity gave way to more serious political contestation. However, as I will now explain, for all the tumult and upheaval that undeniably took place during the counterculture years, many of the key features of 1950s teenagerdom not only endured but intensified.

From 'campus wars' to a generational apocalypse: The Sixties and the long march to adulthood

Few decades divide opinion like the 1960s. For those on the liberal left, 'the Sixties' was a golden age of protest and societal transformation, an unprecedented coming together of counter-culture ideals and political agitation that upended the conformity and suburban ennui of the 1950s.[6] For those on the conservative right, what happened in the 1960s was nothing less than an assault on the established social order; a *decennium horribilis* of moral decline, permissiveness and inchoate anti-authoritarianism. More than fifty years on from 'the Summer of Love' and little has changed. Today, the struggle among academics and commentators for the ideological soul of the 1960s is as contested as ever. But by simply retracing these debates and rehashing the same schisms, we miss important analytic opportunities. This is absolutely the case when it comes to tracing the historical and cultural emergence of infantilisation; for if the socio-cultural tendencies that gave rise to the elevation and celebration of youth culture first emerged in the 1950s, it was in the 1960s that they rose to prominence.

The goal of the rest of this chapter is to offer an alternative, less trammelled narrative of the 1960s, a narrative capable of recognising that the endless debates over the 'culture wars' have obscured a related but arguably no less important conflict. I refer here to the on-going generational wars of the late twentieth and early twenty-first century – the most important casualty of which has been the paradigm of adulthood itself. Here I don't simply mean a battle *between* age groups – the tension between youthful exuberance and adult authority that exists in every generation. Rather what I wish to suggest is that, following the post-war baby boom and the subsequent expansion of the youth market in the 1950s, the culture wars of the 1960s were actually *wars of occupation*, territorial disputes over what was at stake in the then established categories of 'adult' and 'youth'. For example, not only did the Sixties redefine what it meant to be young in Western society, the youthful rebellion that characterised the era also set in motion a series of cultural tendencies and market logics that would go on to undermine the ancient belief that wisdom, farsightedness and moral acumen are characteristics principally associated with adult experience. While we rightly remember the 1960s as a time when protesters challenged everything from the primacy of Cold War militarism to the 'naturalness' of exclusion and inclusion in relation to the (then) established constituencies of race, ethnicity, gender and class, we must also bear in mind that the flames from the culture wars also engulfed the established generational order. And nowhere was this conflagration more apparent than in the realm of mass education.

In the early 1960s, a small, dedicated team of behavioural psychologists undertook a now largely forgotten study of the public high-school system in Eastern Kansas. Gathering swathes of data as they criss-crossed the farming communities and military towns of the central plains, the team's goal was to identify the extent to which high-school size impacted the lives and behaviour of students. With the baby boom in full flow, the study took place against a backdrop of heated discussions about 'school consolidation' and the creation of mass public high schools. Running against the tide of the times, the team concluded that, when it came to student competences such as sense of 'commitment', 'contribution', 'individual participation' and 'involvement and feelings of responsibility', the small-school model was the obvious superior of its bigger cousin. Furthermore, the 'extra richness' of experience that one might assume would result from a greater array of activity options available in large schools did not materialise.[7] But despite concluding that assumptions about the superiority of the consolidated schools were mostly false, the move to large schools in Kansas and beyond was unstoppable. Baby-boom demographics ensured that the supersized school was a necessary evil, most obviously in the US, but also in the UK, where in the mid-1960s, the sprawling comprehensive-school model was introduced. The consequences of this development have exercised pedagogues and youth-studies scholars ever since. For our purposes, however, the key thing to note is that by the middle of the 1960s, it was not just the size of school buildings that was increasing, but *the gap between student and adult*, a point Thomas Hine makes with characteristic clarity:

> it's difficult not to see some connection between the growth of the large, bureaucratized high school and the student alienation that became increasingly evident as the 1960s went on. The promise of the comprehensive school was exposure to an array of courses and specialized teachers. The price may have been an environment where teachers and students found it very difficult to establish relationships with one another, and increasingly saw themselves as adversaries. Although teachers' influence on students had been declining for years, the large bureaucratized high school could only strengthen the influence of the peer-group culture.[8]

This creeping estrangement from adults and its corollary, the retreat into the peer group, went well beyond the standard concerns about the emergence of a 'generation gap'. There was a further, more pressing dimension to consider. Around this time, the noted educationalist Kenneth Clarke coined the term 'vestibule adolescence' after noticing that American children were spending 'year after year of their lives in vague preparation for a distant future'. Clarke was on to something extremely important. He had identified the first steps in what has since been called 'the long march to adulthood' that would go on to characterise not just the late 1960s but every decade since.

Another educational institution standing, or perhaps more accurately cowering, in the direct flood path of the baby-boom tsunami was the university. In the United States the expansion of higher education in the 1960s was simply phenomenal. By 1962, six out of ten American high-school graduates were campus bound. Consequently, by the end of the decade, college enrolment had almost doubled to 7.5 million.[9] This expansion of the university system created a self-confident generation that was not only better educated than any previous generation in history, but also acutely aware of its own political and cultural significance. Such confidence in their influential place in the world was well founded, for it was born not just of education, but of the sense of entitlement that comes from being raised in a world of rising prosperity and increasing consumer comfort. The expansion of university places also had an important democratising effect, as growing numbers of female and later ethnic minority students bolstered each new matriculating year. It was this potent combination of diversity, a sense of entitlement, and sheer demographic heft that contributed to the perception that a youthful revolution was under way. No surprise, then, that the university campus emerged as the battleground on which many of the culture wars of the Sixties were fought.

The numerous campus demonstrations that punctuated the 1960s in the US and elsewhere were often truly riotous affairs attended in the main by groups of seriously committed people.[10] Opposed to political leadership, especially in relation to the rapidly escalating Vietnam War, campus unrest during the 1960s was a powerful phenomenon that involved millions of university students across the globe. But for all the passion displayed by the student radicals, this was no revolutionary moment. To start with, the political causes that animated protesters were often lost on the wider population – not least because of the way important issues such as anti-imperialism were often protested alongside campus-specific concerns about curfews or restrictions on co-educational fraternisation. Furthermore, despite all the talk of 'takeover' and 'revolution', the counterculture protests never actually had the support of the bulk of the population, but instead reflected the interests of small, albeit very influential, cultural groups.[11] In reality, most Baby Boomers were not campus rebels or hippies. Nor did they spend the 1960s linking arms at political sit-ins or criss-crossing the country in psychedelic love buses. Instead, they remained committed to the established democratic order and did their best to make their way in the world. The reason for this lack of mainstream support has already been explained: the rising prosperity and increasing consumer comfort being experienced by all demographic groups in Western economies. It was a tension that was present right from the outset. For at the very moment ideological authors like Herbert Marcuse were formulating their critique of the coercive and alienating nature of modern life in Western consumer society – what Marcuse described as 'the total-izing universe of technological rationality' – the majority of Baby Boomers were enjoying childhoods of unprecedented wealth and prosperity. It is a disparity that haunts the Sixties – you might even describe it as *the* most important culture clash of the era.

Consider, by way of example, the novelist, political commenta-tor and scion of the New Journalism of the 1960s, Norman Mailer. Embodying the spirit of the counterculture, Mailer described himself as a 'radical intellectual' who, through his writings and appearances, was dedicated to bringing about 'a revolution in the consciousness of our time'. However, there was an inherent contra-diction at the heart of the well-crafted Mailer persona. As Christopher Lasch observed as early as 1965, for all his 'revolu-tionary sincerity', the Harvard- and Sorbonne-educated Mailer remained 'far too committed to the culture he claims to despise to be an effective critic of it, either from within or without'.[12] Whether it was his willing involvement in the cult of the 'literary superstar', his dalliances with the film industry and the Hollywood set or his various attempts to insert himself at the epicentre of professional sporting spectacles, Mailer was palpably in love with the very culture that elsewhere he was savaging as oppressive and 'totalitarian'. However, despite this ambiguous position, there were many things that Mailer did get right. In his now controversial essay 'The White Negro', Mailer praised the bohemian hipster for 'giving expression to the infant in himself'. Here Mailer presaged the real story of the Sixties, the preference for hedonistic self-expression rather than adult maturation; a tendency that ultimately ensured the counterculture revolution would be more about youthful excess than substantive political transformation.

As the 1960s wore on, this contradiction between increasing Western prosperity and the revolutionary imperative only intensified. Throughout the decade there was a great deal of concern and mostly middle-class talk of 'alienation', be it as a motif of youthful hipsterism, á la Mailer, or as the curse of the suburban housewife. Yet, as the author and critic Tom Wolfe would later comment, this era of unprecedented affluence was also responsible for a 'Happiness Explosion', a feeling of positivity and boundless opportunity that was apparent in everything from the speeches of John Kennedy to pop art. This exhilarating sense of a freedom born of material comfort was clearly the impetus for much of the creativity and expressivity that characterised the alternative music and literature of the Sixties, but it also gave the politics of the period a particular feel. Unlike today, the assault on the political and social institutions that took place in the early 1960s resulted not from postmodern cynicism (or irony), but from a sense of unbridled, carefree possibility. And as David Farber has commented, 'In such a boundless universe, to whom did one listen for guidance and for ordering principles? Cultural authority – the power to set the rules of proper conduct and behaviour – was up for grabs in the midst of the Happiness Explosion and the nuclear age.'[13] It was this search for a new set of ordering principles that fuelled Sixties student radicalism and triggered the assault on adult authority. This is never more apparent than when one delves into how some of the university protests were undermined by inchoate politics or impractical objectives.

Reflecting on being asked to write down his political goals at the height of the protests, Todd Gitlin, student radical and author of a bestselling account of the Sixties, recalled, 'I agonized for weeks about what it was, in fact, I *wanted* . . . I puzzled endlessly about *who we were*.'[14] It is an honest statement and one that speaks volumes about this era of radicalism and its ultimate inability to form a viable political agenda. Another Sixties chronicler, Thomas Hine, remembers picking up a flyer from the street during a Chicago demonstration that declared 'YOUTH WILL MAKE THE REVOLUTION'. But a revolution based on what exactly? The panoply of protest slogans – 'Stop the Vietnam War', 'Legalize Pot', 'Women's Rights', 'Say "NO" to all Leaders', 'Black Power', 'Student Power', 'The University is a Factory' – suggested that everything was up for grabs: a clear reflection of the tangible sense of possibility that was such a feature of the 1960s, but also the lack of focus that ultimately compromised the radicalism of the era. There was one issue, however, on which the radicals were unequivocal: whatever form the putative revolution would take, it was the young who were going to call the shots. Sure, some of the intellectual inspirations of the Youth Movement were getting on by the high point of student protest (Marcuse was in his late sixties; Mailer his mid-forties), but such individuals were figureheads. At street level, as it should be, it was a young person's struggle.

From the outset, the Sixties revolution was very much the product of a youthful imagination. Noisy, excitable, making up rules as they went along, the student protests of the era were characterised as much by wanton excess and Dada-influenced performativity, as they were by clearly articulated political demands or a bona fide revolutionary manifesto. Moreover, as Seymour Martin Lipset points out in *Rebellion in the University*, the student radicals made no attempt whatsoever to connect with established political parties. Why would they? In an Oedipal struggle, you kill the father; you do not lend weight to his political cause. Other generational elements were also evident in the protests, not least the total rejection of the donnish authority and the *in loco parentis* mindset that characterised the old university establishment. This last development is particularly interesting in that it highlighted the generational self-interest that characterised the later years of Sixties radicalism – something famously articulated by Paul Goodman's ridiculous statement in *Growing Up Absurd* that middle-class students were the 'major exploited class' in society.

The volatile nature of the youth movement meant that by the decade's end there had been a veritable explosion of interest in generations and generational theory. The life-course scholar Richard Braungart, for example, saw the wider counterculture as an assault on traditional institutions that created a favourable environment for 'generational conflict', while the Rutgers University sociologist Ted Goertzel had the perspicacity to recognise that, for many involved in the student protests, generational consciousness was as important as class-consciousness. One philosopher, Lewis Feuer, who was teaching at the University of California during the Berkeley student uprising, even developed an 'Oedipal theory of student protests' to explain the 'de-authorisation' of older generations that took place during this period. But while these scholars were correct to frame the protests in terms of a clash of generations, they stopped short of declaring the obvious winner.

It was not until the early 1970s that the triumph of youth would be fully acknowledged, with some astute commentators even recognising the onset of cultural infantilism and the fact that established life stages were coming under threat from this assault on adult authority. Reflecting on the youth movement's attempt to 'de-institutionalize the existing adult world', the historical sociologist Philip Abrams remarked that, 'The forms of social organisation they typically envisage are simple, direct, face-to-face, a reaffirmation of the world of kin, community, rural innocence *and childhood*.'[15] Likewise, the social psychologist Kenneth Keniston highlighted how societal concern about unruly youth was expanding to include unruly mature *adults*: 'No longer is our anxiety focused primarily upon the teen-ager, upon the adolescent of Hall's day . . . Today we are nervous about the new 'dangerous classes' – those men and women of college – and graduate-school age who can't seem to 'settle down' the way their parents did, who refuse to consider themselves adult, and who vehemently challenge the social order.'[16] Famously, Erich Fromm even penned a short essay critiquing 1960s radicalism entitled 'Infantilization and despair masquerading as radicalism'.

But while Abrams, Keniston, Fromm and others seemed concerned about the direction this current was taking, authority figures on campus could only swim with the cultural tide. Rather than confront this emerging infantilisation with adult forbearance, the reaction of most universities served only to further erode the opposition between established life stages. For example, in *Coming Apart: A Memoir of the Harvard Wars of 1969*, Roger Rosenblatt argued that the campus protests at America's oldest institution of higher education were only possible because of the passivity of the adult order:

The odd thing is that none of the destruction would have occurred had there not emerged a strange conspiracy between those who wanted power and those who readily ceded it to them . . . *they [the student radicals] never could have created so much chaos at Harvard had the administration and most of the faculty not allowed them to . . .* [f]or the most part, they offered no opposition to that which they disagreed with, as if to tell the students: 'If you want it, take it.' Liberalism rolled over on its back like a turtle awaiting the end. I do not know why, but there was an impulse running under the events of that spring to let things go to hell, and it was acted on by young and old alike.[17]

The fact that most university elders were not confident enough to exert their authority confirmed something that would have been unthinkable only a decade earlier: that a reversal of cultural and moral power was taking place between adults and young people and that, rather than doing anything to stop it, many in the establishment were inadvertently hastening its arrival. Whether it was junior staff attracted to the protests by the celebration of disorder and the prioritisation of playful hedonism and spirituality over adult autonomy and restrained rationality, or the simple cowardice of senior institutional figures, many Anglo-American universities had started, if not to submit completely, then certainly to genuflect to the cult of rebellious youth and its value system.

But while the student radicals may have gained the upper hand in the generation game, their attempts at revolution were far less successful. By the end of the decade, the practical political element of the project had splintered under the weight of its own incoherence.[18] Against a backdrop of rising prosperity and the stark realisation that the state was far too powerful to be confronted head-on, the youth movement had failed in its bid to overthrow the capitalist system and its supposed apparatus of control and manipulation. However, this did not mark the end of the Sixties' transformative sensibility. Far from it. Elsewhere, a real revolution was taking place – a revolution of the self that was based not on campus riots and political placards, but on lifestyle consumerism and psycho-spiritual therapeutic programmes.

Turn on, tune in, drop out – of adulthood: Counterculture consumerism and *The Conquest of Cool*

We have perpetuated youth.

Mary Quant[19]

Gore Vidal once commented that 'Until the rise of American advertising, it never occurred to anyone anywhere in the world that the teenager was a captive in a hostile world of adults.' Vidal was referring to the rise of television advertising in the 1950s, but his comment also captured the fact that, by the end of that decade, the youth market had successfully instantiated pseudo teen rebellion at the heart of Anglo-American society – so much so in fact, one could argue it was *the* commercial trend of the decade. By 1964, the youth market was thought to be worth $25 billion in the US alone, as the tastes and consumer choices of Baby Boomers set national trends and emerged as one of the driving sectors of the economy. But this growth was not simply due to a combination of the economic might of teen demographics and the logic of the 'rebel sell'. Something more profound was happening. The Baby Boomers were the first generation of teenagers who carried their teenage tastes and youthful passions with them into adulthood. In so doing, they expanded not just the youth market but also the very concept of youth itself. By the end of the 1960s, youth culture was no longer the preserve of the young. *The youthful adult had arrived.*

To understand exactly how this came about we must undertake a related but very different reading of the 1960s from the one sketched out above. It is an important story for two reasons. First, it undermines Baby Boomer orthodoxy that sees the Sixties as a perpetual fountainhead of political radicalism and anti-authoritarianism. Second, it highlights a pair of very important cultural tendencies that first appeared in the 1960s which then went on to become key drivers of twenty-first-century infantilisation and adultification: ersatz rebellion and the rise of the personal lifestyle.

My notion of ersatz or pseudo rebellion is rooted in Thomas Frank's 1997 book *The Conquest of Cool: Business Culture, Counterculture, and the Rise of Hip Consumerism*. Frank's text is fascinating in that it starkly contradicts the liberal view of the 1960s as the apotheosis of progressive resistance to mass culture. Like the shotgun blast that took out 'Captain America' (Peter Fonda) and 'Billy' (Dennis Hopper) at the denouement of *Easy Rider*, Hopper's overrated 1969 counterculture movie, Frank's book punches a terminal hole through hippy ideals about supposedly 'authentic Sixties resistance'. While it appears deceptively simple, Frank's argument in *The Conquest of Cool* is at once sophisticated and counterintuitive in that it goes well beyond standard conservative critiques of the 1960s to present the most nuanced interpretation to date of what counterculture apologists have termed 'co-optation theory'.

There is a familiar refrain voiced by rebel leftists that goes something like this: 'Back in the Sixties, resistance *meant* something. We were out to change the world, and the only thing that stopped us was rapacious commercial speculators [often referred to as "The Man"] who turned our revolutionary dreams into commodified mulch.' Such logic is used to explain everything, from the 1994 and 1999 Woodstock revival festivals to Bob Dylan's appearance in a Victoria's Secret TV commercial. So goes the standard narrative associated with co-optation theory: that there is something out there – usually originating from the cultural forests of the 1960s

– that can be called *authentic* resistance, which over time has its legitimacy undermined by the market and a series of degrading commodification processes that eventually evacuate any revolutionary potential from said authentic cultural form. Frank asserts that the actual story is considerably messier. He claims that, rather than there being an original counterculture dogged by a fake countercultural doppelganger ('a commercial replica that seemed to ape the original's every move for the titillation of the TV-watching millions and the nation's corporate sponsors'), in reality the original and the fugazi countercultures were *one and the same*. Indeed, far from being a soulless, conservative machine, post-war American business culture 'was as dynamic a force in its own way as the revolutionary youth movements of the period, undertaking dramatic transformations of both the way it operated and the way it imagined itself'. In other words, the *real* revolution took place not in the realm of politics but in marketing practice, management thinking, and ideas about consumer creativity.

In the late 1950s and early 1960s, leaders of the advertising and menswear businesses developed a critique of their own industries, of over-organisation and creative dullness, that had much in common with the critique of mass society which gave rise to the counterculture. Like the young insurgents, people in more advanced reaches of the American corporate world deplored conformity, distrusted routine, and encouraged resistance to established power. They welcomed the youth-led revolution not because they were secretly planning to subvert it or even because they believed it would allow them to tap a gigantic youth market (although this was, of course, a factor), but because they perceived in it a comrade in their own struggles to revitalize American business and the consumer order generally. If American capitalism can be said to have spent the 1950s dealing in conformity and consumer fakery, during the decade that followed, it would offer the public authenticity, individuality, difference, and rebellion.[20]

For advertising executives, copywriters and marketing managers, the dynamism and creative energy of the counterculture provided a fresh language and a new set of hip symbols through which to express and promote their innovative vision of consumer capitalism. Rejecting the mass conformity and suburban blandness of the 1950s, their plan was for a new, more liberating, heterogeneous form of consumerism, based around pleasure, self-expression and a creative sense of individualism. To bring forth this new age of consumerism they appropriated the two dominant tropes of the counterculture: youthful expressivity and rebelliousness.

Earlier I documented how the turn to youth in the 1950s was the result of the demographic change associated with the post-war baby boom. By the mid-1960s, however, the advertising industry had woken up to the fact that 'youthfulness' had an appeal that transcended established teen demographics. Ad men and their corporate paymasters recognised that young-mindedness was no longer the sole preserve of the biologically young, a sentiment writ large in this 1965 quote by columnist Jerry Fields in what was then the bible of the advertising industry, *Madison Avenue*: 'Our solution to this problem is a very simple one – don't grow old. Think young. That's a pretty square and corny statement, but we mean it. We see old men of 35 walking into our office and we see young men of 50 coming in. It all seems to be based on a state of mind – a healthy enthusiastic approach to life in which you never seem to run out of *élan vital*.'[21] In other words, old age was for squares. By getting adults to 'think young', the youth market could be extended in all sorts of ways to all sorts of people. In the words of Frank, 'No longer was youth merely a "natural" demographic group to which appeals could be pitched: suddenly youth became a consuming

Plate 9: The revolution will be advertised. (h.i.s.)

position to which all could aspire . . . The conceptual position of *youthfulness* became as great an element of the marketing picture as youth itself.'[22]

But this appropriation of counterculture values for the purposes of dynamic economic expansion would only be complete when commercialised youth culture fully incorporated the sense of free-wheeling liberation and non-conformity associated with Sixties-style rebellion – something that corporations latched onto with tremendous creative gusto. For example, consider Plate 9. The advertising copy in this image perfectly illustrates how, by the end of the 1960s, it had become quite normal for corporations to appropriate separatist political slogans and use terms like 'anti-establishment' in their campaigns. If the 1950s was the decade when popular cultural expressions of cool rebellion and delinquent, existential restlessness were first sold *en masse* to the young, it was in the 1960s that these appealing sensibilities were normalised to such an extent that they began to undermine the established generational order. However, like the 1950s, the mode of rebellion employed as the emblem of this new age of hip consumption would once again have nothing to do with adult forms of political transformation. Rather what was to be sold was a more juvenile form of cultural 'resistance' – a form of ersatz rebellion heavy on countercultural signifiers but light on actual political significance.[23] Once again Frank perfectly captures the mood of the times:

Advertising and menswear executives seized upon the counter-culture as the preeminent symbol of the revolution in which they were engaged, embellishing both their trade literature and their products with images of rebellious, individualistic youth . . . In its hostility to established tastes, the counterculture seemed to be preparing young people to rebel against whatever they had patronized before and to view the cycles of the new without the suspicion of earlier eras. Its simultaneous craving for authenticity and suspicion of tradition seemed to make the counterculture an ideal vehicle for a vast sea-change in American consuming habits. Through its symbols and myths, leaders of the menswear and advertising industries imagined a consumerism markedly differ-ent from its 1950s permutation, a hip consumerism driven by disgust with mass society itself.[24]

Consider the decade's most prominent and enduring form of creative rebellion – rock music. While only a small number of radicals actively contributed to the political landscape of the counterculture, tens of millions bought the soundtrack. Unlike the rock 'n' roll of the 1950s, this was music with 'a message'. The new breed of Sixties rock stars liked to jam, but they also liked to question social conformity and the square adult values that underpinned it. But for all its rebellious intent, Sixties rock music did little to undermine Western society's established power geometries. In line with Frank's analysis, any subversion that rock and other contemporaneous musical genres did manage to generate was not just accommodated by corporate culture but often served as its soundtrack – and not after the fact, as Boomers like to suggest, but right from the outset. For example, even the much-touted free underground music press of the era was often funded by backdoor payments from music industry executives.[25] Rock 'n' roll music may have flourished on the back of the images and sensibilities of counterculture rebellion, but for the most part, like so much of the art of the 1960s, it was a story of unfettered commercialism; so much so in fact that by the end of the decade, rock music was generating bigger profits than the movie industry.

So, if rock 'n' roll wasn't posing much of a challenge to 'The System', what exactly was it doing? By now the answer should be obvious. If rock music was about anything, it was about the preeminence of youth. Against such a cultural backdrop, growing up (and its corollary getting old) began to look decidedly unfashionable. Consequently, the young and the not-so-young began looking not to the adult establishment for their values and ways of being, but to the new rock-star heroes and icons of mass popular culture. Whether they realised it or not, the faux-rebel celebrities of the Sixties were indeed inspiring a politicised generation; the only problem was the target of this politicisation was not the State or the capitalist structure, but something much closer to home – adult authority. As we will see later in the book, this was a strategy destined to result in both generational confusion and political stagnation. The charismatic musical mavericks of the Sixties were just not into growing up – intellectually and politically many of them never would. In truth, all they would ever offer to the expanding number of adults in their enthralment was a sugary cocktail of rock 'n' roll bombast and infantile politics.

Sadly, this tendency was not limited to music. One only had to glance at late-1960s and early 1970s culture more generally to realise that the dominant trends in the media and the commercial world were also linked to the mythology of youth and the designer angst associated with ersatz rebellion. The adult state may have crushed the young rebels on the streets, but it could not expunge the cult of youth from the shop window and the magazine cover. Only a decade earlier, youth-oriented products, films and musical forms had been overwhelmingly the sole preserve of teenagers, but by the end of the 1960s they had invaded, occupied and dominated the mainstream, their influence spreading across the generations. The values of freedom, hedonism and non-conformity that had been so central to the counterculture movement were poised to become the raw material for the new 'post-counterculture lifestyle'.

'Socialism in one person': The California soul rush and the post-counterculture lifestyle

Just when you think the southbound Cabrillo Highway near Julia Pfeiffer Burns State Park has reached the very edge of Northern California's majestic coastline, a sharp right-hand switchback takes you down a side road and even closer to the cliffs above the Pacific Ocean. There, at the end of a driveway, you'll find the Esalen Institute, the internationally renowned humanist centre dedicated to meditation, spirituality and self-improvement. The Esalen estate has expanded considerably from its humble

beginnings in 1962 when it was founded as a small retreat special-
ising in the psychoanalytic teachings of Wilhelm Reich and the
Gestalt therapy of Fritz Perls. The centre now includes swimming
pools, hot tubs, meditation rooms and massage decks. The growth
of Esalen is unsurprising given that from the mid-1960s onwards
it was part of a new psychotherapeutic vanguard that included the
Human Potential Movement and other similar forms of 'self-
revelation therapy' that supposedly helped individuals 'take back
ownership of their lives' from the coercive state and its systems of
oppression and manipulation. With the endorsement of high-
profile Sixties celebrities like Joan Baez and Ken Kesey, and the
support of the leading American psychotherapists and psychologists of the era, Esalen and the Human Potential Movement
quickly became national and then international phenomena, as
hundreds of thousands of people from all walks of life bought into
this new world of encounter groups, mind–body connection
experimentation, and personal transformation through self-
ownership. By 1971 the Esalen Institute was the template for
nearly a hundred similar centres known as 'Little Esalens'.

The hot tubs of Esalen and the campus clashes of the 1960s
might appear to be unconnected but look beyond the mythology
of the counterculture and it becomes clear they have more in
common than first meets the eye. As we saw above, the 1960s were
about much more than political upheaval; they were also about
unprecedented levels of wealth and material comfort. This new
affluence elicited widespread feelings of freedom and possibility,
sensibilities that were much in evidence in the art, music and
especially the alternative politics of the era. In this sense, key
aspects of the Human Potential Movement (and subsequent
related systems of personal transformation) were not at odds with
the established values of the counterculture, but a critical component of them. From its inception, the counterculture had placed

considerable emphasis on attaining 'personal self-fulfilment' and a 'higher state of consciousness', usually through the false promise of drug experiences or dippy spiritual practices, and so this new preoccupation with self-expression was seen by many as simply the latest twist along a familiar axis.

> In the mid-1960s there was a general feeling in circulation that something exciting and important was happening . . . It manifested itself in individual lives chiefly in the form of a heightened sense of consciousness, a belief that you could rather easily change yourself, or society, or both. Hadn't the students at Berkeley gotten themselves organized and forced the administration to change its rules about political activity on the campus? Hadn't the blacks in Watts, in a spontaneous outburst of rage, made the world pay attention to their community and its pain? Couldn't you similarly grab your own life and create for yourself a new appearance, a new occupation, a new (1960s term) *lifestyle*? Couldn't you ingest this or that chemical and change your very consciousness? . . . even the doubters participated in that exhilarating sense of motion and opportunity, that feeling of ground shifting beneath the feet.[26]

The above quotation was written not by a social theorist or a Sixties musician, but by Walter Truett Anderson, a former group leader and historian at the Esalen Institute. It is instructive for several reasons. First, it nicely evokes the unbridled positivity of the era: the pervasive sense that times were indeed a-changin'. Second, it recognises how important the term 'lifestyle' is for understanding the second half of the 1960s. And third, it understands that the sensibilities and values of the counterculture were not limited to a select few – be they the original student radicals or the founders of places like Esalen – but extended outwards to 'the doubters', the masses, the mainstream, the rump of the population so effectively targeted by the copywriters and marketing managers described by Frank in *The Conquest of Cool*. In short, it hints at a seldom-discussed symmetry between the selling of hip rebellion to the new 'youthful adult' and the selling of 'self-transformation' as a new mode of personalised politics. Taken together, these symmetrical developments did indeed represent a revolution – just not of the type envisaged by the original architects of Sixties radicalism. Instead of liberating the oppressed of society from poverty, class exploitation or racial marginalisation, the culture wars of the 1960s instead simply *set the self free*. They liberated individuals *to be individuals*. No bad thing, you might say, and of course you'd be right, but like all liberations there was ultimately a price to pay. In this case, one of the things put to the sword by the new psycho-politics of post-counterculture consumerism was the previously hard-learnt lesson that real social change only comes about through adult forms of *collective* politics.

The self-transformation movement was an incredible commercial success. Thanks to a raft of bestselling self-help books, widespread enthusiasm for this approach among sympathetic university psychologists, and frequent TV appearances by charismatic encounter group leaders,[27] the atomised mantra of self-empowerment and the notion of 'the limitless self' became staples of Western middle-class (consumer) culture. The following quotation by another chronicler of the Esalen movement highlights their impact on wider society:

Millions of contemporary Americans search for personal and spiritual fulfilment through meditation, yoga, and other practices that engage simultaneously their bodies, minds, emotions, and spirits. Today, these activities are commonplace, unremarkable. Yet, before the sixties, they were rare options for most people

134

outside the upper class or small groups of educated spiritual seekers. The contemporary soul rush for self-transformation and individualised spirituality began on the central California coast at Esalen Institute. Its founding generation made myriad options for spiritual experiences and personal growth available to ordinary Americans . . .[28]

Marion Goldman's memorable phrase, the 'soul rush for self-transformation and individualised spirituality', bears repeating as it aptly summarises the growth of the psychotherapeutic self-improvement movement: its countless encounter groups, spiritual centres and personal growth clinics; its idiosyncratic caravan of therapists and psychic gurus; its reliance on narcissistic primal-scream therapy and other 're-birthing' rituals (here it is interesting to note that primal-scream therapy seeks to go beyond even infantilisation – 'to get in touch with the child inside you' – and into the realm of embryonisation, i.e., a return to the 'oceanic contentment of the womb');[29] and its unremitting emphasis on 'ways of being' and 'self-expressivity'. It is this latter aspect that is most important. As Peter Marin has suggested, the new therapies spawned by the Human Potential Movement and subsequent iterations like EST (Erhard Seminars Training) and its European variation, Exegesis, projected the ideal that 'the individual will is all powerful and totally determines one's fate', further intensifying the 'isolation of the self'.[30]

The psychic 'soul rush' was of course good for business. Personal transformation principles such as the idea of the 'limitless self', with its emphasis on self-expressivity and individual autonomy, were the perfect confederate for the now established marketing tropes of youthfulness and ersatz rebellion. One could even argue that the two logics were essentially peddling the same dream – the perpetuation of youthful vitality via hip opposition to the mainstream. From here it was a short step to the new consumerist world of the *personal lifestyle* and the creation of a highly individuated identity. Indeed, far from challenging the 'totalitarian' nature of capitalist society, the competitive individualism of the new psycho-politics of 'being oneself' fitted perfectly with the existing aspirational framework of Western capitalist society.

It was an irony not lost on Stew Albert, one of the original members of the Sixties revolutionary group the Youth International Party, or Yippies.[31] Never slow to recognise and hijack a trend, Albert realised that as counterculture politics lost out to the rise of lifestyle culture and the personal desire to go 'deeper and deeper into the self', many of his friends and collaborators had started to prioritise their own personal 'journey', and feel good about it.[32] If it was no longer possible to transform society, he argued, then one must instead strive to be 'happy and fully self developed' on one's own – or, in Albert's deeply flawed but unforgettable phrase, '*Socialism in one person*'.

This is not to say that people stopped caring about major causes such as race relations or the environment. It is simply to point out that the practical and political collective activism surrounding these and other causes waned in the 1970s. The ad men's assault on rebellion and the psychotherapeutic movement's prioritisation of selfhood had taken its toll on what remained of the counterculture. No longer was political activism about collective struggle. Instead, it had become the responsibility of the individual to be the unit of change. Again, this shift is succinctly expressed by Stew Albert: 'People who had been politically active were persuaded that if they could change themselves and be healthy individuals, and if a movement grew up just aimed at people changing themselves, then at some point all that positive change going on ... well, you could say quantity would become quality, and there would be a sort of spontaneous transformation of society, but political action was not required.'[33]

This shift, arguably the defining legacy of the counterculture, also goes a long way to explaining the apathy and apoliticism common among many of today's young adults. Indeed, five decades later this type of thinking is everywhere. Consider the smug bumper-sticker aphorism 'Be the change you wish to see in the world'. The logic here is simple: as long as the individual makes the change, typically through some form of self-reinvention, then the need for social transformation is redundant ('I drive a Prius. What are you doing?'). And so, more than half a century on from the 1960s, the contemporary Kidult is confronted by a political landscape characterised by the demise of collective activism and its replacement with a personal (psycho) politics based on the myth that self-transformation is the best route to social transformation. No wonder the default setting for so many young people today is the unedifying choice between rebellious posturing, a highly personalised identity politics or, worst of all, depoliticised disinterest.

By the end of the 1960s, coherent examples of adulthood were not only unfashionable but increasingly difficult to find – at least in the overlapping arenas of consumerism and popular culture. This expanding preference for products and styles associated with the tastes and interests of the young has been captured astutely in Marcel Danesi's concept of *juvenilisation*, the process by which the cult of youth exploded as a mainstream, cross-generational mode of self-expression.

By the 1960s, the desire to be young meant the desire not only to stay and look healthier for a longer period of one's life but also to act and think differently from 'older' people. Being old meant being part of the corrupt and morally fossilized 'establishment', as the consumerist way of life was called by the counter-culture dissidents of the era. By the end of the decade, the process of juvenilization had reached a critical mass, on the verge of becoming *the* defining feature of Western groupthink . . . What appealed to the young would shortly thereafter appeal as well to the old. It became a collective state of mind.[34]

It is this feature of the Sixties, and not the mythic politics of the era, that should be remembered. What started out as a cultural and political revolution ended meekly, but not unproblematically, in an atomised 'rebellion of the self' – a form of psycho-political personhood that by the 1970s had found expression in populist forms of psychotherapy and an unhealthy infatuation with youthful consumerism.

What better way to conclude this short history of the ascendance of youth than with a quote from the most beloved Sixties icon of them all, John Lennon. 'How can I bring up my son,' pondered Lennon in 1969, 'if I haven't brought up myself properly yet?' In highlighting his own insecurity about growing up, Lennon exemplifies the undeniable but too often unspoken truth about the 1960s: although the young radicals lost the political battle, they unequivocally won the generational war. But as Lennon's words make clear, there was a problem. The winners of the generational war, the pop-culture icons and the worrier kings of the new popular psychology, had not devised an effective post-victory strategy. Or maybe they had? In keeping with James Miller's assessment that 'the Sixties' represents less a specific time span and more a vague period in which youthful recklessness and romantic spirit burst into public life,[35] perhaps the unwritten plan was simply the continuation and expansion of a reckless youthful spirit; to carry teenage tastes and interests into adulthood in a bid to stay young for ever.

Just maybe this was what the rumbustious Yippie leader and Sixties icon, Jerry Rubin, had in mind when at the zenith of the counterculture he unashamedly declared: 'We ain't never gonna grow up! We're going to be adolescents forever.' Rubin may have been one of the more controversial figures of the counterculture (in the 1980s he famously rejected political activism to trade stocks and shares), but on this point he was entirely correct. The Niagara of youthful rebellion had carved through the ancient bedrock of adult authority and crashed down with tremendous force on established intergenerational norms such as deference for elders and the propriety associated with adulthood. The result, as is typically the case at the base of any waterfall, is a turbulent, unstable current that can bring about a reversal in the laminar flow of the river. In this instance, the political turbulence of the late 1960s reversed the flow of the generational order, making youthful self-indulgence more important than adult self-discipline. From this point forward, the Anglo-American world would be as much adolescent as adult-directed. Troubled waters indeed.

PART II

RULE OF THE KIDULT

In July 2019, Carol Blymire, a communications and branding executive from Washington, DC provoked a minor Twitter storm with a (now deleted) thirty-two-tweet story about a workplace incident she overheard. As Blymire tells it, in an office cubicle a young woman in her late twenties was receiving feedback from her elder boss about an article she'd been tasked with editing. What follows is a paraphrased summary of the Blymire thread:

> They had been speaking in low tones, but their volume got louder toward the end of the conversation because the young woman was getting agitated about a particular edit. That particular edit was correcting the spelling of 'hampster' to 'hamster' . . . The young woman kept saying, 'I don't know why you corrected that because I spell it with the P in it'. The boss said (calmly), 'But that's not how the word is spelled. There is no P in hamster'. *Young woman*: 'But you don't know that! I learned to spell it with a P in it so that's how I spell it'. *The boss*: 'Let's go to dictionary.com and look it up together (this is a woman in her late twenties, not a fifth grader) . . . I can see the young woman is fighting back the

tears . . . She moves to another table in the common workspace area, drops all her stuff loudly on the tabletop, and starts texting. A minute later her phone rings. It was her mom. She had texted her mom to call because it was urgent . . . She then . . . PUTS HER MOM ON SPEAKERPHONE. IN THE WORKPLACE. She bursts into tears and wants her mom to call her boss and tell her not to be mean about telling her how to spell words like 'hamster'. The mother tells her that her boss is an idiot . . . and she should go to the boss's boss to file a complaint about not allowing creativity in her writing . . .[1]

Blymire is right to be worried about such moments of intergenerational drama. The problem, as Blymire openly admits in her initial tweet, is that she's at a loss to explain why such incidents occur. Unsurprisingly, the various comment threads provoked by Blymire's story threw up a host of potential explanations. For many, the hamster meltdown story was a result of 'helicopter parenting' – a form of over-parenting in which mothers and fathers 'hover over their college students, ready to intervene at a moment's notice to protect and micromanage their emerging adult's personal and academic life'.[2] Also discussed was 'lawnmower parenting', the notion that parents are today operating out in front of their kids, mowing a path for them so they never find their own way or learn how to do things for themselves. In recent years, these terms, along with synonyms like 'hothouse parents', 'snow-plough parents', 'cosseters' and 'tiger moms', have been mobilised to explain the rise of the sort of brattish, self-entitled behaviour described in Blymire's tweets. It is a point of view backed up by academic research,[3] a good deal of which suggests this mode of twenty-first-century over-parenting is the inevitable consequence of an American society fixated with safety and shielding – what Greg Lukianoff and John Haidt refer to in their book, *The Coddling of the American Mind*, as the 'foolishness of overprotection'. But while these practices go some way to explaining both the cause and proliferation of this sort of behaviour, they do not, in my opinion, provide Blymire with the answers she's looking for.

As a late-modern morality tale, the Blymire vignette is an all-too-vivid example of what happens when the juvenile world of fantasy and emotional fragility meets the real world of adult employment. Yet, if we wish to understand it, we need to look beyond the parent–child relationship and consider other key causal factors that have helped create and instantiate the Rule of the Kidult. Yes, it's true that the aspiring writer in Blymire's story is in part a product of helicopter parenting: the instantaneous aggrievement, the emotional incontinence, the public display of petulance and, most tellingly, the telephone call – a psychological distress flare – to her tiger mom to score a fix of consolation and validation, all scream trophy child. But what interests me more is the young woman's unflinching insistence that there is indeed a 'P' in 'hamster'. For many, this might not seem the significant part of the story, but it's actually very instructive when it comes to thinking about contemporary infantilism. The imaginary 'P' is symptomatic of a new illusory cognitive state that has emerged as a result of society's collective failure to challenge individuals and correct their erroneous beliefs. It is a form of imagined-thought-made-public that is the product not simply of hothouse or helicopter parenting, but a far more deleterious combination of over-protection, cultural narcissism and flights of autobiographical fantasy that have been set free by the dual dynamics of advertising and technologically induced puerility.

In the previous chapter, we traced the trajectory of juvenilisation back to the assault on adulthood that took place in the 1950s and 60s. It's time now to return to the present and what I believe are the principal drivers of culturally induced infantilisation: postmodern advertising tropes designed to encourage childish narcissism; the rise of 'safetyism' and related risk-aversive belief systems; the fantasy-normalising life worlds associated with social media platforms; and, perhaps most importantly, the capitulation of adult authority in the Anglo-American education system. Only when we consider each of these themes in detail will we be in a position to comprehend fully the seductive allure of twenty-first-century infantilisation.

Chapter 4

'Come on, ungrow up': From Lifestyle Advertising to Life Stage Dissolution

Teen tastes have become the tastes of all because the economic system in which we live now requires this to be so, and it has thus joined forces with the media-entertainment oligarchy to promote its forever young philosophy on a daily basis. In a phrase, youth sells!

Marcel Danesi[1]

The food manufacturing giant Nestlé has produced white chocolate Milkybars for over a century. Since 1961 they have employed a successful advertising campaign featuring the 'adventures of the Milkybar Kid', a bespectacled young blond boy, dressed in a cowboy suit, whose catchphrase is 'The Milkybars are on me!' In 2010, however, the Milkybar Kid received a TV makeover. His familiar blue glasses, blond hair (now a wig) and cowboy hat remained. The big difference was that the Milkybar Kid was no longer a freckle-faced young boy. He had been usurped by an adult – or more accurately a whole host of men and women aged from seventeen to seventy. Nestlé's goal, of course, was to expand their customer demographic, a gratuitous commercial move encapsulated by the new strapline – 'Come on, ungrow up.'

147

Unsurprisingly, the rapid ageing of the Milkybar Kid drew little attention at the time. Why should it? It's only a chocolate commercial, after all. Yet might there be something symbolically significant in the generational transfer of Milkybar Kid to Milkybar *Man*? I believe there is and that the 2010 Milkybar campaign is symptomatic of a pronounced trend within contemporary advertising and its attendant marketing processes. I speak here of the move by advertisers to use various forms of lifestyle consumerism to actively undermine and erode the inherent opposition that exists between established stages of the life cycle in a deliberate attempt to boost corporate profit.

There's nothing new about pointing out the fatuous nature of advertisements. George Orwell, for example, famously described advertising in 1936 as 'the rattling of a stick inside a swill bucket'. But have you noticed that recently adverts have become more stupefying than normal? When you turn on your TV or computer do you get the sense that, rather than being addressed as a mature adult, advertisers are communicating with you as if you were, well, a child? Given you've read this far, I suspect that not only are you painfully aware of this infantilising tendency, but you don't much like it. You don't like it when banks use characters from children's cartoons to tell you how much they care about your retirement. And you don't like it when pay-day loan companies mask their exorbitant interest rates with fairy-tale storylines and cutesy jingles. Of course, whether you like it or not is beside the point. It's already a thing. It has arrived. It is everywhere. The 'it' in question is the infantilising sensation you feel when addressed as an *adult-child consumer*, and *it* is only going to get worse.

The creation and instantiation of the adult-child consumer is a fundamental goal of contemporary advertising. It is the main reason why we inhabit a world where major corporations like Microsoft and British Gas (masquerading as thermostat-control purveyor, Hive, in a bid to soften its image) think it's perfectly acceptable to hawk their wares to adults with this type of babyish gobbledygook:

As warm as the sun, as silly as fun,
As cool as a tree, as scary as the sea,
As hot as fire, cold as ice,
Sweet as sugar and everything nice, [. . .]
All I Wanna be,
All I Wanna be, [. . .]
Is everything, everything at once.

Advertisement for Windows 8 (2012)

Why aren't you surfing on a cab,
Going to visit your mad dad,
Or shopping for some trousers,
When it starts snowing on your schnowsers,
While Hive is busy controlling your heating at home.

You could be making origami,
From a slice of beef pastrami,
Or having a kick about,
With a team of giant trout,
While Hive is busy controlling your heating at home,

Being naughty in the park,
Or racing badgers for a lark,
Taking your parrot to Milan,
With absolutely no idea or plan,
While Hive is busy controlling your heating at home.

TV Advertisement for Hive (2014)

We have already seen just how rampant infantilisation is within contemporary popular culture. But for all this proliferation, one area stands out as the spiritual home of the twenty-first-century Kidult – lifestyle advertising and marketing. When it comes to infantilism, the advertising industry has not simply swum with the cultural tide, it has played a pivotal role in inculcating the phenomenon as an established and acceptable societal norm. In this chapter, I look at how this situation came about and outline some of the main visual, textual and auditory elements that advertisers use to embed infantilisation within the collective conscience.

But before we start, I should state that my concern here is not whether advertising actually works in terms of an economic return on investment – the so-called 'bottom line' debate that's raged for decades in fields like marketing science and economic psychology. Rather my interest is more closely aligned with what media-studies scholars call 'cultivation analysis' and specifically whether the cultural messages and contradictions set in motion by commercials and marketing campaigns influence human behaviour and thus affect broader social change. In plain terms, does advertising actually *shape* culture as opposed to simply reflecting it? On this point, my view is that advertising is not merely a way of selling goods, but rather a powerful form of modern social communication that people use to make sense of society and everyday life within it.[2] This is not to suggest a simple determinism, or to venture any definitive or universal claims about advertising's 'influence' or 'effect'. It is instead to suggest that adverts and marketing messages become, in the words of Michael Schudson, 'molds for thought and feeling' or 'equipment for living'.[3] It is from this perspective that I interrogate the ways in which advertising projects a vision of a social life increasingly characterised by the diminution of generational differences.

So how and when did the advertising industry decide that dissolving life stages would be a good way to move product? To answer that question, we need to know something about how marketing and advertising have evolved over the last few decades.

Advertising and the postmodern condition

As we saw in the previous chapter, the 1960s was a pivotal moment in the history of the advertising industry. At that point, advertisers started to develop new forms of consumerism based on self-expression and the psycho-politics of 'being oneself'. The key dynamic in this more sophisticated way of 'speaking' to consumers was the creation of lifestyle brands linked to social status and differentiation. For advertisers, this involved marketing products and services that seemed to possess ideals, aspirations and aesthetics that the customer believed in and would use, not simply for adornment or emulation, but as building blocks to construct a supposedly meaningful consumer lifestyle.

As a tool for stimulating demand in the 1970s and 80s, lifestyle advertising was incredibly successful, but it quickly became clear that it came at a social cost, a point made forcibly by the American cultural historian Christopher Lasch in his bestselling 1979 book, *The Culture of Narcissism*. Lasch's focus was not on advertising methods per se, but with how consumption, as both a practice and a 'theatrical' mode of self-expression, had emerged as the primary index of identity for virtually all strata of society, establishing status but more importantly imbuing individuals with a narcissistic sense of who they are. Of course, advertisers, then as now, care little if at all about whether their output might also inculcate cultural narcissism. Their objective is to stimulate demand, something that in the minds of advertising creatives can only be achieved if the industry stays ahead of cultural trends and uses the most sophisticated messaging forms available. It is precisely for this reason that advertisers and marketers welcomed a second radical transformation of their industry in the 1990s – this time provoked by the cultural values and aesthetic sensibilities associated with postmodernity.

A complex thing to pin down, postmodernity is best described as a socio-historical epoch characterised by disruptions and fluctuations in the realm of culture, aesthetics, technology and production, and political and economic practice. The term first emerged as an aesthetic movement ('postmodernism') in art and architectural theory in the early 1970s, before later spreading to philosophy, the humanities and the social sciences. In its early iteration, 'postmodern' simply meant a rejection of the ideologies and modes of thinking associated with aesthetic modernism. However, the term expanded during the 1970s and 80s to encompass a much broader array of social and importantly economic shifts that took place in advanced capitalist societies – including, most significantly, the shift from 'Fordism' to 'post-Fordism'.

The term post-Fordist was initially developed by economists to describe the replacement of fixed industrial (modernist) methods of production (such as standardised, assembly-line manufacturing) with more adaptable and innovative (postmodern) modes of 'flexible accumulation' that allowed companies to better respond to the vicissitudes of demand in consumer societies. However, it soon became clear that practices like niche production, design experimentation, the ability to diversify product lines quickly, etc., could be adapted for use in other economic sectors, and so the logic of post-Fordism was used as a catalyst to transform everything from financial services to regional planning. At this point and drawing on the earlier postmodern turn in art and architecture, left-critical commentators started to argue that developments associated with post-Fordism were also finding expression at a more general, *cultural* level. In a series of groundbreaking works, scholars such as David Harvey and Fredric

Jameson described a new 'cultural dominant' that rejected the relatively stable aesthetic of modernism in favour of a new 'postmodernist aesthetic that celebrates difference, ephemerality, spectacle, fashion, and the commodification of cultural forms'.[4] It was within these influential texts that advertisers and marketers found the tropes and narratives needed to renew their creative palette and reimagine advertising for the *fin de siècle*.

It was clear by the mid-1990s that the advertising industry had a problem. The rapid growth of the internet meant that consumers were being bombarded with an unprecedented amount of media content. As a result, advertisers risked losing the gains they had made from lifestyle advertising, and thus potentially their ability to influence consumers and shape demand. A new approach was needed; something that would allow advertising to stand out in a new digital age characterised by information saturation. The creative wing of the advertising industry turned to postmodernism for a solution, inventing an entirely new style of 'postmodern advertising'. But which aspects specifically?

Broadly speaking, postmodernity is associated with the following cultural characteristics: pastiche; irony; fantasy; ahistoricism; superficiality; the importance of spectacle and simulation; the notion of the 'decentred self'; the compression of space (think of the term 'global village' or the Samsung mobile-phone strapline 'imagine the world as your living room'); and the flattening out of time, so that 'the present is all there is'. At first glance, it might seem difficult to embed such abstruse themes within something as ephemeral as a commercial endorsement. But as a visual and semiotic medium, advertising was well equipped to create promotional content rich in postmodern symbolism and aesthetics.

Obviously, advertisers and marketers also had another more fundamental reason to embrace postmodernity. As the creative arm of capitalism, the advertising industry must, by definition, replicate and reinforce the systemic logic of its (primarily) corporate paymasters. To do otherwise would be to commit commercial suicide. So, if post-Fordism was now the preferred economic model of advanced capitalist societies, advertisers had little choice but to reflect the values and principles associated with this form of capitalist accumulation. Hence the emergence in the late 1980s and 90s of a host of explicitly postmodern tropes within advertising. The importance of this postmodern turn cannot be overstated. Today, not only is postmodern advertising the favoured style for almost all major promotional campaigns but it also provided the cultural manure out of which sprouted the adult-child consumer.

Much has been written about postmodern advertising, both by industry insiders and critical theorists keen to understand how the market went about articulating and weaponising postmodernity. All agree that the best way to conceptualise postmodern advertising is via a series of recurring motifs and tendencies. Very often, in a reflection of postmodernism itself, these characteristic themes overlap, borrow from each other, and generally avoid straightforward categorisation. However, to simplify things, I have chosen four themes that usually appear in one form or another within postmodern advertising.

The first and most universally agreed upon theme is *hyperreality*. The starting point here is the argument that, in capitalist societies, the importance of a commodity lies not in its usefulness, but in its value as a *sign*. This situation is so developed we now inhabit a semiotically chaotic world in which symbols and signifiers 'float' so freely from their original referent, they eventually come to represent something that doesn't actually exist. The French postmodern philosopher Jean Baudrillard termed this inability to separate reality from a simulation of reality, *the hyperreal*; a condition – or a way of experiencing the world – that is hugely

154

advantageous for advertisers. If signs and symbols are now essentially self-referential, and hyperreality shapes consciousness by blurring the distinction between what is considered real and what is considered imaginary, then it's much easier for marketers to fabricate a false sense of 'reality' around their brands. Or, in the words of Firat and Venkatesh, to create hyperreal brand narratives and associations that appear '*more* real than real'.[5] Hence the enduring appeal of Disneyland's 'realistic' streetscapes, or the popularity of Nike sports apparel with sedentary individuals who never darken the doors of a gym or set foot on a playing field. In terms of infantilisation, hyperreality is a key concept as it explains why advertising aimed at the adult-child consumer is all about spinning imagined situations and scenarios divorced from actual reality.

A second pronounced theme in postmodern advertising is the use of *bricolage and juxtaposition* to further transcend a product's simplistic use-value associations. Originally articulated in the structural anthropology of Claude Lévi-Strauss, the concept of bricolage came to prominence in the 1970s when cultural studies scholars used it to make sense of the way youth subcultures of the era (Punks, Skinheads, Mods, etc.) appropriated everyday consumer goods and imbued them with alternative, supposedly oppositional, symbolic meaning. From here, the concept of bricolage spread to several creative arenas, including most famously architecture, before eventually being picked up by art-school flunkies working in the advertising industry. For advertising creatives, bricolage, along with synonyms like 'eclecticism' and 'hodgepodge', had at least two applications. Most obviously, it could be used to influence the *passive* consumer by surrounding a product with abstract representational associations, coded messages and 'older' symbols, to create a new product 'text' or 'narrative'. More importantly, given the dynamic nature of lifestyle consumerism, bricolage was also used by advertisers to make consumers more *active*. By forcing the consumer to think differently, to 'improvise' and deploy 'cunning and guile' when interpreting and experiencing advertising, bricolage creates active consumers who then themselves develop the capacity to 'reappropriate', 'recycle' and 'recreate'.[6]

The intertextual nature of bricolage facilitates a third key feature of postmodern advertising: *pastiche and parody*. Identified as a distinct trope in advertising as far back as the mid-1980s, pastiche is today perhaps the most common style of contemporary advertising. For example, it is evident when historic symbols or icons such as famous artworks or long-dead movie stars are attached to contemporary products. While both pastiche and parody are deployed in advertising via self-referential, playful symbolic codes, it is the former that is more commonly used today – and for good reason. Historically, a parody – whether a work of art, popular song, or form of writing – is a deliberately exaggerated stylistic imitation of someone or something for the purposes of comic effect, ridicule, irony or sarcasm. In contrast, a pastiche celebrates rather than mocks the work it imitates. Thus, while pastiche and parody both wear a playful 'stylistic mask', pastiche is better at fabricating fantasy because of its ability to operate ahistorically. In this sense, pastiche is truly postmodern. By exacerbating a commodity's drift further away from its utility function, the practice of pastiche in advertising opens the door to a range of new symbolic strategies for eliciting positive sensations, including desire, imaginativeness, surprise born of incongruity and, most importantly, the emotional comfort of nostalgia.

The final element of postmodern advertising is less a theme and more an unarticulated mission statement. Here, I refer to the way today's advertisers seek to develop and sustain a *decentred subject* or fractured consumer. Superficially, advertisers claim that postmodern advertising's extreme eclecticism is just another technique for exciting the senses. What they actually wish to achieve is to detach the consumer from a sense of reality; to elicit thought processes, desires and forms of subjectivity that are unconnected to any universal theme or unified notion of history. In other words, to create ahistorical consumers whose representation of self is divided or fragmented, thus heightening the constant need for personal self-reinvention through commodities. It's a process that has been under way since the inception of postmodern advertising, but in the twenty-first century, the ideal of perpetual identity-based self-reconstruction has become much more intense, as social media in particular refabricates the real as the hyperreal and creates more open, fluid and ultimately plastic forms of subjectivity.

Together, these four features revolutionised the branding and marketing industries. But why was this reconfiguration needed? What was it about the condition of postmodernity that demanded both a distinct mode of advertising and the cultivation of a new type of consumer? The answer to these questions lies not in the semiotic and aesthetic froth that advertisers slather their campaigns with, but in the underlying realities of capital accumulation. As early as the late nineteenth century, Marx recognised that, if profits were to be maintained once capitalism satisfied the immediate needs of the people, producers must stimulate new 'imaginary needs' not based on material necessity. Fast forward a century or so, and economically nothing has changed. In overproducing capitalist markets, privileged Western consumers must be constantly provoked into further consumption by any means necessary. For most of the 1970s, this task was achieved by the type of lifestyle consumerism discussed in the previous chapter. But by the mid-1980s, the emergence of another overproduction crisis ensured the need for further demand defibrillations. It was at this point that capitalist economies turned first to post-Fordism (in a bid to address supply-side inefficiency), and then to cultural postmodernism (in the guise of postmodern advertising) as ways of switching up the bait in the consumerist trap. In the ensuing years, capitalism has buttressed these developments by normalising short termism, spontaneity and a general culture of impulsivity, but even this hasn't been enough to maintain required levels of demand. Consequently, the advertising industry was once again tasked with abstracting the concept of need – this time by associating it with forms of reality distraction linked to irrationality, indolence and the active promotion of childlike immaturity.

'Midriffs', 'Mooks' and 'Middle Youths': Postmodern advertising and the 'Infantilist ethos'

Frozen in time, ageing adults remain youth consumers throughout their lives . . . while toddlers and preteen 'tweens' are converted into 'adult' consumers as they come 'on line' at an ever younger age. Thus capitalism in its late consumerist phase postpones its rendezvous with destiny and survives at least another generation or two.

Benjamin Barber[7]

In *Consumed: How Markets Corrupt Children, Infantilize Adults and Swallow Citizens Whole*, the political theorist Benjamin Barber wastes no time getting to the nub of his argument. On the very first page he confidently declares that capitalism is being radically transformed by a powerful new 'cultural ethos' that is working to sustain childishness and create 'a new species of perennial adolescent'. Barber's choice of the word 'ethos' is no accident. It is used deliberately to evoke the distinction between centuries of *productivist* capitalism based on what the German sociologist Max Weber famously termed 'the Protestant ethic', and a new strand of *consumerist* capitalism that Barber calls 'the Infantilist ethos'. For Barber, this new era of 'induced childishness' is no faddish development or simple variation of lifestyle consumerism. It is a 'potent' new corporatist 'ideology' that legitimates a set of habits, preferences and attitudes linked to childlike values and a state of 'lifelong puerility'. No longer will the consumerist economy be hampered by the old virtues of the Protestant ethic – deferred gratification, ascetic self-denial, stoicism, hard work and thrift. Instead, by 'regressing' mature adults to the level of children, capitalism is free to promote an almost diametrically opposed set of values, including impulsivity, profligacy, vulnerability, and a fixation with leisure and hedonistic self-expression. In plain terms, infantilisation is good for business.

Importantly, for Barber, the Infantilist ethos is not a random phenomenon or inadvertent by-product of postmodernity's fascination with play and creativity. It is the result of a premeditated strategy by corporations to reconfigure the nature of consumer culture, a point he makes very clear in the following passage:

> Those responsible for manufacturing and merchandizing goods for the global marketplace, those who are actually researching, teaching, and practising marketing and advertising today, are aiming both to sell to a younger demographic and to imbue older consumers with the tastes of the young ... At the same time, these avatars of consumer capitalism are seeking to encourage adult regression, hoping to rekindle in grown-ups the tastes and habits of children so that they can sell globally the ... consumer goods for which there is no discernible 'need market' other than the one created by capitalism's own frantic imperative to sell.[8]

Barber's primary concern is with the way the market targets children as adult consumers. The first decade of the twenty-first century saw major changes in the way advertisers interacted with young people. In the mid-1990s, it was estimated that the average child was exposed to approximately 150,000 advertisements between the ages of four and eighteen. A decade later, and because of the internet and the growth of viral advertising, that number had mushroomed to an estimated 10 million. But it's not just a question of bombardment. Around this time, market research companies also started to develop an entirely new arsenal of promotional techniques. These included everything from 'neuro-marketing' and influencer advertising to refined promotional campaigns involving carefully selected 'cool' teenagers deployed as playground and chatroom shills to push newly released products. Among its many strengths, *Consumed* serves as an excellent guidebook to this brave new world of product placement and psyche manipulation. Barber is at his most compelling when describing a commercial architecture replete with marketing conferences on 'Youth Power' (that include panel sessions entitled 'Reaching Kids through Causes: An In-Depth Tutorial on How to Market with a Heart'), and craven advertising executives whose *raison d'être* is to help brands achieve the same level of worship and devotion as displayed by followers of religious cults. But as the subtitle of *Consumed* suggests, the 'corruption' of childhood by such practices is only half the story.

As we have seen, there's nothing new about advertisers and marketers targeting and exploiting young children in an effort to elongate the youth market. However, in the twenty-first century, it's more appropriate to think in terms of cultural domination than market elongation. Today, as Juliet Schor argues in *Born to Buy*, 'Kids and teens are now the epicenter of American consumer culture . . . Their tastes drive market trends. Their opinions shape brand strategies.'[9] The consequence of this creeping imperialism is clear: *youth culture is now the culture of all*. It has broken free from the constraints of childhood and teenagerdom and now operates unfettered across almost all stages of the life course. For Barber, this rapid cross-generational expansion of youth culture is the other half of the infantilisation story. Hence, in contrast to other commentators whose analysis is limited to concerns about the erosion of childhood, Barber extends his critique to include the way perpetual childishness is being 'grafted onto adults'.

Once again, Barber chooses his words carefully. Just as a graft is a deliberate procedure involving specific processes of manipulation, the infantilisation of adult tastes and interests is for Barber no chance occurrence. In *Consumed* he shows how adults are targeted – you might even say groomed – *like* children. In previous eras, the infantile imagery associated with child/teen-specific marketing was limited to specific youthful domains (children's television, magazines, etc.). This all changed at the end of the twentieth century when advertisers and marketers started saturating all parts of the mediascape with childlike and teen-centric marketing. The logic behind this new approach was clear. The desire and wants of children are not only more fantastical and boundless than those of adults, but they are also more intense and, importantly, more easily instilled and incited. In contrast, mature adults have historically been characterised by higher levels of forbearance (in its original sense of patient self-control), discernment and financial restraint. Hence, if capitalism's goal is to endlessly stimulate demand beyond established levels, then it makes complete sense to encourage adults to think and act more like immature youngsters.

Drawing closely on Barber's work, the Turkish media-studies scholar Bengü Başbuğ describes this process as '*controlled* infantilisation'. If Barber's *Consumed* is widely considered the core text on the political economy of infantilisation, then Başbuğ's lesser known but more recent and more specific work, *When Brand*

Communication Becomes Childish: Infantilization in 21st Century Advertising, is without doubt the most sophisticated cultural analysis of how the phenomenon has been deployed by advertisers and marketers. Her identification of an entirely new classification of consumer – the 'child-like adult' – is of considerable importance when it comes to understanding the nature and form of twenty-first-century infantilism. The childlike adult is an ideal type; an imagined hybrid consumer who has the financial clout of a mature, working adult, but the tastes, interests and low self-control levels of a malleable juvenile. The bastard brainchild of brand gurus and marketing managers the world over, the childlike adult is the market's desired end-product of Kidult consumerism – a perpetually puerile consumer who carries his youthful pursuits, pastimes and pleasures with him into adulthood. In Başbuğ's account, the childlike adult has emerged as the *'prototypic* figure' of late-modern consumer culture; a 'perennial adolescent' endowed with all the characteristics 'vital to the market', including 'suggestibility', hedonistic irrationality, an endless desire for 'objects that have no utilitarian purpose', thoughtlessness about 'the needs of others' and a 'lack of long-term thought patterns'.

In their respective analyses, Barber and Başbuğ both place considerable stress on how the market encourages what they call behavioural regression. By this they mean the Infantilist ethos is directly promoting pre- – or more accurately, stalled – adulthood as a distinct lifestyle choice. It is an argument that immediately evokes the concept of emerging adulthood as discussed in Chapter One. According to its founder, the developmental psychologist Jeffrey Arnett, emerging adulthood is a new 'life stage' that applies to the years eighteen to twenty-five, a period which he suggests is 'neither adolescence nor young adulthood but is theoretically and empirically distinct from both'. But while the Infantilist ethos and the emerging adulthood paradigm both zero in on stalled adulthood, their respective stance vis-à-vis the phenomenon could not be more different. Generally speaking, Arnett's intention is to promote a sympathetic understanding of what he calls emerging adulthood's distinct subjectivity. Hence he and his supporters stress a generally positive set of psycho-emotional elements such as 'self-exploration', optimistic 'self-focus' and 'identity formation'. In contrast, although advertisers and marketers are also heavily invested in the idea of a delayed transition to adulthood, their goal instead is the promotion of a more corrosive set of psychological traits designed to deliberately induce childishness. Shortly we will explore how these traits manifest themselves in the very latest forms of advertising, but first we need to go back to the mid-to-late 1990s when advertisers started to recognise the value and power of the Infantilist ethos.

As mentioned above, a growing problem for the advertising industry in the final years of the last century was how to get noticed in a message-laden digital age. No surprise, then, that advertisers chose this moment to commence their assault on mature adulthood. Exaggerating some of the key themes associated with earlier postmodern advertising, most obviously irony, parody and fantasy, advertising and marketing creatives began producing a new style of twenty-first-century commercial. Key to this was an emphasis on themes such as jokiness, scepticism, cynicism and puerility; the goal being to create consumers who were sardonic, apathetic, even indolent and thus all too happy to eschew the responsibilities associated with adult life. It is a mode of advertising exemplified by the wildly successful Budweiser 'Wassup?' campaign (1999–2002), which involved nothing more than a group of adult male slackers sitting around watching TV and screaming 'Wassup?' to one another in increasingly irritating ways.[10] Countless campaigns quickly followed along similar lines. Indeed, the approach became so popular the advertising industry developed two fabricated demographic profiles – the 'Mook' and the 'Midriff' – to use as templates for this type of commercial.[11] The Mook was originally designed to reflect a combination of the on-screen personas of slacker-slob movie stars like Adam Sandler, Owen Wilson and Seth Rogen, and the cultural logic behind then-popular TV shows like *Jackass*, *The Dudesons*, *Wildboyz* and *The Tom Green Show*. Initially a stalwart of focus-group proving grounds, the Mook subsequently went on to become one of the most ubiquitous characters in early twenty-first-century advertising. Crude, slothful and unashamedly based on the concept of arrested adolescence, Mooks (of all ages) now haunt our screens: the quintessential male expression of the Infantilist ethos.

Equally familiar to advertising executives the world over is the construct of the 'Midriff': a prematurely adult, openly sexual teen figure used by advertisers as a new form of feminine 'empowerment' – think Britney Spears, Miley Cyrus or, more recently, K-Pop sensations like Kim Seol-hyun and Enubi. Female stereotypes have always moved product, but with the Midriff advertisers created a figure that could activate dual market demographics simultaneously. Not only is the Midriff deployed as a way of prematurely ageing – adultifying – pre-teenage girls, but the nymphet cliché can also be used to appeal to what is commonly referred to in advertising circles as the adult woman's inner child.

Discussion of the Mook and the Midriff inevitably raises important questions about how one might go about organising and disaggregating infantilising advertising messages along gendered lines. But irrespective of whether it's beer-swilling slackers or commercially weaponised Lolitas, the key thing to recognise is that Mooks, Midriffs and the other so-called 'Middle Youth' stereotypes emerging at the start of the twenty-first century were only the advance shock troops of the infantilism invasion. Waiting in their wake to storm the beachhead was a bigger and much better-equipped force of childlike adult characters. The struggle for the soul of the late-modern Kidult was about to ramp up from a peripheral guer-rilla campaign to something more akin to total war.

'Silly stuff. It matters': Advertising and the childlike adult

As advertising straplines like 'Give a little time for the child within you' (Toyota), 'Be a kid again' (Forest Holidays) and 'Recommended by kids for active grown-ups' (Alpro Soya) suggest, after more than half a century of elongating the concept of youth in an effort to expand corporate profits, the advertising industry has succeeded in normal-ising infantilism across the life course. But what specific techniques and themes do advertisers use to concretise what Danesi calls 'forever young syndrome' within the contemporary popular imagination? My analysis of the use of infantilising tropes in twenty-first-century advertising points to three distinctive representational features.

The first and most identifiable trope is what Eric Konigsberg described as the 'conscious abdication of adult responsibility'. Here, I refer to advertisements that feature characters in their twenties, thirties, forties and now even their fifties who have aban-doned any sense of seriousness or sincerity and instead exhibit a contrived attitude of casuality and juvenile insouciance. This tendency to eschew adult commitment in favour of an elongated youth characterised by apathy, indifference, irony and mischief was first identified by Andrew Calcutt in his turn-of-the-millen-nium book *Arrested Development*. Since then, the theme of young people opting to exist in a suspended – or better still perpetual – sense of adolescence, rather than transitioning to adulthood, has been associated with a host of neologisms, including 'Rejuvenile', 'adultescent', 'Boomerang Kid' and 'Parasite single'. But it is within the realm of advertising and marketing that the 'abdication of adult responsibility' trope is most pronounced.

A second key feature is age regression via a symbolic portal to childhood. Writing in a 2002 edition of the marketing bible *Brandweek*, US advertisers Becky Ebenkamp and Jeff Odiorne reported on a then emerging industry trend: 'People in their twenties and thirties are clamoring for comfort in purchases and products, and sensory experiences that remind them of a happier, more innocent time – childhood.'[12] Two decades later and this approach is now a core feature of adult marketing campaigns. As Başbuğ explains, the use of childhood symbols and 'child-centric aesthetics' in adult advertising is not simply a manifestation of postmodern irony. Rather, it is part of a stealthier campaign to unconsciously manipulate adults by triggering psychic processes 'which stimulate a desire for the product by activating existing knowledge and evoking positive memories and emotions'.[13] But why 'stir up' and 'excite' adult consumer psyches in this way? In simple terms, because being 'youthful' was getting old. After nearly a century of use, the concept of teen youthfulness, as imagined and exploited by advertisers, had largely lost its symbolic power as a lifestyle motif. At the same time, the West was experiencing yet another revival of the cult of the child – this time in the form of a compensatory cultural reaction to the erosion of adult subjectivity 'in the active, history-making sense'.[14] Taken together, these developments suggested that the advertising industry needed something new, something fresh and untrammelled – and what's more unsullied than childhood innocence?

As a result of the advertising industry's pivot from youth to childhood, many of today's commercials now resemble the inside of a child's nursery, with toys, playthings and childish metaphors all commonly mobilised as symbolic portals to regress grown-ups back to an idyllic childlike state, absent of adult anxieties (see Plate 10 which provides a literal and figurative example of the portal motif in advertising). It is a strategy as deliberate as it is depressing. By simultaneously glorifying childishness and eroding the belief that adult interests are distinct and something worth aspiring to, this mode of 'controlled infantilisation' represents the epitome of cultural dumbing down, a point made forcibly by Başbuğ: 'The invitation to return to a child-like state, engage in youthful activities and consume entertainment considered to be immature just a few decades before, is meanwhile not perceived as inappropriate, but very welcoming with the consequence that a growing number of adults accept the invitation without any hesitation.'

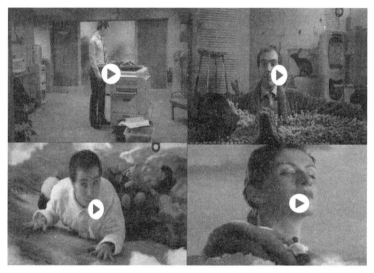

Plate 10: From boring adult office work to a Kidult paradise of adult romper suits, pillow fights and omnipresent mother figures, Trident Soft Gum's 'Be a kid again' advert exemplifies the portal to childish oblivion that is now a common feature of contemporary advertising. (Trident)

The final feature of contemporary infantilised advertising is the colonisation of nostalgia via sophisticated forms of postmodern pastiche. As noted above, a key element of postmodernism is how

it de-historicises history by recycling popular imagery and stereotypes from the past. It is a tendency evident in all manner of postmodern cultural production, but one that reaches its zenith in forms
of contemporary advertising that seek to regress adults back into a
fantasy realm of symbolic childhood. Often folded in with one or
both previous elements, instantly available (or synchronic) nostalgia is used – both in its cloying and ironic forms – to evoke unconscious desires and stimulate positive emotions associated with
earlier, more innocent moments in the life course.[15] From a marketing perspective, these emotional associations are extremely powerful in that they not only induce feelings of safety, happiness and
escapism, but they also 'trigger childlike and irrational thought
processes in adult consumers' decision making'.[16] In other words, by
making nostalgia a central component of infantilised advertising,
consumer capitalism has found yet another way to stimulate desire
by creating a false sense of loss among late-modern Kidults keen to
escape the harsh socio-economic realities of everyday life.

'*Silly stuff. It matters.*' That was the strapline for a 2013 TV ad
campaign for UK mobile internet provider Three. Created by the
advertising agency Wieden+Kennedy, and featuring a moonwalk-
ing Shetland pony, the campaign was designed specifically 'to
celebrate frivolous acts', as this quote by Wieden+Kennedy
employees Freddie Powell and Hollie Walker makes clear:

> All that seemingly stupid, funny and downright daft stuff we look
> at online on a daily basis . . . it's not silly at all. It's this stuff that
> we pass around, that we share, that connects us to one another . . .
> We wanted to do more than just hold up a mirror to all the crazy
> stuff online. We wanted to actually contribute to it and a moon-
> walking pony felt like something that people on the internet
> would gravitate towards. So we took that concept and put it on a
> pedestal, lavishing it with cinematic glory. We wanted to make

something people would want to share, which is where
PonyMixer.com came in – a tool which allows users to play with
Socks and create their own little piece of joy, something personal
that they would want to pass on to others.[17]

The form of thinking described by Powell and Walker is now
dominant across whole swathes of the advertising and marketing
industry. As a result, we are all now forced to live, whether we like
it or not, in a commercial world where *silly stuff matters* – a lot.

Plate 11: Dancing fools. Recently, alongside the various
infantilising tropes outlined in this chapter, a new trend has
emerged where everybody in adverts seems to be dancing, all
the time, no matter what the context. Clearly drawing on the
mistaken belief that dancing is universally popular – a view held
no doubt by those police officers and hospital staff who regularly
post TikTok videos of themselves doing formation dance routines
– the use of dance in contemporary advertising is yet another
deliberate device by which advertisers seek to undermine mature
adulthood by turning every space/situation into a potential site
of expressive youthful performativity. (Maskot/Getty Images)

To illustrate this point, let's turn now to three common styles of advertising designed to speak explicitly to the adult-child consumer. In each case, I urge you to reflect on whether these modes of messaging are examples of benign silliness – harmless fun created to evoke positive sensations in the audience – or whether they are instead part of a more calculated and cynical strategy of controlled infantilisation?

Toyification: On the homepage of www.rejuvenile.com, Christopher Noxon's popular website, the following text is posted: 'Once upon a time, boys and girls grew up and set aside childish things. Or so the story goes. Nowadays, adults buy cars marketed to consumers half their age, dress in schoolyard fashions and play with their children in ways adults of previous generations would have found ridiculous. Most have busy lives and adult responsibilities. They are not stunted adolescents. They are something new: "rejuveniles".[18] Noxon was among the first commentators to identify the so-called toyification of society – the proliferation and increasing prestige of toys in adult spaces such as offices, museums and licensed premises. In his book *Rejuvenile*, Noxon writes that 'everyday adult stuff is getting less utilitarian and more toy-like'. It is a statement that accurately describes the transformation that has taken place in twenty-first-century advertising. From high-street banks (Santander: LEGO bricks; Barclays: a children's bouncy castle) to comparison insurance websites (comparethemarket.com: stuffed Meerkat toys; moneysupermarket.com: 'Epic Action Man'), everywhere you look, companies are using toyification to market their goods and services. Toys even featured recently in an advert for something as serious and adult as writing one's last will and testimony (Will&Quill.com). To illustrate the sheer scale of this tendency, consider the advertising content of mobile-phone network providers, a group of companies who have consistently leant on infantilising advertising since the industry got off the ground in the mid-1990s: inflatable dolphins and balloon animals (Orange 'Pay as you go'); toy soldiers and toy robots (TalkTalk); kites, crayons and giant ribbons (Orange 'Good things should never end'); children's jetpack and Star Wars Yoda doll (Vodafone); doll's house and the 'spin-the-bottle' game (Orange 'Magic numbers'); teddy bears and toys (O2); family members represented by toy figures (Orange broadband); robot toys ('search O2 shop').

Fairy tales, fantasyscapes and fabricated nostalgia: In one of the most insightful essays on the subject, Eric Konigsberg describes infantilisation as 'an antidote to the uncertainties of the day. Age regression is a protective shield.'[19] This astute observation finds expression in contemporary advertising that uses fairy-tale and fantasy tropes to create nostalgic feelings of childhood safety and security. Consider again some examples of mobile-phone advertising. For whatever reason, it is now almost standard practice for companies in this industry to align their brands with symbols and motifs rooted in childhood fantasy. Alongside Three's aforementioned 'PonyMixer.com' commercial, other examples include O2's bizarre 'Be More Dog' campaign (2013–16), and advertisements that feature cartwheels and tumbling (T-Mobile), nursery-rhyme jingles (O2) and pink elves (T-Mobile). Başbuğ also identified a pronounced reliance on fairy tales, fables and myths in her detailed analysis of infantilisation in Turkish advertising. In advert after advert, from thirty-something man-boys playing pirates and dress-up in Captain Morgan and Bud Light commercials, to UK government newspaper ads about global warming that use nursery rhymes as their central motif, the advertisers' message is clear and universal: abandon your 'outer adult' and instead seek to satisfy and sustain your 'inner child'.

Cartoonification: In a similar vein to toyification, countless adult products and services now routinely feature cartoon characters and animated figures in their advertising. Prominent examples here include the Geico gecko; General Insurance's 'The General'; the Duracell/Energizer Bunny; Halifax Bank's Flintstones campaign; Lloyds TSB's long-running 'For the journey' series; Vodafone's Freebees and ZooZoo campaigns; confused.com's cartoon character 'Cara Confused'; Heinz ketchup's use of Looney Toons characters; ING's 'Vole, donkey, bear' animated commercials; and Android's 'Be together' campaign. At one level, this development could be dismissed simply as a reflection of the popularity of animation in society generally (as Noxon pointed out some time ago, more American adults ('18–49') watch the Cartoon Network than CNN). But is it really that straightforward? Or is the cartoonification of adult advertising being driven by something more instrumental and insidious? I believe it is and that by mobilising lovable cartoon characters and cutesy talking animated animals, advertisers are deliberately attempting to stupefy their audience – to make them think and act like children. This is, after all, the underlying goal of the Infantilist ethos – to create consumers who are capable of framing the world only in the most simplistic terms imaginable. While this might seem far-fetched, conspiratorial even, consider this line of copy from yet another mobile phone commercial: 'My Lumina saves my life . . . judging by the bright pink, I'm feeling very happy'. Thirty years ago, addressing adult consumers in such a way would have been inconceivable. Today, it's now almost the norm – and the cartoonification of advertising has played a major part in this normalisation process.

The techniques and styles outlined in this section are everyday staples of brand marketing. For example, Table 2 illustrates how pronounced these tendencies have become in just one market sector – Anglo-American automobile advertising, where adults, it seems, are marketed to as if they were still in high school. But whether it's by colonising nostalgia, creating portals to more inno-cent times, or via specific styles such as toyification and cartoon-ification, the goal behind this mode of advertising is always the same: to appeal directly to the child in the adult-child consumer and thus switch on 'the ego state' associated with pre-adulthood. By adopting a 'playful', 'naughty', or 'fun-loving' sensibility, these commercials all bypass adult rationality and by doing so greatly intensify the process of infantilisation.[20]

CAR MANUFACUTURER/MODEL	INFANTILISING TROPE
Mercedes Benz C Class	Skateboards, trikes and children's bikes; strapline 'Adults are just kids with much, much better toys'.
Citroën C4	(Car depicted as) child's 'Transformer' toy.
Škoda Fabia	Car constructed out of a child's birthday cake. Soundtrack: 'My Favorite Things' by Julie Andrews from *The Sound of Music*.
Škoda Fabia	Soundtrack: 'Bibbidi-Bobbidi-Boo' by Verna Felton from the Disney children's film *Cinderella*.
Honda 'Gift to remember' campaign	Six TV advertisements featuring classic children's toys, including Skeletor, Jem Doll and Stretch Armstrong.
Toyota RAV4	(Car takes part in a) child's go-kart race.
Nissan Note	(Car features as part of a) children's ghost train/house of horrors.
Nissan Qashqai	(Car used as) skateboard; (Car bombarded by) paint balls and water balloons.
Vauxhall Corsa ('C'mon, Follow that car' campaign)	(Car driven by and marketed via) a collection of knitted toy figures called 'The c'mons'.

Vauxhall Corsa	(Car depicted in) *Wacky Races* cartoon theme.
Vauxhall Corsa	(Car depicted in) game of hide and seek.
Toyota	2009 product line launched with strapline 'Give a little time to the child within you'.
Renault Twingo	(Car as) child's toy competing in a game against other familiar children's toys.
BMW Z4	(Car used as a) child's paintbrush in painting.
Vauxhall Zafira	Campaign based on role reversal in which adult roles are played by children and vice versa.
Chrysler Town and Country	(Car advertised using) *Jimmy Neutron* cartoon characters.
Dodge Grand Caravan	(Car advertised using) *Shrek* cartoon characters.
Toyota 'The Journey' campaign	Animated cartoon characters and a Santa letter.
Peugeot people carrier	(Car advertised using) *Toy Story 3* cartoon characters.
Ford EcoSport	*Guardians of the Galaxy* toy.
Peugeot 208	(Car depicted in) *Wacky Races* cartoon theme.
Renault KWID Outsider	Dungeons and Dragons characters.
Citroën C3 Visiodrive	Car converted into children's swing on cargo dock.
Toyota Highlander	*Muppets* characters.
Honda 'Harmony' campaign	(Car advertised using) childlike cartoon dream sequence.
Peugeot 407	LEGO cars, clockwork cars, toy cars; strapline 'Playtime is over'.
Volkswagen ID-Buzz	*Star Wars* characters
Kia EV6	Robotic toy dog as central character

Table 2: The infantilisation of automobile advertising

Advertising and the adultified child

Another very prominent development in advertising today is the role reversal that sees grown-ups positioned in subservient roles to children. Whether it's kids playing adult roles while actual adults are reduced to passive underlings, or smug children tut-tutting and smirking at their parents' stupidity in pretty much every family-based commercial on television, adult authority is continuously being challenged by the rise of the precocious TV child. It is a trend that started almost two decades ago and is exemplified by the much-discussed 2006 Barclaycard 'You're fired' commercial in which a series of all-knowing kids fire their parents for 'errant' behaviour such as working too hard.[21] Since then, this reverse power dynamic has grown ever stronger, not just in advertising but in society more generally. In Plate 12, for example, we see how adultification now manifests itself in commercially sponsored national newspaper content.

 Kristian Niemietz @K_Niemietz Jan 30, 2021

Plate 12: 'They "rebel" against their *Guardian*-reading parents by out-Guardianing them.' Kristian Niemietz comments on Guardian Labs 'generational translator' publication. (Kristian Niemietz/*Guardian News & Media*).

Adultification has even reached the point where babies now assert themselves: speeding along busy highways (Hewlett-Packard, 2010), getting married and giving wedding speeches (E-Trade investments, 2023), singing power ballads (fundingcircle.com, 2021), roller-skating in Central Park (Evian, 2010), trading stocks and discussing portfolio options (E-Trade, 2009–2012), and wearing business suits and ordering subservient adults around in corporate offices (Triple Velvet toilet paper, 2010). Marketers will try to convince you that this type of 'babyfied' branding is just harmless fun, but advertising is not entertainment. It is a process designed to manipulate thoughts, mould behaviour and affect consumer decision making. In this case, the babyfication of advertising is an attempt to attach neotenous traits to goods and services. It is well documented within behavioural psychology that neoteny – the retention of youthful and baby-like physical features within adults – is a powerful driver of attractiveness among humans. Now, it seems, the advertising industry is striving for something similar in the marketplace – cuteness, prettiness and baby-faced lovability as psychological brand associations. Consider, for example, the figures in Plate 13, the Evian 'Live Young' advertisement, which provides a perfect illustration of the blurring of neoteny and fresh-faced adulthood.

In the twentieth century, it was the dynamic, fresh values associated with youth culture that drove advertising narratives, but as a result of its overuse, youthfulness is slowly but subtly being replaced by new forms of universal childishness.

The many examples in this section attest to the fact that, increasingly within contemporary advertising, the passive, stultified adult and the all-powerful, all-knowing child are inversely correlated. If we adopt a traditional critical perspective on advertising, this reversal of authority from adult to child could be written off as just

Plate 13: Neotenous advertising: Evian's long running Live Young
campaign (2009–2018). If these images were not infantilising
enough, just consider the pre-teenage mindset of the people
responsible for developing such campaigns. According to an
Evian spokesperson, Live Young is 'for those who refuse to
settle for just one path. It's for the multifaceted, and we defined
it as those people who want to live young, be what they want
to, try what they want to and do what they want to.'[22] (Evian)

another elaboration of the well-worn logic of capitalist
consumption – goods are enchanted with the capacity to magically offer resolutions to lived experiences of denial and
constraint. From this perspective, the marketing of adulthood
(especially sexuality) to kids, and childish pleasures to adults,
are viewed straightforwardly as forms of escapism from the
normalised constraints imposed on us by the 'mundane real':
for kids, the escape from being denied fully constituted access
to the world of adult pleasures (sex, booze, etc.); and for adults
the escape from rational self-management via a flight to play
and fun. But does this conventional interpretation sufficiently

explain why advertisers are so keen to infantilise their customers? I don't believe it does. Advertising today is doing much more than just interpolating people in terms that appeal to their desire for difference and escape. It is systematically and deliberately eroding generational distinctions in an effort to stave off overproduction and maintain profit. The result is a new form of Kidult consumerism that homogenises the life course and creates what Bengü Başbuğ describes as a new postmodern 'uni-age'.

In the same way as the term unisex enabled products to be sold across genders, the uni-age phenomenon allows children, teens and adults to be addressed simultaneously via the same style of advertising and marketing. The leading edge of this phenomenon was first glimpsed in the early 2000s when infantilising products like alcopops, nostalgia-themed backpacks, Purple Ronnie merchandise, Funko and Hello Kitty adult action figures, and the fashion crime that is the 'onesie' started to appear in the marketplace. The logic behind these and similar items was clearly crossgenerational, but sales were limited because at that point these products appealed only to the emerging Kidult demographic – a narrow group of young adult consumers who wished to stay younger longer. Today, corporations have overcome this problem by encouraging a new type of uni-age consumerism which allows them to sell the same products to customers at *all* stages of the life course. Toy manufacturers, for example, are already offsetting declining Western birth rates by expanding the 'adult toy' market. Thus, it's now possible to purchase everything from replica *Star Wars* neopixel lightsabers costing several thousand dollars to five-hundred-piece 'crystal-meth lab' playsets based on the adult TV series *Breaking Bad*. A similar commercial mindset is evident in Germany, where the world's largest manufacturer of children's food, Hipp, now markets its organic baby purees to 'healthy adult'

Plate 14: The uni-age cometh. (Left: Photo by
Clive Mason – Formula 1/Formula1 via Getty
Images; Middle: Shutterstock; Right: iStock)

customers. Also in Germany, the confectionery company, Haribo, changed their main advertising jingle from 'Kids love it so – the happy world of Haribo' to 'Kids and *grown-ups* love it so – the happy world of Haribo'.[23] But perhaps the most blatant example of uni-age consumerism is Halloween, which has been transformed over the last decade or so from a kids-only holiday to a major adult event with annual sales in the US alone of over $9 billion. Interestingly, much of this expenditure is *by* adults *for* adults. The market for adult Halloween costumes, for example, is now almost half a billion dollars bigger than the market for children's outfits ($1.68 billion/$1.23 billion in 2017).[24] This huge adult market barely existed a generation ago.

Earlier we saw how advertisers use toyification, cartoonification, synchronic nostalgia and other postmodern techniques to enhance the uni-age appeal of various goods and services. These techniques are already being supplemented by a more sophisticated and increasingly subliminal set of aesthetic and auditory markers. But whether cross-generational commercials feature a cartoon character, a talking baby or, as is more likely these days, an ironically confused thirty-something bearded man-boy stumbling through life to a faux-folk ukulele soundtrack, make no mistake about it, the promotional industry is doing everything it can to transform each and every one of us into an unthinking adult-child consumer.

Chapter 5

'No, I *want* to be treated like a kid – adulting is hard': The Infantilising Consequences of a Life Lived Online

We're running around saying we suddenly have a voice [but] the internet infantilises you – you're automatically a teenager when you use any of these [social media] tools. They are geared that way.

DBC Pierre[1]

I suppose it had to happen sooner or later. I had of course seen people wearing onesies (one-piece adult romper suits) before, but this was the first time someone had turned up to one of my lectures in one. The student in question was a nice lad who often made insightful comments, so I felt OK about raising the subject informally at the end of class. 'It's cold, and I like to feel comfy,' he told me when I asked about the onesie's appeal, a statement that met with approving nods from his classmates. Fair enough, but wasn't he concerned about the infantilising overtones of such a garment? His response made it clear that he was not. 'No, I *want* to be treated like a kid. Adulting is hard.' I remember feeling some-what nonplussed by this reply – and not just because it was the first time I'd heard the word adult used as a verb.[2] Why would a university student in his twenties want to be thought of and treated like a child? Why disavow the obvious benefits associated with adulthood? And if it really was just about feeling comfy, why not put on some extra layers as opposed to maundering around campus like an overgrown toddler? Such questions suggest there's something very different about the current generation of university students, something we must explore if we are to understand the rule of the Kidult.

Earlier, I introduced an idea from life history theory that a generation can in part be defined by its shared response to a particular set of historic or socioeconomic factors, including geopolitical events, economic cycles and technological advancements. The young people currently matriculating through our schools and universities are clearly one such generation. Why is this cohort special? Because they are the first to be born after the commercialisation of the internet in 1995 and have thus lived their entire lives in an age of digital connectivity, social media and mobile/smartphone usage. Although commonly known as Generation Z, these 'digital natives' are also referred to as iGeneration (iGen); the 'i' standing for internet, iPod and, most significantly, the iPhone (which was launched in 2007 when the oldest iGen'ers were entering adolescence). As we will see, the young people that constitute iGen have a singular relationship to digital technology that sets them apart from previous generational cohorts, including even their Millennial predecessors. It is to this relationship I now turn, as in its own way it plays an even bigger role in driving contemporary infantilisation than the advertising and marketing techniques associated with the adult-child consumer.

'i' is for infantilisation: From the social-information matrix to the super-connected iGeneration

Concern about the infantilising role of media technology on adult–child relations is not new. Back in the early 1980s, the cultural critic Neil Postman and the communications scholar

Joshua Meyrowitz both identified the deleterious effect television was having in terms of destabilising distinctions between adulthood and childhood. In his classic 1982 work, *The Disappearance of Childhood*, Postman argued that TV had hastened the demise of childhood innocence by functioning as a 'total disclosure medium'. Prior to the emergence of television, children received their information about the world from parents or via content-controlled children's literature. Postman argued that this sense of adult direction was dramatically undermined in the television age. With no meaningful filtration system to shield children from adult programming, television was drip-feeding kids a diet of 'secret' adult information about sex, violence, money, death, etc. As a result, not only were children exposed much earlier to the previously hidden realities of adult life, but they also encountered material in which adult characters were portrayed as weak, flawed and, for the first time, childlike.

A similar argument was set out by Meyrowitz in his 1985 book *No Sense of Place: The Impact of Electronic Media on Social Behavior*. Meyrowitz believed that the shift from 'book culture' to 'television culture' had triggered a fundamental reconfiguration of what he termed the social-information matrix. Influenced by the sociology of Erving Goffman and the media philosophy of Marshall McLuhan, Meyrowitz's social information matrix was a model for understanding human behaviour that looked 'beyond the sequence of *individual* development', to factors like the media that 'influence[d] the behavior of *all* people'. Ideas like this were common in media studies in the 1980s and took a variety of different forms, but what set Meyrowitz's matrix apart was his focus on status and social distinction. Meyrowitz believed that social status was largely determined and controlled by access to information. In other words, higher-status groups maintained their elevated position by restricting access to differentiated 'informational worlds'. By 'thrusting children into a complex adult world', television had elevated their status and freed them from the separate (lower-order) information system associated with childhood. The more adult programming kids watched, the more they became cognizant of what he called the 'secret of secrecy': 'Television's exposure of the "staging of adulthood" . . . undermines both traditional childhood naiveté *and* the all-knowing confident adult role, and fosters the movement toward a uni-age behavioral style'.[3]

It goes without saying that the respective warnings of Meyrowitz and Postman about the corrosive impact of electronic media went entirely unheeded. Postman, for example, recognised that if children were ever to effectively manage the bombardment of messages associated with modern media, they would need to become their own critical editors. For this to happen, society needed to equip kids with the requisite skills to understand and interpret the way electronic media uproots tradition and reshapes cultural norms. Unfortunately, precisely the opposite happened. Rather than encouraging a sense of critical discernment among young people as they negotiate electronic media, society instead promulgated the false message that more (engagement/immersion) must inevitably mean better. As a result, children today are largely left to fend for themselves as they navigate a never-ending stream of digital interactions across sprawling and mostly non-curated informational ecosystems. The results of this social experiment are now all too clear. For all the inestimable benefits associated with digital connectivity, we must also confront what many commentators believe is an epistemic crisis in the way young people today are distinguishing fact from fiction and thus making sense of the world around them.[4]

Of these commentaries, the most important in terms of infantilism is Jean Twenge's analysis of 11 million lifestyle survey responses (compiled from four databases) completed by American youngsters

184

between 1976–2016. Twenge, of course, is best known for being the psychologist who coined the term iGeneration, but her work should also be seen as continuing the tradition of Postman and Meyrowitz in the sense that it too is concerned with how digital media contributes to the diminution of adulthood. Twenge's book has a very, *very* long title – *iGen: Why Today's Super-Connected Kids Are Growing Up Less Rebellious, More Tolerant, Less Happy – and Completely Unprepared for Adulthood (and What That Means for the Rest of Us)*. Given that one of its findings is that iGen'ers rarely read books these days, perhaps such verbosity was not a great idea. One can easily imagine an iGen'er skimming over the book's cover and dismissing it imperiously with that classic text-based acronym, 'TLDR' ('Too long didn't read'). This would be a mistake, as *iGen* offers a fascinating insight – both positive and negative – into the behavioural characteristics of the post-1995 generation. Its great strength is that it's based on an epic sweep of data. Not only does the four-decade-long timeframe enable Twenge to compare one generation with another ('rather than relying on older people's reflections on a time gone by'), but it's also demographically comprehensive, providing detailed information about 'poor teens and rich ones' and kids of 'every ethnic background'. The book also has a broad thematic scope, its coverage extending to subjects such as religious affiliation and political identification. However, as the title suggests, Twenge's primary concern is with technology and, more specifically, with how social media, smartphones and – to a lesser extent – gaming are collectively reshaping young people's lives in the twenty-first century.

The data presented in *iGen* is stark. In 2015, US high-school seniors spent twice as much time online as did their 2006 counterparts. When texting, gaming and internet-based activities are agglomerated, iGen high-school seniors (regardless of economic background) spend on average six hours per day with new media. This level of engagement is itself a cause for concern, but more worrying is what teenagers are *not* doing when they're online. According to Twenge's analysis, today's kids are working less, driving less and volunteering less. They also read fewer books and spend less time on homework – tendencies that no doubt contributed to the decline in SAT scores that began in the mid-2000s (a thirteen-point decline in both writing and critical reading since 2005). Clearly, technology has not supplemented the deep learning and intellectual growth associated with reading, as was enthusiastically predicted by many an overly optimistic tech pedagogue, rather it has supplanted it.

> Apparently, texting and posting to social media instead of reading books, magazines, and newspapers are not a boon for reading comprehension or academic writing. That might partially be due to the short attention span that new media seem to encourage. One study installed a program on college students' laptops that took a screenshot every five seconds. The researchers found that students switched between tasks every nineteen seconds on average. More than 75% of the students' computer windows were open less than one minute. This is a very different experience from sitting and reading a book for hours.[5]

Something else supplanted by technology is going out and getting together with friends. In activity after activity, from shopping with peers to going to parties to just hanging out, iGen'ers spend less time interacting face to face with their friends than any generation in history. Instead, regardless of whether it's early adolescents or college students, iGen'ers are opting for virtual connectivity over in-person interactions. Superficially, it might seem that one form of communication is as good as any other and that as long as young people have access to some sort of supportive friendship network all is well. Sadly, Twenge's survey analysis indicates that teens who spend more time on screen-based activities 'are more likely to be unhappy' than those who engage in 'non-screen activities'. And it doesn't end there. 'Feelings of loneliness' are also considerably higher among kids who spend most time online. Add to this the heightened levels of anxiety and stress provoked by online practices such as cyber-bullying, trolling, doom-scrolling and body-shaming and it's not surprising the US teenage suicide rate spiked by 46 per cent between 2007 and 2015.

Although *iGen* also highlights several positive and clearly very important developments that stem from living a life online, Twenge's primary concern is with how today's super-connected kids are being detrimentally affected by an over-dependence on digital technology. In making this argument, she sets out 'ten important trends shaping iGen'ers and, ultimately, all of us'. Keen to cement the iGen brand in the mind of her readers, each of these trends begins with the letter *i*. Strange, then, that despite having much to say about 'the extension of childhood into adolescence', Twenge chose not to employ the word infantilisation (which, as far as I could tell didn't appear once in the book), opting instead for the more benign rubric 'In no hurry: growing up slowly'. Semantics aside, *iGen* provides further evidence, if more were needed, that something has gone seriously wrong in the way young people are transitioning to adulthood. According to Twenge's findings, iGen teenagers are far less likely than their predecessors to have had sex, drunk alcohol, secured their driving licence, or even gone on a date – all things that, until very recently, were considered ways of differentiating children from adults. Reading Twenge's book it's almost as if iGen'ers have taken a conscious decision that adulthood is not for them, and as a result, the developmental pathway, from childhood to adolescence to adulthood, has slowed, or as Twenge puts it, 'Adolescence is now an extension of childhood rather than the beginning of adulthood'.

Despite the data making it abundantly clear that young people today are eschewing adult activities and avoiding many of the responsibilities that come with early adulthood (working, managing their own finances, driving themselves, etc.), Twenge seems reluctant to apportion iGen any blame. Instead, she rather lets them off the hook, suggesting initially that growing up slowly is a consequence of two overlapping factors: the rise of smaller families (which Twenge claims gives parents more time to 'celebrate' each child and elongate the 'cultivation' period), and what she describes somewhat vaguely as 'a cultural shift toward individualism'. It is only much later that she more fully commits to the real reason teens and even university students are not just acting more and more like children but demanding to be treated as such. According to Twenge, the reason young people have adopted this new 'slow life strategy' is because they have become 'habituated' to the sense of security and control associated with online life words: 'The strongest legacy of iGen'ers' involvement in the online world may be their increased physical safety . . . They are less willing to take chances, and their definition of safety has expanded to include their emotions as well as their bodies.'[6] In other words, the more teenagers have come to rely on online interactions, the more they have distanced themselves from what they perceive to be the unmanageability of the material world.

The fact that iGen'ers appear happy to avoid many of the wonderful experiences associated with adulthood would be a tragedy at any time, but especially now given that, by almost any measure, young people face fewer physical threats than at any point in history. But this, sadly, is the reality Anglo-American society has created. Misplaced fears about the wide world of adulthood have spawned a generation of young people now content to conduct most of their social interactions, indeed much of their lives generally, online. No doubt the safer, more manicured social domain of the online hinterland has its appeal, but it also comes at a huge personal cost. If not carefully balanced with meaningful in-person associations and experiences, digital connectivity risks acting like the sticky, ancient tree resin that trapped insects in amber – only this time it will be young people who are preserved and entombed in a fixed state of pre-adulthood.

'We live in a vacuous world, yet we do so with a feeling of urgency': Online life and the rise of emotional fragility

This is a petrifying moment in our lives. We have never known a world without internet, mobile phones, instant messaging. In other words, we have access to everything at all times and yet all paths seem blocked. We have more tools, more choices, and yet we live as if constantly paralysed . . . There is almost an injunction on today's youth to lead fascinating lives. But if we fail, and most of us are doomed to, we'll be considered losers.

Astrid Bergès-Frisbey[7]

Juliette is a 2013 film about a French woman in her twenties who keeps postponing the moment when she'll have to make adult life choices. In Pierre Godeau's film, Juliette is not only unable but seemingly unwilling to make sense of her predicament. However, the same cannot be said for Astrid Bergès-Frisbey, the Franco-Spanish actor who plays the eponymous lead. In a promotional interview for the film with the French newspaper *Libération*, Bergès-Frisbey neatly sums up the plight not only of her character but of an entire French generation hemmed in by the economic constraints of the Eurozone credit crunch. In the quotation reproduced above, Bergès-Frisbey manages to capture not just the double-edged nature of a life lived online, but the actual affectual responses triggered by a culture infatuated with social media amplification. It is an erudite and honest statement that perfectly frames the two emotional poles associated with online culture: fantasy and the never-ending imperative to live a 'fascinating life' on the one hand, and the paralysing sense of fear and failure on the other. Later, in the same interview, Bergès-Frisbey comes up with an even more powerful observation that in many ways serves as a fitting epigram for our times: 'We live in a vacuous world, yet we do so with a feeling of urgency'. In this chapter I want to follow this train of thought by focusing first on how Bergès-Frisbey's 'sense of urgency' is manifesting itself in a rising tide of emotional fragility; and second, on the way digital culture propagates the externalisation of fantasy via 'the injunction to live a fascinating life'.

The rapid increase in smartphone use and the growth of social media has provoked a host of concerns about the negative side effects of hyper-connectivity. Generally speaking, these concerns can be placed into two mutually reinforcing camps. First, there is what we might refer to as a hardware problem or, more specifically, the belief held by some neuroscientists that digital connectivity – especially smartphone usage – is having a damaging effect on the brain development of young children. According to Oxford University's Susan Greenfield, the unprecedented exposure to audio-visual stimuli caused by excessive digital connectivity, and dopamine jolts linked to what psychologists call the 'intermittent reward schedule' of screen refreshes and other affirmation feedback mechanisms, are together reshaping the brain's neuronal networks. In other words, just as bad gamblers become addicted to the risk and reward patterns of speculative wagering, children and adolescents can develop intense attachments to the patterned behaviour and habitual interactions (Snapchat streaks, auto-play videos, WhatsApp notifications, etc.) associated with social media. This is not addiction in a clinical sense, rather a form of habituation or 'brain hacking' that if reinforced by excessive daily use can detrimentally impact various parts of a young person's development – including their ability to establish human relationships or even read and interpret the micro subtleties and particularities of face and body language. In terms of infantilisation, Greenfield has argued that these increasingly unbreakable attachments to technology are so all-consuming that they can potentially stop children having 'their own inner narrative, their own inner thought process'. She has even suggested that if the current situation intensifies, 'people are going to be like three-year-olds: emotional, risk-taking, poor social skills, weak self-identity and short attention spans'.[8]

The second area of concern focuses on developments downstream from the neurological research into digital dependency and early childhood brain development. Here critical attention falls on how super-connectivity is affecting teenagers and young adults' mental health and their sense of wellbeing. More specifically, it's argued that excessive use of social media can fuel feelings of anxiety, isolation and depression in young people, potentially leading to everything from sleeplessness to symptoms of psychopathology. Essentially, the problem here is one of overexposure. No one would be such a Luddite as to deny the incredible value of mobile phones, both as a means of communication and as a tool for navigating the world. Likewise, video games provide a great deal of pleasure for hundreds of millions of players across the globe – even for someone as inept with a PS5 controller as me. The issue is more how time spent online/interacting with digital devices is slowly but surely *replacing time spent on face-to-face activities*, especially personal interactions with peers, parents and siblings. By reshaping the social landscape, digital networking has replaced the largely spontaneous aspects of social interaction – bumping into a friend in the street or random encounters with strangers in the pub – with more structured and curated relationships. The journalist Timandra Harkness usefully describes this new way of living as a mixed-dimensional world, 'where your friends can be constantly present even if you haven't seen them in the flesh for months'. Although initially comforting and rewarding, the erosion of happenstance and the structured isolation that emerges from living one's life online can, if not kept in check, become both competitive and unsatisfying – especially for adolescents whose self-esteem is still at a fragile stage of development.

We all know that social media platforms and online spaces are designed explicitly to capture as much of our time and attention as possible. But as more and more aspects of our personal lives become ensnared in social media, it's becoming clear that many young people are paying a high price for constant connectivity. For example, the self-curating nature of much social media is already having an extremely negative effect on the wellbeing of young girls – a fact Instagram's owners, Meta, had long been aware of and shamefully covered up.[9] Already under pressure to meet unattainable beauty standards promoted in these environments, teenage girls now also report rising levels of anxiety linked to 'FOMO' ('fear of missing out') – the gnawing sense, triggered by social media, that elsewhere others are having more fun and living fuller, more spectacular lives.[10] The question is whether or not such developments will result in a full-blown mental health crisis among future generations of young people for whom online life now means so much?

One person who has wrestled with this very question for some time now is the American social psychologist Jonathan Haidt. In his bestselling 2018 book, *The Coddling of the American Mind*, Haidt and his co-author Greg Lukianoff, recognised that, behind the upbeat posts and glossy Instagram images, a sense of anxiety and existential dissatisfaction was lurking in Generation Z. At this point, however, Lukianoff and Haidt were fairly cautious about stating unequivocally that excessive social media use was predictive of impaired mental health functioning. After reviewing the Twenge data, for example, they concluded that, while social media use does indeed produce various insidious effects – Bergès-Frisbey's 'feelings of urgency' – it was important not to confuse correlation with causation. Instead, they claimed that much of the concern about the social media/mental health connection should be seen against the backdrop of changing assessment criteria that have dramatically lowered the bar for mental health diagnoses. This is undoubtedly true; however, more recently, Haidt's position has shifted, and he now firmly believes that online performance platforms are the principal cause of a (post-2010) 'teen mental illness epidemic' that is statistically identifiable across five Anglosphere and five Nordic countries.[11] In terms of infantilisation, this is a notable finding in that it highlights once again just how much more complex the journey to adulthood has become. But there's also something else of great importance in Haidt and Lukianoff's work that helps explain the seemingly contradictory combination of 'paralysis' and 'urgency' that Bergès-Frisbey believes is symptomatic of today's super-connected young generation.

The Coddling of the American Mind is largely concerned with the changing nature of university culture, but, as the authors make clear, problems on campus don't start on campus – instead they are a direct result of 'terrible ideas that have become woven into American childhood and education'. By shielding children from supposedly upsetting, but also potentially character-building moments, society has created a generation of young people incapable of dealing with events and experiences that take place outside of a protective bubble. Or to use Lukianoff and Haidt's own terminology, 'the foolishness of overprotection' has eroded the inherently *anti-fragile* nature of young people: 'The modern obsession with protecting young people from "feeling unsafe" is, we believe, one of the (several) causes of the rapid rise in rates of adolescent depression, anxiety, and suicide'.

For Lukianoff and Haidt, the social media/mental health debate – and the problem of fragility surrounding iGen more generally – is all part of what they term *safetyism*: '"Safetyism" refers to a culture or belief system in which safety has become a sacred value, which means that people become unwilling to make trade-offs demanded by other practical or moral concerns. "Safety" trumps everything else, no matter how unlikely or trivial the potential danger'.[12] In and of itself, this is not an especially new idea; sociologists have been talking about a late-modern culture of risk aversion for decades. What is new is the claim that the high level of safetyism evident among today's young people is the result of changes in neural development linked to the rise of online culture. The key issue here is experience – how very young children get it and why, when deprived of real-world play and the interactive feedback associated with it, they are far less likely to develop into functioning teens capable of effective decision making.[13] In other words, as kids spend more time alone, playing, learning and interacting online, they have less time to 'dose themselves' with the type of risk associated with organic, unsupervised group ('free range') play: 'Children, like other mammals, need free play in order to finish the intricate wiring process of neural development. Children deprived of free play are . . . likely to be less tolerant of risk, and more prone to anxiety disorders'.[14] On this point, Twenge would agree – remember, she described iGen as having become 'habituated' to the sense of physical safety associated with online life worlds. Indeed, it is Twenge who comes up with the most relevant term for understanding the 'feelings of urgency' and 'sense of fragility' that are such key elements behind the rise of infantilism – *emotional safety*.

In the course of her research, Twenge conducted a large survey and a series of in-person conversations with iGen'ers – and these interviews provide valuable biographical context for her data. However, reading the thoughts of these kids, one cannot help but feel a little sad. Whether expressed overtly or in the subtext, many iGen'ers clearly view the offline world with considerable apprehension. Having been taught to place a high value on safety, today's young people now baulk at the prospect of being emotionally upset, preferring instead the controllable interactions of the internet over the more nuanced and thus more complex dynamics of real-world experiences. But as Twenge, Lukianoff and Haidt all make clear, it's one thing to seek safety from accidents and other forms of physical harm, and quite another to hide oneself away from people who disagree with you or challenge your worldview. By conflating physical safety with *emotional* safety, we have created a generation of young people who in Twenge's words 'flinch at the prospect of being emotionally upset'. As we will see in later chapters, this situation is already affecting intellectual and political debate and other important aspects of civil society. However, for now, the key thing to note is the extent to which online culture is fuelling infantilisation by engendering a new type of emotional fragility linked to safetyism.

At the start of this section, I stated that cultural and interpersonal problems associated with super-connectivity are not limited to the fears triggered by safetyism (or 'paralysis' to use Bergès-Frisbey's term). Online culture also propagates a second emotional state that has greatly contributed to the rise of the Kidult. Social media and other forms of digital interaction also encourage – or more accurately normalise – *fantasy*, and it is to the feelings of urgency engendered by this aspect of a life lived online that I now turn.

The infantilising unreality of social media: Online life and the rise of fantasy

> *. . . the possibility of happiness had to exist* if only as bait.
>
> Florent-Claude Labrouste, the central character
> in Michel Houellebecq's novel *Serotonin*

> *Thanks to the internet, we can all play at creating ourselves by believing hard enough. Online, no one can tell whether I'm really who I claim to be. Divorced from our bodies and the semi-random nature of who we know in real life, we are all free to find 'our people' and express whatever we feel our inner selves to be. If a 'true self' or group of 'true friends' starts to chafe, we can find another.*
>
> Mary Harrington, 2020[15]

In 1978, during a TV interview for *The Book Programme*, the revered British science-fiction writer J. G. Ballard warned us about a reversal of reality and fantasy under way in our culture. Even though he was speaking more than a decade before the onset of the World Wide Web Ballard understood that any society obsessed with consumerism and what he called 'brilliant technologies devoted to trivia' was heading for trouble. Few heeded his words. Today, thanks to the make-believe nature of the internet, Ballard's fears about a 'superabundance of fantasy' have fully materialised. By turning millions of people around the world into performative actors desperate for approval, and propagating the fiction that everyone's opinion needs to be heard on every new thing, social media platforms and participatory websites have made fantasists of us all.

As any psychiatrist will tell you, the act of fantasising is a universal component of the human condition. Whether it manifests itself in unconscious dreams or conscious forms of mental idealisation, fantasy plays an important role in how the psyche negotiates and upholds the boundaries of desire and reality. When we think about fantasy we do so in internal, psychological terms – most commonly by referencing the classical Freudian Oedipal tropes that so influenced the European intellectual tradition at the beginning of the twentieth century. Today, however, fantasy, as it is wont to do, has taken flight. Instead of existing as a personal, internal phenomenon, the activity of fantasising occurs more and more in plain sight, set free by the cultural forces associated with the supposedly unfettered universe of the internet.

Consider the digital architecture of likes, followers, friends and retweets that underpins social interaction on Twitter/X, Facebook, Instagram, etc. It is a mode of engagement designed explicitly to excavate thoughts, feelings, emotions *and fantasies* from the interior, private realm, and resituate them online for the whole world to view. If we date the start of this process at 2009 (when Facebook launched the 'Like' button – originally developed as the 'Awesome' button – and Twitter added their 'Retweet' function), it's clear that in little more than a decade there has been a radical shift in what is acceptable in terms of the (re)presentation of self within the public sphere. It's now entirely normal for people of all classes and nations to articulate their dreams, ambitions, crushes and even sexual desires openly on publicly accessible social media platforms. It's a similar situation with celebrities (and on occasion even tenured academics), growing numbers of whom seem to relish the opportunity to use these platforms to tell us about their personal plans for the world, or to articulate bizarre, sometimes career-damaging, flights of the imagination. All sorts of examples immediately spring to mind here, including Spike Lee, Mark Ruffalo and Rosie O'Donnell's conspiratorial musings on 9/11; Kylie Jenner's endless tweets about chemtrails; the feminist writer Naomi Wolf's bizarre online onslaught against vaccinations; Jaden Smith's daily Instagram posts about pyramid

conspiracies and hidden cities linked to the mythical Marvel creation Wakanda; and the actor Terrence Howard's alternative theory of
mathematics ('Terryology'). In years past, none of this stuff would
have made it outside of the drink-and-drug-addled circles of the
private Hollywood party scene. Now, sadly, like cow dung in a field,
it's everywhere. The result of all this is that fantasy and other forms of
self-delusion are no longer associated with the closely guarded
domain of the self but have become something to be unselfcon-
sciously externalised and broadcast to the world.

As we saw in the previous chapter, the idea of fantasy has long
been a component of consumer culture. But recently this relationship has taken on an even greater intensity as digital culture has
penetrated ever deeper into the lives of young people. One of the
many consequences of the commercialisation of the internet and
the rise of social media has been the erosion of people's traditional
sources of identity. In previous eras, individuals found fulfilment
in family, friends, community, religion and, up until fairly recently,
a sense of national culture and tradition. Today, for many people,
these vectors of identity have been replaced with internet-
informed false promises of self-fulfilment and deluded 'you-can-
be-anything-you-want-to-be' forms of fantasising. It is a process
that takes many forms, including at the benign end of the scale
vapid aspirational memes and the various other stale signifiers
associated with YOLO (you only live once) culture (see Plate 15).
However, it's in the way fantasy has been made almost compulsory
by a toxic combination of digital advertising, the 'celebrification'
of social life, and online peer pressure/validation that the real
problem lies. With every corporate-sponsored Instagram upload,
every micro-celebrity influencer post, every self-promotional
TikTok video, young people are skilfully being softened up by
corporations who sell them all the lifestyle consumer accessories
they think they need to create their new selves.

Plate 15: The narcissism of 'Hallmark philosophy' and the valorisation of self (perfection) via instructional digital memes. One of the unfortunate consequences of living in the internet age is that we are surrounded at almost every turn by motto-based memes and self-help mantras. These pithy aphorisms take many forms, but one especially widespread variant is of interest in the way it manages to distil adulthood down to a soundbite. You know the kind of thing; you've seen countless examples plastered over Instagram and clogging up your Facebook feed: 'The best project you'll ever work on is you!'; 'Work harder on yourself than you do on your job'; 'This year I finally know I'm good enough'; and, of course, that contemporary three-word hymn to self-love, 'You are magnificent'. Taken at face value, this sort of feelgood sloganeering might seem innocuous enough, and it may even be a source of positivity for some ontologically insecure souls. But dig a little deeper and it's clear this type of Hallmark philosophy is both narcissistic and infantilising in its suggestion that our lives are essentially little more than a journey towards self-perfection (see Chapter Seven). (Shutterstock)

The fact the market has colonised social media sites is hardly breaking news. Digital advertising affiliate marketing has been baked into companies like Facebook from their inception and thus needs no further coverage here. However, if we look beyond the connivances of corporate sponsorship, it's interesting to reflect on the way online fantasies linked to perceived status are bleeding back into the real world. For example, we have already seen how super-connectivity spawned the fantasy prevalent among many iGen'ers that online communication is superior to real-world interaction because it affords a greater sense of security and control; values which in turn are intrinsic to the damaging deceptions associated with safetyism.

The more social media has permeated society, the more common it has become for individuals to articulate their personal feelings and emotions within the public realm. Whether on Facebook, Twitter/X or other websites that offer comment threads and feedback opportunities, studies have shown that, if one's goal is to stimulate interaction it pays to go heavy on emotionality, hyperbole and moral indignation. Digital sociologists even have a term for the sort of angry, hyperventilated discourse that tends to dominate Twitter/X threads and online discussion forums – online moral grandstanding. The digital equivalent of childish attention-seeking, this form of emotionally charged communication has normalised outrage in the public domain, resulting in a crisis not just of meaning, but of reason itself.

Changes in the way we consume information have further intensified political fragmentation and social atomisation. Here the concern is about *selective exposure* – or how 'echo chambers', 'filter bubbles' and individually curated news streams function to polarise opinion and foster alternative realities – fantasies – within already socially estranged segments of the population. Conspiracy theories in particular have been supercharged by digital connectivity. No longer constrained by their association with obscure subcultural groups or fringe individuals, today's conspiracies thrive as a result of a combination of meme and hashtag culture, disinformation bots, dark and deep web communities and celebrity/social media influencer endorsements. Fed by a sense of incomprehension about the workings of the world, isolated individuals now have the online tools to fantasise about all sorts of exotic scenarios and cataclysmic events, the vast majority of which would have been dismissed as the stuff of a children's comic book thirty years previously.

It's a similar story when it comes to the retrospective fantasising currently surrounding some of the twentieth century's more extreme political ideologies which, thanks to online culture, are once again being recycled, this time to youthful audiences keen to disrupt the 'natural order', as Haidt and Rose-Stockwell explain in the following passage:

> Even though they have unprecedented access to all that has ever been written and digitized, members of Gen Z (those born after 1995 or so) may find themselves less familiar with the accumulated wisdom of humanity than any recent generation, and therefore more prone to embrace ideas that bring social prestige within their immediate network yet are ultimately misguided. For example, a few right-wing social-media platforms have enabled the most reviled ideology of the 20th century to draw in young men hungry for a sense of meaning and belonging and willing to give Nazism a second chance. Left-leaning young adults, in contrast, seem to be embracing socialism and even, in some cases, communism with an enthusiasm that at times seems detached from the history of the 20th century.[16]

Five years on from this quote, the combination of ahistoricism and the desire to embrace something politically outré is evident in everything from the recasting of Winston Churchill as a fascist by Western-hating youngsters to the rise of 'anti-capitalist' forms of neo-paganism to those idiot TikTokers filming themselves reading out Osama bin Laden's antisemitic 'Letter to America'. But the fantasising generated by the eroding distinction between 'mainstream' and 'alternative' worldviews is not limited to conspiracy theories and tarnished twentieth-century political ideologies. The vast medium of personal self-expression that is the internet also facilitates another form of political fantasy – the infantile delusion of solidarity associated with social media protests and other forms of so-called clicktivism.

The dream of the original cyberspace gurus and Californian ideologues who developed the online communities behind the World Wide Web was that peer-to-peer connectivity would reshape the world for the better by enhancing collective decision making. Half a century later, and in one of the great ironies of the twenty-first century, almost precisely the opposite has happened. In stark contrast to the over-confident rhetoric of tech companies – exemplified in Facebook's former mission statement, 'to make the world more open and connected' – social media platforms and other user-generated participatory websites have proceeded to undermine many of the baseline conditions needed to construct a meaningful moral and political consensus. Instead of greater civic engagement, it quickly became clear that, while many people were happy to signal a political stance online, this did not translate to meaningful offline action. Indeed, rather than forging practical, collective strategies to enact change, clicktivist campaigns turned complex issues into symbolic, self-celebratory acts – politics reduced to an on-trend profile picture update.[17] By lowering the transaction costs of political action in this way, online campaigns have eroded collective politics and replaced it with a new style of feel-good moral signalling linked to the self. As a result, 'e-politics' is now little more than a fantasy machine for atomised individuals desperate to experience a sense of community belonging, no matter how artificial or imaginary.

And it is here in the artificial construction of 'community' that social media fantasising reaches its zenith. All of us want to feel loved, and all of us want to feel attached to something meaningful or significant. The genius of social media platforms is that they are brimming with digital mechanisms that allow us to receive support and validation not only from friends and family, but potentially from almost anyone, anywhere. Unlike real life, where affirmation and praise (or conversely criticism and condemnation) are rare phenomena, the online world offers the possibility of a powerful and immediate phatic uplift with every swipe of the phone or notification check.[18] This type of psychological support, received via likes, positive emojis, etc., can function as a form of surrogate, albeit disembodied, community. However, it can also exacerbate extant psychological problems such as self-obsession and other narcissistic tendencies associated with what the American psychologist Paul Vitz once famously called 'self-ism'. It is a highly contagious dynamic that sees more and more people happy to bait their social media accounts with all sorts of personal and emotional content in an effort to experience the contrived sense of happiness – what Eric Fromm would have termed 'pseudo-pleasure' – that comes from positive online endorsements.

In *The Terminal Self*, Simon Gottschalk makes it clear that this type of self-validating intersubjectivity is an infantilising endeavour. By tolerating the user's choices in ways that corroborate their existing beliefs and attitudes, the relationship many individuals have with the always-available online world 'promotes the experience of personalisation by gratifying our impulses, desires, interests, *and fantasies* on demand, and like nobody else does or can. In so doing, it tacitly normalize [sic] the terminal self's infantile impulsivity, fantasies of omnipotence, and sense of entitlement.'[19] This fantasy-supporting dynamic has normalised all sorts of infantilising tendencies. For example, one of the main ways in which the ill-advised over-sharing of private thoughts and fantasies is today psycho-biographically justified is via the popular term '*my* truth'. A by-product of postmodern moral relativism, the phrase 'my truth' is now commonly used online to rationalise a controversial personal stance or action, and importantly to shut down any potential criticism or contradiction. But the use of language like 'this is my truth' or 'know your truth' is itself a form of fantasy, a way of protecting one's arguments and beliefs by deploying an imaginary shield of authentic selfhood. On the face of it, this might not seem particularly infantilising, but the idea that a person can fabricate a version of themselves that must be unequivocally believed and thus free from the possibility of criticism is quite clearly a narcissistic disavowal of the real. In Chapter Seven, I explore this narcissism–infantilism dynamic in much more detail, but for now it's interesting to reflect on what can happen when this sort of delusional self-making is set free within the more bizarre subcultural capillaries of the internet.

Consider, for example, the recent case of the Instagram influencer and some-time singer, Oli London. Born in England to white parents, London has for some time identified as Korean. But not just any Korean. London self-identifies as an already existing person – Jimin, the lead vocalist of the K-pop band BTS. In 2021, after eighteen surgeries on his teeth, hair, eyes and forehead, London finally achieved *his truth* and 'came out' as a 'transracial Korean'. An even more extravagant 'truth' is in the process of being realised by Anthony Loffredo, a thirty-five-year-old Frenchman known as 'Black Alien'. Loffredo has put himself through numerous surgeries and medical procedures (including getting his nose and upper lip cut off and his tongue split) in an effort to realise his bizarre goal of transforming himself into an alien.[20] Obviously, these are extreme examples, but the use of medical procedures and customised invasive surgery to pursue internet-induced fantasies and pathologies is a growing phenomenon as people strive to recreate the personas they project and promote online. But whether the practices associated with body modification are undertaken as part of a quest for fame and celebrity or simply as an escape from the banality of everyday life, such physical transformations are emblematic of the way online culture is facilitating 'a giant transfer of time, attention, and resources from reality to fantasy'.[21]

For many of us, these attempts to defy the objective reality of one's racial lineage (and even species)[22] are hard to fathom. But as Mary Harrington has written, for iGen'ers this reimagination of the self, this 'rapid uptake of "trans" identities' is what can happen when the vast majority of communication and socialisation is conducted within the confines of a social-constructionist, image-based digital landscape: 'Social media has already rewired how the emerging generation understands bodies, selfhood and perception. We can expect the political demands that flow from this digital refashioning of personhood to become more insistent and irresistible, as the Instagram generation matures.'[23]

Elsewhere on the internet, other even more deleterious forms of infantilised make-believe are also being encouraged, accelerated and normalised through internet-based social interaction. For some time now, in the fields of terrorism studies and radicalisation studies, scholars have documented how anonymous digital forums use romanticised subcultural imagery and 'imagined, phantasmic ideas' to recruit supporters, encourage hate and fuel extremism. Although the goal of these sites could not be more serious – to provoke terrorism and other acts of extreme violence – it is interesting to note that, in recent years, these participatory sites have also adopted a more playful, infantilising tone. Consider the story of the British jihadist Ifthekar Jaman, as told by the terrorism scholar Simon Cottee. An active recruiter online for the Islamic State, the privately educated Jaman travelled from his home in Portsmouth to Syria in May 2013 to fight for the Islamic State. Before he left the UK, Jaman livestreamed a video to his social media followers 'in which he professed his admiration for Osama bin Laden ("I think he looks kinda cool") and gave advice on how to wear a turban and how to apply kohl eyeliner – or, rather how to look like a premodern *mujahid* [fighter] . . . In Syria, he sought to live out this fantasy, regularly posting tweets and photos of his new life inside the then-nascent caliphate.'[24] If we set aside the abhorrent violence and medieval politics of the Islamic State, it's clear there's something deeply infantilising about both Jaman's dress-up video and the many comments under his post about how 'cool' he looked. There's nothing new about young men dreaming of becoming famous fighters or celebrated war heroes, but usually these desires remain mercifully private. Today, however, such dreams – along with a whole host of other even more damaging murder, rape and abuse fantasies that thrive in the subterranean recesses of the dark web – are easily accessible across the internet.[25] Whether we take as our benchmark the countless subcultural internet forums that stoke violence and sexual deviance by propagating perverse, fantastical ideas, the creation of imagined or self-aggrandising online personas, the extension of heroic juvenile fantasising into adulthood or the rapid growth of phantastic conspiratorial thinking within society, it's clear that the growing immersion of individuals in physically isolated, self-oriented online lifeworlds has profoundly impacted the way huge numbers of people currently view society and their place within it.

One thing we do know about digital culture is that trends, tendencies and terminology which start out online eventually manifest themselves in real-world interactions. Indeed, it is for this reason that digital sociologists no longer uphold the distinction between online and offline worlds, and instead prefer to think of contemporary human behaviour as a phenomenological exchange or dialogue *between* people and technology. Sadly, there's plenty of evidence to suggest this is also the case with the rise of online fantasy. For example, ultra-realist criminologists have recently identified a new cultural form linked to an inflated perception of status they call 'special liberty'.[26] Special liberty is the belief held by certain individuals that they should no longer be constrained by established social or ethical codes, and instead have a divine right to freely express their unique desires and drives. Those who perceive themselves to be in possession of special liberty are exonerated from the need to acknowledge their harm towards others. Instead, individuals are able to operate under the auspices of a fantasy that elevates them to the status of the most transcendent free individuals. In this way, their social egregiousness is negated by their hierarchical status or perceived ability to drive new cultural trends.

Consider the following examples. Activists and academic hoaxers – 'pretendians' – like Jessica Krug, Rachel Dolezal, Kelly Kean Sharp, Carrie Bourassa (aka 'Morning Star Bear'), Vianne Timmons, Raquel Evita Saraswati and 'H. G. Carrillo' who all cultivated fictitious ethnic identities just because they thought they could (essentially an advanced form of children's dress-up); fake hate-crime perpetrators like Jussie Smollett, Yasmin Seweid and Taylor Volk (a form of infantile abstraction where ends are elevated to justify means); and online influencers and so-called 'pranksters' who care nothing about disrupting traffic, retail spaces and even people's homes in their narcissistic pursuit of likes and content engagement (online pranksters in particular are a perfect example of special liberty in that they think nothing of humiliating and even physically assaulting members of the public in their lame attempts at humour and self-promotion). Here one could even include those passengers who behave obnoxiously on flights and trains as a result of some practical imposition or perceived slight (an increasingly prevalent mode of behaviour in which adult babies mistakenly believe that 'acting out' will eventually get them their own way), to appreciate the extent to which the fantasy of special liberty, born of an online culture fixated with status and celebrity, has permeated society.

Mercifully, these sorts of behaviours remain rare. But for how long? While social media-driven fantasising has emerged as almost the default setting for the way many young people perceive key elements of everyday life, at the moment it still functions primarily at what Robert Pfaller calls the 'interpassive' level, i.e., although young people are constantly implored by postmodern media to be ultra (inter)active – 'YOLO', 'FOMO', etc. – in reality, many remain strangely reactive, even submissive in the face of this cultural bombardment.[27] (Perhaps this is what Astrid Bergès-Frisbey meant when she spoke of 'paralysis'?) However, as opportunities for legitimate life/career development – let alone aspirational goals – continue to shrink in the face of never-ending austerity and the rise of robotic automation, those 'feelings of urgency' associated with the desire to lead a 'fascinating life' that Bergès-Frisbey outlined will only grow more intense. At that point, the 'vacuous world' she astutely describes will be aggressively assailed from all sides by a multivocality of new socio-political forces capable of fuelling fantasy in any number of troubling and potentially dangerous ways.

In his book about the fall of the Soviet Union, Alexei Yurchak developed the term 'hyper-normalisation' to explain a paradoxical state of mind prevalent in the country prior to the communist regime's rapid demise in the late 1980s. According to

Yurchak, years of exposure to authoritarian Soviet propaganda had resulted in a bizarre situation in which the collapse of the regime appeared simultaneously both completely unexpected and completely unsurprising: 'Many discovered that, unbeknownst to themselves, they had always been ready for it [the collapse of communism], they had always known that life in socialism was shaped through a curious paradox, that the system was always felt to be both stagnating and immutable, fragile and vigorous, bleak and full of promise'. In other words, prior to its dissolution, the Soviet Union had become a fake version of a society, a place where, in the words of Mikhail Epstein, 'fairy tale became fact'.[28]

By playing along with the fantasy that things were OK while all around them everything was failing, the last generation of Soviet citizens had become *hyper-normalised* – i.e., they no longer believed anything about the present, while having no meaningful vision of the future. Fast forward to today and it's no exaggeration to suggest that in many ways the online world of infantilised fantasy discussed above resembles another variation of the hyper-normalised state. Inherent in the deep structures of late capitalist modernity there exists another (similar but different) destabilising paradox. This time, however, rather than the paradox being constructed and perpetuated by the authoritarian discourse of Soviet bureaucrats, it is peddled by tech overlords and their celebrity puppets (here the term 'influencer' is extremely apposite). While social media implores us to engage in all sorts of fantasy and consensual hallucination, deep down we know the world that has been created is fundamentally fake and superficial. Likewise, as the constant growth of conspiratorial and anti-establishment thinking makes clear, large numbers of people in declining Western liberal democracies have started consciously and openly to acknowledge that globalised capitalist societies are increasingly unstable and managed by a political class that does not have their best interests at heart. No surprise, then, that we have reached a point where, in the words of Glenn Greenwald, online culture is working overtime to condition us 'to view the warped as normal'. In our infantilised late-capitalist world, where adult thinking is diminished, we have oddly mirrored the last generation of the Soviet Union and succeeded in making a 'fairy tale become fact' – after all, nothing pacifies confused and upset children like a magical story involving a phantastic departure from the real world.

We have arrived at a pivotal moment. Everywhere we turn, we are confronted by a postmodern online culture that simultaneously produces and ameliorates social anxiety. The late French philosopher Bernard Stiegler wrote extensively about this paradox, using the term *pharmaka* to describe how today's network of 'globalized psychotechnologies' are successful precisely because they are the antidote to their own poison.[29] Stiegler was convinced that Western societies are engaged in a vital struggle – what he called a 'battle of intelligence for maturity' – for the future of rational critique, and potentially even 'humanity itself'. In his provocative book *Taking Care of Youth and Generations*, he argued that, if we wish to wrest back control from the toxic 'network of *pharmaka*' that is today's 'symbolic media', we need to embark on a massive programme of educational reform that can equip young people with the cultural apparatus needed to achieve 'a new maturity, a new critique'. It is an argument shared by everyone from the juridical philosopher Giorgio Agamben[30] to 'the father of mobile computing', Alan Kay.[31] The problem for Stiegler and the many other commentators who look expectantly to education to dampen down fantasy and the other forms of unreality triggered by digital culture is that today's instructional institutions, from kindergarten to graduate school, are no longer equipped to carry out such a mission. Indeed, as I will now make clear, rather than fulfilling their original goal of fostering maturity through academic knowledge, Anglo-American schools and universities are now the principal incubators of infantilisation.

Chapter 6

The Infantilisation of Education: How Schools and Universities Turned Themselves into Subsidised Day Care

And indeed it was perfectly clear to Rousseau that every man left free to follow his own inclinations and every society allowed to pursue its inherent tendencies would repeat all the familiar errors of the past.
Judith N. Shklar[1]

A few years back, when I still worked in UK higher education, I began to notice a shift in the way university administrators were communicating with me. It started when I was asked to participate in something called a research funding 'Sandpit'. Here I would be allotted a 'Sandpit Buddy' and given something called a 'Straight-talking Token' which would afford me certain privileges should I eventually gravitate to the Sandpit's 'Straight-talking Room'. Around the same time, I began to receive a flurry of emails informing me about 'The Vice Chancellor's Cup' – a new 'School Sports Day-themed' team-building initiative that would see groups of academics and support staff pitted against each other in events such as the 'egg-and-spoon race', 'wellie tossing' and the 'three-legged race'. (Presumably, the omission of a sack race can be explained by the fact that around the same time my university was also pushing for voluntary redundancies.)

213

By the time I left, this sort of infantilism was so institutionally entrenched that few colleagues even raised an eyebrow when a circular email was sent asking faculty if they would be willing to be filmed clapping, cheering and setting off party poppers as part of a welcome video for incoming students. Where did these initiatives come from? Unless I missed something, I don't recall Hannah Arendt and Theodor Adorno ever teaming up for a three-legged race, or Karl Popper popping party poppers in a university puff video. Even as recently as the late 1990s, when I began my career, such initiatives would have been dismissed as juvenile and frivolous. So how did serious, adult-only universities get turned into institutions that now actively speak to the script of an infantilised society? The answer to this question lies in a series of damaging twenty-first-century pedagogical and andragogical developments that, in my opinion, are responsible for creating not only infantilised students, but much of our infantilised world more generally.

Feelgood High: the demise of adult authority in the classroom

What slowly happened, without any policy or plan, teachers began to see children and young people as emotional rather than thinking beings. They were not seen as having the potential to be independent moral and intellectual individuals but were treated as vulnerable people who needed to constantly have their feelings validated.

Dennis Hayes[2]

In April 2010, the political journalist Michael Deacon used his *Daily Telegraph* column to satirise declining standards in UK education. Claiming to have uncovered a confidential report by the fictitious Institute for the Development of Innovation-Oriented Teaching Skills (IDIOTS), Deacon leaked six exciting

214

new initiatives the quango believed would further enhance student empowerment. At the top of the list was the following:

> Teachers must discontinue their antiquated practice of penalising pupils who do not give so-called 'correct' answers. The concept of 'correct' answers is elitist, as it discriminates against pupils who do not know them . . . The custom of grading pupils according to the merit of their work is divisive as it fosters the outdated belief that it is better to be 'clever' and 'hard-working' than 'stupid' and 'lazy'. *All pupils should be awarded identical grades, irrespective of ability* [emphasis added].[3]

Fast forward a decade and what was once the stuff of political satire is now a reality. In August 2021, the governor of Oregon signed a bill 'eliminating high-school graduation requirements of proficiency in reading, writing and maths' in a bid to 'promote more equity for non-white students'. In the same month, the largest school system in the United States, New York City's Department of Education, embarked on a process of 'remaking the grade', urging schools to 'rethink honor rolls and class rankings' because 'student excellence' and 'class rank' can be 'detrimental to learners who find it more difficult to reach academic success'.[4] What these policies and a growing number of others like them represent is essentially the end of the teacher as arbiter of quality and excellence and the ceding of authority to students (or sometimes parents). But how did contemporary education lose its way to the extent that some schools now seem genuinely reluctant to celebrate academic achievement – even to make a qualified distinction about the intellectual merit of one student compared with another?[5] In this section we look for answers to these questions by tracing recent trends and developments within contemporary education that have served to undermine meritocracy and embed infantilisation as almost a default setting within the classroom.

Whether it's political disquiet about declining academic standards, parental anxiety over excessive testing or teachers' concerns about socially irresponsible parents, today's schools are lightning rods for all kinds of criticism and public anxiety. But as the arguments rage, few stop to consider that many of the issues confronting schools are in fact symptoms of a much bigger problem. Here I refer to the reluctance of contemporary society to value and affirm adult authority in the teaching profession and the wider realm of educational policymaking. The result, as Frank Furedi argued in his provocative book *Wasted: Why Education Isn't Educating*, is nothing less than an ontological crisis in the meaning and aim of education:

> Confusions surrounding the role and status of adult authority have led to a loss of confidence in society's ability to socialize the younger generations. The loss of authority undermines the claim that adults have something important to transmit to younger generations. The crisis of adult authority frequently is experienced as an inability to communicate a shared system of norms and values with clarity and conviction. Often schools are charged with the task of taking responsibility for the socialisation of their pupils, and it sometimes appears that schools are expected to find solutions to problems for which the wider society has no answer. As a result, the problems of society are frequently confused with that of education.[6]

Perhaps the most obvious manifestation of the confusion surrounding adult authority can be seen in the collapse of classroom discipline. In the UK, violent incidents in schools have been on an upward curve for years, but recently the situation has deteriorated to such an extent that many teachers now consider being a victim of assault an occupational hazard. According to one recent teachers' union survey, one in four teachers report experiencing physical violence from their pupils once a week, while another survey by the GMB union reported that up to 70,000 teaching and support staff face violence on a regular basis.[7] The situation in American schools is equally dire. But perhaps the best example of the eroded authority relations between adults and children is found in nursery and primary education. Given the younger age of students in this sector, one could be forgiven for thinking that teachers and carers would find it easier here to instil and uphold a sense of grown-up control. But no. Every year in the UK, thousands of primary-school children aged between five and eleven are given fixed-term exclusions for attacking a member of staff. In the US, it's estimated that around 250 preschoolers are suspended or expelled every day for what the Zero to Three Foundation describe as 'challenging behaviors such as aggression, tantrums, and noncompliance'. Such figures, as Furedi observed over a decade ago, 'indicate that what appears to be a question of discipline is fundamentally an issue to do with the failure to give meaning to what it means to be an adult and to be a child'.

But the disciplinary crisis in schools is not simply about controlling errant behaviour. It also extends to disciplining and cultivating learning habits so that young people develop the necessary intellectual skills and social values that will allow them to proceed successfully into and through adulthood. Unfortunately, instead of sticking to the fundamental task of passing on the knowledge needed for the next generation to advance still further, educational institutions have entirely lost their way and are instead using the classroom as the place to solve society's problems.[8] For example, instead of inculcating a love of knowledge or the value of science, modern educationalists seem more concerned about using the curriculum as a laboratory for all sorts of ideological and political experiments, including the delivery of modish social justice ideas, adapting curricula to include 'Net-Zero Visions', and even urging schoolchildren to adopt vegetarianism.[9]

When education expands in this way, and curricula get tweaked to include faddish political or pedagogic initiatives, we run the real risk that students will end up being taught everything and nothing. If this situation is to be avoided, society should end the current practice of refracting its problems and anxieties through the lens of education and instead stick to the more grounded task of educating and socialising children in a balanced, authoritative manner. Sadly, there is scant evidence this is happening. In fact, the continued expansion and promotion of education within society (inflated and arbitrary university attendance targets, poorly conceived 'lifelong learning' projects, etc.) should be viewed not as an intrinsically positive development, but as a form of unarticulated compensation – 'an attempt to occupy the territory vacated by the retreat of adult authority'.[10]

Further evidence of how grown-ups compensate for their failure to assert adult authority is found in the way pedagogues attempt to duck the issue completely by reconstituting the problems of contemporary education as a 'motivational crisis'. On this point Furedi is once again prescient, most obviously because of how he tethers this issue to the rise of infantilisation:

> The feeble valuation of adult authority leads to a disturbing loss of belief in children's capacity to engage with challenging experiences. In education the assumption that children need constant motivation has encouraged the institutionalisation of a pedagogy that infantilizes them. Many pedagogues claim that children need to be taught material that is directly relevant and accessible to them. Too often children are treated childishly by educators who assume that playing is the ideal vehicle for learning.[11]

218

Let me be clear: I am not opposed to new pedagogic initiatives that can help students express themselves through more open forms of reflective learning. What concerns me is the transformation of schools into nurseries by adopting play-centric practices like prioritising video-watching over reading, the adoption of prize and reward schemes (bribes) to encourage compliant behaviour, the growth of universal certificates of achievement instead of meritocratic modes of assessment, and the widespread use of checklists and worksheets as opposed to exercises that test deeper levels of comprehension. Such practices illustrate the extent to which education has been co-opted by the so-called pedagogy of motivation. Often smuggled into schools under the cover of vacuous mantras such as 'the democratisation of the classroom', motivation-led teaching practices should be seen for what they are – another form of compensation for the erosion of adult authority in education. Having lost the ability to exercise influence confidently over children through adult-directed curricula, contemporary educationalists are left with little choice but to cleave towards what students supposedly *want* as opposed to authoritatively determining what it is they actually *need*. If something is boring, get rid of it. Content too difficult? Replace it with something more likely to appeal to young people's tastes.

Such logic explains why, when the leading UK examination board, OCR, decided to 'radically overhaul' its combined English Language and Literature qualification, they attempted to include a passage of select committee evidence by the comedian Russell Brand, tweets from the journalist Caitlin Moran and a TV interview by the rapper Dizzee Rascal. By introducing pop-culture subject matter with a sell-by date only marginally longer than a pasteurised yogurt, exam boards and curriculum designers are essentially affirming that on-trend motivational gimmicks are more important than the content of education. The efficacy of these gimmicks is, of course, rarely, if ever, quantified – but that's not the point. Motivationally fixated pedagogues aren't interested in testing whether or not their various 'applied learning skills' and novel 'doing' practices actually improve standards or encourage children to explore knowledge for its own sake. Instead, in the UK at least, they hide behind annual examination results which for the last two decades have been rolled out alongside well-worn statements about educational standards being at 'an all-time high'. This, of course, is utter nonsense.[12] As any long-serving (objective) academic will tell you, government claims about year-on-year rises in standards are the biggest educational fantasy story since J. K. Rowling came up with the idea for Hogwarts. The truth is, having semi-consciously abandoned the idea of authoritative adult control, educational policymakers are no longer capable of instilling core intellectual values within the students in their charge. Recognising this, they have turned down a different path and transformed contemporary schooling into something akin to a popularity contest. But as lamentable as this is, it represents only one element of the prevailing orthodoxy that drives the contemporary feel-good educational project.

There is, of course, a fundamental problem that haunts the pedagogy of motivation. What happens when it doesn't work? After all, each student is unique, and so what interests one will not necessarily interest another. At this point, rather than questioning the ontology of their approach, advocates of these new motivational techniques simply double down on the belief that what makes students learn is not rising to a challenge or being encouraged to pursue interests that previously they had not considered, but simply *feeling good about themselves*. It is for this reason that schools today are awash with fashionable therapeutic concepts like 'wellbeing', 'mindfulness', 'emotional intelligence', 'self-esteem' and 'resilience'. From their first day of school to their last, schoolkids are being shaped – I would even go so far as to say indoctrinated – by a new therapeutic culture that is redefining the very nature of Anglo-American education.[13] Head teachers are falling over themselves in the rush to create and deliver lessons and learning programmes based around 'personal needs', 'whole-child wellness' and 'emotional literacy'. The problem is there are only so many teaching hours in a day, and the more you stuff the timetable full of personality development and self-esteem classes – even yoga lessons, aromatherapy, mindfulness 'circle time' and Happiness Diary-writing sessions – the less time you have to cover boring educational basics like grammar and mathematics. But who cares if students turn up at university campuses without the ability to write a critical essay or the application needed to complete basic preparatory reading for seminars (in a discipline *they* have chosen), as long as they've fully inculcated the requisite emotional skills and wellbeing platitudes needed to flourish in today's Feelgood High Schools.

The lurch towards therapeutic education reflects the extent to which traditional notions of schooling based on intellectual pursuits and an adult-directed curriculum have been subordinated by softer, more psychological, anti-academic modes of instruction.[14] It is a process predicated on and designed to achieve a fundamental shift from external (adult) authority to a more 'individualistic orientation to the self' supported by the 'internalisation of emotional skills'. Supporters of this mode of education will point out that it aims to tackle all aspects of children's lives and provide them with a broader educational experience not restricted by the confines of subject-based learning. No doubt there's a degree of truth in this argument. However, what these advocates fail to acknowledge are the numerous problematic side effects that follow in the wake of this approach. For example, by placing so much emphasis on 'happiness metrics' and the positivity associated with the culture of self-esteem, primary and secondary schools are essentially attempting to banish negativity from the schooling experience. This bizarre anti-realism requires an endless stream of false praise and psychological boosterism designed to ensure students constantly feel good about themselves. But when we shield children from criticism to promote self-esteem, we do more harm than good. Most obviously, when children are raised on a repetitive diet of empty praise, it diminishes their ability to meet the setbacks and failures that are an inevitable part of human development.

Equally problematic is what happens to students who for whatever reason do not follow the emotional script dominating contemporary schooling. As mentioned above, discipline in schools is a serious problem, but rather than affirm classroom authority, teachers increasingly hand over the problem to anger-management specialists and other interventionists operating in Orwellian-sounding Behavioural Control Teams or Behaviour Regulation Programmes. At this point, the behavioural psychology so beloved by contemporary educationalists quickly morphs from soft to hard, as more intrusive, coercive techniques are employed to condition the recalcitrant. This more technical and consequential form of psychological control perfectly symbolises the general decline of adult authority in the classroom, but it also opens the door to the type of adultification processes discussed in Chapter Two. For example, for some students the failure to internalise the correct feelings and emotional reactions set out in their school's psychological prayer book will simply mean submission to even more emotional training. But for others, especially students from ethnic minorities or those who attend the failing or poorly performing schools that service the working class, the consequences can be far more serious, as they are handed over to state agencies where, as we have already seen, their status as protected children is often greatly diminished.

The stark contradiction between these more draconian behavioural measures and the type of empathetic therapeutic over-protection outlined above, perfectly illustrates the general sense of ambiguity and confusion that currently surrounds questions about who gets treated as a child and who gets treated as an adult. Earlier, I discussed how in the United States young people of school age are being harshly punished for minor disciplinary infractions that previously would not have warranted criminal sanction. However, it's also clear that a punitive turn is underway in the UK, something evident in everything from the enforcement of absurdly strict uniform codes to the increased use of CCTV inside schools as a tool to combat bad behaviour. But whatever form these adultifying developments take, they all have one thing in common: the sense of over-compensation by an adult society that has lost its way and now exists in an almost permanent state of generational confusion.

When assessed in the round, the therapeutic turn in education has done immense damage to the effectiveness and authority of teachers while simultaneously distracting policymakers from their principal task of intergenerational knowledge transmission. But its corrosive impact doesn't stop there. In its current form, contemporary education infantilises children by fostering a prevailing culture of vulnerability in which pupils are treated not as active, creative individuals, but as passive, emotionally 'at risk' subjects. Making the case that society has elevated safety (including emotional safety) to a sacred value, Lukianoff and Haidt use the concept of 'safetyism' to explain several problems confronting young people, including observable increases in depression and anxiety.[15] However, although they trace the implications of this fixation with safety across various social domains, including most obviously university education, their account of safetyism's emergence misses some important elements. According to Lukianoff and Haidt in *The Coddling of the American Mind*, the cultivation of safetyism stems from a combination of paranoid parenting, the decline of free play, and the failures of university bureaucracies to push back against student demands. Clearly, these are key causes, but what Lukianoff and Haidt fail to consider is the role played by therapy culture in spawning the phenomenon in the first place. This reluctance can be explained, at least in part, by the fact that their own solution to combat student fragility is essentially more therapy – the cognitive behavioural treatments associated with the work of University of Pennsylvania psychiatrist Aaron Beck. This is an important omission because the influence of therapy culture in young people's lives goes well beyond safetyism; it is a key driver of infantilisation in society generally.

'Therapy culture' should be understood not as a clinical technique or the means of curing a specific psychic disorder, *but as a way of thinking.*[16] A society becomes therapeutic when the values and language of counselling and psychotherapy break out from the clinical setting and take hold within the cultural imagination more generally. In a clinical setting it makes sense to stress the importance of individuation and an elevated concern with the self rather than focusing on external factors and social relations. However, if individuals start viewing the problems of the *outside* social world through the prism of the *internal* world of their private thoughts, all sorts of problems ensue, most obviously, the erroneous belief that complex social problems can be solved or controlled by the application of the techniques and semantic vocabulary associated with therapy-based forms of intervention. It cannot be stated enough that the contemporary Anglo-American view of children as essentially fragile beings has its origins in precisely this dynamic.

The therapeutic turn in the classroom and its confederate, the pedagogy of motivation, now dominate policymaking in education. As a result, schooling at all levels proceeds from the premise that *the management of emotion* is the most effective way of controlling behaviour and attaining educational success. If this focus on emotion and identity was used simply to make students feel good about themselves or to instruct young people about how to conduct personal relationships appropriately then there would be little cause for complaint. But as the likes of Furedi, Hayes and others make clear, because the ethos underpinning therapeutic schooling is psychology first, education second, the management of emotion has expanded to such an extent that it's now entirely normal 'to regard children as fragile, emotionally vulnerable things who cannot be expected to cope with pressure and real intellectual challenge'.[17] From here, it's a very short step to the belief that children must be shielded at all times from any potentially upsetting experience, no matter how small; the underlying logic being that the external world, with all its uncontrollable problems and risks, is by definition damaging to the internal world of emotions and self-esteem. It is for this reason that schools are so quick to swallow and uphold the mindset and verbiage of the late-modern health-and-safety industry. It's an alliance that regularly throws up all sorts of bizarre news stories, such as the school that reviewed 'the texture and shape' of their canteen cakes after concerns were raised about the potential danger of triangular flapjacks, to the ban imposed on the 'flossing' dance by a headteacher in Devon who claimed that *Fortnite*-related dance moves were 'intimidating' for pupils.[18]

It is out of this climate of vulnerability and risk aversion that Lukianoff and Haidt's protective bubble of safetyism emerges. But as we have already seen, this is not the only way in which contemporary education infantilises its students and diminishes their ability to meet the challenges associated with adulthood. With the passing of each new term, ongoing changes in schools, such as the

dethronement of adult-directed curricula, a fixation with therapeutic systems of meaning and measurement, the replacement of
meritocratic approaches to learning with forms of instruction
predicated on empty praise and emotional support, and the cultivation of vulnerability as a social norm, are combining to reshape
children's relationship between the self and external reality. None
of this, of course, is the fault of young people. The diminution and
infantilisation of education are entirely the result of the erosion of
adult authority, both in the classroom and at policy level – a
process that itself is a symptom of the much broader intergenerational confusion that characterises the late-modern life course.

At this point, you may be asking what can be done to counter
these tendencies? What policies can we enact to ensure education
returns to its principal task of confidently transferring essential
knowledge from one generation to another? If you spent any time in
the Anglo-American university system during the twentieth century
you might assume the best place to find answers to these and other
questions regarding academic standards would be in our elite seats
of learning. But you would be wrong about that. Very wrong.

'You say, we did': Infantilisation and socialisation in reverse on the university campus

> *They* [students] *are the people who know how best they can be taught.*
>
> Emily Collins, student engagement
> coordinator, Reading University[19]

Something strange is happening at your local university. In the
lecture halls and seminar rooms of leafy college campuses and
metropolitan university buildings, changes are taking place that
threaten not just the quality of higher education, but the very ideal

of the university as the ultimate guardian of reason, scientific inquiry and philosophical openness. The story of the infantilisation of university life has been unfolding for at least two decades, but for much of that time, the majority of commentators and academics either refused, or were simply unable, to join up the dots. Today, however, even the most short-sighted observer can't avoid the disquieting fact that the dots are there and appearing in an ever-thickening mass. Sometimes the dots take the form of high-profile news stories. Like the international coverage of the childish, over-the-top reaction by Yale University students to an innocuous email sent by a college master querying Yale's policy on Halloween costumes: 'It's not about creating an intellectual space! It is not! Do you understand that? It's about creating a home here! . . . You should not sleep at night. You are disgusting.' Other times, they are glimpsed in fleeting but telling Twitter moments, such as when Staffordshire University in the UK thought it would be a good idea to instigate a Twitter poll on 'the BEST chocolate bar EVER?'.[20] And on some occasions, they're just too stultifying to miss, like when Oxford University started handing out free colouring-in pencils to its students so they could 'Give their minds a rest'. But whatever form the dots take, their increased presence illustrates something that can no longer be denied: with each passing semester, universities on both sides of the Atlantic are fast being enveloped by a rising tide of infantilism that is trashing academic standards and diminishing cultural life on campus.

Since emerging in Europe in the early medieval period, universities have played many roles and served many masters, but they always had at least one thing in common: the university was a place where young people were educated and socialised by elder scholars confident of their ability to transfer appropriate knowledge from one generation to another. Today, that legacy is in jeopardy. In every type of university, and irrespective of academic discipline, changes are in train that threaten the very principles universities are supposed to stand for. Many of these changes have not gone unnoticed. Far from it. The university, like the school, remains a site of constant controversy and debate. Yet while commentators repeatedly flag problems like the campus free-speech crisis, the commercialisation of university education and the emergence of the so-called 'Woke university', these concerns are typically treated and reported as separate issues rather than as symptoms of a broader infantilised culture. To some extent, this failure to grasp the bigger picture is understandable. The roots of the infantilism problem do not grow in one obvious direction. Instead, the problems currently blighting universities are the result of a combination of factors in which both adults and young people are complicit. Here it is worth recalling my idea of generational mulch. For if the infantilisation of university culture exemplifies anything, it is the damage caused when key institutions fail to uphold adult authority in the face of intense but unconsidered youthful pressure.

I have already shown how motivation-based teaching and the therapeutic turn in schools combined to reconfigure the form and content of UK secondary education. Two decades on from the initiation of these processes and it's clear that the infantilising side effects of these developments have penetrated deep into the timbers of higher education. The fallout from a school system based increasingly on the imperative of motivation and student empowerment is evident in virtually every area of university life, but perhaps its most tangible manifestation is in the slow death of academic standards. In 2009, while giving evidence to a Commons inquiry, Professor Peter Dorey of Cardiff University caused a minor stir in academic circles when he claimed that many English undergraduate students were 'semi-literate'. Dorey painted a bleak picture of students who openly admitted to having 'read nothing' and thus were not capable of grasping basic ideas that were readily understood by undergraduates 'ten to fifteen years ago'. Dorey's comments were controversial, but he was simply articulating what had long been an open secret.

For years, lecturers had complained that school leavers were arriving on campus deficient in basic skills like essay writing, problem solving and critical thinking. However, rather than address the problem, universities simply adjusted their standards and practices downwards. Instead of using the expertise of the higher education sector to counter schooling practices responsible for producing undergraduates who can no longer complete the same academic tasks that previous generations undertook without difficulty or complaint (and that are completed today – often to a much higher standard – by students studying elsewhere in the world), senior managers decided the best way forward was to make universities *more* like schools.

Re-enrol a university graduate from the 1970s or 1980s on a degree course today and he or she would be shocked at what they found. The greatly diminished workload required on many courses would of course be unsettling, but what would come as an even bigger surprise is the way their subjects have been dumbed down by a twenty-first-century textbook culture that reduces knowledge to bite-sized chunks ready for easy regurgitation. There's nothing intrinsically wrong with a decent textbook, but it's the 'teaching the test' mentality surrounding textbook-based learning that's the problem. Most degree pathways adopt a directed-but-independent mode of study, so when we spoon-feed students with cookie-cutter 'how-to-pass-the-exam' materials we are undercutting a fundamental principle of university education. But the over-reliance on textbooks and simplified reading lists is only one example of the schoolification of higher education.

Consider the poor old lecture. Despite being under threat for years from tech-fixated educationalists and academic staff who are useless at lecturing, the 'sage on the stage' model continues to be the foundation stone of most degree courses – but for how much longer? It may have been around for half a millennium, and it may avoid the very real frustration many students feel when forced to listen to the least informed but most opinionated class-mate in noisy seminar rooms, but so what? Today's university students don't like the lecture – mostly because it separates them from their digital teat of choice for fifty minutes – and so it will likely soon be gone; its departure hastened by the emergence of Zoom, Teams and various other techno-educational monstros-ities. It is a direction of travel that only goes one way. With each passing year, undergraduates (and increasingly postgraduates) are provided with all kinds of 'dynamic' new learning resources and academic support systems designed to enhance 'the student expe-rience', but still, they complain it's not enough. Naturally, these complaints have little if anything to do with academic excellence. Instead, they amount to a Hallelujah Chorus of 'It's all too diffi-cult. Can you make it easier for me?' – and, of course, this is precisely what has happened.

The more we have followed the logic of schools and listened to students, the further standards in universities have plummeted. But just as rising examination results have been used as a smokescreen to hide deep-rooted problems in UK schools, successive govern-ments have brushed aside academics' concerns about the devalua-tion of British degrees and instead upheld the fiction of rising university standards. And it is a fiction. For example, the number of first-class undergraduate degrees awarded at British universities has more than quadrupled since 1990. In 2022, four out of ten students achieved a first-class degree (with one institution awarding 80 per cent of their graduates the top award). Likewise, the number of students graduating with either a first or a higher second-class degree has risen from 47 per cent in 1994 to 79 per cent in 2019.

But while UK governments of all political stripes have chosen to ignore the decades-long degradation of academic standards in higher education, on the ground the fallout is there for all to see. Grades are constantly rounded up, while assessment criteria and reading/pre-class preparation expectations are watered down. Test curves are adjusted downwards to maintain acceptable pass rates, and plagiarism and other rule violations are waved away as part of 'the learning process'. Previously, academic staff were taken to task if their exam scripts and coursework grades were considered statistically too high. Today, the opposite logic applies. Because degree classifications are one of the main metrics that universities use to game the deeply flawed university league table system, UK university bureaucracies regularly mandate minimum acceptable percentages for first and upper second degrees. It all adds up to a recipe for grade inflation with no apparent end in sight.

The self-perpetuating spiral of declining standards is just one way in which universities have mirrored schools and in so doing contributed to the rise of cultural infantilisation. The phenomenon of safetyism that stems from modern society's obsession with protecting children from any potentially unsettling experience has also migrated from school to university. To be sure, a preoccupation with safetyism has been a feature on university campuses for some time, but as Lukianoff and Haidt point out, it was only after iGen'ers entered college in 2013 that the problem started to metastasise.

As we have seen, a defining feature of iGen is the way personhood is often refracted through the lens of vulnerability. No surprise, then, that many of today's undergraduates approach university life not as a challenging new experience but as a site of anxiety and emotional distress. To alleviate this unease, Anglo-American university administrations have spent vast sums developing new programmes and services designed explicitly to address iGen'ers' concerns. But no sooner do administrators address one problem with a new counselling initiative, another university-related mental health pathology emerges to take its place, leaving universities playing a never-ending game of therapeutic whack-a-mole.

Such is the culture of vulnerability among today's undergraduates that the clamour for more mental health programmes has even spread to student politics. When striking Goldsmiths University students occupied Deptford Town Hall in south-east London a few years back, their very first demand was 'Recruit more counsellors'. It was a similar story at both the London School of Economics, where demonstrators called for 'the removal of the standard six-session [therapy] cap', and King's College London, where one of the demands of the OccupyKCL protest group was 'a permanent additional CBT therapist'.[21] But are such demands even necessary? The commitment to student protection is so great that, today, at many universities, administrators, counsellors and the other bureaucratic apparatchiks tasked with student wellbeing outnumber academic staff. What's more, almost no one is prepared to push back against this rebalancing of the university mission. Rather than instilling a much-needed sense of proportionality about some of the more spurious concerns, universities have instead lent weight to the idea that students must be constantly coddled. For example, in the same year that iGen matriculated, the former head of Wellington College and vice chancellor of the University of Buckingham, Sir Anthony Seldon, began what can only be described as a crusade to expose the mental health problems of university students. Drawing on a survey of school leaders at both private and state schools, Seldon claimed that 'there is a belief among vice chancellors that young people are adults and can fend for themselves', but '18-year-olds today are a lot less robust and worldly wise'.[22] Since then, Seldon has gone on to propose a raft of measures that serve only to concretise iGen'ers' sense of fragility – including the introduction of mandatory modules on 'resilience, emotional wellbeing and mental health literacy' for first-year undergraduates, and a 'wellbeing league table' for educational institutions so that 'parents can choose one that's best suited for their child'.

This belief that university life is somehow akin to military combat in terms of its damaging impact on one's psychological health has also permeated government. In 2018, the Conservative higher education minister, Sam Gyimah, articulated what many academics had long feared when he told UK vice chancellors that the main purpose of university was no longer the training of the mind, but ensuring the good mental health of their students. By paralleling each other in terms of the way they conflate safetyism with concerns about mental health, schools and universities have made it increasingly difficult to distinguish one from the other. As a result, many undergraduates no longer view the university experience as a rite of passage on the road to adulthood, but instead demand levels of benevolent care and emotional support more traditionally associated with a nursery school or kindergarten.

Once students have internalised the overlapping beliefs that attending university is a traumatic experience, it becomes normal for all sorts of challenges and everyday upheavals to be viewed through the prism of medicalisation. Hence the talk of an epidemic (it's always an epidemic) of mental health concerns surrounding issues such as 'exam stress', 'homesickness', 'perfection anxiety' and 'handwriting'. Even reading is now medicalised. Despite the fact that outside of university campuses few people if any seem particularly concerned that reading may be a psychologically damaging activity, today's therapeutic pedagogues have convinced themselves that reading can be 'trauma-inducing' and that vulnerable students need protecting from the risks associated with 'challenging' course material.

When common educational activities such as sitting an examination or reading a book are constructed as harmful, even traumatic, experiences, it should be obvious that something has gone badly wrong in our universities. By mobilising the language of trauma and medicalising the student experience, university administrators have created a bloated culture of vulnerability that today knows no bounds. Consider the following examples. In 2019, at Glasgow University, students studying the fairy tales of the Brothers Grimm were warned about the 'violent material' contained within the *children's* stories; in 2021, a group of archivists and self-styled knowledge 'gatekeepers' (note: not custodians) at Homerton College, University of Cambridge, attached trigger warnings to a host of classic children's novels, including *Little House on the Prairie* and *The Water Babies*; by 2023, the culture of educational protectionism had become so normalised at Aberdeen University that trigger warnings had been slapped on everything from the study of the Anglo-Saxon poem *Beowulf* ('ableism', 'animal death', 'black magic') to French language courses ('gender, sexuality and love') to J. M. Barrie's classic fairy tale *Peter Pan* ('too challenging').[23] Meanwhile, at University College London, not content with telling students enrolled on an 'archaeology of modern conflict' course that if they found discussions about historical events 'disturbing' or 'traumatising' they were free to leave the class, authors of a Bartlett School of Architecture report took the decision to include a lengthy trigger warning – about trigger warnings.[24]

As with safetyism, the urge to manage behavioural norms and police and purify speech acts has been around for some time. But it was only after Millennials and iGen'ers started arriving on campus that the doctrines associated with these early attempts to regulate interactional and language norms really took hold. Whether this takes the form of reading material that might potentially trigger traumatic memories, or the disinvestment of visiting speakers with controversial views, the fixation with being offended has at its core the belief that language and speech acts can inflict real harm and thus students must be protected at every turn from so-called 'toxic words' and other forms of linguistic pollution. The dangers of this development should be obvious. By treating sensitive issues as potential risks to health we not only limit intellectual inquiry and student curiosity, but more worryingly we open the door to a rising tide of illiberal practices – including new forms of insidious censorship, as the notion of being offended provides the moral warrant to ban everything from Christmas songs to scenes of suicide in ballet.

Consider the recent plight of Dr Greg Patton, a professor at the University of Southern California's Marshall School of Business. In August 2020, while teaching a Zoom class on communication in international business, Patton used an example from Chinese culture to illustrate the distracting nature of filler words (like 'um' or 'er') when giving a presentation. Introducing the Mandarin word 'nèige', which literally means 'that', Patton was recorded on Zoom stating: 'Like in China, the common word is *that* – that, that, that, that. So in China, it might be *nèige* – nèige, nèige, nèige. So there's different words that you'll hear in different countries, but they're vocal disfluencies.' Patton had been using this example for years without issue, but he hadn't reckoned on the changing sensitivities of today's students. Within twenty-four hours of the class, Patton was engulfed in a firestorm of protest after an anonymous group of black students sent a letter to the business school's Dean accusing Patton of 'callous' racism by using a word that sounded 'exactly like the word NIGGA'.[25] To calm the situation, Dr Patton gave an interview to the *Los Angeles Times* in which he described the incident as a colossal misunderstanding. It didn't work. Despite a two-decade career of unblemished teaching at USC – an exhaustive trawl of thousands of Patton's student evaluations found not one trace of racial or cultural insensitivity – Patton was summarily suspended. In a statement announcing his decision, Dean Geoffrey Garrett justified the suspension with the now-familiar blend of therapy-speak and mealy-mouthed apology: 'It is simply unacceptable for faculty to use words in class that can marginalize, hurt and harm the psychological safety of our students … Understandably, this caused great pain and upset among students, and for that I am deeply sorry.' Patton was later completely exonerated, but this preposterous incident illustrates what can happen when all-too-easily offended students are appeased and mollycoddled by university leaders obsessed with 'psychological safety'.

Whether it takes the form of language and content purification, the regulation of thought and behaviour associated with enforced inclusivity and diversity training, or the policing of interactions associated with micro-aggressions, all these developments have one thing in common: they are premised on the belief that today's students are fragile beings in constant need of protection and psychological support. Two infantilising consequences inevitably flow from this situation.

First, in shielding students from challenging material and flattening out their social worlds by reducing any potential complexity or existential challenge, contemporary universities are eroding the distinction between school and higher education and in doing so detrimentally affecting what traditional educationalists once called andragogical competency (i.e. adult learning ability). The word 'andragogy' stems from ancient Greek and literally means 'leading man' (as opposed to 'pedagogy' – 'leading children'). At the core of andragogy is the belief that the best way to educate adults is to synthesise academic knowledge with real-world examples and experience(s), the goal being to create self-directed autonomous learners who are on an intellectual journey towards independence. Today, however, this process has stalled. The more universities have replicated modes of therapeutic learning found in schools, the more they have infantilised their students and severed the andragogical link between academic content and *adult* life. This rupture inevitably results in a more anxious learning process, something which naturally makes it harder for students to develop enhanced forms of critical thinking linked to emerging adult self-confidence.

This deficit in andragogical competency is already being felt in the post-university workplace. For example, many employers are now so worried about the low standard of graduate students they have taken to implementing their own pre-employment screening tests in reading comprehension, writing and maths. Meanwhile, employers in the culture industries are already making noises about how Gen Z employees often lack the necessary intellectual skills to debate and disagree with colleagues who do not share their particular political opinions. Early research on iGen maintained that, because of widely adopted liberal attitudes, this generation would arguably be the most tolerant in history. However, as time passes, it appears almost the opposite is true – so much so in fact that some employers now use the neologism 'YIPS' (young illiberal progressives) to describe young staff who appear incapable of seeing the other side of an argument.

The second consequence stems not from the offices of university administrators, but from the students themselves. By leading the charge for trigger warnings and other forms of campus thought and speech management, Millennial and iGen students have ushered in a new era of academic and emotional paternalism that has hastened the drift towards an infantilised campus. For most of the twentieth century, Anglo-American universities upheld the doctrine of *in loco parentis* – the belief that the university stood 'in place of the parent' and thus had a duty of care towards its students that extended beyond the academic element of university life. However, this changed in the 1960s. The student radicals of that era are best known for their countercultural politics and anti-war protests, but allied to these concerns was the less-vaunted campaign to be recognised and treated as adults on campus. Fed up with paternalistic university rules – in particular, stipulations around gender segregation – the student protestors of the 1960s and early 70s set about dismantling the principle of *in loco parentis*. In doing so they transformed the university into a space where students were no longer viewed as wards of the university, but responsible individuals, free to live their lives as they saw best. More recently, however, there has been a distinct slide back towards *in loco parentis*. The interesting thing to note here is the extent to which this resumption of academic moral guardianship has not simply been accepted by students, but actively encouraged – with student union groups being especially shrill in their efforts to mobilise all sorts of new protections around alcohol consumption, drug use and sexual safety. As a result of this manicuring of the university experience, today's students have got exactly what they want: a revanchist paternalism in which the university once again acts as an overseeing parent – only this time, a weak and easily manipulated one who is primed to capitulate to never-ending student demands.

We have already seen how this permissive relationship has impacted academic standards, but it has also reshaped the way universities physically look and feel. It used to be the case that coming up to university was a time when young people learnt 'to put away childish things'. Not any more. Thanks to ever-indulgent university leaders, a walk around many contemporary campuses often feels like you've inadvertently stumbled across the threshold of a theme park or children's play area. Universities proudly proclaim facilities such as LEGO and Play-Doh rooms, 'Chillout Zones', colouring-in spaces and even petting zoos. In the US, nearly a thousand universities offer their students sessions with 'therapy dogs', a ritual designed to reduce the anxiety of academic study. Likewise, in the UK, 'Puppy rooms' have become a must-have campus feature, with Buckingham, Cambridge, Nottingham Trent, University College London, Swansea and London Metropolitan among those deploying psycho-pooches. Middlesex University has even put 'canine teaching assistants' on to the staff in a bid to stop anxious and lonely students dropping out.[26] Incidentally, one of the pivotal studies that established the belief that therapy dogs reduce academic stress – a 2019 study by researchers at Washington State University – was funded by the Mars Group, a global pet-care company with interests in dog food and veterinary surgeries.

Elsewhere, other childlike activities are also encouraged as antidotes to the apparent stresses of attaining a university degree. LARPing, PWA (performance without an audience) and other forms of immersive cosplay all feature prominently on today's campuses, as does Quidditch, the Harry Potter-inspired sport-like activity that requires students to ride around on broomsticks. But perhaps the most obvious example of the transformation of universities into leisure parks can be seen in the increased presence of parents on campus. It started, innocently enough, when parents began accompanying their children to open days, campus visits and interviews (and why not? After all, they're usually the ones footing the bill for today's over-priced degrees). But like crab grass in a veggie garden, the parents of Millennials and iGen'ers proved hard to keep in check. In a further retreat from the *in loco parentis* doctrine, many US colleges have for some time been organising special programmes and events designed specifically to 'encourage parents to become enmeshed ... with their children's lives on campus'.[27] This in turn has led to a phenomenon called the College Family Weekend, a cross-generational gathering at which parents are encouraged to join in university-sanctioned events such as lectures by celebrity speakers, ghost tours, family bowling events and even midnight roller-skating! 'They [parents] really want to be part of their student's experience,' claims Anna Thomas, the director of Vanderbilt University's Parent and Family Program, which regularly organises events involving more than 4,000 family visitors.[28] But the adult search for the student experience is not without its problems. Writing about the College Family Weekend in the *New York Times,* Bruce Feiler documented a series of unedifying developments including the deployment of 'parent bouncers' to eject family members who refuse to leave campus, and printed handouts advising parents not to get drunk and fraternise with students. As anyone who has visited a theme park knows, the defining feature of these Disneyfied spaces is how they actively cater for the whole family *equally*. This same dynamic is now also present in the new infantilised academy, as College Family Weekends and other cross-generation initiatives further normalise generational mulching.

Many of the above themes, including safetyism, paternalism and fantasy, all come together in what is perhaps the definitive symbol of the way universities have been transformed into manicured zones absent of debate and organised instead around identity validation: the safe space. Initially associated with the feminist movement of the 1970s, early safe spaces provided a valuable service by creating a neutral zone for victims of violence and abuse to meet, share experiences and talk through problems. More recently, however, the safe space concept has expanded far beyond its original remit – especially on university campuses where they now function as protective zones for anyone who may be experiencing stress or who might be offended/triggered by content or arguments they find unsettling. This might not seem especially problematic, but once universities demarcate certain spaces as 'safe', they essentially imply that the rest of campus (and, by extension, society) is unsafe. From here a safe space *mentality* quickly takes hold which can result in students and professors clamming up for fear of saying anything at all that might be considered hurtful or controversial. Even worse, as the columnist Judith Shulevitz has argued, by validating the belief that people are likely to be emotionally damaged by 'being upset', or by confronting material they find unpleasant, the creeping capillaries of safe-space culture undermine the ability of young people to counter the sort of setbacks that are a feature of everyday life: 'People ought to go to college to sharpen their wits and broaden their field of vision. Shield them from unfamiliar ideas, and they'll never learn the discipline of seeing the world as other people see it. They'll be unprepared for the social and intellectual headwinds that will hit them as they step off the campuses whose climates they have so carefully controlled.'[29]

Advocates of safe spaces believe them to be 'world-making projects that provide an account of public trauma and a sense of collective vulnerability',[30] but as each year passes it's clear they're nothing of the sort. The safe space, along with its pseudo-therapeutic affiliate the trigger warning, are in fact symptoms of a postmodern culture no longer capable of drawing a meaningful distinction between actual harm and dubious Foucauldian-based assumptions about systemic psychological oppression. By quarantining hypersensitive individuals from subjects, ideas and even 'problematic words', we have, as Shulevitz makes clear, intensified 'student self-infantilization'.[31]

Instead of pushing back against safetyism and a culture that has turned vulnerability into a common feature of everyday biography, late-modern university elders have rolled over in the face of any sort of student demand or complaint. Consequently, what's happening on campuses today is not education but capitulation. We have already seen how this capitulatory stance has resulted in dumbed-down degree courses and declining academic standards, but it's also apparent in other less obvious ways. In the last five years, universities from Berkeley to Bradford have introduced 'diversity' and 'equality' training courses for new undergraduate students. The original versions of these mandatory trainings were well-intentioned exercises linked to Title IX concerns in the US or the UK Equality Act. Recently, however, they have taken on a far more politicised role.

For example, in 2021, the University of Kent (where I taught Criminology for over a decade) was accused of inculcating 'Woke conformism' after it restructured its mandatory online 'Expect Respect' module. Containing a raft of controversial questions and scenarios about 'white privilege', alongside a legally inaccurate section on sexuality that flagrantly misinterpreted the concept of gender as defined in the 2010 Equality Act, the content of Kent's four-hour 'Expect Respect' module was seen by many as indoctrination under the guise of education. The controversy prompted mathematics professor Alan Sokal (who, in 1996, famously published a deliberately nonsensical paper in the cultural studies journal *Social Text* in a bid to debunk postmodern verbiage), to write a detailed critique of the 'Expect Respect' module. Sokal pointed out that, although this type of 'educational catechism' is clearly antithetical to the mission of the university in a democratic polity, the real problem is with university managers who lose control of the content and tenor of these compulsory exercises, and by doing so fail to uphold educational integrity. This point was perfectly illustrated just a few months later when a similar row broke out at the

University of Cambridge. Following the introduction of mandatory online race classes at Wolfson College, several students leaked information about 'white supremacy' questions in the course to reporters, a move that angered student union officials at the college who 'vowed to find and ban the leakers' from the union's official forum. The Wolfson witch hunt made national news and prompted the general secretary of the Free Speech Union to comment: 'The college authorities should be embarrassed. They've relinquished their leadership role and the result is that a student mob is now in charge . . . Why would anyone want to go to Wolfson if the college is now run by a group of Maoist thugs in short trousers.'[32] Once again, it's a matter of capitulation. When senior figures at Kent, Cambridge and elsewhere acquiesce to non-academic bureaucrats – the Student Services office, the Human Resources Department, Equality, Diversity and Inclusivity officers, the Corporate Communications office, etc. – on matters relating to educational content, they essentially undermine their own position in the university hierarchy.

Capitulation, of course, takes other forms. In their constant efforts to accommodate the demands of students, senior university administrators frequently cave in to what they erroneously believe is a growing clamour among the student body for enhanced diversity and inclusion training. On this point, however, they could not be more wrong. By taking the student union as its primary interlocutor on this matter, university management has capitulated not to the student majority but to a small band of minority activists.

Boxed in by their addiction to public money on the one hand, and the ever-growing demands of student consumerism on the other, today's titans of the corporate university have done almost nothing to counter the emergence of the infantilising developments outlined in this section. By cravenly capitulating to bureaucrats and an 'anointed minority of student leaders', these supposed guardians of education have ensured that the creation of mandatory conditioning programmes is now a normalised feature of university education. It is, as Sokal correctly asserts, a recipe for culturally induced infantilisation sanctioned and imposed by 'administrators ensconced in their own echo chambers' – a way of 'teaching 18-year-olds how to play together nicely'.[33]

Top-down infantilism is not limited to students. Today, academic staff are also frequently required to complete various compulsory training courses and so-called upskilling programmes, many of which are so patronising it's as if they've been designed by/for a preschooler. Consider, for example, a recent online General Data Protection Regulation course rolled out across many European universities. Not only did the whole thing look and feel like a children's cartoon, but participants were constantly prompted to interact with 'Data Dave', an animated helper there to reorientate the lost and confused. But when it comes to designing software programmes that treat adults like children, one need look no further than the University of Kent. Not only does their Expect Respect module reward incoming students with 'a Gold Star' if they correctly place a checkmark against all thirteen examples of white privilege, but staff too can now be credentialled with a 'Moodle badge' if they complete all sections of a 2021 online module entitled 'Academic Adviser training'.

While long-serving staff may gnash their teeth at such nonsense, most junior academics have known little else and thus are likely to be unconcerned about being addressed in this manner. Indeed, a cursory scroll through the digital playpen that is academic Twitter/X makes clear that rather than pushing back against these childish modes of management communication, many early-career academics directly collude in the infantilisation party, often speaking and behaving like children themselves. In recent months I have seen academics in my own field announce on X:

- that they categorise their students as 'green elves' and 'white elves';
- that they hide an Easter egg in their online syllabus which, if students find, and then 'send in a picture of an otter', they receive extra course credit;
- that 'This weekend I recreated my fifth birthday cake, because why not';
- and that they bought a Nintendo Switch 'because, you know, I'm an adult, and now all I want to do is play Mario Kart'.

Some academics now even take it upon themselves to act as adult school monitors, reprimanding their colleagues for small micro-aggressions or reporting them to the 'Bias Response Team' for perceived infractions of the latest performative language code. On this point, it's worth reflecting on how emojis and other infantile digital 'stickers' are being used by some academics as a form of activism in sheep's clothing. Just as children use drawings and other modes of play to articulate their underlying goals and wishes, these popular infantile symbols are being used for overt political purposes under the guise of a logic which suggests emojis function as 'a small action towards inclusivity' (as described in a recent email forwarded to me by a fellow academic). But while these cutesy symbols might appear innocuous, they often contain within them the throb of political authoritarianism. For example, in the above-mentioned email, colleagues were also implored to 'show their allyship' by adding an email footer or a door poster 'relating to Black Lives Matter [that] would help black and other racialised students feel seen and supported'. There's a paradox here, of course, in that while such practices are no doubt the work of academics who constantly tout the importance of 'self-reflexivity', they seem utterly in the dark about just how juvenile and patronising these practices appear to anyone at a university who still identifies as an adult.

Academic Twitter/X provides a perfect lens through which to observe the infantilisation of the academy. Just as schoolkids have been conditioned to receive gold stars and merit badges from their teachers, many academics have become addicted to the affirmation of their sense of self that comes from 'likes' about their achievements. The primary vehicle by which to achieve this recognition is, of course, the *humblebrag* – an ostensibly self-depreciating comment designed explicitly to draw attention to one's personal qualities or academic accomplishments. The most common form of humblebrag is the tweet that starts out by declaring how 'humbled', 'proud', 'excited' or 'thrilled' the tweeter is to announce x, y or z. In today's academe, no achievement, no matter how small, is beyond the humblebrag. Even the signing of a publishing contract to write a jointly authored chapter for an outrageously overpriced handbook must be trumpeted on Twitter/X as if it were a Nobel Prize nomination. Sadly, this tendency seems to get worse the higher up the academic chain you go. University vice chancellors and other senior management figures, for example, appear to spend 365 days a year feeling either honoured, inspired, heartened, grateful or privileged. It's a wonder they ever find the time to implement voluntary redundancy programmes or meet with shadowy management consultants about the next meaningless corporate initiative. This combination of being continuously excited and thrilled while simultaneously desperate for attention and digital recognition perfectly captures the infantilised state of many contemporary academics. Little wonder, then, that so few have noticed that, right under their noses, a fundamental shift in power relations is taking place in the Anglo-American university that has irrevocably undermined the very status these infantilised humble-braggers so desperately crave.

Walking around a university in the East Midlands a few years back, I was struck by a poster plastered up all over campus. Produced by the university to curry favour with its consumer-students, the poster's message was short and succinct – 'You say, we did'. It had clearly been designed to draw attention to the fact that university managers had dutifully acquiesced to a host of recent student demands, but it also perfectly encapsulates a more general rebalancing of power that has taken place within the late-modern university. Here I refer to the growing tendency to include student opinion in a range of discussions about what should be taught, how teaching should be organised and delivered and, increasingly, how the university (and its finances) should be run. In pedagogue-speak, this rebalancing is typically dressed up as 'student-led teaching' or 'undergraduate-driven learning'. For those of us who have seen these processes up close, a more fitting description is *socialisation in reverse*. The term socialisation in reverse was originally used to capture a child-centric phenomenon taking place in schools whereby schoolchildren were being entrusted with the (moral) mission of socialising their elders: 'The process of socialisation in reverse works through communicating the idea that children possess knowledge and competence about certain important issues and social experience that is way ahead of their parents'.[34] But with its emphasis on porous intergenerational relations and in particular its contribution to the erosion of the moral status of experienced adults, socialisation in reverse is also a useful concept for understanding the rampant reversal of authority under way in higher education.

The processes associated with socialisation in reverse are evident in almost all areas of university life. Many colleges now include student representatives not only on curriculum design committees but also on working groups and internal boards that wield considerable influence over capital spending. (I once had a conversation with a then UK university vice chancellor who somewhat sheepishly informed me that he had just come from a budget meeting about a new 'Olympic-size swimming pool' because it was one of the primary demands put forward by the Student Representative Council.) This inversion of traditional hierarchy structures also takes place via 'learner-led' teaching awards that have the effect of influencing the style and form of andragogic practice based on student preference (which usually boils down to either more recorded lectures or requiring lecturers to adhere to a homogenised template that typically involves PowerPoint or some other form of academic karaoke). It's even been suggested that student evaluation data should be tied to academics' salaries and promotion prospects. University libraries also increasingly take their lead from students, actively promoting so-called Student Driven Acquisition policies under the strapline 'You read, we buy'. In the UK, there is even a specific organisation, Student Voice, dedicated to better integrating students into university decision-making structures. The ethos underlining all this authority reversal was perfectly captured by Steve Outram, a senior advisor for the Higher Education Academy's 'students as partners' programme, when he declared that 'It's a different mindset. It's not "This is what we will do to you". It even goes beyond "This is what we will do with you". It's "Tell us what you would like us to do". [35]

Any form of socialisation in reverse is music to the ears of student union reps. For decades, the National Union of Students in the UK has been lobbying for a bigger seat at the university decision-making table – typically to promote activist views that lack any real support among the wider student body. Consequently, Anglo-American student unions are often prime movers when it comes to advocating for new modes of governance based around socialisation in reverse. The problem, of course, is that student union representatives, along with most of the students they supposedly represent, do not have the requisite experience – of life generally, but of other universities specifically – to play a meaningful role in the day-to-day running of a higher education institution. Undergraduate students in particular are entirely unqualified to evaluate the quality of the education they receive until after they've received it. Relatedly, while there is obviously much to be gained from course evaluation feedback and other inclusive techniques designed to capture student opinion, it has been argued that the current penchant for embedded forms of learner-led teaching creates more problems than it solves. For example, in an insightful article entitled 'Recentring pedagogy in an age of narcissism', the clinical psychologist Ann O. Watters claims that the student-centred pedagogy associated with today's 'student-as-consumer' culture has contributed to the rise of narcissism in society generally, and in recent (US) college cohorts specifically. According to Watters, by constantly striving to enhance student self-esteem, universities have over-valorised the student voice at the expense of academic expertise. Consequently, 'instead of successful student-centered approaches or a middle way between teacher-centered and student-centered, instructors report widespread resistance to critical feedback, let alone critical evaluation. They increasingly note the devaluation of instructor expertise, not to mention authority, and the assumption that all opinions are equal and equally valid, rather than that all have equal rights to express opinions.'[36]

In the glossolalia at the end of his novel *Player One: What is to Become of Us*, the novelist Douglas Coupland introduces a concept called 'Post-adolescent expert syndrome': 'The tendency of young people around the age of eighteen, males especially, to become altruistic experts on everything ... "Kyle, I never would have guessed that when you were up in your bedroom playing *World of Warcraft* all through your teens, you were, in fact, becoming an expert on the films of Jean-Luc Godard'. Coupland was worried about what society might look like if post-adolescent expert syndrome ever leached out from its bedroom stronghold – but in a way it already has. On British and American university campuses, over-confident youthful experts increasingly call the shots, whether by demanding academic staff include their gender pronouns when introducing themselves, or more generally asserting that 'They are the people who know how best they can be taught'.[37] In previous eras, such 'expertise' would have been treated with caution by learned academics who would then consider the evidence prior to making a decision about what was in the next generation's best interests. However, after two decades of uncontested socialisation in reverse, pressure from below has become so normalised that – as the 'You say, we did' rubric suggests – today's techno-bureaucratic university managers now function as little more than a glorified rubber-stamping outfit.

So, what of the future? Where will these various trends and developments eventually leave the late-modern university? In many ways, it's a future that's already arrived. In an article entitled 'The Rise of the Comfort College', the philosopher Steven B. Gerrard outlined what happened when an elite private university compromised its principles in response to pressure from below. Williams College in Massachusetts was founded in 1793 as a free school with 'a transcendent Christian purpose'. In the intervening years, the college proceeded through several distinct eras, usefully characterised by the Williams historian Frederick Rudolph as 'the Christian college', 'the Gentlemen's college' and, most recently, 'the Consumer college' (of the late twentieth century). However, since 2016, Williams College, like many Anglo-American universities, has been convulsed by a series of controversies, including protest marches, a volatile free-speech crisis, several no-platforming incidents, and threats made against faculty members who simply sought to uphold liberal values. Having personally been caught up in these events, Gerrard believes that collectively these campus disturbances herald the emergence of an entirely new era for the college, based on the emotional sensibilities and political views of iGen and Millennial students.

> Elite private education in America is on the cusp of this new era. The controversies over free speech, safe spaces, trigger warnings, microaggressions and the like are symptoms of this shift. They are currently considered controversies because the colleges are in transition, and many do not realize that the old standards no longer hold. Once the transition is complete, the 'correct' side of the controversies will become central to a school's identity – just as faith was to the Christian college, self-confidence was to the gentlemen's college, and alumni devotion and achievement were to the consumer's college. Some have suggested naming this new college 'the therapeutic university' or 'the woke college.' *I prefer 'the comfort college,' because it combines the emotional component of the first with the political elements of the second.* Our students are comfortable in their opinions but uncomfortable with their lives, finding their world and the Williams campus a threatening place. Once Williams' transition to comfort college is complete, the students will expect to find their college truly comfortable in all respects [emphasis added].[38]

Gerrard freely acknowledges that, in many ways, by promoting the voices of previously under-represented groups, the comfort college version of Williams is a more inclusive and progressive institution than previous iterations. Indeed, his issue is not with identity politics per se, but with an 'agenda that runs counter to true diversity and inclusion, [and] has (often silently) accompanied these positive changes': the assault on knowledge that is the corollary to today's student politics. By buckling to pressure from interest and activists' groups, and by giving in to student demands on issues such as no-platforming and the forced imposition of censorious tribal language, Williams College officials have sacrificed rational argument and the pursuit of knowledge on the altar of weaponised political correctness. And so, an irony. By aligning itself with a set of 'correct' opinions, the new Williams (Comfort) College starts to resemble its original iteration, the Christian college, in that it is now organised on the basis of a transcendent dogma ('unwritten but understood by all'), and that anyone who deviates from the script(ure) in thought or deed must be constructed and demonised as a heretic. Rather than a beacon of progressivism, the comfort college model shuts down debate, free inquiry, and diversity of opinion, creating instead an atmosphere of intellectual fixity: 'Students are now absolutists. Students, administrators and some faculty know what is right (and who is wrong). Any challenge to their views cannot be in pursuit of knowledge or even clarification. It can only come from the desire to crush and oppress.'

If the 'comfort college' signposts a future of university education predicated on a combination of socialisation in reverse and safetyism from alternative opinions, what about the other elements of the infantilised campus – the demise of academic standards and the transformation of university facilities into themed leisure parks? Here again, we have a vision of the future that is already with us. In 2012 there was much media fanfare surrounding Dale Stephens and the 'UnCollege movement'. Stephens – who was home-schooled from the age of twelve – was given $100,000 by Peter Thiel, the PayPal founder, to skip university in America and do something important in the real world instead. Based on the correct premise that a university education is not necessarily the best way for many young people to learn and develop, Stephens used Thiel's money to set up a pilot programme (costing $12,000 per 'Un-student', or 'hackademic', as he preferred to call them) that would involve subscribers creating their own support network and working out what their employable skills were. So far, so good. Claiming (without any substantiating evidence) that the UnCollege movement would offer 'meta skills' 'above and beyond' any university curriculum, his programme involved spending 'the first 10 weeks living in a shared house and learning how to find mentors and access educational resources. After this, they [UnCollege subscribers] have $2,500 to spend on a trip abroad of their own design . . . followed by a three-month internship. The course ends with a personal project creating something 'that someone will pay for in the real world'.[39]

Puffed up in the media by the usual mix of futurists and anti-bricks-and-mortar tech ideologues, Stephens targeted what he called the disgruntled 'too-cool-for-school type' and had grand plans for UnCollege campuses in San Francisco and London. It quickly became clear, however, that what Stephens had created was neither practical nor desirable for most of his students, and recruitment to the UnCollege programme fell away almost as quickly as the media hype. Five years on from its launch, and UnCollege was unceremoniously rebranded as a one-year gap programme based entirely on a lengthy overseas stay designed 'to prepare students for life at university and in the world of work'.

The UnCollege experiment provides a vivid example of what happens when you devise a new mode of educational experience based on a combination of the hubris associated with 'post-adolescent expert syndrome' and the erosion – in this case the virtual eradication – of robust, quality-assured academic standards. In contrast to the type of intellectual journey that used to characterise a university education, the UnCollege programme wound up being nothing more than a glorified holiday from real life, free from all those pesky academic tasks like reading, writing and passing exams.

In 1994, two psychologists at the University of Massachusetts at Amherst conducted an experiment into how undergraduate students responded to being treated like children.[40] The aim of the study was to help students overcome unfavourable attitudes towards older members of society who are often treated in patronising and infantilising ways. But the three-decade-old experiment also illustrates the extent to which student attitudes have changed regarding infantilising practices. In the study by Susan Whitbourne and Erin Cassidy, 138 undergraduate students were subjected to an unannounced exercise which involved the instructor informing the class they had been selected to colour-in pictures to be used to decorate the faculty building. During the colouring-in process the instructor used exaggerated, high-pitched speech to praise and patronise the students. Any student who did not follow the rules was told they were a 'troublemaker' and would 'be sent back to their rooms'. At the end of the crayon experiment, the students were asked a series of questions based on their experience. Overwhelmingly (76 per cent) the respondents described the session in extremely negative terms ('degrading', 'dehumanising', 'insulting', 'embarrassing', etc.). However, what was even more interesting was that they also expressed concern about how, during the experiment, 'they experienced hostility [towards the instructor], regressed behaviourally, and became territorial [over the sharing of crayons]'. Clearly, for these students, being infantilised was not just demeaning but a threat to their intellectual and personal maturation. How times have changed. In the contemporary university, as we have seen, many students seem only too happy to be treated as infantilised supplicants in need of protection. No surprise, then, that behavioural regression and student hostility towards academic authority figures are such common features of campus life.

Given that universities are our most elevated seats of learning, you might have expected them to counteract the many problems caused by changes in twenty-first-century secondary education. But the plain truth is that, for the most part, they have made the situation worse. Consequently, we now produce battalions of graduates with neither the intellectual capacity nor the interpersonal capabilities required to function effectively in adulthood. It is a situation that should concern us all.

In December 2021, my university in Denmark held something called a 'Global Development Day.' One of the events featured was a session entitled 'What could the world look like if students were in charge?' Leaving aside the fact that, in many institutions, to all intents and purposes this imagined scenario has already transpired, the programme for the day had much to say about what a student-led world would likely prioritise. Alongside some wonderfully vague soundbite-type panel sessions ('Dig deeper and relate wider', 'Doing Development Differently') there were 'free samosas', a beer-based 'science slam', a lounge for networking with globalist charities, a gathering around the university Christmas tree culminating in 'A wish list for [the] rector' and for good measure a bit of culturally appropriated ersatz spiritualism in the form of a closing 'Baraka'. Everything except meaningful critical debate and attention-demanding scholarship.

These last two things, as we have seen, are typically not very popular in contemporary universities that seem unable or unwilling to stem the rise of socialisation in reverse. The same is true in Anglo-American schools, where such is the reversal of adult authority, many teachers now face the dreadful predicament of ensuring they are not viewed as 'oppressive' or 'non-progressive' by their increasingly self-righteous students. In previous eras, when a teacher corrected a student on a point of issue, that student might have made an extra effort in the future to win back the place of esteem with the teacher. Now the teacher is likely to retreat from such an encounter, feeling instead that they've committed some sort of grievous offence – the offence of deviating from the script of empty praise and restrained criticism that has become normalised within many contemporary schools.

For well over a century, Anglo-American society had been able to count on schools and universities to deliver adult-directed content and educational programmes designed to socialise young people and instil within them the uncontroversial idea that they will need to adjust their behaviour and adapt to the world if they are to function effectively within it. Today, however, modern education no longer operates in this way. Instead, thanks to a confluence of therapeutic teaching practices based on 'everyone's a winner' credentialism, and the commensurate capitulation of adult authority, schools and universities have become places where self(ish) entitlement and the irrational worldview of the infanti-lised child are not just tolerated and reaffirmed but seemingly actively encouraged.

PART III

THE PATHOLOGIES OF INFANTILISATION

I n *Against the Double Blackmail: Refugees, Terror and Other Troubles with the Neighbours,* the provocative philosopher Slavoj Žižek used the term 'zero-level protest' to describe the three weeks of rioting and civil disorder that shook various cities across France in the autumn of 2005. In contrast to those commentators who claimed the riots were motivated by socio-political concerns, Žižek argued that what actually defined the 2005 French riots was a 'deplorable near-absence' of 'radical emancipatory politics'. This was a sustained act of violent protest that demanded absolutely nothing. Instead of any unified political vision, there 'was only an insistence on *recognition,* based on a vague, non-articulated *ressentiment*'.[1] Although socially marginalised, the rioters had not been subject to exceptional levels of poverty. Instead, the riots were 'a blind acting out', a self-destructive pulse of violence directed inwardly against their own marginalised community. Since 2005, this type of 'zero-level protest' has become increasingly common: an expression if ever there was one of a late-modern society devoid of any meaningful political vision. My concern here, however, is not with the underlying causes of today's riots, but with Žižek's use of the term 'acting out' to describe a new style of political expression.

In psychological circles, the term acting out has several meanings. In the treatment of behavioural or substance addiction, acting out – the excessive display of addictive behaviour – is viewed by councillors and clinicians as an illusory attempt by the addict to take control of their downward-spiralling situation. For psychiatrists, the practice of acting out is a 'defence mechanism', a way of protecting oneself from anxiety-producing thoughts and feelings related to internal conflicts and exterior stressors. In developmental psychology, acting out is viewed slightly differently. In the early years of child development, temper tantrums and episodic screaming rages are understood as techniques to alert parents to perceived needs and to gain their undivided attention. In describing the French riots as a form of blind acting out, Žižek was seemingly drawing on elements from across these interpretations. Most obviously, the riots can be seen as a flawed attempt to take control: a psycho-cultural defence against external stressors (police violence, marginalisation, etc.). Importantly, as is the case with addiction, this position also involves a perceived sense of victimhood: the view that, behaviourally, one is being unnecessarily constrained and is therefore justified in acting out. But what's interesting about Žižek's account is he also understands that urban disorder which demands nothing and lacks a defined emancipatory politics is essentially an infantilised cry for help; a highly disruptive and frequently self-destructive form of communicative attention-seeking.

I start the final part of this book with a brief discussion about why much contemporary disorder should be understood as a form of acting out because it hints at some of the more generalised psychological and political pathologies – victimhood, narcissistic attention-seeking as a communicative strategy, angry infantilised political outbursts – that have been spawned and encouraged by the rise of infantilisation. It should be clear by now that we have a problem. Over the next two chapters, I attempt to set out the full extent of this problem and what it means in terms of the way infantilised people see themselves and the wider community that surrounds them.

Chapter 7

The Destructive Dimensions
of the Infantilised Self

What's going to happen to the children
When there aren't any more grown-ups?
. . .

Hushabye, hushabye, hushabye my darlings,
Try not to fret and wet your cots.
One day you'll clench your tiny fists
And murder your psychiatrists.
What's, what's, what's going to happen to the tots?
Noël Coward 'What's going to happen to the tots?', 1955

The Japanese tennis star Naomi Osaka is a sporting phenomenon. Aged just twenty-six, she has already won four Grand Slam titles and is generally acknowledged to be the highest-paid female athlete *of all time*. But despite the international adulation and eye-watering riches, all is not well with Ms Osaka, who frequently speaks about her ongoing mental health problems. Although the exact nature of these problems is unclear, one thing is known, they tend to manifest themselves in a very specific context: the post-match media conference room where, in recent years, she has broken down on a number of occasions. In emotional statements, the tennis star has made it clear that being forced to answer questions about her performance from journalists is a source of considerable anxiety, as this tweet posted after she announced she would not take part in any press events at the 2021 French Open makes clear: 'I've often felt that people have no regard for athletes' mental health and this rings true whenever I see a press conference or partake in one. We're often sat there and asked questions that we've been asked multiple times before or asked questions that bring doubt into our minds and I'm just not going to subject myself to people that doubt me.'

Following a self-imposed hiatus from tennis press conferences, Osaka returned to answering journalists' questions after winning the Western and Southern Cincinnati Open in August 2021. It didn't go well. After only four questions, Osaka broke down in tears following what she later described as an 'aggressive question' by veteran *Cincinnati Enquirer* sports columnist Paul Daugherty. No footage exists of the question being posed, so we can't assess whether Daugherty did bully Osaka as her agent, Stuart Duguid, later claimed. What we do know is that Daugherty had no interest in serving up the usual softball questions favoured by most tennis journalists. Instead, he addressed inconsistencies in Osaka's decision not to talk to the tennis media: 'You are not crazy about dealing with us, especially in this format, yet you have a lot of outside interests that are served by having a media platform. I guess my question is, how do you balance the two . . .?' Osaka attempted a reply before tearing up and exiting the press room. Within hours, Twitter was atwitch with messages of support for Osaka, while Daugherty was condemned as a 'hater' and an 'asshole'. But surely Daugherty had a point. For example, after winning a match at the 2021 French Open, Osaka cited mental health issues as an excuse to blow off her press obligations, only to then give a lengthy interview to Wowow, a Japanese broadcaster that pays her for her time, access and words. And then there's the issue of selectivity. How can it be that media work is the source of such profound anxiety in one sphere of Osaka's professional life – contracted press inter-actions at tennis tournaments – but apparently not in another? The famously introverted Osaka certainly apportions a fair bit of her free time to media-facing activities, whether it's co-chairing the Met Gala, promoting her own skincare line or posing for magazine covers such as *Vogue* or *Sports Illustrated Swimsuit Edition*. For example, shortly after her loss in the final of the 2022 Miami Open, Osaka took part in a photoshoot at her Airbnb rental house – Airbnb is coincidentally one of Osaka's sponsors – to promote her new line of personalised swimwear. What Daugherty was gently circling around was something others had already considered: that Osaka's refusal to field questions from the tennis press might be due to her attitude as well as to her mental health. Only Osaka can answer that question. What we do know is that, around the same time she was complaining about the media pressure that comes with her life as a high-profile tennis star, she was filming a three-part Netflix documentary about her life as a high-profile tennis star. What this suggests is that, rather than media work being the source of unmanageable anxiety, Osaka's problems might occur more when she doesn't have control of the narrative.

I open this chapter by discussing Naomi Osaka for two reasons. First, because it provides a vivid illustration of the way iGen'ers like Osaka attempt to manicure and manage their social worlds to avoid the calibrating effects of life that are a vital part of the transi-tion to adulthood. Remember, Osaka is a twenty-six-year-old woman, not a precocious teenage prodigy. As every other seasoned professional tennis player knows only too well, part of the job is servicing the media in ways you can't always control or foresee. What's more, without the press there's not only no pro tour, but there are also no sponsors and thus no personalised swimsuit and skincare lines. Second, Osaka's behaviour may be seen as illustrative of two related emotional tendencies that are increasingly prevalent within our infantilised world. I refer here to the destructive emotional forces associated with victimhood and narcissism. By this, I do not mean to suggest that Osaka is a narcissist per se. Nor do I see her as someone who considers herself a passive or oppressed victim – if this were the case, she could hardly function as a world-class athlete. Rather, what I mean to suggest is that her self-absorbed stance towards the media could be suggestive of the type of sub-clinical *cultural* narcissism described by Christopher Lasch. In what follows, I build on Lasch's work by exploring and updating some of the tendencies and pathologies associated with the concept of cultural narcissism – victim signalling, look-at-me attention seeking, emotional manipulation, etc. – to show that, if infantilisation means anything, it means the coming together of a sense of vulnerability with narcissistic forms of self-indulgence and self-pity.

I, victim: The cult of victimhood and the denial of adult autonomy

> But victimizing oneself is like a drug – it feels so delicious, you get so much attention from people, it does *in fact define you, making you feel alive and even* important *while showing off your supposed wounds, no matter how minor, so people can lick them . . . The fact that one can't listen to a joke or view specific imagery (a painting or even a tweet) and that one might characterize everything as either sexist or racist . . . is a new kind of mania, a psychosis that the culture has been coddling.*
>
> Bret Easton Ellis[1]

One of the strengths of Andrew Calcutt's book *Arrested Development: Pop Culture and the Erosion of Adulthood* is his analysis of the connections that exist between infantilisation and victimisation. According to Calcutt, the 'elevation' and 'celebration' of victimhood has been one of the primary forces undermining the concept of adult maturity. Writing in 1998, he stated:

> The victim and the child are the two leading cultural personalities in today's society. They complement each other in that they are joined together by the common element of powerlessness. Abused and defenceless, the victim and the child are attractive personae in that they represent life beyond the discredited struggle for power between competing, self-interested adults.[2]

Calcutt asserted that, although traces of heroic vulnerability clearly existed in the literature (Camus, Salinger, Kerouac, etc.) and popular culture (Dean, Clift, Brando, etc.) of the 1950s, it was in the 1960s that the virtues of victimisation and self-oppression really gained traction in Anglo-American society. Using examples such as the penchant for new forms of self-therapy and the supposed emotional fragility of Sixties icons like Dylan, Lennon, Bruce and Burroughs, Calcutt believes that a sense of regressive vulnerability was 'an essential element in both the public make-up and the private persona of most countercultural anti-heroes'. He even goes so far as to suggest that, while the Sixties is typically framed as a paroxysm of radical ambition, it was equally an era defined by emerging feelings of vulnerability, confusion, even fear: 'For all the rhetoric of social transformation in the radical counterculture, the embrace of vulnerability should be seen rather as the renunciation of the transformative potential of humanity since it connotes an idea of selfhood which is primarily receptive and essentially passive.'[3] And it is this *passivity* – i.e., the idea that individuals have become cultural 'receptors' as much as active agents – that is key to understanding the widespread combination of victimisation and infantilisation that is so commonplace today.

In 1997, Damon Albarn, the lead singer of the UK band Blur, declared, 'If there's going to be an epitaph for the nineties, it will be by the end, we all felt like victims.' For most people, Albarn's statement was just another hyperbolic rock 'n' roll soundbite. Not for Calcutt. Echoing Albarn's observation about the expansion of victimhood during the 'nervous nineties', Calcutt drew on a range of examples – the contrived vulnerability of 'heroin chic' fashion models, the appropriation of miserabilist victimhood by musicians like Sinéad O'Connor, Morrissey and Courtney Love, and the rise of the 'autopathography' literary genre (autobiographies based around illness, frailty and victimisation) – to illustrate a powerful co-dependency gathering momentum in the pop-cultural peatlands of postmodern society: the mutually reinforcing relationship between the preoccupation with vulnerability and a pervasive desire for safety and security.

But the hipness of helplessness came at a cost. By emphasising vulnerability and normalising victimhood, end-of-millennium society spawned a new postmodern personality – the 'at risk' individual whose ability to assert agency in the face of putative threats was greatly diminished. In a lengthy case study at the start of the book, Calcutt uses the induced feelings of safety associated with the infantilised 1990s ecstasy drug scene to illustrate the coming together of immature vulnerability and a rising preoccupation with personal safety:

Drug culture was not always so 'banal' or 'smug'. In the 1960s Dr Timothy Leary's acid-driven 'politics of ecstasy' entailed an abortive attempt to transcend the ego. For the safety-conscious ravers of the 1990s, however, the special joy of E is that it allows the user to 'take your ego with you'. It seems to soothe today's fragile psyche in the same way that the infant Linus draws comfort from his security blanket in the *Peanuts* cartoon strip.[4]

By constructing 'an idea of ourselves as vulnerable and child-like', Anglo-American culture had struck a blow against the concept of mature adulthood. The agentic, history-making adult subject of modernity was being eclipsed by a more vulnerable postmodern figure whose obsession with popular culture was only surpassed by a fixation with risk aversion and personal well-being. Two decades on from Calcutt's *Arrested Development*, and the relationship between victimhood and infantilism has grown even stronger. By giving vulnerability a pop-cultural sheen, society has successfully transformed victimhood into something perceived as advantageous, a resource that many now seem to covet. How did this situation come about? How did we get to a point where neologisms like 'victim Olympics', 'oppression politics' and 'grievance mongering' had to be invented to describe the panorama of preposterous victimhood that currently engulfs us?[5]

As the culture of vulnerability expanded in the last third of the twentieth century, many observers grew concerned about how victim status was being constructed as a sort of 'agentic straight-jacket', a categorisation that brought with it 'overtones of passivity and powerlessness'.[6] It was for this reason that various victims' groups sought to replace the term 'victim' with that of 'survivor'; the logic being, if victimhood is something one suffers *passively*, then survival is achieved through endurance, through exerting *agency*. Unfortunately, this well-intentioned attempt to empower the powerless was soon co-opted by all sorts of spurious lobby groups and self-interested individuals. As a result, by the 1990s, the concept of victimisation had largely been hollowed out of its original meaning. This tendency to appropriate victimhood for personal gain has continued ever since, so much so in fact that, in a striking irony, contemporary claims of victimisation have indeed triggered a revanchist sense of agency – albeit one that now pits 'victims' against each other:

> Critics of our culture of victimhood are often attacked as abusers themselves, perpetuating a culture of harm and assault. Frequently, the response of that embattled critic is to assert that they are a victim as well. Men criticized as sexist for challenging radical feminism defend themselves as victims of reverse sexism, people criticized as being unsympathetic proclaim their own history of victimisation. In courts, during sentencing, it is common, even de rigeur, for felons to proclaim that their history of victimisation contributed to their harmful, illegal actions. In our culture of victimhood, victims can be excused for victimizing others, taking away the rights, freedoms, and autonomy of others, in service to their victimisation.[7]

Commonly described as 'victim signalling' or 'competitive victimhood', this tendency to flag one's victim status is found in almost every realm of contemporary society. Thirty years ago, in *A Nation of Victims*, Charles Sykes pointed out that if you added up all the people who belonged to oppressed minority and victim groups in America, the cumulative figure would come to nearly four times the population of the entire United States. Today, given the concept's elasticity, the number of people who consider themselves to be victims would be almost impossible to calculate. But why do so many people feel the need to tether their identity so firmly to the concept of victimhood?

The use of victim signalling to boost one's moral status is not especially new. As early as 1984, Christopher Lasch observed that 'the victim has come to enjoy a certain moral authority in our society'. Likewise, signalling suffering or a sense of trauma has long been used to justify acts of retribution or to excuse the wrongdoings of victims themselves. However, in recent times, the benefits – both moral and economic – of victimhood have increased immeasurably. To start with, as Calcutt noted, many well-known personalities, 'from footballers to princesses' understand that they 'cannot hope to retain their celebrity unless they come up with a story in which they play the victim'. Consequently, our magazines and TV screens are full of suspiciously well-timed stories about celebrities tackling the latest psychological disorder or coming to terms with a history of addiction and substance abuse. From hypocritical, fame-hungry actors who claim that being in the limelight is damaging to their mental health, to tearful professional cricketers who suggest that the rigours of overseas touring in hostile environments like Australia and the Caribbean cause stress and homesickness, hardly a day goes by without another celebrity, sportsperson or politician ramming their innermost tales of suffering and victimhood down our throats. For many celebrities, publicising trauma is a way of maintaining their 'brand', of staying relevant in overcrowded media markets. But for others, victimisation is used more as cultural capital, a resource for garnering sympathy and visibility – or as a duplicitous tactic to deflect criticism.

Many journalists and politicians, for example, now respond to mildly critical comments that appear after they've said something specious or inaccurate by claiming they are victims of 'abuse' and that the online criticism they received constitutes a form of 'persecution'. This practice, sometimes referred to as cry-bullying, perfectly illustrates not just the dysfunctional and increasingly cyclical nature of contemporary victim culture, but also its infantilised state. By simultaneously acting first as bully, and then as victim (usually by mobilising a psycho-biographical experience or

271

identity trait), the cry-bully degrades public debate, turning it into something resembling primary-school playtime, complete with tell-tales, bullies and playground monitors.

It used to be the case that only masochists welcomed their own victimisation. But in these late-modern times such can be the rewards of victimhood – sympathy, elevated social status, even financial support – that some high-profile figures have taken to fabricating the victim experience. In 2008, Hillary Clinton flagrantly lied about having to run for cover from sniper fire after her plane landed in Tuzla, Bosnia in 1996. The sniper story was concocted in the run-up to the Democratic presidential candidate election to imply that Clinton was someone with battle-hardened foreign policy credentials. But the story backfired when it was later revealed that Clinton had fabricated the entire event and that the only thing pointed at her on that Bosnian runway was a camera lens at an organised photoshoot. Clinton's outrageous deceit barely registered with the public, suggesting perhaps that a shift in society's relationship to agentic victimhood was already under way. Certainly, in subsequent years, the tendency to elaborate on or even exaggerate a victim experience has become a common occurrence, especially in the world of celebrity where it's been suspected of many from Jussie Smollett to Elizabeth Warren, Bubba Wallace to Amber Heard. But claims of victimisation are by no means the preserve of public figures. In his extensive research, the Kentucky State University political scientist Wilfred Reilly has documented hundreds of claims of racial victimisation that subsequently turned out to be either 'flamboyant misunderstandings or out-and-out fakes'.[8]

This desire to embody victimhood, to use it as a sort of prestige good or form of cultural currency, has also gained popularity among children and adolescents. On TikTok it is common for young people to self-diagnose (usually erroneously) quite serious mental health disorders, especially those involving trauma experienced during childhood. If there's one thing we know about teenage interests, it's that they are especially susceptible to fads and fashions, and this is clearly the case with the subsection of young people who, for whatever reason, now crave association with serious mental illness. In 2021, the dubious clinical syndrome dissociative identity disorder (DID) started trending on TikTok, with one controversial video racking up over 5 million views. These daft videos, full of childish talk of so-called 'alters' (alternative personalities handily complete with their own gender pronouns) and 'systems' (the complex network of personalities that DID sufferers struggle to control), are often posted by flamboyant characters who seem equally interested in matters relating to gender fluidity.[9] The attention-seeking videos at the heart of the online 'DID community' are mostly absurd and almost certainly fake, but this hasn't stopped countless youthful TikTokers flocking to watch and often bizarrely identify with these immature tales of faux psychological trauma.

By manufacturing victimhood in such ways, Anglo-American society has turned vulnerability into almost a default existential position, 'a badge of honour' in the words of the Greek sociologist Nikos Sotirakopoulos. This ever-present sense that 'we are all victims now,' has made it much easier to scale victimisation and oppression at the broader social and political level – something that is already having infantilising consequences. For example, while hate crimes sadly remain a frequent occurrence in the UK, in recent years the concept has been fundamentally undermined by the ever-expanding legal definition of what constitutes 'hate'. In the UK, thanks in large part to a series of poor decisions by senior police managers, almost anything can be classed as a hate crime. In West Yorkshire, a swimming teacher was landed with a police record after a child's mother claimed her son had been allowed to bang his head against the side of the pool 'due to his ethnicity'. Similarly absurd was the Buckinghamshire pensioner who in 2018 was investigated by police for a 'racially aggravated public-order offence' after she beeped her horn in a supposedly racist manner at a black driver on a petrol station forecourt. Thousands of such 'offences' are now recorded each year under the dangerously elastic term 'non-crime hate incidents' – social or online interactions recorded by the police which, although offensive, do not meet the legal hate-crime threshold, but which leave those charged with a police record that can potentially remain on file for up to six years. Here, the criteria for deciding whether an incident is hateful or not are simply decided by the accuser, an ill-conceived victim-first principle that potentially turns even the most microscopic offence or resentful comment into a police matter.

When victimhood is constructed as a virtue and, more importantly, when it is considered to be something *always there*, a sort of cultural entity residing just below the surface, it's hardly surprising that many people have come to internalise vulnerability as their default worldview. It is perhaps this sense of resignation in the face of late-modern life and its apparent oppressive dangers that accounts for why so many people enthusiastically welcomed lockdown after lockdown during the Covid-19 outbreak. As vulnerable beings, confronted at every turn by potentially oppressive experiences, too many appeared delighted to accept the pandemic discourse with its childish gesture politics ('Clap for carers', 'We're all in this together'), mawkish media coverage, and infantilising instructions about how to wash your hands or to be 'jolly careful' at Christmas – when Christmas wasn't cancelled entirely (see Plate 16). But it's when collective feelings of victimisation get mixed up with personal, identity-based concerns that things really start to spiral out of control.

Plate 16: So pronounced were the themes of vulnerabilisation and infantilisation during the Covid-19 crisis that even superheroes were turned into supplicants. (Craig Perkins/SWNS)

Earlier, we saw how the university campus has once again emerged as a febrile site of political upheaval and student militancy. Typically underpinned by transcendent, crypto-Marxist dogma, the new student left views the world and its problems through a binary lens of the 'privileged' and the 'oppressed'. The problem with this dialectic is that because it's predicated on the notion of identity politics, the victim-centric worldview of the new campus thought-police is for the most part an infantilised one. Both in terms of its inherent authoritarianism (ideological transgressors must be punished, heretical voices silenced, etc.) and its factional elitism, the 'Social Justice Warrior' perspective too often appears like a childhood morality tale: a fantasy meta-narrative divorced from the day-to-day realities of the marginalised groups these student activists claim to represent. This sense of estrangement from ordinary people and their actual concerns is in large part a product of the demographics and intellectual backgrounds of the Woke movement's self-appointed spokespeople. Long gone are Antonio Gramsci's 'organic intellectuals' – working-class political thought leaders capable of representing the problems of their own class stratum – replaced instead with a university-ordained ministry of intersectional clerics whose primary mode of reasoning is to scream their demands like children in the run-up to Christmas. Mostly the offspring of the privileged and pampered middle class, what these synthetic revolutionaries lack in popular political support they make up for in Woke victimhood, often bathing in the rewards of their self-confessed oppression online via carefully coordinated Twitter/X and Instagram networks.

What these political movements miss is the fundamental truth that, for progress to become a reality, mass public buy-in is a prerequisite. For that to happen, one has to offer something more substantial than a lexicon of post-structural buzzwords. Likewise, simply adding the adjective 'critical' in front of pre-existing academic subjects or reducing complex socio-political problems to three-word slogans might work in the university seminar room when surrounded by fellow activist-students, but it's not going to garner support from voters dismissed as 'deplorables' or heteronormative racists. But in a victim-based politics that favours censoriousness and top-down cultural hectoring over materialist analysis, does this even matter? Why forge meaningful links to the working-class if the goal is the creation of a new ruling intersectional elite whose power is derived not from the ballot box but from a Gramscian 'long march' through the corporate and cultural institutions? And herein lies the issue. How much of the new politics of Wokecraft is truly socially transformative, and how much simply about subverting existing social norms in the interests of divisive victim-based identitarianism?

In an infamous 2013 essay entitled 'Exiting the Vampire Castle', the social theorist Mark Fisher described these posh-left moralisers as 'neo-anarchists'. Drawn from 'a petit-bourgeois background, if not from somewhere even more class-privileged', neo-anarchists have 'experienced nothing but capitalist realism', and as a result operate without any meaningful sense of class consciousness. According to Fisher, the natural habitat of the neo-anarchist is the university campus and Twitter/X, a bourgeois-liberal configuration that he wryly termed 'the Vampires' Castle': 'The Vampires' Castle specialises in propagating guilt. It is driven by a *priest's desire* to excommunicate and condemn, an *academic-pedant's desire* to be the first to be seen to spot a mistake, and a *hipster's desire* to be one of the in-crowd.' Fisher hoped the Vampires' Castle would eventually be toppled by a revanchist working-class left capable of 'comradeship and solidarity instead of doing capital's work for it by condemning and abusing each other'. However, a decade on from his article and precisely the opposite has happened. Instead of collapsing, the Vampires' Castle has added all sorts of new battlements, keeps and gatehouses. Consequently, victimhood is even more normalised, and oppression as an interpretive framework for understanding the world has largely replaced material exploitation as the dominant form of political analysis/explanation. Fisher committed suicide in 2017 and thus is no longer here to comment on the sheer scale of the contemporary Vampires' Castle. But his writing was perspicacious enough to recognise the dark pathologies that today take place within its catacombs: 'This priesthood of bad conscience, this nest of pious guilt-mongers, is exactly what Nietzsche predicted when he said that something worse than Christianity was already on the way. Now, here it is . . .'[10]

In *Ordinary Vices*, the political theorist and Nietzsche scholar Judith Shklar wrote about this precise point, albeit at a different moment in history. She warned us that cruelty and physical violence are not the sole preserve of the state and its officials, but can also be undertaken by those who claim to *oppose* oppression. According to Shklar, individuals and groups who believe they are fighting against injustice or cruel forms of inequality also have the capacity to degenerate into authoritarianism. Shklar called this tendency 'moral' or 'pious' cruelty. One need not look too far to see evidence of Shklar's pious cruelty in our current political moment.[11] The incomprehensible chaos of the world and its resultant inequalities mean we have entered volatile, disorienting times. However, rather than confront this situation in a clear-sighted way, many instead resort to forms of emotive politics based on moral victimhood, a strategy that, although superficially well intentioned, functions only to further divide already fractured communities.

Currently, when we think of this mode of politics, we associate it with 'neo-anarchistic' forms of Woke activism, but victim-based political narratives are also a common feature of other highly charged political ecosystems. Many far-right extremists, for example, construct their victimisation through exactly the same political and cultural lenses as traditional liberals. It's a similar story with the so-called 'incel' movement – the fringe online masculine subculture that trades in misogyny, victimhood and fatalism, and which occasionally spits out dangerously troubled individuals who seek to overcome their sexual misery by engaging in acts of extreme violence. As Simon Cottee points out, while incels range in form and type, one thing – perhaps the only thing – that unites them is their shared sense of victimisation:

The incel subculture is a brotherhood of the shipwrecked and the defeated. Incels portray themselves as accursed victims who are triply wronged: first, by genetics (they lament that they are not tall enough, that they are not good-looking enough, that they are not fit enough etc.); second, by women, who they blame for

278

rejecting them; and third, by society at large, for the contempt and indifference it exhibits toward incels. These wrongs are described by incels in catastrophic language as deep wounds and traumas to the self. Indeed, the incel subculture is first and foremost a wound culture that thrives, indeed engorges, on the psychological suffering of its members.[12]

The poster boy for many incels is Elliot Rodger, the twenty-two-year-old university dropout who murdered six people and injured fourteen others during a spree killing in Santa Barbara, California in 2014. Over many years of embodied inceldom, Rodger essentially succeeded in inverting the classic perpetrator–victim dyad, viewing himself as a wronged victim as opposed to the murderous, shame-filled loser he actually was. Before commencing his attack, Rodger posted a video online justifying his actions. It is, in Cottee's words, 'saturated in self-pity, narcissistic self-regard, resentment, shame and rage'. But it also points to something else. It highlights the infantilised worldview of incels and other prominent alt-right 'manosphere' subcultures: the deep-rooted victim mindset, the emotionally immature desire for never-ending revenge, and the childish sense of entitlement and expectation that the world must revolve around them and their often pathetically adolescent sexual requirements.

And of course, no account, no matter how brief, of the way victimhood has been mobilised in contemporary politics would be complete without mentioning Islamist terrorism and the radicalised losers of Western jihadism. Much has been written about the young men (and occasionally young women) who carry out the Islamic State- and Al Qaeda-inspired attacks that intermittently convulse cities across the globe. Typically, this commentary relies on a series of media clichés to describe these terrorist actors ('evil madmen', 'quiet loners', etc.). Yet, if we look beyond the stereotypes, it's clear that many of the perpetrators also epitomise the conflation of victimisation and infantilisation outlined in this chapter. To start with there's the bristling sensitivity to the slightest slur or challenge to their worldview. Then there's the way jihadists are regularly seduced by the mythic narratives and childish 'heroic fantasies' associated with so-called 'jihadi cool' (with its attendant fashion, poetry, *nasheeds* and dream interpretation). Indeed, as numerous terrorist scholars have pointed out, radical jihad, with its juvenile badassery, offers troubled emerging (Muslim) adults an alternative narrative to the secular materialism of the West: an exciting and immersive subcultural universe forged out of perceived victimisation and a quest for existential meaning.[13] Even the term 'Islamophobia' is infantilising – a dismissive way of deflecting legitimate criticism about radical Islam's role in perpetuating medieval forms of discrimination and encouraging violent extremism.[14]

From the moral crusades of illiberal liberals to the moral cruelty of fanatical jihadists, we see how manufactured victimhood exacerbates emotionality and diminishes the capacity of adults to act rationally. Leaning on Fisher's Vampires' Castle metaphor in a recent article about his former days as a Marxist student activist, the writer Tobias Phibbs describes the current political moment as an 'ouroboros of emotional manipulation'. It is a powerful and succinct summary that captures not just the lamentable state of contemporary politics but also the psycho-biographical insecurity that often resides just below the surface of these infantilised pseudo-political outbursts.

Whenever a clip goes viral of a person, clearly in some mental distress, repeating the usual platitudes, it is impossible not to see the anxieties of life under late modernity writ large. They are there in the voice, constantly on the point of breaking, in the incredulous,

280

widening eyes, and in the earnestly furrowed brow. It is a recognisable form of distress, but not one found among those at the sharp end of genuine political tyranny or destitution. It is hard not to conclude that a whole generation has been terribly misled about how best to pursue a life of meaning and resilience.[15]

As our society has afforded victimhood greater and greater prestige, the emotive signalling of self-declared oppression has become a prominent feature of public discourse. Whether it's screaming in the face of an opponent at a political rally, or cry-bullying your way out of a Twitter/X faux pas, victimhood yields a host of personal benefits. No surprise, then, that behavioural scientists have recently identified a distinct new personality type that consciously co-opts victim status for personal gain. After conducting a series of moral experiments, researchers at the fabulously named University of British Columbia's Immorality Lab identified that those who regularly signal personal victimhood (whether real, exaggerated or false), are more prone to lying, cheating and other forms of deception to advance their own interests. More worryingly, Immorality Lab researchers also found that individuals possessing the 'Dark Triad' of behavioural traits ('Machiavellianism, Narcissism, Psychopathy'), 'more frequently signal virtuous victimhood, [after] controlling for demographic and socio-economic variables that are commonly associated with victimisation in Western societies.'[16] In short, signalling victimhood or emitting self-oppression have become *manipulative strategies* that can be used either to attain personal rewards or as a powerful symbolic resource to be deployed in the trenches of the twenty-first-century culture wars.

In *Arrested Development*, Calcutt had much to say about the emergence of a new cultural personality, something constituted out of a convergence of, on the one hand, the childlike young adult unwilling to transition into an adult world of rationality and responsibility, and on the other, a permanently 'at risk' individual unable to assert agency in the face of putative risks. Twenty years on, and while Calcutt's prognosis is still unfolding, it's clear that key aspects of his formulation are already with us. By celebrating a new type of agentic victim, Anglo-American culture has undermined the idea of young adults as strident, history-shaping subjects, substituting instead a culture of infantilised, reactive vulnerability. Two problems inevitably stem from this situation.

First, and most obviously, if we are indeed 'all victims now', it makes it considerably more difficult to identify genuine victims of abuse and alleviate their suffering via established forms of victim support. Second, when citizens act victimised and childlike, it becomes much easier to remould 'the individual's relationship to the state in accordance with his supposed immaturity'.[17] In other words, and as we will see in the final chapter, just as religious leaders prefer compliant, unquestioning followers, there are major advantages both for the state and for corporations to have large numbers of people whose primary sense of agency is wrapped up in childlike narratives of narcissistic victimisation.

At the end of *Arrested Development*, Calcutt posed the reader a question: given an emerging new political order 'in which the victim is supreme, and adults are treated more like children . . .' will 'adulthood go into abeyance' or can 'the end of adulthood be resisted by a critique of infantilism and the reclamation of subjectivity'? In the two decades since Calcutt wrote these words, infantilism has only continued to grow, untroubled for the most part by any serious socio-political critique. Over the same period, however, there has indeed been something of a 'reclamation of subjectivity'. The problem, as we shall now see, is that it is nothing like the type of prosocial subjectivity Calcutt was hoping for.

The narcissism-infantilism dynamic: Christopher Lasch and 'the infantile illusion of omnipotence'

I feel like I'm the worst, so I always act like I'm the best.

Marina and the Diamonds, 'Oh no!', 2010

One of the consequences of being a criminologist is that you get to experience all sorts of unusual and sometimes dangerous spaces. Over the years, I've spent time in US neighbourhoods wracked by street gangs and crack cocaine, criss-crossed favelas and slums, and visited an array of prisons, including Rikers Island in New York City and Brazil's biggest penitentiary, the notorious Presídio Central de Porto Alegre. On leaving these environments my first thought, usually over a stiff drink in the closest bar I can find, is how desperate and fragile life is in these places. Recently, however, among some of my criminological colleagues, I've noticed a rather different reaction to fieldwork experiences in challenging locations. Instead of foregrounding the plight of the inhabitants of prisons, bad neighbourhoods, refugee detention centres, etc., they instead prioritise how the experience affected *them*. Indeed, it's now quite common for academics, often under the guise of auto-ethnography, to write *entire papers* on how they themselves have been 'traumatised' by what they term 'the emotional labour' expended during a visit or research stay. On this point, criminologists are not alone.

The tendency to insert oneself into the narrative has become an all-too common feature of contemporary cultural life. Consider the recent Russian invasion of Ukraine. As the bombs rained down on Mariupol and Kyiv, a cavalcade of US celebrities lined up to make the conflict all about themselves and their own personal issues. In the US, *The View* co-host Joy Behar, for example, showed her caring side by saying she was 'scared' the troubles in Ukraine would scupper her upcoming Italian vacation plans. Pro-wrestler and actor John Cena likewise weighed in, using the geo-political tragedy as an excuse to promote his new HBO series *Peacemaker*, gratuitously tweeting 'If I could somehow summon the powers of real life #Peacemaker, I think this would be a great time to do so.'[18] Not to be left out, British celebrities James Corden and Holly Willoughby expressed their anguish about the invasion. Not so much about the actual victims of the bombings. Instead, for the privileged multimillionaires Corden and Willoughby, the central problem was how *they* were going to have to explain the violence to *their* children. But the cherry on top of the celebrity narcissist parfait surely went to former *90210* actress and budding foreign policy expert, AnnaLynne McCord, who uploaded a two-minute video to Twitter in which she narrated a self-penned poem addressed personally to Vladimir Putin. According to McCord's sonnet, none of this nasty invasion business would have happened if she had been there to nurture Putin as a child ('*If I was your mother, you would have been so loved, held in the arms of joyous light . . .*').

The only surprising thing about all this weapons-grade self-indulgence is that it's no longer surprising. For well over a decade, scholars from various disciplines have talked about a growing 'epidemic' of narcissism. The type of behaviour outlined above is just further proof that, in Hollywood and elsewhere, the only way many people can view the world and its troubles these days is through the lens of self. In this section, however, my goal is not to dissect every aspect of narcissism as a psychiatric phenomenon, but to focus instead on its specific role in buttressing late-modern infantilism.

The classical myth of Narcissus has been used by psychoanalysts for over a century to explain behaviour such as all-enveloping vanity and the excessive admiration of the self. The term was first appropriated by the sexologist Havelock Ellis in 1898 but came to prominence within psychiatry in 1914 when Sigmund Freud stated, somewhat confusingly, that narcissism was both a necessary feature of human personality development and a potential source of pathology. For the next fifty years, narcissism existed as something of a contested psychological category, as analysts attempted to resolve the ambiguity at the heart of the Freudian framework. Despite the often-intense nature of this debate, it remained the case that narcissism was largely a specialist psychiatric concern. All this changed, however, in the 1970s, when two psychoanalysts exposed the subject to wider public attention.

The 'new narcissism' of the 1970s was in large part kickstarted by Heinz Kohut, who gave the concept a particularly American sheen by emphasising the progressive aspects of self-admiration. Sympathetic to the Sixties counterculture movement, Kohut 'applauded the rising generation's search for intense inner experience, whether abetted by surrender to the intoxications of drugs and music or by immersion in the teachings of Eastern philosophy'.[19] Like Freud, Kohut believed narcissism was a necessary element of the human condition, but in the latter's hands the concept was set free from its roots in early childhood ego development and used as justification for the rising tide of gratification and self-absorption that had become a characteristic feature of American society by the end of the 1960s.

The second key figure in the emergence of narcissism was the pioneer of transference-based psychotherapy, Otto Kernberg. Based in the early part of his career at the Menninger Foundation in Topeka, Kansas, the Vienna-born psychoanalyst Kernberg had treated a large number of patients with severe personality disorders and this experience had given him a far more negative view of narcissism than the more generative version promoted by Kohut. For Kernberg, the narcissist was a 'malignant' figure, a seductive, superficial actor who was unable to maintain deep relationships, and whose high regard for himself trumped everything else. But importantly, the narcissist's exaggerated and unending search for personal supremacy was a form of personality subterfuge, a way of masking a deep-rooted sense of existential inadequacy and psychological emptiness.

The fact that Kernberg and Kohut differed in their respective analyses of the narcissistic personality did not stop the concept from becoming incredibly popular during the 1970s. On the contrary, it was the term's very plasticity that allowed it to be used as a catch-all explanation for many of the ills blighting American society at that time.

It is generally acknowledged that the prime mover in the popularisation of narcissism in America and beyond was the cultural historian and polemicist Christopher Lasch. In his bestselling book, *The Culture of Narcissism: American Life in An Age of Diminishing Expectations*, Lasch blended the psychiatric literature on the narcissistic personality with sociological, historical and literary references to launch a full-on assault on the American way of life. He portrayed America at the end of the 1970s as a broken, almost debased society, undermined by a combination of consumerism, moral relativism, a fixation with therapeutic culture and fashionable forms of New Age spiritualism and, perhaps most importantly, the devaluation of family values and other traditional concerns which he believed were essential in providing young people with strong and effective ego ideals. To make sense of what he described as 'the disintegration of public life' and its replacement with a culture of 'asocial individualism', Lasch seized on the psychiatric concept of narcissism. But rather than sticking to the clinical ideal of narcissism as an inner, psychic experience associated with the early stages of human development, Lasch expanded the concept so that it could be applied at a *cultural* level.

For some commentators, this conceptual slippage was

problematic, but for his growing number of readers and supporters – which included incumbent US President Jimmy Carter, who drew heavily on Lasch's arguments in his famous 1979 'malaise' speech – the use of narcissism to explain the prevailing form of social life in 1970s America was a masterstroke. It's perhaps because of Carter's speech that *The Culture of Narcissism* is best remembered today as a searing critique of consumer culture. Yet the book is much more complex than that. Often overlooked is the fact it also had a fair bit to say about infantilism – or what Lasch termed the 'infantile illusion of omnipotence'. This being the case, no account of the postmodern Kidult would be complete without a discussion of Lasch's work.

As already mentioned, prior to Lasch, narcissism was primarily a diagnostic term used by clinicians in relation to certain personality disorders. The genius of Lasch was to recognise that, 'in a more subdued form', narcissistic traits and other forms of self-admiration had become normal features of the late-1970s 'cultural scene'. But what caused this proliferation of behavioural narcissism? In its classic Freudian formulation, ('primary') narcissism is a normal psychic defence mechanism against the feelings of helpless dependency experienced in early life. Over time, these feelings of grandiosity and self-centredness dissipate as the child comes to understand their place within a wider latticework of social relations. However, in Lasch's account, modern capitalist society has prolonged 'the experience of dependence into adult life', and by doing so encouraged 'milder forms of narcissism in people who might otherwise come to terms with the inescapable limits on their personal freedom and power'.

According to Lasch, the undermining of the family unit and the subsequent destabilisation of traditional parental functions had severed the prevailing sense of historical continuity, bringing about a collapse in established, psychologically engrained ideals – including 'the internalisation of others' expectations and of the traits we love and admire in them'. As a result, the need for recognition and approval was no longer linked to fixed figures but could be sourced from elsewhere – most obviously, popular culture. (Interestingly, it was around this time that the construct of 'self-esteem' emerged as a flawed substitute for the collapsing forms of recognition linked to the father or other traditional generational figures.) For Lasch, the individual was further 'privatised' by the false promises associated with the self-empowerment movement, as religion and community were beaten back by the rise of what he termed 'the therapeutic sensibility':

> People today hunger not for personal salvation, let alone for the restoration of a golden age, but for the feeling, the momentary illusion, of personal wellbeing, health, and psychic security. Even the radicalism of the sixties served, for many of those who embraced it for personal rather than political reasons, not as a substitute religion but as a form of therapy. Radical politics filled empty lives, provided a sense of meaning and purpose.[20]

These transformations in the psychic and moral fabric of the American character were significant enough in themselves to be ontologically destabilising, but as Lasch pointed out, they were closely accompanied by a host of other then-emerging cultural phenomena – sexual permissiveness, the anti-authoritarianism associated with drug use and other 'deviant' subcultures and, at the end of the 1970s, the rise of the self-actualisation movement with its emphasis on material success and self-admiration – that together helped fashion a new type of inward-directed individual. If every age creates its own forms of pathology, then according to Lasch, the post-1965 period had normalised the narcissistic pursuit of the self as the primary source of value.

The wider social consequences of this situation were disastrous. Despite all her restless energy and 'permissiveness', the new cultural narcissist of the 1970s was minimised by inescapable feelings of emptiness – or what Lasch called a 'void within' – that she tried to fill with a confection of self-esteem, hedonism and playful consumerism. But such pursuits do not provide the authentic connection to the world that comes from meaningful work, family or a sense of generational continuity. Lingering below the surface was the feeling that something important was missing: specifically, a lack of commitment to something bigger than the self, the absence of a sense of love as self-sacrifice, and the moral validation one receives from being connected to community groupings or prosocial institutions.

There was, of course, one beneficiary of the hollowed-out interior life associated with the new age of cultural narcissism: the market. The rampant individualism and personal entrepreneurship that are inevitable by-products of self-aggrandisement were the perfect fit for a capitalist system which by the early 1970s had already deftly repackaged youthful inhibition, freedom and other key tropes associated with Sixties counterculture in the form of lifestyle consumerism.

In making these arguments, Lasch often confronts the subject of infantilism head on. For example, not only is there much talk of the 'grandiose, narcissistic, infantile, empty self', but he also expresses concern about the 'fantasies of omnipotence' associated with 'eternal youth', as well as 'the dread of old age and death' that, he claimed, was in some ways 'the most characteristic expression of the times'. Lasch's preoccupation with Freudian thought also saw him expound upon how the 'well-known cult of youth' reordered family life and destabilised generational continuity by making it more difficult for children to relate to older generations. These themes were developed further in his lesser known but equally insightful 1984 book, *The Minimal Self: Psychic Survival in*

Troubled Times. Primarily concerned with how 'the self contracts to a defensive core' as a hedge against economic and emotional adversity, *The Minimal Self* also deals with another subject that is often overlooked in his work, the erosion of generational differences.

Lasch claimed that 'the glorification of youth' and 'weakened parental authority' had combined to create a tautological family dynamic predicated on the illusory ideal 'that *everyone* should be equal'. In his account, the modern American family of the 1980s was increasingly predicated on 'a collective fantasy of generational equality' – a fashionable 'child-centric' phenomenon that is 'the product of egalitarian ideology, consumer capitalism and therapeutic intervention'. It is a critical observation that closely resonates with my own concept of generational mulch, as the following quote makes clear: 'Reluctant to claim the authority of superior experience, parents seek to become their children's companions. They cultivate a youthful appearance and youthful tastes, learn the latest slang, and throw themselves into their children's activities. They do everything possible, in short, to minimize the difference between generations.'[21]

Despite such observations, Lasch's insights into infantilisation (and adultification) are often subsumed in his more general argument about the emergence of cultural narcissism as a pervasive social characteristic. This is a mistake, for there is much to be gained from his thinking in this area. To illustrate this, I will now develop some of Lasch's ideas by situating them within contemporary culture. Taken together, these three elements constitute what I term the contemporary *narcissism–infantilism dynamic*.

1. *The transformation of parenthood and the erosion of the family as the last bastion against capitalist encroachment*: On parenting, as

with so many of today's other cultural hot topics, Lasch was incredibly perspicacious. For example, in the following quote from *The Culture of Narcissism* he pre-empts concepts like 'helicopter parenting' and 'safetyism' by some forty years – and in so doing perfectly explains the intergenerational pantomime that perplexed Carol Blymire in the vignette that opened Part II of the book:

> The mother in particular, on whom the work of childrearing devolves by default, attempts to become an ideal parent, compensating for her lack of spontaneous feeling for the child by smothering him with solicitude. Abstractly convinced that her child deserves the best of everything, she arranges each detail of his life with a punctilious zeal that undermines his initiative and destroys the capacity for self-help ... His idealistically inflated impressions of the mother persist unmodified by later experience, mingling in his unconscious thoughts with fantasies of infantile omnipotence.[22]

As early as 1979, Lasch understood that family life was being crushed by a combination of mass culture and fashionable forms of behavioural parenting that sought to erode generational differences. He identified the emergence of an entirely new child-rearing culture in which 'narcissistic parents' either conceal their familial shortcomings 'beneath an appearance of continual solicitude' or, worse still, overcompensate by fuelling their child's fantasies rather than their developmental or interpersonal needs.

Forty years on from Lasch's observations and it's generally acknowledged by contemporary scholars that the primary source of narcissism and self-entitlement is indeed over-indulgent parenting. In their bestselling book *The Narcissism Epidemic: Living in the Age of Entitlement*, American psychologists Jean

Twenge and W. Keith Campbell are in no doubt that 'a new parenting culture' is to blame for the contemporary narcissism crisis. Having the advantage of several decades of empirical data based on the Narcissistic Personality Inventory (NPI), Twenge, Campbell and their co-researchers analysed eighty-five samples of 16,275 American college students who filled out the NPI between 1979 and 2006, noting that: 'by 2006, two-thirds of college students scored above the scale's original 1979–85 sample, a 30% increase in only two decades . . . In other words, the narcissism epidemic is just as widespread as the obesity epidemic.'[23]

Twenge and Campbell deploy several colourful terms to describe the processes and products associated with the over-indulgent/over-praising parenting style, including 'raising royalty', 'Indigo children' and 'princess parenting'. According to their research, modern parents have been seduced by the tyranny of self-esteem, believing incorrectly that self-admiration bolsters confidence as opposed to what it actually creates – subclinical cultural narcissism. Their research also provides empirical evidence for something else Lasch hinted at: the reversal of the obedience dynamic so that parents find themselves on an equal, if not at times subservient, footing to their offspring. Drawing on fifty years of survey data, they show that, while mothers and fathers in the 1950s and 1960s prized obedience in their children above all other characteristics, their twenty-first-century counterparts have very different priorities. In fact, today's permissive parents appear more interested in being their child's friend rather than acting as a source of generational authority.

Lasch also identified another influential force acting to erode family life and encourage generational mulch. However, this time, rather than the concern being about how the family is being corroded from within, the focus is on the 'appropriation of family functions by outside agencies', particularly bloated state bureaucracies and the self-appointed experts of the health and therapeutic industries. One of the striking features of contemporary social life is the way our sense of self is filtered through a combination of expert opinion and the new ideologies of self-care linked to therapeutic forms of social policy and governmental advice. At almost every turn, we are invoked to change our ways, to moderate our lifestyles, to adopt 'mindful' practices that accord to someone else's view of optimal human behaviour. Even the notion of happiness itself is today quantified by self-styled 'happiness experts' who trade in wellbeing metrics and other poorly conceived abstracted affect-based calibrations.[24] How did this situation come about? Why do so many people diminish their autonomy by cleaving to the fashionable vicissitudes of expert advice?

One of Lasch's central arguments is that, while modern capitalism 'severed the ties of personal dependency' that bound us to the kings, priests and landed overlords of 'the old paternalism', it quickly reconstructed a new mode of dependence, this time 'under cover of bureaucratic rationality'. A fundamental feature of this 'new paternalism' was the rise to prominence of what he termed the 'helping professions': the 'practitioners of a new form of 'priest-craft' that 'undermined the family's capacity to provide for itself'. For Lasch, these new experts diminished the family in several important ways, not least by replacing fundamental human qualities such as 'the mother's instinct for childrearing' with 'a body of esoteric lore accessible only to the initiated'.[25] In this new world of the parental expert, every traditional aspect of child-rearing is picked over and questioned, from how to direct children's play to who is deemed a suitable babysitter. This expansion of the jurisdiction of child-care experts and mental health practitioners has resulted in a risk-driven state of affairs which has served to exacerbate parental fears about things they previously took for granted.

In the same way the therapeutic-bureaucratic expert has assumed responsibility for children's healthcare and lifestyle management, the school has taken over many of the family's traditional instructional functions, often turning the classroom into a site of moral indoctrination or, as we saw in the previous chapter, a playground laboratory designed to solve society's problems. (The entrenchment of bureaucratic dependency in the form of a commitment to professional expertise and hierarchical social ordering is further galvanised by the fact that the late-modern education system now extends further and further into the life course.)

But while the 'democratised' school is big on virtuous posturing and promoting fashionable liberal orthodoxies, it typically has less to say these days about family values, personal responsibility or historic and civic continuity – ideals that are essential if we are to counter the narcissistic trend of our culture and uphold a sense of generational stability.

2. The infantile narcissist's dependence on the 'intricate, supremely sophisticated life-support systems' associated with consumerism: In *The Minimal Self*, Lasch develops his earlier critique of consumer culture, asserting that 'culture organised around mass consumption encourages narcissism – which we can define, for the moment, as a disposition to see the world as a mirror, more particularly as a projection of one's own fears and desires – not least because it makes people grasping and self-assertive but because it makes them weak and dependent'.[26] By using the term 'the world as a mirror,' Lasch is evoking that early stage of human emotional development (what Freud termed 'primary narcissism') when the subject is in love with the image of themselves and their own bodies and which precedes the love of others. Over time, during normal childhood development, such feelings of self-centredness should dissipate as the child begins to understand that they are part of something bigger than themselves. However, as Lasch explains, under late-capitalist conditions, the fascination with self-image endures and now manifests itself in infantile feelings of dependency and the constant need for gratification in adult life. It is a state of being that has long been recognised within advertising circles and was memorably characterised as early as 1983 by the psychologist Dan Kiley as 'the Peter Pan Syndrome'. According to Kiley, the Peter Pan-adult is characterised by narcissism and an apparent carefree playfulness, but also by corresponding feelings of deep-rooted emptiness which he attempts to mask with over-confidence, personal fantasies that bear no resemblance to social reality, and an excessive interest in personal appearance and self-image. And it is this sense of excessive self-care that is one of the more recognisable traits among today's narcissistic Kidult consumers.

As Twenge and Campbell make clear in *The Narcissism Epidemic*, this infatuation with vanity and observing the self is evidenced by the year-on-year increases in invasive plastic surgery, the huge credit card debts accrued purchasing luxury clothing and other high-status products (what they nicely term 'the cascading [economic] consequences of narcissistic spending') and the spectacular expansion of self facilitated by the ability to broadcast one's image on social media. These are all obvious indicators of an intensifying culture of narcissism, but beyond these data points, what does this culture look like at street level?

Consider the contemporary vanity pandemic shaping Anglo-American society. From the rise of the male metrosexual to the penchant for physical extensions (hair, eyelashes, nails) and bodily adornment (piercings, tattoos, branding, lip volumisation, scarification, tooth filing/contouring, ear conching, surgical implants), it's clear that, for many people, the only self that matters today is the one that is purchased and projected. On this point, consider the rise and rise of the tattoo. Once largely the preserve of sailors, convicts and gang members, today tattoos are as ubiquitous as Nike trainers. No doubt, as Slavoj Žižek has pointed out, much of tattooing's appeal stems from the fact that, because of its permanence and painful application, the tattoo represents a visceral attempt to symbolise the un-symbolical (Lacanian) Real. But given tattooing's incredible popularity, it's clear that something else must also be going on. By adopting the perspective of Christopher Lasch, we can see that society's current fixation with tattooing is *a narcissistic attempt to externalise the self*, either via the symbolisation/stylisation of a personal narrative or private obsession, or as a figurative attempt to project an idealised self-image onto the world. In either case, tattooing should be understood as a form of what I term narcissio-glyphics (glyphic here originating from the Greek adjective γλύφω, meaning to carve or engrave a purposeful mark or incision).

An even more obvious example of infantilised appearance management is the fixation (across all genders) with unnaturally groomed pubic hair. Often seen as stemming from the desire to replicate the so-called 'porn-star look', this trend in fact exemplifies a society whose infantile feelings of helplessness are now taking on a physical manifestation. Interestingly, most if not all of these developments are highly individualised fashion statements as opposed to being associated with any form of developed (youth) subculture. Indeed, it's interesting to note that, rather than opposing or challenging mainstream consumerism, these practices represent a form of generalised narcissistic peacockery entirely in keeping with postmodernism's obsession with identity, something very much in evidence in the changing nature of public masculinity.

In the twenty-first century, although the productive aspect of youth culture has virtually stalled as evidenced by the lack of new musical genres or unique subcultural configurations, Anglo-American society has thrown up at least one new ubiquitous 'youth' cultural phenomenon: the narcissistic late-modern hyper lad. Adopting specific transatlantic forms born of different national antecedents, the hyper lad or, more prosaically, 'bro' (and sometimes 'brah' or 'bruh') culture is a brash, loud, body-and-sex-obsessed sub-variant of the Kidult phenomenon that emerged first in the US – the so-called 'American bruh' – before taking hold in Britain. Rooted in a mix of ra-ra frat-boy culture and semi-ironic patriotism, the American bro is a shredded-and-tanned, backward-baseball-cap-and-hoody-wearing, sports-obsessed alpha male, whose capacity to remain 'amped', 'stoked' and 'pumped' is only surpassed by his dedication to pre-loading, pre-gaming and partying. Desperate to be socially acknowledged and digitally immortalised, the American bro is a walking assemblage of the characteristics Lasch identified as being symptomatic of the narcissistic actor. In an unforgiving description by the writer John Saward, the unappeasable appetite, the promiscuity, the superficial insouciance and the unsatisfied oral cravings are all well to the fore:

It is almost 9 AM on St. Patrick's Day, and he is on the Metro North train to Manhattan . . . He is pulsing like the mercury on a cartoon thermometer; he is ready to explode through the glass. It seems impossible for a human being to care this much about recreation, to care this much about celebrating something so tiny, so contrived, but that is why he is alive. He will come, he will see, he will conquer. He will vomit out the window of a taxi. He is the American Bro . . . He is all about CONSUMPTION. Every decision is dictated by the pursuit of this. He consumes women, exploits weaknesses, spends 23 dollars at In-N-Out and posts a picture of the receipt to Instagram. To him, everything is a dick pic, a flex, a look-how-hard-I-get, a watch-me-fuck-the-universe . . . He doesn't simply celebrate his existence; he celebrates how much better his existence is than everyone else's. No one goes as hard as he does; no one has killed it like he has.[27]

Over the years, no cultural outlet has had more to say about bro culture than *Vice* magazine, and so it wasn't surprising that in 2014 one of its more insightful writers, Clive Martin, came up with a moniker for the American bro's UK counterpart – 'the modern British douchebag'. Describing them as 'the sad lost children of the metrosexuals and the miners' and 'looking like Ken dolls dipped in tea and covered in biro', Martin paints an excoriating picture of the British bro, but one that ultimately – and this is important – is not unsympathetic. Channelling his inner Tyler Durden, Martin recognises that behind all the excessive preening, waxing and over-caffeinated cocktails, the modern British douchebag is essentially a masculinity crisis in ripped jeans:

The institutions that gave British men a sense of well-being have been ripped apart. Nobody trusts the police anymore; nobody wants to join the army because no one believes in its wars; traditional industries have been decimated, and the only thing to replace them are stifling, mind-numbing positions in service and retail . . . Because of this, British men have tried to reimagine masculinity, in a hyper-realized, childish desperate way. A new kind of machismo, built on fake bravado and vanity . . . when nobody wants you, you can do what you want.[28]

At this point, it is instructive to revisit Oliver Smith's account of life in the booze-and-brawl landscapes of the British night-time economy, as discussed in Chapter Two. Drawing on first-hand accounts of thirty- and forty-year-old binge drinkers, Smith

298

showed how, because of declining meaningful employment opportunities (the 'age of diminishing expectations' outlined by Lasch), his sample had almost given up on the maturation process, existing instead as 'infantile narcissists' unable to resist 'the shallow pleasures of the night-time leisure experience'. And Smith is not the only criminologist to have identified how the narcissism–infantilism dynamic manifests itself in socially destructive behaviour. In *Criminal Identities and Consumer Culture*, Steve Hall, Simon Winlow and Craig Ancrum undertook a series of lengthy ethnographic interviews with young urban criminals in the marginalised estates of post-industrial north-east England. It is interesting to note that the age profile of the consumerism-obsessed young people interviewed by Hall and his colleagues perfectly maps onto Jeffrey Arnett's 'emerging adulthood' cohort. However, rather than the type of positive journey of 'self-focused exploration' reported by Arnett, Hall and his colleagues found life stories characterised by entrenched disaffection, narcissistic consumerism and, revealingly, infantilisation.

> Our data revealed that for so many who are deeply absorbed in consumer culture, adulthood is now a continuation of narcissistic aspects of the infantile world, and as this simulated faux-adulthood is imposed on the child from an early age [via advertising], we are seeing the end of both traditional childhood and adulthood; distinct life-course stages that are now melding into a single differentiated consumerist form.[29]

By documenting the lives of young criminals in the north-east of England, Hall and his colleagues provide evidence of how consumer-driven narcissism is functioning to propagate new emotional states, feelings, and desires that contribute to *both* the depreciation of mature adulthood and the adultification of very young teenagers whose lifestyle choices and activities involve sexual activity, drugs, criminality, etc. that previously were the preserve of young adults. Evidence, then, of the bidirectional processes of life stage dissolution in action. The work of Smith and Hall et al. is concerned with consumption-driven transgression and predatory criminality respectively, but one could just as easily extend this line of thinking to include the type of hedonistic excess, incivility and narcissistic self-absorption commonly displayed by the hyper lads of American and British bro culture.

3. *The propagation of infantile dreams of fame and glory via media-centred technologies*: Early in *The Culture of Narcissism*, Lasch describes a new type of 'patient' who seeks psychotherapeutic counselling despite not showing any signs of clinical neurosis. Instead, this new breed of analysand manifests only 'vague and ill-defined complaints' linked to a 'hollowed-out interior life' which they then attempt to fill with unhealthy levels of self-absorption. One strategy used to achieve this is, of course, fantasy – but a particular form of fantasy linked to 'nothing more substantial than a wish to be vastly admired, not for one's accomplishments but simply for oneself, uncritically and without reservation'[30] Lasch was writing two decades before the onset of mainstream social media, but it's not hard to see how, yet again, his thinking was astonishingly prescient – this time, prophesying the epidemic of infantilised online narcissism that currently envelops us.

Here, we must return to Twenge and Campbell who, like Lasch, recognised the significance of the psychological symbiosis between fantasy and narcissism. One of the consistent themes in *The Narcissism Epidemic* is the way fantasy in the form of infantile desires, overclaiming and grandiose aspirations has increasingly encroached on reality.[31] According to Twenge and Campbell this process has been ongoing for some time, triggered by a combination of abundant credit and loose lending, a deeply entrenched culture of self-entitlement, a switch from deep to shallow interpersonal relationships, and 'the new Wild West' of the Web 2.0. Even though Twenge and Campbell were writing in 2009, well before the mass explosion of social networking – their main site of analysis was MySpace.com, remember that? – they understood one of the fundamental truths of online culture: that social networking sites and comment-based platforms are the perfect breeding ground for propagating and promoting narcissism.

> First, users can choose to present only the most attractive or cool pictures of themselves – some people call this 'the angles' (for example, you show your good side, or if you're overweight you only show your face) . . . Second, the sites emphasize only certain aspects of people's lives and only certain aspects of their person-alities. Almost invariably, these are the behaviors and traits consistent with narcissism, such as partying, looking hot, having a good-looking boyfriend or girlfriend, or winning a competi-tion . . . Just as animals evolve and change to fit their environ-ments, young people are becoming more narcissistic to fit the demands of the new digital world.[32]

From here, it's a very short step indeed to what Lasch described as the desire 'to be vastly admired, not for one's accomplishments but simply for oneself' – or what four decades later has come to be known as *the will to celebritise*.

According to the NPI, narcissists score highly when responding to statements such as 'I like to be the center of attention', 'I get upset when people don't notice how I look when I go out in public', 'I think I am a special person' and 'I like to show off my body'. No surprise, then, that one of the by-products of social network culture is how many young people are today disproportionately consumed with an infantile quest for fame and celebrity. It is a quest that can take some very dark twists and turns. Thanks largely to social media, we are now regularly confronted with the spectacle of individuals and groups performing, recording, sharing and publishing their acts of deviance – everything from schoolyard bullying to acts of rioting and even terrorism. Again, this is not entirely new, but what is interesting is the way that the nexus of user-generated content and the desire of individuals to aggrandise themselves through self-representation has itself become a motivating factor for deviant behaviour. The criminologist Majid Yar has called this tendency the 'will-to-represent', a new kind of causal inducement to transgress the rules that stems from a 'desire to be seen, and esteemed or celebrated, by others for their criminal activities'.

Twenge and Campbell made a similar point, arguing that social networking has intensified a trend towards seeking fame by hurting someone else. Describing narcissism as a psychological 'cousin' of antisocial personality disorder and psychopathology, they show how 'narcissistic aggression' does not have to be directly physical but can also take the form of 'verbal aggression', i.e., being cruel in an online context – either via practices based around the urge to dominate like cyberbullying, trolling and gaslighting, or simply in the form of generalised spiteful commentary. Narcissists believe their needs and aspirations take precedence over everybody else's. Consequently, they have found a natural home on the internet's comment-based platforms and social media streams, where their desire to be heard, to promote their agenda at all costs, is effortlessly and shamelessly set free via fake (typically anonymous) tough guy-speak and other modes of toxic self-aggrandisement.

In the same year Lasch published *The Culture of Narcissism*, another very different book about narcissism hit the bookstands.

Now largely forgotten, Jules Feiffer's *Tantrum* was a pioneering graphic novel about a forty-two-year-old family man and office worker named Leo Quog who, over the course of 183 cartoon-panelled pages, narcissistically screams himself back to infancy as a way of avoiding adult responsibility. Although Feiffer and Lasch had little in common politically, both writers understood the effect narcissism was having on modern society. However, when it came to concretising the specific cultural link between narcissism and infantilism, Feiffer went even further than Lasch, understanding the fundamental 'pull of infantilisation and its promise to magic away responsibility'.

In a thoughtful commentary on Feiffer's work, Paul Williams argues that *Tantrum* 'develops two themes apparent across Feiffer's oeuvre: male regression back to childhood and the child traversing the adult world unaided'. As with Lasch, a fundamental concern for Feiffer was the new forms of psychotherapy associated with the 'consciousness movement' of the 1960s. In particular, how faddish developments like primal-scream and re-birthing therapies fed into an emerging culture of American narcissism. This concern is vividly illustrated two-thirds of the way through *Tantrum* when Leo – who throughout the graphic novel is depicted as a two-year-old infant who retains the thoughts and speech patterns of an adult – is forced to travel to an Esalen-style retreat in Palm Springs to rescue his sister-in-law, who has become dangerously diminished by alternative therapies that have ravaged her body and corroded her mind. If the story concluded there, 'a Laschian reading would see *Tantrum* as a straightforward morality tale: a fulfilling life is possible if older males embrace their authority over younger family members.'[33] But Feiffer's reading goes well beyond Lasch's argument that narcissism is simply a new form of social pathology. Instead, he makes it clear that, such is the developed state of Leo's personality regression, he is incapable of jettisoning his infantile self. In the final pages of *Tantrum*, Leo abandons his children entirely and strides off into the sunset with his equally regressed adult wife.

By ultimately 'exposing his ill-disciplined children to the emotional vacuum of his own youth', Leo Quog is not just emblematic of American narcissism, he represents an early cultural expression of an adult figure *who wilfully adopts permanent infancy* – both in terms of unreconstructed childishness and the prioritisation of the pleasure principle over the reality principle. Feiffer's Leo Quog is, of course, literally a caricature, a graphic tool for articulating many of the same trends and tendencies outlined in *The Culture of Narcissism*. But beyond that, by emphasising the latter element in the narcissism–infantilism dynamic, *Tantrum* presages precisely the type of life stage dissolution discussed in Chapter Two, as Williams makes clear in the following quote: 'Leo Quog occupies a genuinely indeterminate status, reasoning and conversing like an adult while occupying the physical body (and vulnerability) of an infant.' Proof, if proof were needed, of the power of satire to identify social deformities even before they are fully manifest in society.

On the subject of cautionary satirical observations, most of us will be familiar with the tragic myth of Narcissus, the Greek tale of a young boy who was so impossibly handsome that he fell in love with his own image reflected in a pool of water. In the original version from Greek mythology, Narcissus, unable to tear himself away from the pool, withers away from despair, dying ultimately of thirst and starvation. In the Roman version, the story has a different, more violent ending, as Narcissus is killed for spurning the advances of the beautiful nymph, Echo. In either case, the moral is the same: fixating on the self to the detriment of all else brings with it tragic consequences, whether in the form of slow decay or violent upheaval. Lasch understood this better than anyone. For him, the worst excesses of narcissism, including self-righteous victimhood, produced what he called 'a dying culture' – a society that convinces itself it no longer has a viable future. Under these conditions, any functional sense of community shrinks and is replaced by self-preservation and other new forms of what he called 'psychic survival'. In this new world characterised by individualism, resignation and paranoia, any collective sense of political relations recedes into oblivion, as individuals execute their own emotional retreat from society, fuelled by the fallacies of personal growth and the fantasies of lifestyle consumerism. In the final chapter, I explore this situation in detail, arguing that the inevitable consequence of infantilism is a selfish and stupefied politics that can no longer confront the many juvenile illusions that today pass for insight in our world of unarrested arrested development.

Chapter 8

Pantomime Politics: The Stupefaction and Degradation of the Public Sphere

pantomime: *Brit.* A theatrical entertainment based on a fairy tale.
Oxford English Dictionary

[Pantomime] *does not appeal to our fine perceptions of beauty or wit. Its sentiments are, of course, mostly ludicrous; it is invariably blatant and jingo in its patriotism; its humour has little subtlety.*
A. E. Wilson, 1934[1]

I sat and watched those guys
Debate each other on TV
Politicians, wrestlers
They're all the same to me
Hey, I don't give a damn
Which idiot runs this country
Since I'm the last man on Earth
It don't matter to me
Loudon Wainwright III, 'The Last Man on Earth'

In a July 2023 by-election, the good people of Selby and Ainsty elected twenty-five-year-old Keir Mather as their new Labour MP.

As the country's youngest parliamentarian, and also perhaps because of his head boy-like appearance, the press was quick to resurrect and apply the old moniker 'the Baby of the House' to Maher. However, it wasn't long before he lived up to that sobriquet for an altogether different reason. After Mather was criticised in some quarters for being too young and inexperienced to be a politician, his mother leapt to his defence, protecting her son in the media against such unfair 'ageism'. Not content with telling all the nasty bullies off, she gave another interview where, like a glowing tiger mom at a family gathering, she happily speculated about Maher becoming a future Labour Party leader. There was a time, not so long ago, when politicians didn't need their mums to fight their battles or conduct their PR – but that was a time when politics was still a serious adult business, as opposed to the infantilised clown show it has become today.

In one of the ironies of the age, the more elected officials of all stripes blather on about the importance of 'grown-up politics', the more the political class act like juveniles at a demented high school. Whether it's behaving like attention-seeking adolescents on TikTok, playing *Pokémon GO* or watching porn in parliament, or endlessly parroting childish soundbites in place of actual policies, it's clear that a deep infantocratic impulse exists at the heart of contemporary politics.[2] To make matters worse, this impulse is not limited to politicians. Bereft of any positive moral leadership, too many members of the public also exude an emotive, anti-adult form of political expression that helps explain everything from the toxic fallout over Brexit to 'Trump-derangement syndrome'. Viewed through this lens, then, infantilisation represents something far more serious than just the elongation of youthful pursuits. It suggests a new way of viewing the world that's already shaping our history by damaging democracy and pitting citizens and communities against one another.

In this chapter, I outline the corrosive impact infantilism is having on contemporary political life. By focusing on themes such as the increasingly prominent role of celebrity culture in politics, the high-energy pantomime that today passes for political debate, the growth of conspiratorial and affective online political content, and the emergence of forms of activism and resistance based on infantile emotionalism, I argue that a new *infantocracy* in politics is propelling us in a very dangerous direction that, if left unchecked, could bring about the end of democratic politics as we know it.

Welcome to the infantocracy: The juvenilisation and celebrification of politics

There is, it appears, a worldwide epidemic of infants in positions of political power, and everyone is telling everyone else to grow up.

Samuel Earle[3]

It's not important what famous people say. No. We have to speak about things in the right manner. Not people with no knowledge, like me, talking about something that people with knowledge should talk about.

Jürgen Klopp

Any functioning adult. These three words were a common sight on lawn signs and bumper stickers across the United States in the run-up to the 2020 Presidential election. The slogan was meant as a not-so-subtle commentary on the credibility of the two main electoral candidates, Donald Trump and Joe Biden. But beyond the frustration about the state of American politics, the words captured something else, something deeper: the palpable sense of anxiety in the United States and beyond that twenty-first-century society had entered a distinct new phase that we might call the twilight of judicious adult oversight.

For all the talk about the decaying state of Anglo-American politics, surprisingly little has been written about the role infantilisation has played in this process. One notable exception is a short but insightful article by the novelist and commentator Samuel Earle, in which he deploys the term 'infantocrat' to describe a new breed of contemporary politician who, not content with treating *us* like children, now behave themselves in disturbingly infantile ways.[4] Earle sees Donald Trump as 'the biggest child politician of them all', but unlike most liberal observers he also recognises that the problem of childishness in politics runs much deeper than the forty-fifth president of the United States, who in many ways is simply the inevitable end-product of politico-cultural tendencies that have been under way since at least the mid-1990s.

In *Arrested Development*, Andrew Calcutt recounted the story of the Conservative MP George Walden, who, after announcing he would not be seeking re-election in the 1997 general election, remarked that those in political power were 'treating the public like children with learning difficulties'. Walden was rightly concerned about the way late-twentieth-century politicians had stopped respecting the electorate and were viewing them instead as 'social inadequates . . . incapable of making rational decisions on their own behalf'. Twenty-five years later, and while Walden's comments still ring true,[5] a second, even more worrying infantilising dynamic has emerged to further diminish Anglo-American political relations. This time, however, it doesn't involve top-down derogatory opinions of the voting public, but the infantilisation of the political class itself.

Having previously worked as a public relations executive for a media company, former UK prime minister David Cameron was extremely adept at managing his image. Desperate to come across as an energetic man-of-the-people, the Eton-educated Conservative was a master of the soundbite and the orchestrated photo-op. During his tenure, hoodies were hugged, husky dogs petted, and he made sure he was regularly photographed jogging, surfing, and cycling to work. Given this attention to image management it seemed strange, then, that in 2012, just as his government was facing the dual challenge of the rise of Islamic State and the Eurozone economic crisis, Cameron's PR team drip-fed the press a story about his fixation with *Angry Birds*, the video game in which a flock of animated birds try to save their eggs from green-coloured pigs. The fact that a UK prime minister was burning daylight on such a trivial pastime angered many observers, not least because he had already garnered a reputation as someone with a penchant for 'chillaxing'.[6] On this occasion, however, they needn't have worried. Cameron's *Angry Birds* addiction was, like so much about the man, a contrivance: a calculated attempt to burnish his everyman credentials. However, while UK politicians as far back as Harold Wilson have used pop culture to broaden their electoral appeal, Cameron was the first UK politician to initiate full-on infantocrat mode by unashamedly associating himself with an online children's game.

In Chapter Five I discussed the work of the media theorist Joshua Meyrowitz in relation to how changes in electronic media had contributed to the infantilisation of young people, and it's instructive to draw on his work once again here – this time in relation to what he calls the 'de-imperialising' nature of modern political media coverage. As Meyrowitz notes, historically there have been two main ways to study the image and the rhetoric of political leaders. The first approach involves examining the content and form of speeches and policies. The second focuses more on the situational context in which leaders perform their roles, i.e., less emphasis on political rhetoric and more on the general environment that surrounds those in high office. Meyrowitz favours the latter approach, and thus argues that the declining standards of American politicians has less to do with the individuals themselves, and more with 'a [changing] communication environment that undermines the politician's ability to behave like, and therefore be perceived as, the traditional "great leader". In other words, what is deemed acceptable or 'symbolically appropriate' behaviour for politicians is determined not by their statesmanlike qualities, but by the prevailing 'means of communication and the forums of interaction'.[7] In modern liberal democracies, the political communication environment is shaped by, and increasingly tailored to, social media feeds, soundbites, screen crawls and short-term news cycles, and thus our politicians have inevitably adapted to the 'staging contingencies' associated with this mode of information dissemination. In a mediascape contoured by uncurbed rapidity, what matters most is action rather than adult deliberation, 'delivery' instead of considered enquiry, and image management and 'brand' recognition more than traditional values like integrity, character, and experience. Such tendencies, as we have seen throughout this book, are highly symptomatic of our infantilised world, and so it's hardly surprising that many of our political leaders now engage in symbolic behaviour that is itself infantilised.

In *Peril*, their bestselling book about the final years of Donald Trump's presidency, Bob Woodward and Robert Costa recount the moment when Trump tried to enlist Vice President Mike Pence in his attempt to overturn the 2020 election result. When Pence refused, Trump rounded on him: 'No, no, no! . . . You don't understand, Mike. You can do this. I don't want to be your friend anymore if you don't do this.' Given some of Trump's other adolescent antics, such as his penchant for bestowing infantile nicknames on his political enemies and bragging about the size of his penis on the campaign trail, this is bland stuff. It does, however, neatly illustrate the depths of his childishness. In the words of CNN analyst Chris Cillizza, Trump 'wants what he wants when he wants it. And when he doesn't get what he wants, he throws a temper tantrum.' For Woodward, Costa, Cillizza and countless others, Trump's personality and political style are an affront to politics. But as Samuel Earle makes clear, while Trump is the obvious exemplar of the contemporary infantocrat, he is in no way unique. In fact, as a political trend, infantocracy started well before Trump and extends far beyond him. Consider for example Plate 17, which shows former UK government ministers Ed Balls and Andy Burnham gleefully riding a tyre swing at the opening of a new children's play area as far back as 2008 – a physical manifestation of the new politics of the playground if ever there was one. And then there was former Dutch prime minister Jan Peter Balkenende, who tried to curry favour with the electorate by cashing in on his supposed likeness to Harry Potter. One could even go back as far as the late 1990s, and former Conservative Party leader William Hague's ill-fated promotional strategy that involved plunging down a theme park waterslide wearing a dodgy baseball cap with his own name on it and bragging about drinking fourteen pints of beer a day as a teenager.

Plate 17: 'Playground politics': New Labour ministers Andy Burnham and Ed Balls mix policymaking with a play break at a south London children's park in 2008. (PA Images/Alamy Stock Photo)

When these daft political PR stunts first appeared they naturally stood out against the backdrop of more sober forms of political self-promotion, but a decade and a half later and they are now a commonplace feature of the mediascape, so much so in fact that several contemporary leaders essentially base their political image on juvenile characterological traits. Obvious examples here include Boris Johnson, whose persona is essentially a composite of the-scruffy-kid-who-never-grew-up and a mischievous-public-school-prefect; Silvio Berlusconi, who spent his entire political career playing a rejuvenated pantomime villain; George W. Bush, a breezy, lightweight figure more interested in listening to 'his gut' than his brain; Rishi Sunak, whose urchin suits and nerdy demeanour (the man tried to make a virtue out of his Coca-Cola memorabilia collection for Pete's sake) made him appear more like a wide-eyed sixth-form prefect than an adult statesman; and Justin Trudeau, the self-satisfied Canadian premier who likes nothing better than a bit of make-believe dress-up (Superman, Sikh, Hans Solo, Chinaman, cowboy, black-faced minstrel, etc.) to enhance his 'United Colors of Benetton' political mindset. The problem with this type of infantocracy is that, not only does it degrade the status of high office, but it brings down everything else around it.

For example, instead of adopting the role of a grown-up politician during the 2016 election campaign, Joe Biden often ended up countering Trump's juvenile antics with his own brand of geriatric infantilism. Biden, for example, 'spoke of wanting to "take Trump behind the gym" and made gestures accordingly with his fist – "*if* I were in high school".'[8] Tough talk from someone who used a teenage asthma diagnosis to get five draft deferments from the Vietnam War (despite being fit enough to work as a lifeguard and play college football). And the 46th President's childish behaviour didn't stop there. By 2024, the old duffer was so bereft of adult ideas, he was retweeting Elmo from the children's TV show *Sesame Street*, adding: 'I know it is hard some days to sweep the clouds away and get to sunnier days. Our friend Elmo is right: We have to be there for each other ... Even though it's hard, you're never alone.'[9] It's difficult to know what Amtrak Joe thought was to be gained from engaging with a children's muppet monster, but then again, having himself been ventriloquised for four years, perhaps he'd just grown empathetic towards other puppets.

This playground slide-like descent to the bottom is also evident among female politicians. As the feminist journalist Jill Filipovic has pointed out, women in American politics have long been subjected to condescending and infantilising linguistic attacks by their male colleagues, a process she terms 'girlification' (Nancy Pelosi: Princess Nancy; Elizabeth Warren: Betsy Wetsy/Pocahontas).[10] Today, however, such are the seductions of infantocracy that some female politicians are actively embracing self-infantilising actions in ways that mirror themes favoured by male political Kidults.

In 2017, Hillary Clinton, as desperate as ever to stay relevant, posted a ninety-five-second video message to Twitter in which she likened herself to the DC Comics character Wonder Woman. Given Ms Clinton's long track record of attaching herself to other people's achievements, few were surprised at such gratuitous self-promotion. What is more surprising is the extent to which other female political figures have also associated themselves with superhero culture. Sarah Palin, Michelle Obama, Caroline Kennedy and, of course, Clinton herself have all featured as comic-book superhero characters. Outside of the usual wishy-washy blather about 'empowerment', the logic behind this sort of cartoonification is never made entirely clear. However, what *is* clear is that, as a tool for advancing the political ambitions of these women, these covers have been woefully unsuccessful – and yet the trend continues. In 2019, the high-profile US politician and self-styled activist Alexandria Ocasio-Cortez declared she was humbled (naturally!) when it was announced that, along with other female members of 'The Squad' (four women elected to the 2018 US House of Representatives), she would be the subject of a comic-book series by Devil's Due Comics (see Plate 18). It's easy to make fun of these superhero renderings, but they illustrate an important point – that many of today's politicians (not necessarily those in these illustrations) actually believe that voters will be won over by a juvenile mash-up of comic book aesthetics, 'Girl Boss' power stances and thinly-veiled sexualisation.

Plate 18: 'Narcissists assemble': Alexandria Ocasio-Cortez and the cartoonification of politics. (Devil's Due)

Given the prominent position of superhero films and fiction in contemporary culture, this melding of politics with comic-book characters was perhaps to be expected; another showy by-product of a postmodern world that dissolves everything in a vast, undiscriminating vat of pop-cultural symbolism. Yet if we take a step back from the low-lying ground fog of infantile popular culture that surrounds us, it's clear that the only thing these comic-book super-hero references reinforce is the childish reputation of today's politicians. Consider again Alexandria Ocasio-Cortez. It's not bad enough that her own political proclamations are often childishly over-dramatic – in 2019 she compared ICE border detention centres to Holocaust concentration camps and declared that 'only Nazis oppose open borders' – she must now negotiate her political career against a backdrop of comic-book crusader hype.

The superhero mindset has even permeated UK politics. For example, the Labour MP Jess Phillips's book *Truth to Power: 7 Ways to Call Time on B.S.* is so full of childish references to superheroes, superpowers and 'dark [political] forces', it prompted one reviewer to comment, 'The really striking thing about these passages is what they say about Phillips' regard for her readers and supporters: this is not how you would speak to someone you consider your equal, it's how you would talk to a child.'[11]

The infantocratic impulse of today's political class is further normalised by the shallowness of contemporary media. Not so long ago, it was a common sight on our television screens to see well-informed politicians, seated in leather chairs, debating the issues of the day in a considered fashion. Today, this type of head-to-head discussion has all but disappeared. In its place has emerged a very different form of political discourse attuned instead to the instantaneous demands of rolling news and whatever's trending on Twitter/X. In this world of denuded debate, political speech comes to resemble something akin to a cartoon bubble, a format-dictated mode of expression that functions as the enemy of nuanced, non-patronising communication. Even worse, within the frantic blur of twenty-four-hour news and social media scrolling, complex political issues get flattened out into childish slogans and hashtags ('pizzagate', 'smeargate', 'partygate', 'beergate') and important matters of class and social policy are boiled down to one-dimensional buzzwords and infantile call-out phrases ('Karen', 'gammon', 'Chad').

Such transformations and distortions of political communication can be seen as part of a wider development that Nicholas Carr calls the third big technological makeover of modern electioneering (radio being the first in the 1920s and TV the second in the 1960s). In this new political arena, what matters most is a particular style of message that captures the attention of the perpetually distracted: a glib sound-bite, a catchy phrase or a marketable/Instagrammable political person-ality that is always at the forefront of the discussion, but which para-doxically does not require any 'steady concentration'. In Carr's words, politics conducted via social media 'favors the bitty over the meaty, the cutting over the considered. It also prizes emotionalism over reason. The more visceral the message, the more quickly it circulates and the longer it holds the darting public eye.'[12] In this distorted political context, politicians end up acting and sounding like attention-seeking teenagers desperate to be heard and validated at an out-of-control house party. The consequences of this type of political showing off are predictably embarrassing. Almost every day some politician or other shoots themselves in the foot, either by displaying their ignorance after chiming in on geo-political incidents about which they have no exper-tise, or by getting embroiled in tawdry Twitter/X spats that have all the decorum of a fraternity hazing. Indeed, the very fact that Twitter/X has become the number one source of political news for many people speaks volumes about our infantile times.

Twitter. Even its very name is infantilising. In the mid-twentieth century, Tweety Pie was a children's cartoon character – but now we have the absurdity of people going around declaring 'I've just tweeted something' as if it were an achievement, a mean-ingful contribution to knowledge/society. Any serious politician would immediately recognise the limitations of this mode of trun-cated communication and use it sparingly and judiciously. Not today's infantocrats. More interested in soundbites than structured arguments, and desperate to virtue signal their latest fashionable observation, many of today's demi-witted politicians seem oblivious to the potential danger of instantly blogging their often ill-considered micro thoughts. Later, I will look more closely at how Twitter/X and social media have infantilised political discourse by transforming it into a reductionist like/dislike space with no room for nuanced discussion. But for now, suffice it to say that by helping to dissolve the distinction between fake and real news and giving a platform to every hair-trigger commentator and instant non-expert out there, Twitter/X has played a key contributory role in the rise of the infantocracy.

There is, of course, an alternative, more positive reading of technology's role in reshaping political communication, and that's the tech utopian's view that social media has broken down barriers with authority and by doing so 'democratised expertise'. But as Tom Nichols points out in *Death of Expertise: The Campaign Against Established Knowledge and Why it Matters*, rather than triggering a new era of democratised scientific or civic engagement, social media has achieved the opposite, lowering the bar on expertise to such an extent that anyone with a laptop and a Twitter/X account can today brand themselves an authority on almost anything. In previous times, governments would counter pseudo-expertise by asserting their own scientific evidence and using democratic institutions as sites of coordinated messaging and information dissemination. But in the age of the infantocrat, politicians lack a rational, adult vision of the future and consequently are incapable of formulating a coherent social policy strategy. Instead, in a futile attempt to shroud their political emptiness with something gaudy and eye-catching, they hasten the death of expertise by engaging in an infantilised process known as the celebrification of politics.

In recent years, the late-modern cult of celebrity has been the subject of much discussion. One of the features of this development has been the increased prominence of celebrities of all types within the political sphere,[13] a transfer of power made all the easier by many politicians who appear and act more like celebrities than elected officials. Yet even though one can't move these days for concerned celebrities 'spotlighting' this or 'advocating' for that, as Mark Harvey makes clear in his recent book *Celebrity Influence: Politics, Persuasion, and Issue-based Advocacy*, it remains to be seen just how effective all this celebrity agenda-setting actually is.[14] But in terms of understanding infantilism in politics, we need to look beyond questions about the persuasive power of celebrities per se and focus instead on how their increasing influence is both a cause and a reflection of our stupefied and degraded political culture.

In 2007, just before leaving Downing Street, Tony Blair launched a ferocious verbal attack on the UK media. Veteran political journalists Howard Rosenberg and Charles Feldman recount the story:

> Taking no prisoners, Blair charged that journalists had created a supercharged atmosphere driven by twenty-four-hour news technology and an emphasis on 'impact' and 'heat.' He said they stressed 'sensation above all else.' He declared, 'We are all being dragged down by the way media and public life interact.' He equated news media to a 'feral beast, just tearing people and reputations to bits.'

The hypocrisy of Blair's words stuck in Rosenberg and Feldman's craws, who commented, '. . . inescapable here was the irony of Blair, the ardent media spinner, now outraged by media spin; Blair, the maestro of manipulation, now complaining bitterly of being manipulated by media.'[15] That Blair seemed especially agitated about 'impact' and 'heat' was particularly ironic given he had cosied up to celebrities more than any other British politician before or since. Like so many of New Labour's ideas, the decision to associate so closely with celebrities came from Bill Clinton, a politician who wrung every last drop out of his pop-cultural credentials. Clinton played the sax (badly); Blair strummed his guitar (horrendously). Clinton liked to be seen palling around with as many black celebrities as possible – Aretha Franklin, Arsenio Hall, Oprah Winfrey, etc. – to deflect attention from the abject racism of many of his criminal justice policies; Blair invited musicians and salt-of-the-earth celebrities to Downing Street parties in the hope of gaining a bit of working-class credibility. In both cases, celebrity culture was unsubtly sucked into political culture, as politicians eager to appear youthful and on-trend gripped, grinned, and gratuitously bathed in the light of shimmering celebrity faces.

Much of the literature on the celebrification of politics is concerned with how politicised celebrities ingratiate themselves with and then use politicians to further their own activist agenda. Clearly, this is an important issue, especially given that much celebrity activism is driven by elephantine levels of narcissism rather than any rational or considered policy agenda. However, my concern here is with how celebrity is being used in the opposite direction by politicians fixated with appearing contemporary and youthful when rolling out new policy initiatives. For example, a favourite New Labour tactic was to launch policies in tandem with a celebrity-laden 'task force'. In the subsequent years, this politics of popularity has expanded to such an extent that it's often harder to find a new government initiative that's not celebrity endorsed than one that is. Consider the following list of UK examples:

- *Carol Vorderman* (TV quiz show host): appointed by both Tony Blair and David Cameron to separate task forces on improving maths teaching.

- *Jamie Oliver* (celebrity chef): appointed by Tony Blair to advise on new school meal policy.
- *Tanya Byron* (host of parenting-skills TV show): appointed by Gordon Brown to head a government inquiry into the effect of porn and violent videos on children.
- *Kirstie Allsopp* (TV property show host): shared a platform with David Cameron on the issue of scrapping Home Information Packs.
- *Loyd Grossman, Alain Roux, James Martin and Stephen Terry* (celebrity chefs): all appointed at various points to government initiatives aimed at improving hospital meals.
- *Mary Portas* (TV host and retail expert): appointed by David Cameron to lead a government review on the future of the high street.
- *Alan Sugar* (entrepreneur and host of *The Apprentice*): made Gordon Brown's new 'business and enterprise tsar' before being made a Labour peer.
- *James Caan* (entrepreneur and TV judge on *Dragon's Den*): recruited by the coalition government to launch Open Doors, a government initiative to improve social mobility.
- *Martin Lewis* (TV money-saving expert): contacted by the Conservative chancellor of the exchequer, Rishi Sunak, in 2022, for advice about how to announce a package of government measures to ease the cost-of-living crisis.

Similar tendencies are evident in my own field – criminology – where it's not uncommon for anti-crime policies/initiatives to be sprinkled with a bit of celebrity stardust. When the former mayor of London Boris Johnson constituted his knife-crime task force in 2009, he decided not to bother with the advice of professional criminologists, preferring instead to get input from not one but two *en vogue* celebrities. Not content with enlisting former

EastEnders soap star Ross Kemp, Johnson swooped to recruit singer Lily Allen after reading on her Myspace page that she was keen to help stop citizens 'stabbing each other in the UK'. It was a similar story a few years later when UK Prime Minster Theresa May announced £18m to combat knife crime. The funding was triggered by a report authored by Brooke Kinsella, another former *EastEnders* soap star who had been recruited as a knife-crime advisor to the Home Secretary after her brother was stabbed to death in 2008. Similarly, perhaps one of the reasons why Gordon Brown's Labour government was happy to ignore the advice of the Advisory Council on the Misuse of Drugs (something that ultimately resulted in the resignation of its head, Professor David Nutt, one of the country's leading academic drug scientists), was because they had previously received 'expert' testimony on the international cocaine trade from taxi-driver Mitch Winehouse, the father of troubled singer Amy Winehouse, at a Home Affairs select committee.

Star-spangled expert testimony got even glitzier in 2012, when comedian and former heroin addict Russell Brand testified at a Home Affairs select committee on drug addiction. The chirpy cockney that he is, Brand unsurprisingly used the opportunity to get some barbs in at the committee's expense, but in truth the whole thing was an unedifying sideshow, and not simply because of Brand's presence. The select committee at which Brand testified was chaired by MP and moral chameleon, Keith Vaz, who at the time was Britain's longest serving Asian MP. Vaz, however, is no longer involved in politics. In 2016, the *Sunday Mirror* reported that he had engaged in unprotected sex with male prostitutes telling them that, if they wanted, he would also pay for their cocaine use. It goes without saying that shabby figures like Vaz do immense damage to the public's opinion of parliamentarians, but so too in their own way do governmental hearings involving well-intentioned but unqualified celebrity 'experts'. By allowing the cult of personality to creep into the heart of governmental inquiry and public policy, the only thing these political publicity stunts really achieve is the further erosion of the moral distinction between politics and celebrity culture.

Given all this endeavour by politicised celebrities, one might be forgiven for thinking the UK's numerous social problems would be in sharp decline. Sadly, however, for all Lily Allen's emoting, stabbings in London and elsewhere in the UK have climbed to an all-time high. Likewise, despite the massive injection of intellectual firepower and policy nous delivered by a kitchen-full of cocksure celebrity chefs, food in National Health Service hospitals remains as grim and grey as ever. But is this really surprising? The idea that somehow attaching a celebrity to a complex policy problem will inevitably improve the fortunes of such initiatives is the political equivalent of those quick-fix TV makeovers on *Ramsay's Kitchen Nightmares*. A lick of paint, a bit of tinkering with the menu and a large dollop of celebrity chef razzamatazz and, hey presto, the restaurant's fortunes are radically transformed, and everybody lives happily ever after. Unfortunately, as any student of government will tell you, in the real world, entrenched and complex social problems are rarely resolved quickly, and if and when they are it's due to ideas put forward by experienced experts rather than soap stars or TV cooks.

The whole phenomenon of the activist-celebrity class is a triumph of media hype over material transformation. This might be tolerable if not for the fact that most of this spurious political activism is driven not by a deep or well-researched commitment to the issues, but by a thin carapace of narcissism and hypocrisy. How many more times, for example, are we to be lectured about the environment by celebrities who spend their lives criss-crossing the planet on private jets, or talked down to about the evils of capitalism from movie stars whose entire career essentially involves shilling for global media conglomerates? In celebrity land, famous people are rarely, if ever, told that their views on geopolitics are not as insightful or erudite as they assume, or that perhaps it would be a mistake for them to take on that role as the new autism tsar. Instead, puffed up by the uncritical support of hangers-on and social media sycophants, these self-righteous limousine radicals now proceed through life subscribing to the narcissistic fantasy that in their hands lies the power to change the world. There is, of course, something deeply infantile about all this, something that perhaps stems from the fact that actors, musicians and reality-TV stars all necessarily inhabit performative, make-believe worlds. Having chosen to ignore the fact that being a celebrity does not automatically mean you know what you're talking about, these 'pretend politicians', to use Tanya Gold's term, need reminding of an important but too often overlooked truth: nothing important is ever changed by celebrities: 'They do not salvage the climate; they do not end rape in war; they do not bring the equality or fairness they beg for. They have simply allowed their vanity to gouge a hole in our politics, where serious politicians and an informed citizenry should be.'[16]

Celebrities, we are told, 'democratise' politics, and it is precisely for this reason that the UK's most popular weekly debate show, *Question Time*, regularly includes a celebrity on its panel of politicos. In a *Question Time* debate following Brexit, the comedian Jo Brand stated: 'I'm not sure I can justify it [a second Brexit referendum], I just want it'. Brand's statement is interesting because it perfectly highlights two important aspects of celebrity politics. First, it illustrates that, for celebrity activists, what matters most is not reasoned critique or persuasive argument but the narcissistic assertion of mere opinion ('I [insert celebrity name] believe it, and given my feted position in society, this is reason enough for you to believe it too'). It is an objectionable form of argumentation that has conquered large tracts of the contemporary media, resulting in a situation wherein being opinionated is itself considered reason enough to justify one's commentator status – a process we might call the Piers Morganisation of news media.

This emphasis on attention seeking and hollow emotionality inevitably opens the door to the second symptomatic feature of celebrity politics: the rise of pseudo-expertise and the downgrading of specialised opinion. It should be clear by now that the first casualty of our celebrified politics is the slow death of sapiential authority. But how exactly did this situation come about? Like almost everything else in the contemporary mediascape, it's simply a question of supply and demand. In terms of demand, celebrities are booked as talking heads on news and current affairs shows primarily because of their likeability, or what's known in TV and advertising circles as their high Q-score. On the supply side, sadly, there are just more and more celebrities who labour under the delusion that their opinions must be heard, irrespective of a lack of related expertise. It can only be for this reason that the UK population is constantly bombarded with the bizarre musings of celebrities on random issues, including, for example, the former Sex Pistol John Lydon on who should succeed Boris Johnson as prime minister (his answer? Jacob Rees-Mogg), soap star Ross Kemp on the optimum size of the British naval fleet, and the fashion designer Vivienne Westwood on the nuclear power debate. This development is largely the consequence of the fact that today's celebrities are artificially buoyed by social media affirmation. As a result, many celebrities now believe popularity in and of itself bestows upon them an innate ability to say something profound.

What we are witnessing is a cultural manifestation of what psychologists call 'the Dunning-Kruger effect'; essentially the idea that the *less* skilled or competent the person, the *more* confident that person is that what they are saying is correct. Or, in the words of Dunning and Kruger: 'Not only do (such people) reach erroneous conclusions and make unfortunate choices, but their incompetence robs them of the ability to realize it'.[17]

There's something else about today's activist-celebrities that's even more concerning. Here I refer not to the style of celebrity politics but its content. In Chapter Five, I introduced Alexei Yurchak's concept of hyper-normalisation, the paradoxical state of mind in which, under certain stagnating political circumstances, individuals and groups can hold two mutually exclusive and seemingly contradictory positions in their head simultaneously. Yurchak formulated this concept to explain the mindset of many Russians during the final years of the Soviet Union, but it also has value when thinking about activist-celebrities. From Sean Penn to Susan Sarandon, Jane Fonda to Jon Stewart, the overwhelming majority of celebrity activists emanate from the liberal left. Often heard raging against capitalism or decrying Western values to anyone who will listen, these liberal firebrands with their luxury opinions simultaneously manage to exist very comfortably and profitably within the system they appear to hold in such contempt. As such, what they represent is not real resistance but the postmodern appearance of it.

It's a similar situation with celebrity eco-activists and environmental campaigners. In their minds and on their social media platforms they consider themselves to be radical thinkers, brave rebel disrupters kicking against the traces of the avaricious corporate machine. The problem for these green crusaders is that most major corporations have already shot their fox by virtue signalling their own eco-credentials at every opportunity. It's the same scenario with most of the other issues that traditionally animate liberal celebrities – gay rights, plastics in the ocean, transgenderism, etc. They have all been effortlessly co-opted by capitalism and fully integrated into their marketing machinery. Thus, while celebrities play at being anti-capitalist activists, they are in fact simply upholding the economic status quo by promoting what is now the bland establishment position. In other words, with their fairy-tale version of political 'resistance', twenty-first-century politicised celebrities should be thought of as *hyper-normalised non-radicals* whose only real achievement has been the further popularisation of a form of anti-materialist politics that Slavoj Žižek nicely describes as 'spaghetti structuralism'.

Given the challenges confronting us, what we need is a committed political class capable of forging practical policies of substance and vision. Instead, we have an emergent infantocracy in which governments, regulatory bodies and elite celebrity influencers, exhausted of any meaningful ideology, now act more like a trendy, youthful friend than a guiding and knowledgeable patrician. This situation, caused in large part by the ideological black hole that is Third Way centrism, has created a crisis of confidence in the political class themselves, but more importantly in the public's faith in how they are being governed. Concerned only with popularity, today's infantile political elites appear bereft of both confidence and experience and, as a result, half-baked, short-term decision making is now the norm – a bit like being a teenager really.

Polarising distractions: Falsehoods, fantasies, and factional enmity

All empty souls tend to extreme opinion.

W. B. Yeats

In *Empire of Illusion: The End of Literacy and the Triumph of Spectacle*, the Pulitzer Prize-winning war correspondent Chris Hedges takes a blowtorch to what he calls 'the high energy pantomime' of contemporary American culture. Drawing on Daniel Boorstin's work on the rise of the spectacle and specifically his concept of the 'pseudo-event' ('in contemporary culture the fabricated, the inauthentic, and the theatrical have displaced the natural, the genuine, and the spontaneous, until reality itself has been turned into stagecraft'), Hedges documents a culture in steep moral and political decline. The targets of his critique are broad. Hedges eviscerates everything from the Californian porn industry to academic psychologists who make their living peddling 'happiness' metrics, but throughout the book one theme reverberates loudly: the idea that in both the political and pop-cultural spheres we are being 'fed illusions', comforting myths that 'destabilize the truth' by creating their own semblance of reality. Hedges explains his position in the following passage:

The flight into illusion sweeps away the core values of the open society. It corrodes the ability to think for oneself, to draw independent conclusions, to express dissent when judgment and common sense tell you something is wrong, to be self-critical, to challenge authority, to grasp historical facts, to advocate for change, and to acknowledge that there are other views, different ways, and structures of being that are morally and socially acceptable. A populace deprived of the ability to separate lies from truth, that has become hostage to the fictional semblance of reality put forth by pseudo-events, is no longer capable of sustaining a free society.[18]

As this quotation attests, Hedges' principal concern is with how the American people are being *distracted* from economic and structural reality by celebrity culture, consumerist mythology and emerging forms of political demagoguery. Importantly, Hedges was writing before the full impact of social media had taken effect.

Thus, he could not have predicted how online platforms have contributed to a marked rise in tribalistic and hyper-partisan politics. In this section, I update the line of argument set out in *Empire of Illusion* in light of developments in online culture. I argue that *polarising distractions* are contributing to the infantilisation process by creating a new type of worldview based not on any shared or coherent political vision, but on speculative stories and illusory tropes that circulate unencumbered by reality within today's 'post truth' mediascape.

Only the most fervent tech ideologue would dispute the claim that social media companies have contributed to a world of over-torqued partisanship. In study after study, across a host of disciplines, it has been shown that interactive digital platforms damage civility and intensify political discord. But while the internet, as Silicon Valley entrepreneur Paul Green has commented, is a medium that engenders disagreement by design, it would be wrong to assume that our disputatious age is the product solely of online culture. In the UK, the US and elsewhere, modern politics and all forms of public discourse have been subjected to a decades-long campaign of degradation. This assault on the public sphere takes different forms in different contexts,[19] but one constant feature in the process has been the dumbing down of news media. If two key features of infantilism are shallow outrage born of juvenile indignation and an immature mindset that stops individuals from adjusting their arguments in light of new information, then it's not hard to see how both these characteristics have been provoked and reinforced by a corrosive style of news making that, for at least two decades, has prioritised the controversial and the inflammatory over the measured and the genuine. There are many aspects to this development, of course, but in terms of the connection between pantomime politics and infantilism, two processes stand out.

The first is the slow demise of what one might call hard news and the rise of a more showy, infantile soft news constituted from 'churnalism', instant blog factoids, clickbait headlines, superficial vox populi ('street meat') and hyperventilating news anchors. Initially used to plug gaps in twenty-four-hour rolling news schedules, this more polemical style of news collation/dissemination quickly emerged as the template for many 'all-news' stations in the early 2000s. In simple terms, it should be seen as a shift away from information to entertainment, a slippage that set the table for the more general deterioration of the news media that would follow in the online era. Today, as a result of this prioritisation of sensationalism and emotionality over fact-gathering and cautious restraint, the news cycle moves faster than the actual news, with anything longer than a soundbite dismissed by audiences raised on digital instantaneity as a ponderous intrusion into their world of self-focused information processing.

The second process, which inevitably flows from the first, is the rejection of complexity in favour of brazen and unapologetic partisanship. Described by Michael Massing as the 'Fox News effect', this style of reporting involves shearing stories of all nuance and subtlety and framing them instead in crude, black-and-white terms designed specifically to elicit an emotional response from viewers. Although this type of newscasting has been around for some time, it really took off in the aftermath of 9/11, as stories about the 'war on terror' unfolded like cautionary tales written for vulnerable children. It is interesting to recall that shortly after the attack on the Twin Towers, Susan Sontag wrote, 'The disconnect between last Tuesday's monstrous dose of reality and the self-righteous drivel and outright deceptions being peddled by public figures and TV commentators is startling, depressing. The voices licensed to follow the event seem to have joined together in a campaign to infantilise the public.'[20] Whether it was entirely unsubstantiated reports about the detonation of 'dirty bombs' or panic-ridden stories about potential Al Qaeda attacks on plutonium stores at nuclear power stations, speculation about what could happen quickly morphed into news stories couched in terms of imminent danger. In the intervening years, this type of news-as-fevered-fantasy has become almost standard practice on many all-news stations, pushing Anglo-American society further away from the realm of rational analysis and into a moribund world of worst-case-scenario thinking.

These and other related developments have combined to create an increasingly emotive style of late-modern news coverage. For example, in the fast-moving, highly competitive world of twenty-four-hour rolling news, content that includes visceral public outrage is often seen as the key to sustaining audience interest. To that end, as the sardonic media critic Charlie Brooker has pointed out, journalists working in this field have fashioned a power reversal between themselves and the public such that, today, 'Instead of offering us a factual summary of events that we can then form an emotional opinion on, they [reporters] now ask us for an emotional opinion, and then incorporate it into their factual summary of events'. With its user-generated content and MTV-style graphics, 'its easy hate figures, its selective storytelling and stupid viewer votes', TV news has come to resemble a popularity contest in which the viewers themselves manipulate the characters and vote out content they don't like or find too challenging or disturbing.[21]

Crime reporting in particular has been affected by such developments, especially when it comes to one of the themes discussed in the previous chapter – contemporary victimhood. For example, drawing on the criminological concept of the 'mediated victim', Butler and Drakeford talk about the way high-profile crime victims are hastily associated with larger themes and issues, thus becoming *dramatis personae* in a late-modern morality play involving archetypal heroes and villains – pantomime characters? – who get pushed onto centre stage for us to 'boo' or 'cheer' at.[22]

As divisive as the Anglo-American news media has become, it's nothing when compared with the hostile spectacle of good and evil that passes for the public sphere in today's online world. The factional enmity provoked by social media and its associated tools of virality have combined to propel us beyond even the illusory diversions described by Boorstin and Hedges and into a contemporary mediascape dominated by what I term *polarising distractions*. While polarising distractions are similar in many ways to pseudo-events, they differ in one important respect: they involve an *active* dimension as opposed to simply being something – a spectacle – that is passively received or consumed. And it is this active element that we need to consider here if we are to understand why public discourse has become so infantilised.

The dream of the original cyberspace gurus who developed the online communities behind the World Wide Web was that immediate peer-to-peer connectivity would reshape the world for the better by enhancing collective decision making. But as we have seen, instead of creating a new mode of digital democracy capable of giving voice to the masses, social media platforms and other user-generated participatory websites have functioned to undermine the baseline conditions required to construct a meaningful political consensus. In terms of social media, it's not difficult to see how this happened. By placing a premium on emotionality, hyperbole and moral indignation, social media functions to polarise opinion and propagate alternative realities – fantasies – within already socially estranged segments of the population.

Up until fairly recently, it was typically assumed that this rise in political fragmentation and social division was the direct result of changes in the way we *consumed* online information ('filter bubbles', 'echo chambers', individually curated news streams, etc.).

This quote from 2012 by the Canadian communication expert Allan Gregg, for example, sets out the established view that, as a result of specific funnelling processes, the digital world is limiting people's exposure to alternate opinions:

> If I believe the world is flat, the internet now puts me in touch with legions of fellow flat earthers and reams of pseudo-science to support that belief. As importantly, if I am so inclined, I never have to be exposed to any contrary views and can find total refuge in my community of flat earthers. The Internet therefore, offers me the opportunity to have a completely closed mind and at one and the same time, fill it full of nonsense disguised as fact. In a brand new way therefore, the Internet democratises not just individual opinion but legitimizes collective ignorance and spreads a bizzarro world of alternative reason. When this occurs, prejudice and bias is reinforced and the authority of real science and evidence is undermined or even more likely, never presented.[23]

However, more recent research has challenged this view. Rather than social media users being trapped inside the narrow confines of self-confirming filter bubbles, there is growing evidence to suggest that users of social media actually encounter a more heterogeneous set of political views than non-users who remain committed to 'old' media formats.[24] Unfortunately this alleged exposure to a broader range of opinion has not resulted in a new Eden of mutual understanding and public tolerance – far from it. A quick scroll through political Twitter/X or the comments section underneath a breaking news story and it instantly becomes clear that what passes for public discourse today is mostly childishly inane retorts, mawkish feel-my/your-pain language and emotionally charged political commentary that minimises macro social problems while maximising speculative risks and unsubstantiated threats. Or, as Ian Leslie puts it in his book *Conflicted: Why Arguments Are Tearing Us Apart and How They Can Bring Us Together*, 'Instead of creating [filter] bubbles, the internet is bursting them, generating hostility, fear and anger'.

In 2018, three data scientists from the Massachusetts Institute of Technology published findings from the most comprehensive ever study of fake news stories on Twitter. After analysing 126,000 stories, tweeted by 3 million users over the entire timeframe of Twitter's existence, the MIT team's conclusions were stark and depressing: 'falsehood diffused faster than truth'.[25] The paper, published in *Science*, was written in complex statistical language, but such was its importance, it became the subject of a feature article in *The Atlantic*, where Robinson Meyer helpfully summarised the study's key findings:

> A false story reaches 1,500 people six times quicker, on average, than a true story does. And while false stories outperform the truth on every subject – including business, terrorism and war, science and technology, and entertainment – fake news about politics regularly does best. Twitter users seem almost to *prefer* sharing falsehoods. Even when the researchers controlled for every difference between the accounts originating rumors – like whether that person had more followers or was verified – falsehoods were still 70 percent more likely to get retweeted than accurate news . . . Fake news could put together a retweet chain 19 links long – and do it 10 times as fast as accurate news put together its measly 10 retweets.[26]

The reason for this is simple: controversial negative stories evoke strong, *emotional* reactions that grab our attention and make us want to disseminate this type of information with others. This deep-rooted human attraction to negative threats (this time in the guise of fake news) is then set free by the informational architecture of social media, as Meyer explained:

On platforms where every user is at once a reader, a writer, and a publisher, falsehoods are too seductive not to succeed: The thrill of novelty is too alluring, the titillation of disgust too difficult to transcend. After a long and aggravating day, even the most staid user might find themselves lunging for the politically advantageous rumour. Amid an anxious election season, even the most public-minded user might subvert their higher interest to win an argument.

This all sounds entirely plausible as an explanation for why fake news is so prevalent in late-modern society, but what it doesn't sound is very adult.

The problem with amplified, distracting untruths is that, in a social media world where emotions are afforded such primacy, falsehoods can quickly turn into fantasies. It's not an original observation to state that we live in the age of conspiracy, but what is new is social media's unprecedented capacity to mainstream fringe conspiratorial beliefs which previously would have existed only on the very peripheries of society. Consider QAnon, the conspiracy theory that originated in 2017 on the blogsite 4chan. Essentially QAnon adherents subscribe to a variant of the conspiracy theory that Donald Trump is in league with a small band of brave military intelligence officers who are waging a deep-state resistance war against a shadowy Satan-worshipping, child-eating paedophile cabal, all of whom just happen to be either high-profile liberals or Democrat politicians. Two decades ago, this would have remained the stuff of a graphic novel or perhaps the over-wrought imagination of the Swedish crime writer Stieg Larsson, but today, thanks to the virus of conspiracism, QAnon is practically a household name, both in America and beyond. In 2020, a Pew Research Center poll documented that the number of Americans who had heard about QAnon rose from 23 per cent in March 2020 to 47 per cent in just six months. In an article about the need to inoculate US military personnel from the influence of QAnon, Christina Bembenek writes: 'despite bans by Facebook and Twitter, QAnon-affiliated groups continue to emerge across social media. After Facebook's initial ban on QAnon content in August . . . 100 QAnon groups were still achieving over 600,000 likes and posts per week.'[27]

Christopher Hitchens once described conspiracy theories as 'the exhaust fumes of democracy', the toxic smog that proliferates when too much of the wrong type of emotionally charged information circulates among a large number of people. The problem we face today is that conspiratorial smog is everywhere, making it ever harder to breath the clean air of political reason and objective science. When bad ideas abound, and the means of challenging them is diminished by the assault on reality-based institutions, it's no surprise that many individuals choose to embark on a psycho-cultural descent into the unknown via conspiratorial beliefs. Whatever else they are, conspiracy theories are ultimately escape routes, whether in the form of a dream or a nightmare. In both scenarios the conspiratorial thinker is comforted by the belief that, if not in control, then they are at least in possession of a secret code or hidden agenda known only to a select few. In previous eras, such thinking was the preserve of religious zealots, the psychologically impaired or children and teenagers hiding from adult reality. In late-modern society it is now the way millions of people attempt to make sense of the world and their place within it.

The second noteworthy thing about polarising distractions is that, while they are clearly energised and set free by developments in online culture, in essence they remain a manifestation of human nature. As Ian Leslie points out, what lures people into destructive online conflict in the first place is usually a struggle over *who they are*: 'When a debate becomes volatile and dysfunctional, it's often because someone in the conversation feels they are not getting the face [the public image a person wants to project in a social interaction] they deserve. This helps to explain the pervasiveness of bad temper on social media, which can sometimes feel like a status competition in which the currency is attention.'[28] It is a tendency that most of us will recognise from our youth, only now social media has extended the idea of a status competition into the always-on, me-focused world of the internet – with all sorts of negative consequences. In the inflamed, disputatious world of the online public sphere, the first casualty of status competitions is reason itself, not least because in inter-Kidult disputes neither party typically knows how to disagree well. It is at this point that something else all-too-human occurs. Having abandoned reason, the outraged loser (or winner) of the status competition looks to his or her tribe for support, praise and a sense of wider understanding. Humans are tribal creatures and as such few behavioural patterns are more engrained or emotionally gratifying than pitting a virtuous 'us' against a malevolent 'them'.

In his recent book, *Identity Politics and Tribalism: The New Culture Wars*, Nikos Sotirakopoulos advocates a slightly different position to most of the established sociological and psychological literature on tribalism. More specifically, he asserts that, while tribalism inevitably damages the public sphere, it also diminishes one's ability *to think*. This is certainly the case in online contexts replete with polarising distractions. Desperate to overcome the chaos of contemporary society and its associated feelings of emptiness and isolation, the online actor searches for something meaningful – a sense of 'psychic survival' in Laschian terms – in the shared energy and in-group narratives of tribalistic thinking. If this also means having to embrace conspiratorial beliefs, so be it; the collective effervescence of the tribe, expressed in likes and other acts of viral support, will provide the necessary phatic scaffold needed to resist any suggestion of specious or contradictory thinking. It is for this reason we are witnessing not just the revival of infantile fantasies of puritanical righteousness and fictive kinship, but entirely new forms of weird political syncretism, such as the fusion of right-wing conspiracy theory with New Age spirituality, something that American religion scholars have usefully termed 'conspirituality'.[29] If pantomime politics needed a hothouse in which to grow, polarising distractions provide it. In a world where vaudevillian political rhetoric is effortlessly and uncritically amplified, and where fractious and hyperbolic modes of interpersonal communication are normalised, the likelihood of cultivating socially aware and politically accomplished actors is small indeed.

In *Empire of Illusion*, Hedges correctly pointed out that human beings' infinite appetite for distraction frequently results in what he termed 'a culture of illusion'. But importantly, beyond the 'happy thoughts' and 'manipulated emotions' provoked by pseudo-events, he also understood that in a diminished public sphere characterised by unsubstantiated fearmongering, unabashed hyper-partisanship and clickbait journalism, something else is likely to be lurking. That something, although it might not ultimately prove to be full-blown totalitarianism, looks an awful lot like it.

Thy Woke Kingdom come: Infantilised performative politics in the era of new clichés

In J. G. Ballard's dystopian novel *Kingdom Come*, washed-up advertising man Richard Pearson attempts to find out what happened to his father who was gunned down by a spree killer in a Surrey shopping mall. Set against a backdrop of celebrified politics, suburban ennui and the bleak and soulless landscapes of consumer culture, Pearson's quest for answers leads nowhere until he meets enigmatic local psychiatrist Dr Maxted. While Maxted is evasive about the psychological state of the gunman, he waxes philosophical about a new 'social pathology' that he believes is emerging out of the post-religious, post-consumerist era:

> People feel they can rely on the irrational. It offers the only guarantee of freedom from all the cant and bullshit and sales commercials fed to us by politicians, bishops, and academics. People are deliberately re-primitivizing themselves. They yearn for magic and unreason, which served them well in the past, and might help them again. They are keen to enter a new Dark Age. The lights are on, but they're retreating into the inner darkness, into superstition and unreason. The future is going to be a struggle between vast systems of psychopathologies, all of them willed and deliberate, part of a desperate attempt to escape from a rational world and the boredom of consumerism ... Consumerism creates huge unconscious needs that only fascism can satisfy. If anything, fascism is the form that consumerism takes when it opts for elective madness. You can see it here already.[30]

In this passage, Ballard deftly blends reality with futurology, his aim being 'to dip a toe into the waters of psychopathology to provide the kind of high-tension excitement that people need, because everyone in the consumerist world is very bored.'[31] In *Kingdom Come*, Ballard recognises intuitively that, when the fictitious lifeworlds of consumerism lose their shimmer and promise, something else must necessarily emerge to fill the void. It is an intriguing argument and one which I believe has considerable application for understanding a third element of pantomime politics: the rise of infantilised forms of political expression and performative activism. My argument in this section is that much of the supposed political resistance we see today is in fact an ironic by-product of the very same illusory emotions that drive late-modern consumerism. To understand what I mean by this we must first explore the repertoires of feeling and forms of radicalism that are very often at the heart of the contemporary activist mindset.

Over the last decade or so, Anglo-American politics has been fundamentally transformed by the emergence of a new assemblage of ideas and ideological mantras that used to be known as left-liberal identity politics but is now more commonly referred to as Wokeness. Earlier we saw the damage done to higher education as a result of the emergence of the so-called 'Woke university' and its related modes of cultural infantilisation. Here, we widen the frame of analysis beyond the confines of the college campus to consider the impact of Woke politics more generally.

At its core, and as originally articulated in African American vernacular, the term 'Woke' simply meant a state of 'being aware', especially of social problems such as racism and inequality. More recently, however, the term Wokeness has expanded in all sorts of unanticipated ways with all sorts of unexpected consequences. To make sense of this situation, we need to pause briefly to consider the history of Wokeness, and in particular how it was co-opted by primarily white, educated liberals to serve a particular set of elite ideological interests.

One starting point on the road to Wokeness was the work of a very influential group of critical theorists, including Michel Foucault, Gilles Deleuze, Jacques Derrida and Judith Butler. Based in large part around the concept of power, the ideas and concepts associated with these postmodern thinkers quickly gained a committed following in university humanities departments in the 1980s and 90s. Although each theorist had their own specific sphere of interest, all were bound together by a central premise: that modernist 'truths' – including even scientific objectivity – and post-Enlightenment ideals of progress, justice and rational ethics, were essentially forms of oppression (capitalist, colonialist, bourgeois, patriarchal); the ultimate goal being the comprehensive rearrangement of modern Western society such that all forms of privilege and hierarchy are flattened out via new platforms of progressive egalitarianism. These theories spread like so many bacilli across the social sciences and beyond. But despite their growing academic influence, seldom did these thinkers penetrate mainstream culture. All this changed, however, in the 2010s, when a series of events catapulted watered-down versions of these ideas onto centre stage.

The economic slowdown that followed the financial crisis of 2008 unsurprisingly provoked a new era of anti-capitalist and anti-government protest. Beginning with the Occupy movement in 2011, the first half of the 2010s was marked by a series of organic street-level protests, including the Indignados movement in Spain, the Movimento Passe Livre in Brazil, and major political demonstrations in Greece, Turkey, Tunisia and elsewhere. Inevitably, these events galvanised a new generation of student radicals concerned about the state of the world and its intensifying inequality. However, not for the first time with student politics, the fundamental issue of political economy was quickly abandoned in favour of matters relating to culture and identity. Rallying around the somewhat vague banner of 'social justice', a small minority of leftist students in Anglo-American universities succeeded in directing attention away from corporate greed, the profligacy of

342

the banking sector and economic inequality, and towards issues of race, gender and sexuality. The 'Great Awokening' had begun.

In 2014, protests erupted in Ferguson, Missouri, following the police killing of Michael Brown. One of the consequences of the Brown shooting was the rise to prominence of the Black Lives Matter (BLM) movement. Founded in 2013 to raise awareness of police brutality in black communities, BLM was quickly bracketed with Wokeness, not least because of the group's prominent use of the Twitter hashtag #StayWoke. At this point, the term Woke was still largely the preserve of the African American community. This changed, however, when student activists and other liberal elites started to appropriate the term as a synonym for the broader concept of social justice. Two consequences followed. First, the original meaning of the concept was greatly diminished as the label 'Woke' was attached to anybody who expressed any sort of interest in intersectional inequality. Second, as a result of its overuse by all sorts of identity-based groups, Wokeness took on a secondary use as an epithet; a term of derision deployed by right-wing critics to undermine the claims and demands of what they saw as a new authoritarian left on the march in Anglo-American society.

The sense that what students and other leftist activists were engaged in at this time was as much a moral campaign as it was a political one was further validated by the emergence of what has since become the principal intellectual schema of Woke politics – critical race theory (CRT). A defining feature of postmodern critique was the frequent use of arcane terminology and jargon-ridden prose, a style of discourse deployed not so much for the purposes of clarification, but as a shield against 'the malicious attacks of real things', to quote Françoise Thom. This tendency to use language both as an obfuscation tactic and as a sort of secret code to distinguish the initiated also features prominently in contemporary CRT. Most closely associated with the work of Robin DiAngelo and Ibram X. Kendi, CRT asserts that not only are the United States and Europe 'white supremacist societies', but that every white person, irrespective of context or circumstance, is a de facto racist.

While CRT is almost always couched in political terms, the solution to systemic racism proffered by the likes of DiAngelo and Kendi is fundamentally a moral one. Indeed, with its quasi-spiritual redemptive message, its prescribed actions (taking the knee, raising the fist), its creedal language, and its sense of heresy and original sin (to be born white is to be born evil), CRT has far more in common with a liturgy or a eucharistic rite than it does with an established political ideology. But perhaps this was to be expected.[32] Postmodern theory/critique was never big on political consensus building. Rather, its stated aim was to 'deconstruct' ideology and 'decentre' all forms of knowledge associated with power and tradition. No surprise, then, that the works of DiAngelo and Kendi found their main audience not with working-class people of colour who suffer the bulk of racial injustice, but with educated, Foucault-obsessed white liberals who use CRT for what is – a form of racialised pseudo therapy.

There is much one could say about the rise of Wokeness and the various purposes it serves. How it has replaced the materialist language of economic exploitation with the more nebulous concept of oppression. How it has spawned a new class of pseudo-elites and salaried thought-managers who labour in the service of Astro-turfed postmodern concepts and a fairy-tale moral hierarchy. And how its intolerant illiberalism breeds moral absolutism, especially among young people who today use Woke ideas in the same way previous generations used provocative youth subcultures to differentiate themselves from and antagonise the adult world. But my aim here is not to catalogue the many problems and contradictions associated with Wokeism, it is rather to understand its relationship to infantilisation. To do this, we must spend some time on something often overlooked about today's intersectional activists. That just as the counterculturalists of the 1960s were a refracted version of contemporaneous developments taking place elsewhere in consumer society, many of the Woke activists of the 2020s are themselves direct by-products of late-twentieth-century consumerism.

The parallels between radical Woke politics and the counter-culture are fairly obvious. Both place a strong emphasis on the old Sixties activist logic of consciousness/awareness raising, and both believe the existing structural order is intrinsically oppressive and corrupt. However, they also share something else in common that's not so immediately self-evident. Just as the spirit and values of the counterculture were quickly captured and redirected by lifestyle advertising, today's radicalism has also been effortlessly absorbed by the market. One could even go so far as to say that the moral insurgency supposedly being waged against the establishment by today's pseudo-rebels is the first leftist revolution in history to be fully endorsed, some might even say underwritten, by the forces of capitalism. It is for this reason that Wokeism is evident everywhere from Hollywood award ceremonies to the boardrooms of Disney, Ben & Jerry's, Gillette and the countless other major corporations who constantly feel they must take the lead in the re-education of their ignorant customers. But how did this situation come about? How was corporate capitalism able to take on board (and monetise) the very same words, views and slogans of the allegedly anti-capitalist social justice warrior class? The answer to this apparent contradiction is to be found within the swirling currents and fast-moving riptides of late-modern consumerism. Three overlapping themes stand out.

First, an important feature shared by Wokeism and consumerism is the way both phenomena create and cultivate new forms of concomitant subjectivity based around newness, immediacy and impulsivity. One of the central tasks consumer culture sets itself is the production of subjects who are constantly on the lookout for new commodities and experiences. The sociologist Zygmunt Bauman famously described this late-modern form of subjectivity as 'sensation gathering' – a mode of being characterised by what he called 'neophilia' and driven by a culture of (market-induced) dissatisfaction and a narcissistic fixation with personal growth. In addition to being insatiable, consumer culture also cultivates a desire for immediate rather than delayed gratification. Both these dual aspects of consumerism are much in evidence in Wokeism.

Postmodern gender studies, for example, has been virtually colonised by neophiliacs. Want to appear de rigueur and progressive in this field? Simply invent a new sexual orientation or identity category and you're almost guaranteed high status in the seminar rooms and lecture halls of today's captured universities. The love of the new is similarly evident in race and ethnicity studies. A few years back, the neologism BME (Black and Minority Ethnic) fell out of fashion only to be replaced with the term BAME (the 'A' standing for Asian). Today, however, BAME is also increasingly seen as 'problematic', and no doubt will soon be replaced by the latest acronym du jour. The 'if it's new it *must* be good' sales logic has also affected implicit racial bias training, an industry now purportedly worth $8 billion in the United States alone. Rolled out initially under the rubric of workplace inclusivity training, this new form of corporate mind control quickly morphed first into race awareness training, then diversity training, and now unconscious bias training – remarkable, really, given the entire enterprise is based on a prejudice metric derived from 'implicit association tests', which study after study have shown to be flawed and non-replicable.[33]

It's a similar story with instant gratification. One of the consequences of a culture predicated on instantaneity has been the emergence of 'do-somethingism' – the misguided belief that urgent intervention is everything. A feature of Woke campaigns generally, this tendency is most evident in climate activism where, rather than a measured, scientific debate about the specific threats posed by global warming, we are bombarded with *Mission Impossible*-style ticking timeclock metaphors and doomsday scenarios linked to the somewhat vague instruction to 'act now'. The problem with poorly thought out do-somethingism is that it almost always produces the wrong policy outcomes for the problem. This is especially true when it comes to corporate Wokeism. For some time now, the professional managerial class has assumed its role is to *manage everything* – and by manage here I mean transform. Buoyed by the purity of opinion associated with Woke values, these high-minded corporate thought leaders now erroneously believe they have the justification needed to expunge society of any notion of homeostasis or tradition. In this belief they are, of course, fundamentally wrong, but this matters not to the technocrats and self-styled disrupters whose status and wealth ensure they are always shielded from the damaging consequences of their hubris.

A second example of the relationship between consumerism and Wokeism is the shared reliance upon branding practices, including the use of dedicated, sloganistic language. Anyone who has ever studied Woke culture knows very well that it relies to a large degree on a combination of icons and symbols backed up by a lexicon of insider terms and phrases. Prideful flags, childish emojis, hashtags, quasi-revolutionary iconography (the Resist fist, the Che Guevara silhouette) and, of course, that ever-changing weathervane of herd thinking, the social media ident photo (black square, Charlie Hebdo, Ukraine flag, etc., etc.) all are used to express identity and signal political affinity. Often these things are deployed collectively in a single tweet or on an individual social media profile in something resembling a neo-heraldic Woke coat of arms. On their own these symbols have little transformative power, and so in the same way advertisers use straplines and marketing copy to reinforce brand associations, specialist semantics are used to prop up this elite symbology and pressure off-message thinkers into compliance. Consider, for example, the following phrases, all of which feature prominently in online comment posts as potent rhetorical devices: 'Right side of history', 'stay in your lane', 'we see you', 'silence is violence', 'educate yourself', 'this isn't a good look', 'read the room', 'repeat after me', 'it's not OK', 'do better', 'do the work'. None of this, however, achieves anything practical in terms of actually reducing social problems. Instead, it simply shifts the focus of the struggle away from the root cause of structural problems towards errant individuals whose personal opinions must be brought in line with the latest daft linguistic fabrication ('Latinx', 'chestfeeder', 'BoPo', etc.). Politics reduced to gatekeeping opinion and the virtuous display of infantile emojis.

The final way in which Wokeism can be seen as a by-product of consumerism is the emphasis both place on the construct of 'lifestyle'. If postmodern consumer culture was about anything it was about projecting a largely imagined sense of hierarchical difference via the adoption of a lifestyle sensibility. Today, however, instead of choosing a particular commodity or brand, do-something activists and Wokeists select a set of pre-scripted political opinions which they then mobilise via performative political gestures into something resembling a cultural lifestyle. One part virtuous badge of honour, one part power fantasy, this type of performative political signalling is just an alternative form of elaborate status differentiation. In the case of corporations, it's less about hierarchical ordering and more about using lifestyle politics and other forms of identity-based political signalling as tools to launder their fundamental goal of profit maximisation.

These three developments are part of the reason why contemporary leftist politics is in such a pitiful state. However, my concern here is not with 'the death of the left' per se,[34] but with how pantomime politics more generally is diminishing our potential to build a better society based on adult political decision making. To make sense of how this situation came about, I turn now to some of the infantilising moral and emotional shifts that have transformed politics from a serious, grown-up pursuit into something resembling a cross between a children's morality tale and a performative therapy session.

One of the underlying themes in this section has been the resurgence of morality in politics. This is true for all sorts of clannish and identitarian behaviour right across the political spectrum, but never more so than when it comes to one particularly prevalent form of gestural politics. I refer here to the phenomenon of 'virtue signalling', a term coined in 2015 by the British journalist James Bartholomew to describe the act of expressing fashionable opinions – whether sincerely or insincerely – in a bid to curry favour with strangers and improve one's social standing or popularity. The concept of projecting one's virtue had featured previously in religious studies, but what Bartholomew did was to give the term a pejorative meaning, as illustrated in the following passage: 'No one actually has to do anything. Virtue comes from mere words or even from silently held beliefs. There was a time in the distant past when people thought you could only be virtuous by doing things . . . [that] involve effort and self-sacrifice.'[35] In the few short years since, virtue signalling has crept into common parlance, used as code to describe everything from greenwashing companies to online 'slackivists' who champion political issues on social media but do nothing practical to support these causes. Here I want to focus on its specific role in the infantilisation of politics.

In his book *A Left for Itself: Left Wing Hobbyists and Performative Radicalism*, David Swift takes aim at what he describes as the 'obnoxious' and 'unreflective' behaviour of today's identitarian left. Describing this generational cohort of activists as 'political hobbyists', he claims these often middle-class, university-educated, virtuous pseudo-rebels have caused immeasurable damage to centre-left politics by abandoning the economic concerns of the working class in favour of an obsession with issues 'around race, gender identity and the Middle East'. As he acidly puts it, 'this section of the left doesn't care about the "man on the Clapham omnibus" so much as the man on the Shoreditch unicycle.'[36] In such statements, Swift understands that at least part of what makes 'attention-seeking' virtuousness so popular is that it holds many of the same attractions as lifestyle consumerism.

In the previous chapter I spent time making the link between narcissism and infantilisation and how, within this dynamic, consumerism is used to overcome feelings of deep-seated emptiness. I made the point then that infantilised narcissistic consumers commonly attempt to mask their personal sense of inadequacy with over-confidence, childish fantasies that bear no resemblance to social reality, and an excessive interest in self-image and its projection. It seems to me that a very similar set of characteristics are also present when it comes to political virtue signalling. The natural home of the infantilised narcissist is the internet, where comment-based platforms and social media streams provide the perfect canvas to promote personal agendas (no matter how impractical or fantastic) and sate the narcissist's desire to be heard. In previous times, many of these same desires would have been worked out in dynamic youth subcultures, but as these are almost non-existent today, a new mode of shouty, online performative politics has emerged as the main space in which individuals now live out their fantasies of resistance and rebellion.[37]

The cultural hierarchy of virtue is not, of course, just the preserve of individuals and radical activists. It has also been enthusiastically embraced by corporations, NGOs, governing bodies, educationalists, HR departments and the celebrity-industrial complex. As a result, we inhabit a world where, like consumerism, virtue signalling has penetrated practically every area of society. Attend a concert or football match and be prepared to be bombarded with what are essentially wall-to-wall advertisements for organisations and causes predicated on iden-tity politics – or even unreconstructed Marxist revolutionary politics in the case of BLM. Seek refuge from the perpetual storm of virtue branding in formerly politically non-aligned spaces likes libraries, galleries, universities and museums and you'll be similarly deluged by a confetti of tiresome social justice messag-ing. All of this, of course, is highly infantilising. It suggests that at every turn your underdeveloped, childlike mind must be prompted to think and act in certain proscribed ways – a bit like being forced to take part in a Woke Pavlovian social experiment. Or to put it another way, life today is less about learning from experience and finding a unique path through the world, and more about being conditioned by exposure to a set of carefully curated messages passed down from on high by a holy order of unaccountable managerial overlords.

Morality, of course, does not exist in a vacuum. It is triggered by thoughts and feelings associated with extant ideas and perspec-tives and elicited in the context of emotions. This is certainly the case with the moral discourse at the heart of pantomime politics.

In the previous chapter, I discussed the pivotal role that narcissism and its supplementary emotions have played in the rise of infantilism, and I return to this subject here in an effort to make sense of the emotive morality that is such a common feature of today's performative politics.

A few years back, I started noticing a distinct new type of photograph staring back at me from the covers of university publications and the pages of glossy style magazines. The image is always the same: it depicts a usually young, unsmiling person, in fashionable, but importantly unbranded, clothing, striking a contrived, unnatural pose designed to exude a sense of power or, in the parlance our times, 'fierceness'. Part activist, part reluctant thrift-store-fashionista, these individuals represent the new cover stars of the social justice movement. The stories that accompany this photogenic wing of Woke agitprop are also strikingly similar. After a bit of psycho-biographical background, the narrative quickly turns to how their particular social cause is being overlooked and how they themselves are voiceless and ignored – despite the fact that they and their particular issue are being featured on the cover of a magazine. The irony of this message is, of course, entirely lost on these individuals, but there's a reason for that: in moments like these, when politics is reduced to an article of consumption, the protagonists often exhibit what Christopher Lasch would describe as 'superficial narcissism'. I am not suggesting those who feature in these articles are narcissists in any clinical sense, rather what these articles exemplify is a form of neo-Laschian cultural narcissism in which political causes/issues are used as a vehicle for the projection of self. In a society that affords considerable prestige to identity-based victimhood, there is a great deal to be gained from collapsing together and then emotively signalling broad political causes with style cues and branding techniques drawn from the much-cheapened world of celebrity culture. The infantilising effects of this *merger of politics and cultural narcissism* are already affecting society in all sorts of different ways, but its most obvious and potentially damaging manifestation is in the performative signalling associated with contemporary political 'resistance'.

As we saw in Chapter Three, the radical currents associated with the Sixties counterculture fundamentally transformed the idea of political protest in the US, the UK and elsewhere. In particular, as astute commentators like Barbara Epstein have pointed out, the rebellious nature of countercultural politics represented a flight from collective, organised resistance towards a politics that instead tended to emphasise self-expression.[38] As a result, politics was no longer 'about the subordination of self to some larger political cause; it [had become] . . . the path to self-fulfilment'.[39] The decision by many on the left to follow a narrow path of self-fulfilment rather than the broader boulevard of collective politics, led ultimately to the world of self-interest and self-identified action groups that we now associate with the term identity politics. Over fifty years on from the libertarian excesses of the Sixties counterculture, and forty years on from the emergence of identity politics, the destructive impact of these dual developments on collectivist politics is painfully apparent. Not only did the counterculture gloss over the complex nature of most social problems, but ultimately it made it more difficult than ever to galvanise a meaningful democratic opposition to corporate power and the vested interests of the establishment. Consequently, there now exists a confused, almost schizophrenic relationship between the individual and the issue, something most apparent in the way symbolic, narcissistic politics have triumphed over more practical, collective forms of instrumental political action.

As a criminologist, the subjects of resistance and transgression are naturally of considerable interest to me. However, over the last decade or so, I have come to realise that much of what passes for political resistance today is in truth little more than 'lifestyle activism', or what I have described elsewhere in a co-authored article as faux resistance.[40] This 'radical gesture' phenomenon is observable across the entire political spectrum, but it has especially imprisoned the left, ensnaring it within what Lasch described as 'a politics of theatre, of dramatic gestures, of style without substance – a mirror image of the politics of unreality which it should have been the purpose of the left to unmask'.[41] Today, this type of narcissistic political theatre involving the acting out of leftist fantasies of resistance is everywhere.[42] Consider the following examples: Flamenco dancing flash mobs in Andalusia organised by the anti-capitalist group Flo6x8 as a protest against the excesses of the banking system; Extinction Rebellion activists LARPing as characters from the TV series *A Handmaid's Tale*; the topless/nude protests of the 'sextremist' group Femem; Palestinian supporters wearing blueface and donning the clothes of the Na'vi tribe from the film *Avatar* to raise awareness of the Israeli border wall; the US politician and activist Alexandria Ocasio-Cortez cosplaying being arrested (by faking 'air [hand] cuffs') at a 2022 protest outside the Supreme Court; the identitarian Young Boy Dancing Group, whose goal is to 'challenge gender and sexuality' by writhing around on the floor with laser lights stuck between their buttocks; the self-righteous soup and super glue activism of Just Stop Oil philistines; and, of course, who can forget the 2017 Pussy Hat phenomenon?[43] Clearly, some of these examples are more absurd than others, but what they all have in common is the combination of infantilisation and cultural narcissism outlined above – a tendency that sadly is already over-represented in other areas of political resistance.

Attend any sort of demonstration or rally these days and you cannot fail to be struck by the ludic nature of the protest.

Face-painting, drum circles, biotic baking, burlesque, 'craftivism', juggling, masking, performative dance, Zen mysticism and other specious types of New Age-ism, inefficient 'people's mic' speeches and endless childish fancy-dress (sorry, I mean costumed resistance) – it's almost as if the protestors, many of whom are drawn from disparate and often contradictory causes, believe they can conceal the complete absence of any delineated political principles behind these directionless displays of 'subversive creativity'. Advocates of this type of street-theatre-as-politics argue it constitutes a form of 'tactical carnival'. Others believe these street-party demonstrations offer a glimpse into a new 'horizontal political culture'. But for those looking on from the outside, these events appear like sideshows on the deck of a sinking ship. No doubt for the semi-professional activist class who turn up at demonstrations on stilts or wearing huge papier-mâché heads these events offer a brief moment of carnival. But the plain truth of the matter is that no amount of face-painting or fire-breathing is going to help rebuild the labour movement or regulate the egregious behaviour of the financial sector.

Unfortunately for career activists and rebel academics, the adult world of democratic change requires major public buy-in and for that to happen groups must come up with more sophisticated messaging than the type of magical thinking mantras ('Stop oil now', 'Capitalism is crisis' and 'Repeat after us: trans women are women') that proliferate today. Similar tendencies have even spread to that old bulwark of leftist solidarity, the picket line. Strikes in my own field, higher education, for example, now feel more like children's play dates than industrial action, with university staff bragging on Twitter about how striking lecturers are busy drawing chalk Christmas trees on the pavement, doing Zumba and filming TikTok dance routines. In 2019, Strathclyde UCU even sent out a tweet, complete with requisite infantilised emojis, advising those new to picketing to bring along: 'a big coat', 'a warm hat', 'two gloves', 'sensible shoes', 'musical items', 'pets', 'solidarity', 'witty chants' and 'a cuddly toy'!

As far back as the early 1970s, Lasch was writing about what he called 'the cult of participation', in which the experience of protesting is what protesting is all about. Half a century later and it seems something akin to the cult of participation has enveloped not only the committed activist, but a much broader cross section of society. For example, the leftism of today's metropolitan middle classes is characterised by an easy, throwaway moralism that is signalled at every turn with little sense of reflexivity about how it looks to anyone struggling to live on a state pension or stay above the poverty line on a sink estate. In 2020, the writer Neil Davenport coined the term 'cutesy radicals' to describe middle-class leftists whose political symbolism is so infantilised they now rely on primary-school imagery – children's rainbow paintings with the words 'Our NHS Heroes'/'PPE now' or the eco-doom classroom daubings of their kids – to flag their anti-government stance. Davenport sees this development as part of a wider adult attachment to what he calls 'primary-school aesthetics':

> Primary-school imagery has also become a marketing device for big companies. Ice-cream company Ben & Jerry's (part of the Unilever corporation) has long used kiddish paintings on marketing campaigns, including those associated with its One World/One Heart campaign. Then there is the Innocent Drinks company (owned by Coca-Cola), whose images and fonts resemble a primary-school reading book. Delivery service Ocado has a fleet of vans that resemble a children's toy set – all blaring primary colours and 'A is for Apple' images. The overall effect of all this is to make big companies appear like small cottage industries, and ones that also champion good ethical and environmental causes. Primary-school images, then, have become code for virtue.[44]

This combination of infantile virtue signalling and dinner-party activism is also evident in other forms of supposed middle-class protest. Consider the type of political posturing that occurs every year at contemporary music festivals like Glastonbury, Parklife and Coachella. The well-heeled, increasingly middle-aged nostalgia junkies who flock to these gatherings – the average age of the UK festival-goer is thirty-six – inevitably wind up making some sort of sweary but predictably safe left-wing statement ('Fuck the Tories', 'Fuck the Supreme Court', 'Oh, Jeremy Corbyn', etc.). No doubt these collective political gestures feel good in the moment, but like most of the acts that headline Glastonbury these days, it's ultimately bland, middle-of-the-road stuff; these events are a comforting annual ritual for metropolitan liberals no longer capable of drawing a distinction between entertainment and politics.[45] The problem here is that, whether it takes the form of resistance fantasies at music festivals or cultural memes and online campaigns with the lifespan of the average housefly, cutesy radicalism is less about meaningful politics and more about self-expression and identity projection.

It's important to acknowledge that not all forms of protest have devolved into cutesy or synthetic radicalism, and that many countries in recent years have experienced a major resurgence in more animated, coordinated and often unrepentantly violent forms of social protest. This is especially true in the United States, where the country has been shaken by a series of activist-led political controversies, including: the most sustained student protests on university campuses since the 1960s; the 2020 BLM demonstrations; the rise of the militant Antifa movement in the Pacific Northwest and elsewhere; and a revival of ultranationalist and white supremacist direct action. These movements all clearly involve highly motivated individuals, many of whom are prepared to commit acts of violence and risk arrest and imprisonment in the name of their chosen cause. It is wrong, therefore, to assume that contemporary political activism is no longer a powerful force. That said, such is the pronounced state of our pantomime politics that even these more serious forms of protest have been undermined by cultural infantilisation.

In previous eras, unless you were personally caught up in the white teeth of a political protest or civil disturbance, it was impossible to understand the emotional and behavioural dynamics that shaped these events and gave them meaning. Today, however, as a result of video uploads and live streaming at rallies, we have access to countless videos that show the close-up reality of late-modern protest. They do not make for edifying viewing. For example, videos of student protests on US campuses often depict young adults screaming, wailing and crying: their voices teetering on the edge of anxiety and mania, their faces displaying the same signs of distress (the arched eyebrows, the incredulous widening eyes) as that of a child who can't get his own way. At one level, this degree of emotionality can be understood as a normal by-product of political contestation, but at a deeper level, underneath the surface aesthetic of campus rebellion, it lays bare the look-at-me superficial narcissism that Lasch warned us about. In these and numerous other videos of recent university demonstrations, so pronounced is the sense of anxiety and emotionality on display, it's sometimes difficult to tell if this generation of activist students is waving or drowning.

A similar but even more intense pattern of behaviour is evident in viral videos that show Antifa members clashing with police, rival protestors or local residents over practices such as unlawful traffic stops and attempts to create urban 'autonomous zones'. One video in particular sticks in the memory. It shows a middle-aged woman in a pink vest being assaulted by a group of protestors in downtown Los Angeles in July 2021. The lone woman had turned up at a rally with a hand-written sign stating she didn't want to see trans women's penises in women's spaces; a statement that in itself is enough for some trans-rights activists to see her not just assaulted but burnt at the nearest stake for gender heresy. Isolated on a side street, the woman is quickly confronted by a baying crowd, including masked, black-clad Antifa activists. Just like when high-school bullies pick on the weak kid after class, the crowd of *adult* men and women home in on their chosen target, jostling and humiliating her, swearing in her face and repetitively chanting 'Go home, transphobe'. They trash her stuff (hat, sunglasses) and throw water in her face, all the time giggling manically as they feed off their victim's growing fear. Skateboards, backpacks and adolescent cosplay all add to the high-school-like feel of the incident. This is street politics so no one should expect Socratic dialectic, but what occurs in this video and many others like it is crass, desperate and above all adolescent stuff – a reboot of *Lord of the Flies* for the Millennial generation.

The infantilised state of protest and resistance is equally evident at the other end of the political scale. Scroll through videos of hard-right Trump supporters clashing with Antifa groups or the Proud Boys antagonising all-comers at Second Amendment rallies and Patriot Prayer meetings, and you can't fail to be struck by the juvenile nature of some of the antics. Patriot LARPing, frat-boy hollering, the childish repetition of platitudes and irrational 'conspirituality' theories: all are on display in these videos, despite the fact that most of those involved are a generation older than their leftist antagonists. But whether they stem from the left or the right, these examples all illustrate the pantomime-like nature of much contemporary political resistance. At this point, however, even the pantomime metaphor seems strained. Given the pyretic emotions that underpin these now increasingly common moments of political rage, perhaps it would be better to frame things in terms of a passion play: a late-modern dramaturgical performance of faith and devotion in which two equally tone-deaf factions square off in a contrived battle of good versus evil.

Good and evil? It is not the first time the frenzied morality of our current political moment has been framed in these binary terms. Several commentators have already made the comparison between today's more extreme Woke militants and those who were drawn to anarchical millenarian movements of the late Middle Ages.[46] Similarly, much has been made of the way many contemporary right-wing groups in the US and elsewhere lean on eschatological Christian theology and other revivalist forms of chiliastic fantasy. Parallels between both these groups and earlier apocalyptic traditions that believed society had to be destroyed before it could be remade anew certainly bear examination. But in terms of tying contemporary political resistance back to some of my earlier arguments, of more importance here is the way today's activists often exhibit forms of neo-puritanical moral reasoning. By this I do not mean a revival of high Protestantism, but simply the emergence of a secular high-mindedness linked to the unwavering belief in a singular worldview which is then used as a justificatory framework to repudiate any form of alternative or dissenting opinion.[47]

The most obvious manifestation of this mindset is the purification ritual, something that featured prominently during the BLM protests. Often involving symbolic acts such as public officials washing the feet of protestors, or groups of white middle-class self-styled 'allies' prostrating themselves like medieval penitents seeking to join the company of the Elect after the Rhapsody, these moments of moral purity achieve nothing practical nor offer any meaningful vision of an alternative future. Instead, they function as make-believe cleansing ceremonies that, as the late Angelo

Codevilla pointed out, are not only self-defeating but potentially dangerous:

> The Americans who confess other people's racism absolve themselves inexpensively by a moral mechanism common to humanity: the more I profess to hate evil, the more I showcase my own goodness. Such confessions, however, have a particular history of tragedy in Christian civilisation. Again and again over the centuries, persons who have imagined themselves cleansed by ritual confessions have believed themselves elevated above the rest of humanity and, hence, entitled to oppress or even annihilate those around them. Today's self-purifiers, arms outstretched in supine submission, who then countenance violence against persons, property, and cultural symbols, are mostly unwitting protagonists in yet another chapter of a hoary history.[48]

The rise of a neo-puritanical mindset was precisely what J. G. Ballard had in mind in *Kingdom Come*. In the passage quoted earlier, Ballard predicted that, in post-consumerist, secular societies, people will eventually backslide into what he described as 'the inner darkness' of 'superstition and the irrational'. Confronted with the emptiness of their situation, they will 'yearn for magic and unreason' and the type of rituals which 'served them well in the past and might help them again'. We can already see this tendency in some of the actions of the more fanatical Woke activists: it is there in the ritualistic demand for atonement for actions and events that took place centuries previously; it is there in the urge to purge contemporary culture of much-loved books and TV shows on the basis that they fail to adhere to language standards set yesterday; it is there in the social media 'pile-ons' that function similarly to the auto-da-fé shaming festivals of public penance carried out by Spanish Inquisitors; and it is there in the censoring, de-platforming and cancelling of individuals who have transgressed social codes to do with race, sex, interpersonal behaviour and even humour no longer deemed acceptable by the self-ordained high priests of social justice. Such developments suggest that the will to punish and to purify, to enthusiastically stoke the fires of an all-consuming late-modern bonfire of the vanities, is already with us. But it also points to something else, something already discussed in another context: the mainstreaming of fantasy as a psycho-political strategy.

One of the features of both puritanical and millenarian movements was that although they typically emerged out of ordinary struggles, the solutions they offered always relied upon myths of rapture and revolution. Here, once again, the similarity with today's activist insurgents is striking. Instead of clearly articulated goals, we are offered secular-theological slogans ('Hands up, don't shoot', 'I can't breathe', 'Language *is* violence', etc.) that function more like sacred scripture than political ideology. And instead of harnessing the genuine sense of outrage that originally sparked the BLM protests to forge viable coalitional alignments, the hyper-moral activists who claim to speak for the protestors fixate on dismantling existing systems of language and other types of cultural 'tone policing'.

Political choices have consequences. In the case of BLM, the main consequence is that four years after it held the world's gaze it has achieved virtually nothing of long-lasting practical importance. Seattle's CHOP (Capitol Hill Occupation Protest) 'autonomous zone' quickly devolved from a well-intentioned socialist cooperative into a chaotic site of gun violence and lawlessness. The many murals and impromptu shrines that appeared on the street corner where George Floyd was killed did nothing to stop the surrounding south Minneapolis neighbourhood's descent into violence after it was temporarily declared a no-police zone. And the Wall of Moms protest vigil in Portland, Oregon was equally short-lived after the organiser was rounded on for allegedly 'sanctifying white motherhood'. A sense of fantasy also surrounded many of the demands BLM organisers made in the wake of the protests. Eye-catching calls for lots of free stuff and quixotic abolitionism serve a performative purpose, but for these goals to become a reality, a sense of proportion and an ability to compromise are necessary. And herein lies the problem. Because it prioritises the motifs of redemption, purification and self-righteous destruction over ordinary politics and practical policy solutions, all extreme Wokeism can ever offer is the juvenile politics of fantasy, a neo-puritanical, almost metaphysical orthodoxy which believes – just as the anarchical millenarians of the late Middle Ages did – that the only way to save society is to destroy it.

In their book *On the Edge: Political Cults Right and Left*, Dennis Tourish and Tim Wohlforth argue that cultic forms of organisation and belief have infected the realm of late-modern politics. They argue that, on both sides of the political divide, political extremists should best be understood 'as cults on a par with the Unification Church (the Moonies), Scientologists, and other bizarre groupings who regularly capture media headlines'.[49] Tourish and Wohlforth were writing in 2000, long before the emergence of today's fanatical Woke militants. Yet their analysis of earlier political groups that fell into the trap of cultism makes for interesting reading when thinking about the moral and political framework of contemporary neo-puritanical activists. Consider the following list of abridged characteristics set out in *On the Edge*:

Create your own social reality: 'Cults short-circuit this process by eliminating all sources of information other than that provided by the cult ... In time, their vocabulary shifts, so that cult-sanctioned words and expressions predominate.'

363

A rigid belief system: 'In the case of left-wing religious cults this belief system suggests that all social, natural, scientific, political, economic, historical, and philosophical issues can be analyzed only from within the group's theoretical paradigm.' [Something] which 'removes the need to seek intellectual sustenance outside the group's own ideological fortress'.

The cult of confession: 'this requires people to confess their inadequacies . . . and the many ways they have let the organisation down.'

Loading the language: the extensive use of 'repetitive phrases' and 'the thought-terminating cliché' . . . 'as interpretative shortcuts.'

In light of recent media allegations about leading figures within BLM purchasing expensive houses and giving lucrative contracts to relatives, one further characteristic of political cults pointed out by Tourish and Wohlforth is also worth mentioning: 'A belief in equality, combined with the accumulation of enormous privileges for the cult leaders'.

Whatever Wokeness is, it's clearly too broad and nebulous a phenomenon to be thought of simply as a destructive cult. But like the many cults that flourished in the second half of the twentieth century, the tendency to judge oneself, and others, entirely through the prism of the group is something shared by today's zealous social justice warriors. Likewise, the lapse into political fantasy, including dreams about the destruction (the cancellation?) of one's enemies, is also a shared defining feature of both cultism and Wokeism.

Clearly, many will not welcome this comparison. They will claim my analysis of the contemporary identitarian left is too harsh. My response to such critics is simple: switch off Twitter/X and take a long, hard look around. Not only has the working class and much of the middle class lost any type of political agency (and is without any obvious way of reacquiring it), but the only thing the major parties of the left can offer these days is a warmed-over stew of technocratic managerialism posing as politics, and condescending, out-of-touch candidates (encapsulated in Michelle Obama's staggeringly contemptuous 'when *they* go low, *we* go high' maxim) of a type favoured only by coastal Democrats and metropolitan Labourites. Greatly facilitated by the rise of the internet and the inability of the contemporary infantocracy to mobilise any meaningful political alternative, we have begun the slow descent into the dark, gloomy swamps of what can only be described as a new era of ambient anxiety – perhaps even mass paranoia, hysteria and, in the longer term, violence and brutality.

In our outwardly glossy but inwardly hollow world of pound-shop politicians, hyper-confident pseudo-experts and demi-witted celebrities, where obvious lies and falsehoods become 'truths' simply because enough fools believe them, and where pantomime politics and other forms of cultural infantilisation have created the perfect conditions for the propagation of fantasy, there's little room left for the community values and histories of trust and shared interest that used to galvanise people into co-operative political alliances. In their place has emerged a new self-righteous and more performative form of identity-based political expression in which outgroup members are demonised and interpersonal relations are viewed as potential sites of enemy engagement. To make matters worse, the chance of political course correction is blocked by a high-school-like public sphere in which any challenge to the mandated rules and behavioural codes is seized upon by social media hall monitors and other identity-obsessed laptop warriors whose desire to convince or persuade has long since given way to the urge to purge and humiliate.

If it wasn't so desperately serious, you could be forgiven for thinking it was all just a bit, well, childish.

Christopher Lasch's Angry Ghost (CLAG) is one of a new breed of anonymous online public intellectuals – sometimes referred to as pseudonymous social critics. In 2022, s/he published a Substack article entitled 'Cringe dialectics' about the rise of a new style of political 'display of high awkwardness that can often generate an intense feeling of second-hand embarrassment – or even shame – in having witnessed it'.[50] According to CLAG, this new undignified cringe politics is apparent everywhere from NHS-promoting TikTok dance videos to images and memes of the costumed and face-painted 'QAnon Shaman', Jake Angeli, rampaging through the US Senate in 2021. Mobilising elements such as 'glib humour', 'narcissistic fantasy', 'emotionalism' and 'simplified truths and stylised realities', CLAG argues that the politics of cringe is best understood as a form of kitsch, a highly sentimentalised style of artistic representation characterised by questionable taste and low-rent aesthetics.

One does not need a deep grasp of political theory to recognise the obvious parallels that exist between cringe dialectics and pantomime politics – or for that matter some of the imagery and mawkish prose that has accompanied the rise of identity-based narcissism and the cultural construction of victimhood. All these developments are clearly reflected in and intensified by the emergence of this mode of un-satirisable kitsch simplification. CLAG acknowledges this, of course, stating at one point that cringe dialectics, packaged as it is 'according to the platform logics of the social media era', is at once 'disconcertingly ingenious and infantilising'. But s/he also understands something even more important. By pitting emotion against intellect and eroding the public sphere to the extent that only the burnt-out shells of empathy and honesty remain, cringe politics has pushed open the (back) door to creeping authoritarianism: 'Perhaps this is why the use of kitsch aesthetics in authoritarian politics can be so effective – it means people don't take these movements seriously until it's too late.'

Writing in 2018, Simon Gottschalk noted astutely that an infantilised culture is one that leaves its flanks open to the incursions of soft authoritarianism: 'While we might find it trivial or amusing, the infantilist ethos becomes especially seductive in times of social crises and fear . . . It's not difficult to imagine an infantile society being attracted to authoritarian rule.'[51] Gottschalk is correct to make this association. Six years on from his comments and the coming together of infantilisation and authoritarianism has only grown more intense. Most obviously, as Gottschalk notes, our interaction with smartphones and other 'high-tech pacifiers' has fostered an ever-more 'submissive attitude' to being watched over and manipulated. We 'surrender to their requirements', agree 'to "terms" we do not understand', and unthinkingly hand over sensitive personal data to corporations that routinely violate our privacy and surveil us at every turn. It's a similar story in the modern workplace, where employees are increasingly monitored, tracked and treated like children to be punished or rewarded depending on the whims of our all-seeing corporate nannies-in-chief. This employer-as-controlling-parent dynamic has even been described by one observer as a new form of 'co-dependency'.[52]

This type of *patrician infantilisation* is also at the heart of the so-called 'nudge agenda'; the use of behavioural science techniques by governments around the world to influence their citizens into adopting certain 'preferred' courses of action. Even if we set aside the fact that considerable doubt has been expressed about the efficacy of using behavioural science as a policy tool, it's not difficult to see that what nudge ultimately represents is a patronising form of soft authoritarianism masquerading as libertarian paternalism, its unstated but undoubted aim being to replace individual, adult autonomy with a form of governance that views individuals as passive, childlike actors who must constantly be watched over and told what's best for them, lest they think independently and go against the grain of the ruling technocratic orthodoxy.

An interesting metaphor for all this behavioural nannying and loss of adult agency is the phenomenon of the self-driving car. In the not-too-distant future, cars will no longer be something the driver controls, but instead will be packed with sensors and AI monitors that will manage not just the steering but every function inside the cabin, from climate control to the automatic downloading (i.e., purchasing) of new software updates for all the unnecessary high-tech gizmos that now clutter up the driving experience. Like all tech-led revolutions, self-driving cars will be rolled out on the basis of safety and the misguided premise that the algorithm knows best. Yet despite more than $100 billion of investment, these auto-driving schemes remain highly inefficient and, in many cases, downright dangerous. How many more billions will be wasted on such quixotic ideas before we wake up to the fact that driverless cars, like many other types of urban 'smartness', and even the concept of behavioural science itself, are all essentially high-tech pacifiers for the infantilised generation? Alternative policy initiatives designed to coerce and control adult-children, so they behave appropriately in the performative government spaces that we used to call society.

The famous German jurist Carl Schmitt once observed that 'If a people no longer has the strength or will to maintain itself in the political sphere, that is not the end of politics in the world. It is only the end of weak people.' It remains to be seen whether or not infantilism's current pathologies – narcissism, victimhood and the emerging infantocracy – will collectively produce a populace so weakened and civically anaemic that it loses the sense of its own power and ends up being trapped in a downward spiral of anti-adult policies enacted by infantilised politicians. But whatever happens, as Schmitt makes clear, some sort of post-cringe, post-pantomime politics will emerge. The problem, of course, is that against a constant thrum of fear, conspiracy and dystopian catastrophism, it won't take much to turn the soft authoritarianism associated with patrician infantilisation into something much harder that ends up destroying the very principles underpinning our democracy.

Epilogue

Ten Rules for a More Grown-up Society

W hat are we to do about our infantilised world? How should we combat the rise of the Kidult and the problems associated with the emergent infantocracy? Here I offer some brief reflections on how to push back against the ever-encroaching forces of infantilisation and adultification.

1. View adulthood as an aspirational destination rather than something to be avoided at all costs: No matter how deep the Kidult buries himself in the pop-cultural toybox, an infantilised life is ultimately a pathetic one, a form of existential escapism devoid of distinction, struggle or meaning. It is therefore essential you do all you can to reaffirm adulthood as a valued destination rather than something that exists forever beyond the horizon.

What can you do, then, *as an individual*, to pump the brakes on the runaway infantilism juggernaut? Start by accepting the fact that the current situation is not going to be turned around by our captured cultural elites and infantocratic governments. You're going to have to take a stand and adultify yourself. This means seeking out films, books, museum exhibits and other cultural products that reflect the complexities and vitality of adult life as opposed to sophomoric, self-righteous art or stories that exist entirely in the realm of childish fantasy. To be successful in this endeavour you'll need to ignore the hectoring advice of today's joyless culture police whose creeping censoriousness now encompasses everything from Charlotte Brontë to Dr Seuss. Instead, create for yourself an unashamedly adult cultural world based on the premise that it's better to study and learn from the past than to airbrush it out of existence. The achievements of history's great writers, musicians, scientists and philosophers will serve as a far better guide to the future than any offered by today's sanctimonious 'sensitivity readers', neophile influencers or fly-by-night 'thought leaders'.

Reject self-absorbed, identitarian novels written to appease inclusivity and diversity quotas, and instead explore great works of literature, from Homer to Houellebecq, Austen to Atwood, that have something universal to say about life and its vicissitudes. Likewise, develop a more balanced cinematic diet by swopping out green-screened franchise movies for more challenging films by thought-provoking directors like Kubrick, Kurosawa, Tarkovsky, Reichardt, Herzog, etc. These canonical works will not only give you a window on the adult world, they might even change your life.

Here I should be clear, I am not suggesting you shun all forms of cultural escapism; that would be absurd, and elitist. My intention is simply to call for a long overdue rebalancing – something which, of course, is easier said than done. Entertainment corporations, for example, have little interest in initiating change. It's far easier for them to keep churning out endless brand-based sequels and retellings of familiar tales than it is to take a chance and develop challenging and characterful stories that say something valuable and timeless about the human condition. The truth is, the only way to stem the children's-stories-as-adult-entertainment tsunami is if we as an audience demand more from our cultural producers. As a consumer you have a choice – it's time to exercise it if you want to recreate a more adult world.

2. Protect childhood against those who seek to erode it as a distinct stage of the life course: Whether it's educational institutions that facilitate the 'school-to-prison pipeline' or those that recycle their adult obsessions about sex and gender through the lives of toddlers and children, it's clear that the traditional legal and cultural boundaries associated with being a child are under threat. It's vital therefore you defend without compromise the category against those who, for whatever reason, are actively trying to undermine childhood innocence. This point should be self-evident. The fact it no longer is tells you everything you need to know about the morally confused state of contemporary society.

3. Reject identitarianism. It's not only tiresome, but it blocks the path to progressive political change: From the five-day week to gender discrimination laws, these campaigns achieved their stated aim not because they drew on autobiographical proclamations or the cult of personality, but because they galvanised widescale support via the traditional, tedious process of grassroots political organisation. These days, however, such methods are out of fashion with the identitarian class. Instead, what passes for 'resistance' is often little more than a form of moralistic psycho-political emoting that advocates more for the self than for the cause. If social justice is indeed the aim, then this must change. Relinquish your fixation with identity-based politics and instead lend weight to something more universal and adult, something capable of bringing people together rather than fracturing them into a million intersectional shards. It won't sit well with the identitarian rebels out there, but the truth is that the only way to bring about real social change is to (re)create collective political movements that stress mutuality and community rather than obscurantist issues linked to tribal identity.

4. In today's world, unsubstantiated fear and over-the-top anger are everywhere. Be adult about it and don't catastrophise, don't panic: From various iterations of terrorist threats to dystopian accounts of environmental devastation to fearmongering about the next global pandemic or looming financial crash, we are constantly bombarded with highly charged news stories that predict imminent catastrophe. It matters not that by virtually every metric Western societies are safer, healthier and less prone to natural disaster than at any point in human history, many people still live their lives in a constant state of agitation, working themselves up over putative threats and doomsday scenarios that fly in the face of statistical or scientific reason. Such flawed thinking has more in common with the mindset of a child than a rational adult. It's normal for children to frighten themselves with stories about monsters, ghosts and scary animals, but a big part of growing up is overcoming such irrational fears. Too many adults today, however, seem unable to move on from their own particular source of anxiety, whether that's Covid-19 maximalism, Trump-based hysteria or Just Stop Oil apocalypticism. As a result, they blunder through life like an eight-year-old suffering from a bad case of the night terrors.

It's a similar story when we look at the angry state of contemporary political debate. One of the most depressing features of our infantilised world is the adolescent nature of the public square. In a mature adult society, individuals implicitly understand that screeching at the top of your voice or emotionally bullying people into submission is not an effective way to bring about positive social change. Unfortunately, too many people seem only too happy to resort to childish emotionalism to make their point: to yell, curse and abuse – and when that doesn't work, to belittle, smear and cancel.

Any society that replaces political reasoning with fear and anger risks permanently stalling the dialectic. Do not contribute to this toddlerisation of democracy. The next time you feel yourself being manipulated by media scare stories about new or growing risks to your health and safety, try not to overreact. Chances are you aren't anywhere near as 'unsafe' or 'at risk' as you think you are. Likewise, when you find yourself getting angry at someone you've never met just because their opinion differs from yours, don't take it as a personal affront to the non-negotiable subjectivities of 'your truth'. Take a moment to process the fact that, their opinion, like yours, has a right to be aired – whatever you may think of it. In other words, when entering the public square, try not to let your emotions get the better of you – it's the adult thing to do.

5. Be wary of any school or university that has allowed its educational principles to be captured by politicised ideas based on fashionable groupthink: Education should be the frontline of defence in the battle against infantilisation. Unfortunately, in the UK and the US, this essential barrier has not only been breached but overrun. Consequently, instead of schools and universities capable of instilling in students the intellectual capacity and habits of thought required to function as responsible, self-determining adults, contemporary education resembles, in the language of Christopher Lasch, a 'watery blend' of 'mind-emptying ideology' and pseudo self-fulfilment. Part of the problem can be explained by the simple fact that too many pedagogues labour under the delusion that the classroom is the best place to solve society's social and political problems. This fashionable reprioritisation of the mission of education has ensured that values crucial to the meritocratic ideal, such as resilience, resolve and emotional reasoning, are devalued and, as a result, late-modern education is no longer countering the infantilising and narcissistic currents abroad in our culture.

Think twice, then, about paying a large sum of money to embark on a humanities or social science degree taught by biased ideologues who favour indoctrination over education. And think thrice about attending any university that does not staunchly defend heterodox opinions or that kowtows to students who claim to be traumatised by content or speakers that do not align with their particular worldview. (If this means that a small number of students are upset or claim to feel unsafe, then so be it).

And finally, if governments aren't capable of upholding and enforcing the sacrosanct principle that education should be undertaken objectively and not in a manner that endorses a specific politicised outlook, then you must make your presence felt in the sector – whether that means holding local educational authorities to account or actively boycotting universities that fail to protect academic standards and the free exchange of ideas.

6. Reject the coddling and cosseting that is the by-product of a culture obsessed with safetyism: Prior to the twenty-first century, few parents of a toddler thought it necessary to child-proof their home by fitting it out with safety devices such as padded foam corner-and-edge bumpers, window guards, electricity outlet covers or anti-tip appliance anchors. Today, however, parents who don't engage in this type of child-centric health and safety are considered almost criminally negligent. In recent years, this fixation with overprotection has steadily crept up the life course to include school-aged children, teens and even young adults. This pervasive culture of safetyism is one of the primary contributing factors in the rise of infantilism and must be arrested as part of any meaningful de-infantilisation strategy. By turning safety and risk aversion into the unspoken ideology of our times, the professional managerial class has created a world in which household gas stoves are deemed dangerous and university students must be protected from characters in fairy tales. Don't let yourself be corrupted by this mindset. Growing up means rising to challenges – and, yes, taking risks. Equip your kids with the necessary skills to successfully transition to adulthood by subjecting them to age-appropriate challenges and stressors. And equip yourself with the good sense to know that, when someone uses a phrase like 'out of an abundance of caution' or 'safety is a lock, but you are the key', they are often doing so for ideological reasons or as a means of exerting control.

7. *Lifestyle advertising is an adulthood repellent. Limit your exposure to it by changing your viewing habits and reducing time spent online*: By definition, advertising is patronising. Not only do advertisers presume to know what it is you want, they also believe they are capable of telling you what it is you *should* want. This is not new, but recently have you noticed you're being patronised even more than usual? There's a reason for that. Since at least the turn of the century, lifestyle advertising has been systematically undermining adulthood and destabilising intergenerational relations. At least three strategies have been used to achieve this goal. First, the fabrication and widescale deployment of the 'fun-loving', 'ironic' and often 'bewildered' *adult-child consumer* has allowed advertisers to bypass adult rationality and establish a new, ever-expanding stage of pre-adulthood consumption. Second, marketers and advertisers have deliberately undermined established cultural archetypes and hierarchical role models which in previous eras functioned as examples of well-defined adulthood. Third, because the advertising industry has spent decades undermining adult knowhow, we now consider it entirely normal to purchase competencies, services, and expert advice for everything from dog training to financial record-keeping to child-rearing. As a result, the fully socialised postmodern consumer has become a childlike, skill-free dependent. Advertising is obviously a necessary evil, but this does not mean you should have to put up with a constant stream of 'ironic' adult bashing and downright silliness. Do what you can to limit your exposure to these commercial hallucinations and you'll be all the more adult for it.

8. Cultivate your inner George Orwell and treat pantomime politicians of any stripe with contempt. Carefully scrutinise anyone who seeks or demands a political platform and if you sense the slightest whiff of moral triangulation, take your support elsewhere: Contemporary politics is in a pitiful state. Our professional political class are, for the most part, an out-of-touch ship of fools crewed by self-interested, soundbite-peddling bullshitters, elite captured virtue signallers and visionless human bollards whose only discernible skill is the ability to fail forward. Meanwhile, in the alternative realm of activist politics, we are offered a masochist's choice of, on the one hand, de-civilising environmental apocalypticism, and on the other, variants of victim and identity-based performative politics that are long on ideological purity but short on voter appeal. It's a depressing state of affairs that is most evident when elections roll around and we see just how incapable our inept politicians are of putting forth any kind of clear-sighted, positive agenda for the future.

Given this frustrating situation, it's perhaps unsurprising that many disgruntled voters now look to well-intentioned but typically unqualified personalities to provide some sort of moral direction or policy steer. However, rather than improve the situation, hyper-normalised celebrities serve only to further muddy the political waters. In fact, thanks to the general stupefaction of our politics, we now have a situation where not only are celebrities trying to appear more politician-like, but certain politicians seem keen to ape celebrities. For example, there was a time when you wouldn't follow footballers on fashion, let alone politics. This is no longer the case. Whether it's Marcus Rashford calling for free school meals, Troy Deeney weighing in on the epidemiological risks of Covid-19, or Gary Neville writing books about the role powerful football clubs should play in the vanguard against racism, footballers' opinions feature regularly in the public sphere. Meanwhile, former Conservative Party Cabinet ministers Nadine Dorries and Matt Hancock are happy to appear on *I'm a Celebrity . . . Get Me Out of Here!,* claiming they can do more for their 'social causes' by appearing on a knockabout jungle game-show than they can as Members of Parliament. Such examples lend weight to the feeling that, when it comes to contemporary politics, society is putting its books back on the wrong shelves.

In his famous 1919 essay, 'Politics as a vocation', the great German sociologist and economist Max Weber stated that politicians and political parties must always exude a sense of 'traditional authority' based on 'an eternal past', and that without a certain bearing – or 'grace' – legitimate political rule is threatened. It's hard to know what level of grace the former health secretary displayed when eating a camel's testicle on *I'm a Celebrity . . . Get Me Out of Here!,* but perhaps that's the price grifter-politicians like Hancock are prepared to pay these days 'for connecting with the people'. In the same essay, Weber also warned about the danger of 'vanity' and the problems that ensue when political figures make decisions based on the emotional attachments of 'followers and sycophants' and not on rational reasoning or objective facts. It's an observation that could have been written for the social media age, and one that both media-obsessed politicians and the new breed of celebrity-politicos would do well to remember the next time they feel compelled to clamber onto their soapbox.

What should you as an individual do to help recreate more adult politics? In truth, there's not too much you can do – after all, as the old adage goes, every nation gets the politicians it deserves. That said, just because recent generations of UK and US politicians have vacated any sense of mature, responsible leadership does not mean you should give up hope and retreat into nihilism or a world of fringe conspiratorial beliefs. Quite the opposite. Now is the time to reassert the importance of political principles, to hold your elected officials to account, to defend the rules of democratic elections and to demand leaders that, á la Weber, are serious and vocationally committed to the task at hand. In short, you must reject the allure of pantomime politics and instead seek out and support principled representatives who can put us back on the path to grown-up political discourse.

9. Subject any new technology that wants to watch over you or track and shape your behaviour to the utmost scrutiny – especially if it's being uncritically promoted by political figures or tech industry patricians on the grounds it will enhance public safety or improve security: Far from bringing about a rise in the level of public intelligence, the information revolution has ushered in an era of misinformation, mass distraction, and never-ending culture wars marked by childish squabbles and neo-medieval public shaming rituals. This is not technology's fault – as Melvin Kranzberg reminds us in his famous 1986 paper on technology and history, 'technology is neither good nor bad; nor is it neutral'. In a well-governed adult world, this observation would be reassuring, but in a society overseen by infantocrats and softened up by years of cultural infantilisation, it is not just worrying but potentially dystopian.

For some time now, political theorists and security scholars have expressed concern that developments in predictive applications, scalable AI and smart, self-organising systems pose a risk to the established liberal order. In crude terms, the thinking here is that the greater the networked connectivity, the greater the chance of sleepwalking into a new era of digital-political governance based on biometrics and advanced techno-systems of pre-emption and control. Given the current direction of travel this is not a fanciful scenario. We already know from experience that governments across the globe consistently lag behind 'big tech' when it comes to understanding new developments, their watchdog bodies and hapless select committees flailing around in an effort to exert even a modicum of oversight and regulation. Even more worryingly, the comforting, always-there-to-pacify-you nature of the digital realm has already primed the late-modern Kidult to acquiesce to the algo-rithm, to cave in and cede important aspects of everyday life (and liberty) to cybernetic and computational control. Meanwhile, softly, in the background, ongoing advancements in the field of digital entertainment, especially virtual reality gaming, will further infan-tilise end users by tapping into the fantasies and aspirational self-delusions spawned by social media. Day-by-day, with each auto-matic software update, each ignored terms-and-conditions template, each failed government attempt to rein in the power of big tech, we allow not only our privacy and agency to be eroded, but, more importantly, that sense of ourselves as independent, sequestered beings – all things that, in theory, should increase as we travel further into adulthood.

Alongside its many benefits, digital culture also breeds a beguil-ing passivity and compliance among its users. Take more of an active interest in this dynamic. It's good to know who is watching you, and why.

10. Finally, be prepared to make a stand against authoritarianism. Always remember that not all tyranny comes at the point of a gun. Often all it takes is a collective shrug of the shoulders: The more infantilised a society, the easier it is to control, coerce and corrupt. Be extremely watchful, then, of any government, corporation or institution that treats you like a child in need of protection rather than a rational adult who knows their own mind. In the same way, do not be indifferent to objective truth, for if you abandon facts in favour of fantasy, you will, to paraphrase Orwell, drift so far from reality that lies seem truthful, and murder appears respectable. In *On Tyranny: Twenty Lessons from the Twentieth Century*, the historian of genocide Timothy Snyder writes, 'You submit to tyranny when you renounce the difference between what you want to hear and what is actually the case.' When children are young, we forgive them for closing their eyes and hoping the bad things will go away. As adults, we know, or at least we should know, that such magical thinking doesn't work. Remember this when next you sense your personal liberty being eroded, or when someone in authority speaks to you like a five-year-old girl talking to her dolls. It might just be that your very freedom depends on your ability to think and stand up for yourself as a competent and confident adult.

Acknowledgements

Like the human life course, books are shaped and marked by many people. It is therefore a pleasure to acknowledge the contributions of the numerous friends and colleagues who have helped take this book from infancy to maturity.

Very early in this book's journey, I was helped in my thinking by Avi Brisman, Frank Furedi, Travis Linnemann and Majid Yar. My thanks to them for their time and insight. I'm also grateful to former colleagues Chris Shilling and Miri Song for reading and commenting on early draft chapters. Many other people have helped me in all sorts of different ways during the writing of this book and I am greatly in their debt: Jordan Shlain and Caroline Eggli-Shlain for fun times in Europe and for giving me a home in San Francisco, on numerous occasions; Jack Katz, for wise counsel and for reminding me it's okay to take your time writing a book; my 'Brazilian team', Salah H. Khaled Jr., Álvaro Oxley da Rocha, José Vicente Tavares-do-Santos, and Tiago Lorenzini for translating my work into Portuguese and for their tireless efforts promoting cultural criminology in Brazil; Diego Héctor Padilla Lobos and Amy Wassif for collating the data and configuring Table 1; Aleksandras Dobryninas and Jolanta Aleknevičienė for their warm hospitality when I visited the University of Vilniaus as part of my sabbatical in 2022; and Olga Petinsteva, Greg Snyder, Alma Melendez, Rita Faria, and Sandra Bucerius for the conversations and good humour.

I am blessed with good friends and two of them went the extra mile and read the completed manuscript. I have written numerous books and articles with Jeff Ferrell over the years, and so it was heartening that my former collaborator and criminological mischief-maker enjoyed this latest solo effort – even though I'm sure he didn't agree with all my arguments. My old friend and fellow English immigrant to Scandinavia, Frank Palser ran his eagle-eye over the proofs, correcting numerous grammatical errors and saving readers from some of my more inscrutable prose. Thanks Frank, for your support and for always being first to the bar in Stockholm and on Swedish skiing trips – a feat of outrageous generosity that few would even contemplate.

As any ex-pat knows, one of the consequences of leaving behind your country of origin is that even longstanding friendships can whither and fade away over time. So, thanks to Owen Neal, Tim Turner, Steve Hall, David Pritchard, Geoffrey Hunt, Tony Jefferson, Larry Herzog, Vince Miller, Larry Ray, Nicola Henderson, and Patrick Foulis and Milya Vered Foulis, for making the effort to stay in touch. Let me tell you, even the briefest of check-ins means a lot during those dark, seemingly endless Danish winters. On the subject of staying in touch, I should like particularly to express my gratitude to James Henderson. Twenty years ago, in my first book, I thanked James for providing 'regular breaks from writing' and amazingly he's still doing it. So, thanks TGOWOTW for all the Twickenham and Wimbledon tickets, the frequent use of your attic guest suite, and for being a stalwart friend since first we met on Q corridor at Fitz all those years ago.

While Copenhagen is a sophisticated and aesthetically pleasing city to live in, Danes, by their own admission, can often be difficult to get to know. Thanks, then, to Heine Kaarsberg, David Brehm Sausdal, Henrik Vigh, and (honouree Dane) Sam Lusk, for good companionship and late-night drinks. If there's a better city in Europe for the latter, I have yet to visit it. However, no one has done more to make me feel at home in Denmark than Jakob Johan Demant, who over the years has helped me with everything from negotiating Nordic grant application portals to sourcing obscure plumbing and outboard motorboat parts. Tusind tak, Jakob. Writing books is a lonely and often frustrating business, and so thanks to Nikolaj Jørgensen, Kim Salomonsen, and the good people of Vesterbronx Gym for allowing me to blather on about my writing woes when I should have been training. Thank you, too, to my friends and hitting partners at B93 Tennis Club. I owe a very special debt of gratitude to all my teammates in the Danish XL cricket league – even the ones I berate for their slow T20 strike rate. My life in Denmark would undoubtedly be much the poorer if not for your positivity, camaraderie, and boundless good humor. Skål boys. I should also especially like to thank two of my colleagues at the Faculty of Law, University of Copenhagen: Beatriz Martinez Romera for her conspiratorial sense of fun, and Amnon Lev for being a daily source of great encouragement, a stand-up guy, and excellent company in Copenhagen's better cocktail establishments. Thomas Basbøll has had much to say about this book over the last five years or so, most of which has been extremely useful. Thanks, Thomas, for your good guidance and for changing my mind about conspiracy theories.

My agent, Matthew Hamilton, deserves much praise both for believing in the project from the start and for giving me the confidence to write for a more general audience. Thanks, Matthew, for your calm reassurance and for taking a chance on a random academic from Denmark.

At Little Brown, Andreas Campomar has been a joy to work with.

I am grateful to him for shepherding me and my manuscript through the complex and unfamiliar ravines of trade publishing. Also at Little Brown, I had the good fortune to work with Holly Blood whose patience and positivity were much appreciated as we worked together to bring the manuscript to completion. Thanks also to David Bamford and Henry Lloyd for their help in this process.

I must, of course, also acknowledge the help and support of my family: Mum, Dad, my sisters Kathryn and Claire, and my ever-generous brother-in-law, Andrew Fowler. My nieces, Isabelle (Millenial) and Eleanor (Gen Z) read parts of the book and it has no doubt benefitted from their respective insights. Similarly, Alice, Dominick, and Rob Balantyne also helped by reminding me that young people today are as bright and inspiring as they have always been.

Finally, my greatest and most persistent debt in writing this book has been to my friends Kester Aspden and Simon Cottee. Remarkable authors themselves, Simon and Kester have selflessly taken large chunks of time out of their lives to listen to my ideas, correct my errant thinking, and offer all sorts of useful suggestions. Simon, thanks, for listening, advising, and cajoling – but, more importantly, for being a fearless, independent thinker and a funny and reliable correspondent. I would need a separate volume to detail all the ways Kester has helped in the writing of this book. At various points, he has acted as sounding post, critic, editor (twice), distractor, deal broker, and decimator of footnotes. Thanks, Kes, for caring about this project across its long and winding life course. But more importantly thanks for all the laughs and for lightening my day with your unique brand of humour – in the lonely world of writing books that matters, a lot.

Keith Hayward

Copenhagen, April 2024

Images

1 *The Big Brother* Kidult-scape. (Shutterstock)
2 Tate St Ives. (© Tate Joe Humphrys & Lucy Dawkins)
3 'Sweet bounce of youth'. Crocs 'Big Yellow Boot'. (Photo by Aruro Holms/Getty Images for NBA 2K24)
4 'Bronies' take it to the streets at BronyCon. (Photo by Andre Chung for The Washington Post via Getty Images)
5 'Silence sucks' campaign, 2017. (Sage Therapeutics)
6 The adultification of criminal justice. (Steve Liss)
7 If I knew you were going to be diagnosed with a neurodevelopmental disorder, I would have baked a cake. (DR Archive)
8 'What happens at day-care stays at day-care'. (Author's own)
9 The revolution will be advertised. (h.i.s.)
10 Trident Soft Gum's 'Be a kid again' advertisement. (Trident)
11 Dancing fools. (Maskot/Getty Images)
12 Guardian Labs 'generational translator' publication. (Kristian Niemietz/*Guardian News & Media*)
13 Neotenous advertising: Evian's Live Young campaign (2009-2018). (Evian)
14 The Uni-age cometh. (Photo by Clive Mason – Formula 1/ Formula1 via Getty Images; Shutterstock; iStock)

Notes

Introduction

1 Bywater, M. (2006: 9) *Big Babies?*, London: Granta.
2 e.g., Coyle, B. (2019) "What the f**k is maturity?": young adulthood, subjective maturity and desistance from crime', *The British Journal of Criminology*, 59(5): 1178–1198.
3 The term 'infantocracy' is associated with the author Milan Kundera who, in *The Art of the Novel* (1986, London: Faber and Faber) defined it as 'the ideal of childhood imposed on all humanity'. A fitting description of our times if ever there was one.
4 Ellis, B. E. (2019: 144) *White*, London: Picador.
5 Definitions derived from collinsdictionary.com, Google's English dictionary and thefreedictionary.com.
6 Gottschalk, S. (2018: 109) *The Terminal Self*, London: Routledge.
7 e.g., Sternbergh, A. (2006) 'Forever youngish: why nobody wants to be an adult anymore', *New York Times*, 3 April; Epstein, J. (2003) 'The perpetual adolescent', *Weekly Standard*, 15 March; Cohen, P. (2003) 'The long road to adulthood is growing even longer', *New York Times*, 12 June; Samuelson, R. (2003) 'Adventures in agelessness', *Newsweek*, 3 November; and Robin Marantz Henig's 2010 cover story for the *New York Times Magazine*, 'What is it about 20-somethings?: why are so many people in their 20s taking so long to grow up?' (*New York Times Magazine*, 18 August).
8 The word 'Kidult' has a relatively longer lineage, first appearing in the 1950s as a term used to describe adults who enjoyed watching children's TV programmes.

9 See Hymowitz, K. S. (2011) 'Where have the good men gone?', *Wall Street Journal*, 19 February; Rose, S. (2012) 'Why are there so many movies about guys who won't grow up?', *Guardian*, 12 May; Noxon, C. (2003) 'I don't want to grow up', *New York Times*, 31 August; Bucholz, T. and Bucholz, V. (2012) 'The Go-Nowhere Generation', *New York Times*, 10 March; Dugan, E. (2014) 'The Boomerang Generation: forced back to the nest by a lack of jobs and high cost of living', *Independent*, 21 January; and Davidson, A. (2014) 'It's official: the Boomerang Kids won't leave', *New York Times*, 20 June.

10 Scott, A. O. (2014) 'The death of adulthood in American culture', *New York Times Magazine*, 11 September.

11 Fry, R. (2016) 'For First Time in Modern Era, Living With Parents Edges Out Other Living Arrangements for 18- to 34-Year-Olds', Pew Research Center, https://www.pewresearch.org/social-trends/2016/05/24/for-first-time-in-modern-era-living-with-parents-edges-out-other-living-arrangements-for-18-to-34-year-olds/ and Wang, W. and Parker, K. (2014) 'Record share of Americans have never married', Washington DC: Pew Research Center, https://www.pewresearch.org/social-trends/2014/09/24/record-share-of-americans-have-never-married/.

12 Office for National Statistics: Statistical Bulletin (2022) 'Childbearing for women born in different years, England and Wales: 2020', https://www.ons.gov.uk/peoplepopulationandcommunity/birthsdeathsandmarriages/conceptionandfertilityrates/bulletins/childbearingforwomenbornindifferentyearsenglandandwales/2020; and Office for National Statistics: Statistical Bulletin (2023) 'Marriages in England and Wales: 2020', https://www.ons.gov.uk/peoplepopulationandcommunity/birthsdeathsandmarriages/marriagecohabitationandcivilpartnerships/bulletins/marriagesinenglandandwalesprovisional/2020.

13 Twenge, J. (2018: 226) *iGen*, Atria: New York.

14 With Latin roots meaning 'to nourish', the word *adolescens* has been in use in the English language since at least the early fifteenth century, primarily as a term to describe pre-pubescent boys who left the family home in search of work in a guild or trade, but also (in a later variant, *adolescentia*) as a cognate term for notions of 'youth', variously defined (Shahar, S. *Childhood in the Middle Ages* cited in Danesi, M. (2003: 7) *Forever Young*, Toronto: University of Toronto Press). However, it was the American psychologist G. Stanley Hall who essentially constructed adolescence as we know it today in his 1904, two-volume, 1400-page magnum opus *Adolescence: Its Psychology and its Relations to Physiology, Anthropology, Sociology, Sex, Crime, Religion and Education*. The legacy of Hall's work lies in the way it presented adolescence as an inherent problem. A keen student of German culture, Hall coined the phrase 'Sturm und Drang' ('storm-and-stress') as a shorthand term for the turbulent process of negative moods, problematic relationships (especially with parents) and risk-taking behaviour associated with the adolescent years.

15 Here I do not mean to suggest that the fundamental biological components associated with adolescence are fixed. Throughout history, the temporal onset of (biological) adolescence has ebbed and flowed as a result of a number of variables, including diet, climate and wealth.

16 Sawyer, S. Azzopardi, P. S. Wickremarathne, D. and Patton, G. C. (2018) 'The age of adolescence', *The Lancet Child & Adolescent Health*, 2(3): 223–228.

17 Pinkstone, C. (2022) 'Childhood can now last until you're 40: Demands of the modern world mean young people are now reliant on their parents for longer, says scientist', *Daily Telegraph*, 11 June, https://www.telegraph.co.uk /news/2022/06/11/childhood-can-now-last-40/.

18 Becker, R. (2022) 'Age queer: why we need queer age now more than ever', changingaging.org, 7 April, https://changingaging.org/ageism/age-queer/.

19 Erikson's eight stages of development are 'infancy', 'early childhood', 'play age', 'school age', 'adolescence', 'young adulthood', 'adulthood' and 'old age'.

20 Feist, J. and Feist, G. (1998: 257, emphasis in original) *Theories of Personality*, Boston: McGraw-Hill.

21 Hayward, K. J. (2012) 'Pantomime justice: a cultural criminological analysis of "life stage dissolution"', *Crime, Media, Culture*, 8(2): 213–229; Hayward, K. J. (2013) '"Life stage dissolution" in Anglo-American advertising and popular culture: Kidults, Lil' Britneys and Middle Youths', *The Sociological Review*, 61(3): 525–548.

22 Stein, J. and Townsend, M. (2021) 'Muslim boy, 4, was referred to Prevent over game of *Fortnite*', *Guardian*, 31 January. In recent years, the mission creep of the UK's Prevent programme has been remarkable. In 2022, Prevent counterterrorism operatives even started to probe school history curricula after concerns were raised that 'ideas about Britain's past could fuel far-Right extremism' (Simpson, C. (2022) 'Prevent officers probe school history lessons for far-Right links', *Daily Telegraph*, 12 June.

23 This bizarre idea was mooted (in a now-deleted tweet) by Flora Gill, a blue-check-marked journalist and daughter of the former UK home secretary Amber Rudd. The tweet went on: 'Young teens are already watching porn but they're finding hardcore, aggressive videos that give a terrible view of sex. They need entry level porn! A softcore site where everyone asks for consent and no-one gets choked etc'. Later, after Gill was dragged on Twitter, she subsequently tweeted that when she said 'children' she did not mean younger children: 'To clarify – children means under 18. I'm talking about 14/15/16 year olds.'

24 See Dastagir, S. (2022) 'What the public keeps getting wrong about pedophilia', *USA Today*, 17 January; Walker, A. (2021) *A Long Dark Shadow*, Berkeley: University of California Press.

25 *Standards for Sexuality Education in Europe* (2010) WHO Regional Office for Europe and BZgA.

26 Milmo, C. (2015) 'Sex teacher Stuart Kerner spared jail after judge says he was "groomed" by 16-year-old girl', *Independent*, 14 January.

27 Grossberg, L. (1992) *We Gotta Get Out of This Place*, New York: Routledge.

28 Sironi M. (2018) 'Economic conditions of young adults before and after the Great Recession', *Journal of Family and Economic Issues*, 39(1): 103–116.

29 e.g., Strimpel, Z. (2022) 'Who wants a middle-aged *Love Island*?: adult sexuality is being infantilised', unherd.com, 27 July, https://unherd.com/2022/07/who-wants-a-middle-aged-love-island/; Crispin, J. (2020) 'Pathologizing desire', *Boston Review*, 2 September. On the infantilisation of women in feminism more generally, see Daum, M. (2019) *The Problem with Everything*, New York: Gallery Books.

30 McWhorter, J. (2020) 'The Dehumanizing Condescension of *White Fragility*', *The Atlantic*, 15 July. See also Hughes, C. (2020) 'Black fragility', *City Journal*, 29 November.

31 Here, I should address a concern some may have about the way American and British examples are used interchangeably. Although the UK and the US differ in fundamental ways, in recent years, culturally at least, they have started to feel less and less distinct – so much so in fact one might even talk about the existence of something resembling a 'British American Culture' (n.b. The idea of a British American Culture is a reversal of the idea of an American British Culture, as set out in Russell Kirk's influential account of how the United States derived its language, mores and political purposes from Great Britain). This conflation is obviously the result of the heft and ubiquity of American mass consumerism. However, it's also symptomatic of a broader trend ushered in by the forces of globalisation, namely the diminution of national values and traditions and their replacement with a newer, more transposable and synchronous Anglo-American culture. Indeed, at a crude level, infantilisation can in part be understood as an all-too-vivid example of what happens when you replace something native and unique with something generic sourced from the Transatlantic pop-culture pound shop.

32 The phenomenon of arrested development has already spawned a range of neologisms around the world. The 'Germans speak of "Nesthocker," Italians of "Mammone," Japanese of "Freeter," Indians of "Zippies," and the French of a "Tanguy" syndrome and "puériculture"' (Barber, 2007: 3). In Japan there is considerable concern about the *otaku* youth subculture, a disaffected, highly individualised section of society that inhabits 'a kind of enclosed, virtual world of computer games and comics' (Bradley, J. P. N. (2015) 'Stiegler Contra Robinson: On the hyper-solicitation of youth', *Educational Philosophy and Theory*, 47(10): 1023–1038). Japanese culture is also replete with examples of adultification, including the problematic trend of 'junior idols' and

'schoolgirl pin-ups': pre-teenage girl singers and wannabe pop stars whose fans are overwhelmingly middle-aged Japanese men. Meanwhile, recent research on twenty-first-century linguistic patterns has identified infantilist trends in language everywhere from Russia to the Mediterranean (Martynnova, I. and Glukhov, G. (2015) 'Exploring the echoes of social change: case studies of language infantilism', *Mediterranean Journal of Social Sciences*, 6(6): 315–322.)

33 Virilio, P. (2006: 94) *The Information Bomb*, London: Verso.

Chapter 1

1 Meades, J. (2014) *Bunkers, Brutalism and Bloody-mindedness*, BBC4.

2 Calcutt, A. (1998) *Arrested Development*, London: Castell.

3 Martin, C. (2014) 'This sad generation doesn't know when the party stops', Vice.com, 1st December.

4 Grose, J. (2010) 'Omega males and the women who hate them', slate.com, 18 March.

5 Hoby, H. (2012) 'The slacker is back – and this time she's a female', *Guardian*, 25 March.

6 Queenan, J. (2013) 'Man of Steel: does Hollywood need saving from super-heroes?' *Guardian*, 12 June.

7 The vampire format (*The Twilight Saga, True Blood*) can also be interpreted as a story about teenagers never having to grow up. Likewise, the revival of the 'body-swap' movie (*The Change-Up, Freaky Friday, 13 Going on 30, 17 Again*) not only reflects a growing uncertainty about what it means to have an embodied identity, but also relies on a narrative form that turns around the uncoupling of generation and responsibility.

8 For an entertaining take on the infantilisation of the adult diet, see Fry, S. (2024) 'In Touch With the Inner Adult', available at: https://stephenfry. substack.com

9 Serrà, J., Corral, Á., Boguñá, M. *et al.* (2012) 'Measuring the evolution of contemporary Western popular music', *Sci Rep* 2: 521.

10 The sharp-eyed/eared among you will have spotted that both these lyrics are from songs by the ubiquitous US rapper Pharrell Williams. When searching for these lyrics online I stumbled across something called 'The Pharrell Williams Freedom Factsheet'. Produced by a company called Eduquas, the Freedom Factsheet perfectly illustrates the type of corporate-approved 'activism' often used in contemporary lyrics so banal they could have been generated by a word randomiser. According to the factsheet, 'Being "different" and rebelling against conformity is a main theme' in the multimillionaire Williams' work, as

is his commitment to political change which it claims 'cleverly combines corporate sponsorship (Apple Music) with social activism (UN International Day of Happiness).'

11 Metzeger, P. (2016) 'The Millennial Whoop: a glorious obsession with the melodic alternation between the fifth and the third', https://thepatterning.com/2016/08/20/the-millennial-whoop-a-glorious-obsession-with-the-melodic-alternation-between-the-fifth-and-the-third/

12 Harris, J. (2013) '*Clampdown: Pop-Cultural Wars on Class and Gender* by Rhian E Jones', *Guardian*, 16 May.

13 Thompson, J. (2018: 20) *The Orange Balloon Dog*, London: Quarto.

14 Greenberger, A. (2020) 'First there was Zombie Formalism – now there's Zombie Figuration', artnews.com, 9 July.

15 Adams, A. (2020) 'Banksy and the triumph of banality', www.thecritic.co.uk, January.

16 Vartanian, H. (2021) 'Kaws is terrible, but thankfully forgettable', hyperallergic.com, 2 September.

17 Davis, B. (2021) 'I looked through all 5,000 images in Beeple's $69 million Magnum Opus. What I found isn't so pretty', *artnet.com*, 17 March, https://news.artnet.com/opinion/beeple-everydays-review-1951656.

18 York, P. (1984: 64) *Modern Times*, London: William Heinemann.

19 Woodward, D. (2023) 'Why massive shoes are the trend of the year', bbc.com, 25 September.

20 Wampole, C. (2016) 'How to live without irony (for real this time)', *New York Times*, 19 December, https://www.nytimes.com/2016/12/19/opinion/how-to-live-without-irony-for-real-this-time-.html.

21 Calcutt, A (1998: 166).

22 Gallagher, J. (2022) 'The big men's fashion trend of 2022? Dressing like a Tween', *Wall Street Journal*, 6 January, https://www.wsj.com/articles/what-is-kidcore-11641485543.

23 Here, one could also point to the *adult* hobby of collecting 'Sonny Angel' dolls. See, for example, O'Neil, S. (2023, 'Why do people love this tiny doll?' *New York Times*, 6 April), in which one female devotee states that collecting Sonny Angel dolls is 'healing my inner child'.

24 The American youth 'super predator' myth was in large part based on a fallacious assertion made by the Harvard criminologist John Dilulio, who stated that by the year 2000, there would be, in his words, an additional 30,000 young 'murderers, rapists, and muggers' roaming the streets of America sowing mayhem. (Dilulio, J.J. (1995) 'The coming of the super-predators', *Weekly Standard*, 27 November). Backed up by conservative criminologists like James A. Fox, the super predator theory, with its semantics of a 'crime wave storm' and an impending 'bloodbath', contributed to a state of paranoia that in turn saw tens of thousands of young black men

swept up, arrested and imprisoned. In 2001, Dilulio admitted he had made a mistake, stating 'I'm sorry for any unintended consequences.'

25 Grossberg, L. (2001: 112) 'Why does Neo-liberalism hate kids?: the war on youth and the culture of politics', *The Review of Education/Pedagogy/Cultural Studies*, 23(2): 111-136.

26 See books such as *Bigger Kids, Bigger Problems: A Practical Handbook for Parents with Grown-Ups* by Paul Avila Mayer and Sasha Von Scherler (1998); *101 Ways to Get Your Adult Children to Move Out: And Make Them Think It Was Their Idea*, by Richard Melheim (1993); and *The Crowded Nest Syndrome: Surviving the Return of Adult Children* by Kathleen Shaputis (2016).

27 See Bolick, K. (2011) 'All the single ladies', *The Atlantic*, November; and for a lengthier discussion Kay Hymowitz's *Manning Up: How the Rise of Women Has Turned Men into Boys* (2011, New York: Basic Books).

28 Mintz, S. (2015: 17–25).

29 See, e.g. Arnett, J. J. (2004) *Emerging Adulthood*, New York: Oxford University Press; Arnett, J. J., Kloep, M., Hendry, L. and Tanner, J. (2010) *Debating Emerging Adulthood*, New York: Oxford University Press; Arnett, J. J. and Tanner, J. (2006) *Emerging Adults in America*, Washington, DC: American Psychological Association.

30 In 1960, 77 per cent of women and 65 per cent of men aged thirty had achieved the five benchmarks associated with adulthood; in 2000, these numbers had declined to 46 per cent and 31 per cent respectively. A further decline was noted for twenty-year-olds; down from 29 per cent (women) and 9 per cent (men) in 1960 to 6 per cent and 2 per cent respectively. Furstenberg, F., Kennedy, S., McLloyd, V. C., Rumbaut, R. G. and Setterston, R. A. (2004: 37) 'Growing up is harder to do', *Contexts*, 3 (3): 31–41. See also Berlin, G., Furstenberg, F. and Waters, M. C., (2010a) 'Transition to adulthood', *The Future of Children*, 20 (1) spring, and more generally the findings of the McArthur Foundation's Network on Transitions to Adulthood which recently stated that 'transitions to adulthood' now end at thirty.

31 Setterston, R., Furstenberg, F. and Rambaut, R. (2005: 5) *On the Frontier of Adulthood*, Chicago: Chicago University Press.

32 The National Institute of Mental Health study followed nearly 5,000 children between the ages of three and sixteen. Initially, it was expected that brain development (including the pruning of the synapses) would have stabilised by age eighteen but follow-up brain scans found that significant changes were still taking place well into the early twenties.

33 See Koganzon, R. (2010) 'Slacking as self-discovery: the rebranding of indolence as 'Emerging Adulthood', *The New Atlantis*, Fall for a thoughtful critique.

34 MacDonald, R., Shildrick, T., Webster, C. and Simpson, D. (2005: 874) 'Growing up in poor neighbourhoods: the significance of class and place in the extended transitions of "socially excluded" young adults', *Sociology*, 39 (5): 873-891.

35 See e.g., Jones, G. (2002), *The Youth Divide: Diverging Paths into Adulthood*, York: Joseph Rowntree; Côté, J. and Bynner, J. (2008), 'Changes in the transition to adulthood in the UK and Canada: the role of structure and agency in emerging adulthood', *Journal of Youth Studies*, 11 (3): 251–268. To be fair to Arnett, in recent years he has attempted to rebalance his account by training more attention on the issue of social class. But for his critics, Arnett's recent conversion to class pattern analysis is unconvincing in that it continues to downplay economic factors associated with employment, race and gender (see Furstenberg, F. F. (2016) 'Social class and development in early adulthood: some unsettled issues', *Emerging Adulthood*, 4, 236–238; du Bois-Reymond, M. (2016) 'Emerging adulthood theory under scrutiny', *Emerging Adulthood*, 4, 242–243).

36 Lerner cited in Marantz Henig (2010).

37 Côté, J. E. (2014) 'The dangerous myth of emerging adulthood: an evidence -based critique of a flawed developmental theory', *Applied Developmental Science*, 18(4): 177–188.

38 Berlin, G., Furstenberg, F. and Waters, M.C. (2010b: 3) 'Introducing the issue', 'Transition to adulthood', *The Future of Children*, 20 (1): 3–18.

39 The document office of a tropical fruit research plant is an unlikely place from which to revolutionise the history of childhood, but that was precisely what Philippe Ariès did in 1960 when, as director of a centre for international fruit commerce, he published his classic work, *Centuries of Childhood*. His (then) controversial argument was that, prior to the sixteenth century, the notion of childhood as a separate time of life simply did not exist. Drawing on examples from French cultural history – especially portraiture and textual accounts – Ariès asserted that childhood has never been about a fixed biological form. Instead, it is contingent on adult expectation and recognition, ascribed duties, functions and obligations, and most significantly material circumstance.

40 The foundational work here is Karl Mannheim's 1928 essay 'On the problem of generations'. Basing his assumptions on the collective shame felt by German society (especially its youth) in the aftermath of World War I, Mannheim argued that a generation could in part be defined by its shared response to a particular historical event. Put differently, a traumatic occurrence or prolonged societal experience can unite a generational cohort into a self-conscious age stratum.

41 Hutchison, E. (2003: 9) *Dimensions of Human Behaviour*, Thousand Oaks, CA: Sage.

Chapter 2

1 Chapman, A. H. (1968: 63) *Put-Offs and Come-ons: Psychological Maneuvers and Stratagems*, London: Cassell.

2 A good example of this logic in practice was a recent decision by the UK National Trust to have their staff and (typically older) volunteers be 'reverse-mentored' by children 'so they can explain the colonial history and slavery links of some of its country houses' (Hope, C. (2021) 'National Trust signs up children to lecture staff on colonialism', *Daily Telegraph*, 9 January, https://www.telegraph.co.uk/news/2021/01/09/national-trustsigns-childrento-lecture-staffon-colonialism/.

3 Twenge, J. and Campbell, W. K. (2013: 102-3) *The Narcissism Epidemic*, New York: Atria.

4 Lancy, D. (2008) *The Anthropology of Childhood*, Cambridge: Cambridge University Press. Lancy's classic 'Agrarian gerontocracy pyramid' has 'ancestors' at the apex, followed by 'elders', 'adults', 'adolescents' and 'children' in descending order. The modern neontocracy pyramid reverses this ordering, with children at the apex and parents and grandparents at the base.

5 See Rapley, G. and Murkett, T. (2014) *Baby-led Parenting*, Ebury Publishing; 'Baby-led weaning: what you need to know' (2021) Cleveland Clinic, 27 October, https://health.clevelandclinic.org/baby-led-weaning/; 'New journeys with toddler-led walks', Montessori Kids Universe, https://montessorikidsuniverse.com/new-journeys-with-toddler-led-walks/.

6 Lockwood, R. and Kelly, S. (2021) 'Young people should have a say in policies that affect their future', *Independent*, 27 December, https://www.independent.co.uk/independentpremium/voices/young-people-politics-covid-climate-change-b1982846.html.

7 For more on how brands and advertisers expand the ambiguity between children and teenagers see Cook, D. and Kaiser, S. (2004) 'Betwixt and Be Tween: age ambiguity and the sexualisation of the female consuming subject', *Journal of Consumer Culture* 4(2): 203–27.

8 Rush, E. and La Nauze, A. (2006) *Corporate Paedophilia: The Sexualization of Children in Australia*, The Australia Institute.

9 Williams, R. (2010) 'Too much too young? Retailers still selling over-sexualised clothing to kids', *Guardian*, https://www.theguardian.com/society/2010/apr/16/children-clothing-survey-bikini-heels.

10 Coughlan, S. (2013), 'Teachers attack "rebranded" sexism', bbc.com, 2 April, https://www.bbc.com/news/education-21990043.

11 Jackson, S. and Vares, T. (2016), '"Too many bad role models for us girls": girls, female pop celebrities and "sexualisation"', *Sexualities*, 18(4): 480–498;

Baker, S. (2001) 'Rock on baby! Pre-teen girls and popular music', *Continuum: Journal of Media and Cultural Studies*, 15(3): 359–371.

12 Birbalsingh, K. (2020), 'Is *Cuties* a dangerous movie?', spiked.com, 1 October, https://www.spiked-online.com/2020/10/01/is-cuties-a-dangerous-movie/.

13 In 2021, Arts Council England found themselves mired in controversy after they awarded funding to *The Family Sex Show*, a gender-awareness theatre group whose repertoire allegedly included a song encouraging five-year-old girls to masturbate. Eventually, following a public outcry, the funded shows were cancelled.

14 Mulholland, M. (2013) *Young People and Pornography*, New York: Palgrave Macmillan; Paul, P. (2005) *Pornified*, New York: Henry Holt.

15 Dines, G. (2017: 4) 'Growing up with porn: the developmental and societal impact of pornography on children', *Dignity: A Journal of Sexual Exploitation and Violence*, 2(3).

16 Needless to say, these figures disproportionality affect children of colour, 'with Black children 8.6 times more likely than their white peers to receive an adult prison sentence, while Latino youth are 40% more likely than white youth to be admitted to adult prison'. (Trolio, M. (2018) 'Locking up youth with adults', Prison Policy Initiative, 27 February, https://www.prisonpolicy.org/blog/2018/02/27/youth/). The situation is made even worse by the fact that, since as far back as 2008, the Department of Homeland Security has been locking up large numbers of undocumented children with adults in immigration centres across the country (Gordon, J. (2013) 'The US is locking up undocumented kids with adults', motherjones.com, 6 June).

17 Although not as acute, the problem of adultification in the criminal justice system is also evident in the United Kingdom. For well over a decade, concern about how children are being treated as adults has been a major issue for several charities and penal reformers. In 2012, for example, the mental health charity Young Minds voiced its concerns about the number of vulnerable children (some as young as eleven) being locked up in adult cells – in some cases for more than twenty-four hours. Likewise, in the same year, a report by the National Association for Youth Justice documented an 87 per cent increase in convictions of ten- to twelve-year-olds between 1997 and 2007. Shortly after, the House of Commons Justice Committee issued a warning about the 'needless criminalisation' of children in care for 'trivial incidents' (on one occasion, the police were called to a children's home over a broken cup!).

18 D'Agostino, R. (2014) 'The drugging of the American boy', *Esquire*, 27 March.

19 In 2012, one health trust in England almost seemed to be bragging about treating its youngest-ever patient – a two-year-old referred for child psychotherapy. Robinson, C. and Fenton, D. (2012) 'Five-year-olds treated for

depression and anxiety', bbc.com, 30 May, https://www.bbc.co.uk/news/uk-england-18251582.

20 Bates, K. (2019) 'Exams may damage teenagers' mental health and restrict their potential', 22 August, https://bold.expert/exams-may-damage-teenagers-mental-health-and-restrict-their-potential/. Interestingly, even when schools have moved away from examinations (as British schools did during the Covid-19 pandemic), the mental health fearmongering continued, with predictive grades immediately constructed as a source of mental health problems. Woolcock, N. (2021) 'Predicted grades "damage mental health of pupils"', *The Times*, 6 September.

21 Bly, R. (1996) *The Sibling Society: An Impassioned Call for the Rediscovery of Adulthood*, Reading, MASS: Addison-Wesley.

22 Unsurprisingly, this criticism is distilled to its essence by Christopher Hitchens in a column for *Vanity Fair*, 'Boomer wasteland', 16 January 1996.

23 Queenan, J. (2006: 27) *Balsamic Dreams,* New York: Picador.

24 There are many obvious social and cultural differences between Millennials and Baby Boomers. However, as the first Millennials reached their forties in 2022, it's interesting to note that, over time, the two cohorts have come to have at least one thing in common. Here I refer to the way both generations were perceived initially in very positive terms, but as time wore on were then recast in a far more negative light. For example, writing in 2000, Neil Howe and William Strauss (*Millennials Rising*, New York: Vintage Books), described Millennials as 'special', 'confident', 'optimistic', un-self-absorbed 'cooperative team players', 'accepting of authority' and the best-educated ('smartest') generation in history. Two decades on from that gushing assessment and it's clear that these observations have not aged well. This discrepancy has resulted in something of a backlash, with the term Millennial – like Boomer – now evoking mostly negative connotations. However, as Derek Thompson has argued, very often this type of pejorative commentary is based more on lazy stereotyping than demographic reality (Thompson, D. (2013) 'How to write the worst possible column about Millennials', *The Atlantic*, 4 November).

25 Bristow, J. (2015: 110) *Baby Boomers and Generational Conflict*, Basingstoke: Palgrave Macmillan.

26 Willetts, D. (2010: xv) *The Pinch*, London: Atlantic Books.

27 Bristow, J. (2019) 'The futility of generation wars', spikedonline.com, 21 June, https://www.spiked-online.com/2019/06/21/the-futility-of-generation-wars/.

28 Wysockly, K. (2012) 'Never-ending block party: Sean Kenney's full-time job is mere child's play—on a mighty grand scale', *American Way*, 1 November.

29 Hayward, K. J. and Turner, T. (2019) '"Be more VIP": deviant leisure, hedonism, and faux luxury culture in Ibiza's party spaces', in T. Raymen and O. Smith (eds) *Deviant Leisure: Criminological Perspectives on Leisure and Harm*. Palgrave.

30 Smith, O. (2014) *Contemporary Adulthood and the Night-Time Economy*, Basingstoke: Palgrave Macmillan.

31 Smith, O. (2015) 'Growing up, going out: adult cultural and aesthetic attachment to the nighttime economy', in Thurnell-Read, T, (ed) *Drinking Dilemmas*, London: Routledge.

32 It is worth noting that Erikson viewed the individual personality not purely as a psycho-biological phenomenon but also as a product of historical and cultural context. Trained in cultural anthropology, Erikson frequently utilised both anthropological research and sociological analyses to shape his theories on life cycle development.

Chapter 3

1 Jerry Rubin quoted in Greenfield, J. (1973: 247) *No Peace, No Place: Excavations Along the Generational Fault*, New York: Doubleday.

2 While the tentacles of teen culture and ergo infantilisation are today global in reach, the origins of both phenomena are distinctly American. It is for this reason that the story offered in this chapter takes place predominantly in the United States, for it was in the Petri dish of American twentieth-century popular culture that the teenager and its successor, 'the young adult', first replicated themselves.

3 Rebellious youth culture was not an invention of the post-war years and did not start with rock 'n' roll. As Hine notes in his definitive history of the teenager, by the end of the 1920s a discernible youth culture had already emerged: 'Young people were, for the first time, setting styles in clothing, hairstyle, music, dancing, and behavior on their own, and both adults and children looked to them as leaders. Young people were organizing their own social lives, and adults felt powerless when they rejected previous standards of propriety as irrelevant to modern life. Certainly, people in their teens had had fun before, but in the twenties it became a right.' (Hine, T. (1999: 179) *The Rise and Fall of the American Teenager*, New York: Avon Books).

4 Ibid., 157.

5 Danesi, M. (2003: 15).

6 This standard narrative of 'the Sixties' as a binary opposite of the 1950s was first articulated as early as the late-1960s in bestselling books like Theodore Roszak's *The Making of a Counter Culture* (1969) and Charles Reich's *The Greening of America* (1970), and has largely held sway in the popular imagination ever since.

7 Barker, R. G. and Gump, P. V. (1964) *Big School, Small School*, Stanford: Stanford University Press.

8 Hine, T. (1999: 254).

9 It was a similar story in the UK, where demand for university places outstripped supply to the extent that in 1964 the Conservative government hurriedly created seven bespoke new universities.

10 Much of the political ideology adopted by the student radicals can be traced to a spate of remarkably popular books such as Paul Goodman's *Growing Up Absurd* (1960), a perspicacious text that had much to say about upcoming generational upheaval; C. Wright Mills's *The Sociological Imagination* (1959); Betty Friedan's *The Feminine Mystique* (1963) and most significantly, Herbert Marcuse's *One-Dimensional Man* (1964). Although these books set the political agenda for Baby Boomer student radicalism, in reality they were all products of the 1950s and the critique of 'mass society' associated with post-war America.

11 For example, it is estimated that, for all the anxiety it induced, the 'Black Power' movement never gained more than a 10 per cent approval rating among the black urban poor it claimed to represent.

12 Lasch, C. (1965: 343-4) *The New Radicalism in America*, New York: W.W. Norton.

13 Farber, D. (1994: 2) 'Introduction', *The Sixties*, Chapel Hill: North Carolina University Press.

14 Gitlin, T. (1993: 258) *The Sixties*, New York: Bantam.

15 Abrams, P. (1970: 186 emphasis added) 'Rites de passage: the conflict of generations in Industrial Society', *Journal of Contemporary History*, 5(1): 175–190.

16 Keniston, K. (1971: 5) *Youth and Dissent*, New York: Harcourt Brace Jovanovich.

17 Rosenblatt cited in West, D. (2007: 52, emphasis West's).

18 It should be noted that the analysis of the political struggles of the 1960s presented here is limited to the United States. I recognise that elsewhere, most notably Latin America and Africa, political resistance took a very different form.

19 Mary Quant cited in Calcutt, A. (1998: 80).

20 Frank, T. (1997: 6-7, 9) *The Conquest of Cool*, Chicago: Chicago University Press.

21 Jerry Fields quoted in Frank, 111.

22 Frank, 24–25.

23 Heath, J. and Potter, A. (2006) *The Rebel Sell*, Chichester: Capstone.

24 Frank, 27–28.

25 Chapple, S. and Garofalo, R. (1977: 75) *Rock 'n' Roll is Here to Pay*, Chicago: Nelson Hall.

26 Truett Anderson, W. (1983) *The Upstart Spring: Esalen and the Human Potential Movement*, Addison-Wesley.

27 The Esalen Institute's Will Schutz (whose bestselling 1967 book, *Joy*, went

through nine printings in the late 1960s, and who did more than anyone to place 'Esalen and the human potential movement front and center on the world stage', http://www.esalen.org/page/will-schutz), made three consecutive appearances – including one thirty-minute segment – on America's number-one talk show, *The Tonight Show Starring Johnny Carson*.

28 Goldman, M. (2012) *The American Soul Rush: Esalen and the Rise of Spiritual Privilege*, New York: New York University Press.

29 It is important to recognise the inherently infantilising nature of these practices, as Paul Williams does in his article 'Jules Feiffer's *Tantrum* at the end of narcissism's decade', *Studies in the Novel*, 50(3): 378–399): 'Some of these therapies asked patients to relive birth or infancy: in Nude Therapy screaming naked participants re-experienced birth in the faux-amniotic ambience of California's swimming pools . . . Primal Therapy encouraged patients to cry, thrash, and scream in order to relive deep-rooted Pain and thus remove the neurosis created by that Pain's repression. Janov used childhood props to encourage the reliving of Primal Pain, including teddy bears, baby bottles, and cribs. Patients at Janov's Primal Institute could reportedly "relive the trauma of birth" by clambering through a birth simulator constructed from "tied-together inner tubes"'.

30 Marin cited in Lasch, C. (1979: 9) *The Culture of Narcissim*, New York: W.W. Norton.

31 The Yippies started out with typically grandiose plans to create a 'New Nation' via traditional collective methods such as demonstrations and food cooperatives, but when this failed to get off the ground, they turned to political pranks and crass guerrilla theatre in an attempt to make their often incomprehensible points.

32 In his autobiography, *Growing (Up) at Thirty-seven*, Stewie's fellow Yippie figurehead, Jerry Rubin, talks ad nauseum about his 'journey into myself', observing that 'from 1971 to 1975, I directly experienced est, gestalt theory, bioenergetics, rolfing, massage, jogging, health foods, tai chi, Esalen, hypnotism, modern dance, meditation, Silva Mind Control, Arica, acupuncture, sex therapy, Reichian therapy, and More House—a smorgasbord course in New Consciousness' (quoted in Lasch, C. (1979: 14). And, yet, despite all this industrial-scale self-examination, he still wound up as a stockbroker.

33 Albert quoted in the documentary series *The Century of the Self* (2002) Dir. Adam Curtis, BBC (episode 2, 'There is a policeman inside all our heads. He must be destroyed').

34 Danesi, M. (2003: 12).

35 Miller, J. (1987) *Democracy is in the Streets*, New York: Simon and Schuster.

NOTES

Part II

1 See Green, S. (2019) 'Millennial writer cries at work, puts mother on speakerphone after editor corrects her spelling', pjmedia.com 15 July, https://pjmedia.com/vodkapundit/2019/07/15/millennial-writer-cries-for-mother-at-work-when-editor-corrects-her-spelling-n249160

2 Weiland, D. M. (2020: 16) 'Helicopter parenting and the mental health of iGen college students', *Journal of Psychosocial Nursing and Mental Health Services, 58*(5): 16–22.

3 See Padilla-Walker, L. and Nelson, L. (2012) 'Black hawk down?: establishing helicopter parenting as a distinct construct from other forms of parental control during emerging adulthood', *Journal of Adolescence*, 35(5): 1177–1190; Hesse, C., Mikkelson, A. and Saracco, S. (2018) 'Parent–child affection and helicopter parenting', *Western Journal of Communication*, 82(4): 457–474.

Chapter 4

1 Danesi, M. (2003: ix).

2 Williams, R. (1980: 184-185), *Problems in Materialism and Culture*, London: Verso.

3 Schudson, M. (1993: 10) *Advertising, the Uneasy Persuasion*, London: Routledge.

4 Harvey, D. (1990: 156) *The Condition of Postmodernity*, Oxford: Blackwell; Jameson, F. (1984) 'Postmodernism, Or the Cultural Logic of late Capitalism', *New Left Review*, 146: 53-92.

5 Firat, A. and Venkatesh, A. (1995: 252) 'Liberatory postmodernism and the re-enchantment of consumption', *Journal of Consumer Research*, 22(3): 239–267.

6 Gabriel, Y. and Lang, T. (1995: 139) *The Unmanageable Consumer*. London: Sage.

7 Barber, B. (2007: 18) *Consumed*, New York: W.W. Norton.

8 Barber (ibid.: 7).

9 Schor, J. (2004: 9) *Born to Buy*, New York: Scribner.

10 In 2006 the 'Wassup?' campaign was inducted into the CLIO Hall of Fame and this success clearly influenced Anheuser-Busch's subsequent advertising. However, in 2015, as part of Bud Light's 'Up for whatever' campaign (itself a deliberate attempt to engender a sense of carefree, teenage spontaneity around their beer), the company was roundly condemned for inadvertently promoting 'a predatory rape culture' after adding the slogan 'The perfect beer for removing "no" from your vocabulary for the night' to their beer labels. https://www.entrepreneur.com/article/245608.

11 See the 2001 PBS documentary *Merchants of Cool*. (Dir. Barak Goodman).

12 Ebenkamp, B. and Odiorne, J. (2002) 'Panic regression', *Brandweek*, 28 January.

13 Başbuğ, B. (2019) *When Brand Communication Becomes Childish: Infantilization in 21st Century Advertising*, Grin Verlag.

14 Calcutt, A. (1998: 91).

15 Christy Wampole describes the ironic commercial as 'an ad that calls itself an ad, makes fun of its own format, and attempts to lure its target market to laugh at it and with it. It pre-emptively acknowledges its own failure to accomplish anything meaningful. No attack can be set against it, as it has already conquered itself. The ironic frame functions as a shield against criticism' (Wampole, C. (2016) 'How to live without irony (for real this time)', *New York Times*, 19 December, https://www.nytimes.com/2016/12/19/opinion/how-to-live-without-irony-for-real-this-time-.html).

16 Başbuğ. (2018: 164).

17 https://www.thedrum.com/news/2013/03/01/three-ad-campaign-celebrates-britain-s-love-sharing-silly-stuff-online.

18 Noxon's website is essentially a clearing house for companies who sell toys to grown-ups (adult pogo sticks, office desk toys, etc.), and a space to promote childish activities to adults, including adult skipping clubs and grown-up pyjama parties.

19 Konigsberg, E. (1995) 'Infantilisation', in S. Daly and N. Wise (eds) *Alt. Culture*, London: Fourth Estate.

20 Başbuğ. (2018: 183).

21 Barclaycard has form when it comes to advertising with life stage dissolution as a key theme. See e.g., their 'school's out' commercial (where adult office workers are depicted as rebellious schoolchildren) and their 'contactless technology' campaign, which featured adults 'commuting' on a child's' water slide and a rollercoaster.

22 Wong, S. (2018) 'Evian 'I Wanna #Live Young' campaign marks new chapter for brand', alistdaily.com, 27 August, (https://www.alistdaily.com/lifestyle/evian-i-wanna-liveyoung-campaign-marks-new-chapter-for-brand/).

23 For some time now, Haribo have advertised their products using generational role reversal techniques that see children cast in adult roles and, more commonly, adults cast as children (complete with childish mannerisms and dubbed children's voices). According to their own press release, these 'bring out the child inside' advertisements are designed specifically 'to create moments of childlike happiness'. 'Haribo weighs in with £4m TV creative for Tangfastics' (2021) grocerytrader.co.uk, 3 August, https://grocerytrader.co.uk/haribo-weighs-in-with-4m-tv-creative-for-tangfastics/.

24 https://www.statista.com/statistics/275741/us-halloween-costume-expenditure/.

Chapter 5

1 Quoted in Cummins, A. (2020) 'DBC Pierre: "You can be shut down from life for one mistake"', *The Guardian*, 1 August.

2 The neologism 'adulting' first emerged as a staple of Twitter hashtags and social network memes in 2013, the same year that saw the publication of Kelly Williams Brown's self-help book *Adulting: How to Become a Grown-Up in 535 (Easyish) Steps*.

3 Meyrowitz, J. (1984: 25, 32–37), 'The adultlike child and the childlike adult: socialisation in an electronic age', *Daedalus*, 113(3): 19–48.

4 See Rauch, J. (2021) *The Constitution of Knowledge*, Brookings Institution Press; Carr, N. (2020) *The Shallows*, New York: W.W. Norton; Alter, A. (2018) *Irresistible*, New York: Penguin.

5 Twenge, J. (2017: 64) *iGen*, New York: Atria.

6 Ibid., 177.

7 Poirier, A. (2013) 'France's 'lost generation' of jobless youth finds film portrait in Juliette', *The Guardian*, 21 July. https://www.theguardian.com/film/2013/jul/21/france-lost-generation-film-juliette.

8 Hymas, C. (2018) 'Social media is making children regress to mentality of three-year-olds, says top brain scientist', *Daily Telegraph*, 6 August, https://www.telegraph.co.uk/news/2018/08/05/social-media-regressing-children-mentality-three-year-olds-says/. See also Greenfield, S. (2015) *Mind Change*, London: Random House.

9 Wells, G., Horwitz, J. and Seetharaman, D. (2021) 'Facebook knows Instagram is toxic for teen girls, company documents show', *Wall Street Journal*, 14 September, https://www.wsj.com/articles/facebook-knows-instagram-is-toxic-for-teen-girls-company-documents-show-11631620739.

10 Haidt, J. (2021) 'The dangerous experiment on teen girls', *The Atlantic*, 21 November, https://www.theatlantic.com/ideas/archive/2021/11/facebooks-dangerous-experiment-teen-girls/620767/.

11 Haidt collates his data on the After Babel Substack, a free resource in which he helpfully lists and sorts more than one hundred academic articles on the social media–mental health dynamic.

12 Lukianoff and Haidt (2017: 24, 30).

13 See Gray, P., Lancy, D. and Bjorklund, D. (2023) 'Decline in independent activity as a cause of decline in children's mental well-being: summary of the evidence', *Journal of Paediatrics*, https://doi.org/10.1016/j.jpeds.2023.02.004.

14 Lukianoff and Haidt (2017: 193).

15 Harrington, M. (2020) 'For me, self-identification was a con', unherd.com, 9 December, https://unherd.com/2020/12/for-me-self-identification-was-a-con/.

16 Haidt, J. and Rose-Stockwell, T. (2019) 'The dark psychology of social

networks', *The Atlantic*, December, https://medium.com/the-atlantic/the-dark-psychology-of-social-networks-c6e684a507b5.

17 One only needs to recall the way hundreds of thousands of people cowardly withdrew their 'Je Suis Charlie' social media ident photos at the first charge of Islamophobia to realise that clicktivism is the politics of the weak and the uncommitted. See also Drumbl, M. A. (2012) 'Child soldiers and clicktivism: justice, myths, and prevention', *Journal of Human Rights Practice*, 4(3): 481–485, on the limited shelf life (and value) of global clicktivist campaigns.

18 The imperative to criticise and condemn also fuels another form of online fantasy. Here, I refer to the web detectives and grievance archaeologists who trawl the internet looking for historic tweets and other offensive postings made by celebrities or people who have recently emerged in the public eye. Presumably, such people believe they are acting as a force for good, but in reality, what they are involved in is a petty form of vengeance (often against individuals who naively posted stupid things when they were much younger) while upholding the hubristic fantasy that they are somehow helping to save the world from bigots, racists, etc.

19 Gottschalk, S. (2018: 57 emphasis added) *The Terminal Self*, London: Routledge.

20 More recently, it was reported that Loffredo has even gone so far as to have two fingers surgically removed in a bid to turn his left hand into a claw. Steinbuch, Y. (2022) 'French 'Black Alien' reportedly gets fingers sliced off to create a claw', *New York Post*, 22 November, https://nypost.com/2021/11/22/black-alien-gets-fingers-sliced-off-to-create-claw/.

21 Twenge, J. and Campbell, K. (2009) *The Narcissism Epidemic*, New York: Atria.

22 In Japan, Toko-san, a YouTuber and animal fanatic, spent £12,500 on an ultra-realistic border collie costume. Although not an example of surgical body modification, Toko-san's fixation with fulfilling his 'dream of becoming an animal', is another example of an internet-induced delusion (Crisp, J. (2022) 'Man succeeds in dogged quest to become a Lassie lookalike', *Daily Telegraph*, 26 May, https://www.telegraph.co.uk/world-news/2022/05/26/man-succeeds-dogged-quest-become-lassie-lookalike/).

23 Harrington, M. (2021) 'Gender, nationality, species: everything is fluid for Generation Z', unherd.com, 28 June, https://unherd.com/thepost/gender-nationality-species-everything-is-fluid-for-gen-z/.

24 Cottee, S. (2020: 763) 'The Western jihadi subculture and subterranean values', *British Journal of Criminology*, 60 (3): 762–781.

25 Cottee, S. (2022) *Watching Murder: ISIS, Death Videos and Radicalisation*, London: Routledge.

26 Hall, S. (2012) *Theorizing Crime and Deviance*, London: Sage.

27 Pfaller, R. (2017) *Interpassivity*. Edinburgh: Edinburgh University Press.

28 Yurchak, Y. (2005: 4, 75) *Everything Was Forever, Until It Was Not*, Princeton: Princeton University Press.

29 The term 'pharmaka' is an adaptation of the ancient Greek word *pharmakon* which translates as something that is both *remedy* and *poison*.

30 Agamben has argued that the only way to counter the 'technological barbarism' of the age is with a revitalised university culture. However, as he himself has stated on various occasions, any chance of this happening has already been lost. See, for example, Agamben, G. (2020) 'Requiem for the students.' https://d-dean.medium.com/requiem-for-the-students-giorgio-agamben-866670c11642).

31 Merchant, B. (2017) 'The father of mobile computing is not impressed', fastcompany.com, 15 September, https://www.fastcompany.com/40435064/what-alan-kay-thinks-about-the-iphone-and-technology-now.

Chapter 6

1 Shklar, J.N. (2006: 154) 'Rousseau's images of authority (especially in *La Nouvelle Héloïse*)' in P. Riley (ed), *The Cambridge Companion to Rousseau*, Cambridge: Cambridge University Press.

2 Hayes, D. (2021) 'Five ways to tell if your school is making a therapeutic turn', *Independent Schools Magazine*, www.independentschoolsmagazine.co.uk.

3 Deacon, M. (2010) 'Pupils who plagiarize from the web will get extra marks', *Daily Telegraph*, 5 April.

4 Algar, S. (2021) 'NYC wants schools to rethink honor rolls deemed 'detrimental' to students not making the grade', *New York Post,* 31 August.

5 An increasingly common practice in some US schools is to never give a grade below 50 per cent – even if the assignment is not handed in. In Boston, MA, Cambridge public schools controversially eliminated advance math in middle schools in a bid to reduce the disparity between low-income children of colour and more affluent students.

6 Furedi, F. (2009: 9) *Wasted*, London: Continuum.

7 Sellgren, K. (2019) 'Teachers face weekly violence from pupils, says survey', bbc.com, 20 April. An earlier survey by the Association of Teachers and Lecturers claimed that nearly 57 per cent of state schoolteachers had 'faced aggression from pupils in the last year', with 40 per cent of the respondents considering leaving the profession because of problems caused by student behaviour (BBC News (2014) 'Half of state schoolteachers face pupil aggression', 1 September).

8 A good example of this logic in wider culture was the 2019 documentary

series, *The Great British School Swap* (Channel 4, UK) in which pupils from different ethnic backgrounds were brought together in a superficial attempt to understand racial stereotypes. Promoted using the strapline, 'Can they solve what the adult world has failed to fix?', the show offered no real insights into the roots of racial prejudice and illustrated the futility of looking to children for answers to complex adult problems.

9 Eastwood, N. (2023) 'School children urged to go veggie and listen to whale songs during net zero lessons', *Daily Telegraph*, 28 August.

10 Furedi (Ibid., 5).

11 Ibid., 13.

12 In 2021, grade inflation in the UK reached an all-time high with nearly half (44.8 per cent) of all students receiving an A or A* grade at A-Level (up from 38.5 per cent in 2020 and 25.5 per cent in 2019). To put this in perspective, between 1963 and 1986 only 8–10 per cent of students received an A grade at A-Level.

13 Ecclestone, K. and Hayes, D. (2009) *The Dangerous Rise of Therapeutic Education*, Routledge: London.

14 See, for example, Robert Pondiscio's critical report on the drift towards SEL (social-emotional learning) in American education. Pondiscio, R. (2021) *The Unexamined Rise of Therapeutic Education*, American Enterprise Institute, 13 October.

15 In 2021, 'anxiety' was voted 'Children's word of the year.' In 2014 (when the initiative was launched) the word picked by children was 'Minions' and a year later it was 'hashtag'. The shortlist of words given to children are selected from the Oxford's Children Corpus, 'an online database of material from stories and poems written by children as well as books written by children's authors' (Davies, G. and Stephens, M. (2022) ' "Anxiety" voted children's word of the year', *Daily Telegraph*, 18 January.

16 Bellah, R., Madsen, R., Sullivan, W., Swider, A. and Tipton, S. (1996) *Habits of the Heart*, Berkeley: California University Press.

17 Furedi (Ibid., 189).

18 'Canvey Island School bans triangular shaped flapjacks', BBC News, 23 March 2013 https://www.bbc.com/news/uk-england-essex-21923218; 'School bans 'flossing' dance because Fortnite moves are intimidating children on playground', *Daily Telegraph*, 7 July.

19 Swain, H. (2012) 'Should students be given the power to decide how universities are run?', www.guardian.co.uk, 12 May.

20 Staffordshire Uni (2020) 23 April https://twitter.com/staffsuni/status/1253260864746131458?s=21

21 Gardiner, B. (2015) 'Top of the list of student demands: not lower fees, but more counselling', *Guardian*, 11 May.

22 Brown, J. (2013) 'Universities ignoring binge drinking culture and failing to protect students' wellbeing, say teachers', *Independent*, 6 March.

23 Gair, K. (2022) 'Here might be dragons: Aberdeen University gives Beowulf content warning', *The Times*, 4 August; Simpson, C. (2022) 'French course 'may be upsetting', students told in trigger warning', *Daily Telegraph*, 10 August; Hood, L. (2023) 'Aberdeen University criticised for putting trigger warnings on J.M. Barrie's Peter Pan', *Press and Journal*, 8 January.

24 'We recognise that a trigger warning such as this may also be triggering. That said, we felt it was necessary to include this warning based on the findings and conclusions of our investigation and the summary of our experiences and evidence contained in this report.' https://www.ucl.ac.uk/bartlett/sites/bartlett/files/the_bartlett_school_of_architecture_environmental_investigation_report_june_2022p_6.pdf.

25 McGahan, J. (2020) 'How a mild-mannered USC professor accidentally ignited adacemia's latest culture war', *Los Angeles Magazine*, 21 October, https://www.lamag.com/citythinkblog/usc-professor-slur/.

26 Coughlan, S. (2019) 'Dogs "prevent stressed adults dropping out"', https://www.bbc.com/news/education-48806935 2 July.

27 White, B. (2007: 351) 'Student rights: from in Loco Parentis to Sine Parentibus and back again', *Brigham Young University Education and Law Journal*, 27(2): 321–350.

28 Feiler, B. (2014) 'This weekend, college is for everyone', *New York Times*, 31 October.

29 Shulevitz, J. (2015) 'In college and hiding from scary stories', *New York Times*, 21 March.

30 Bryon, K. (2017: 116) 'From infantilizing to world-making; safe spaces and trigger warnings on campus', *Family Relations*, 66: 116–125.

31 A recent UK poll about safe spaces reported that fewer than half of university students 'consistently support free speech', with two fifths favouring censorship and the no-platforming of controversial speakers. Things are even worse in the United States, where a 2021 survey of 37,000 American college students found that 70 per cent believed a professor who says something that offends them should be reported to administrators. (Woolcock, N. (2019) 'Students turn against free speech amid "culture of conformity"', *The Times*, 11 November; College Free Speech Rankings, Foundation for Individual Rights in Education, 2021).

32 Somerville, E. (2021) 'Cambridge students' union in "witch hunt" over racism classes leak', *Telegraph*, 4 December.

33 Sokal, A. (2021) 'Catechism class at British universities', aeromagazine.com, 26 October.

34 Furedi (Ibid., 40). A good example of socialisation in reverse in practice is the tendency for educational institutions to include students on teacher hiring panels (Griffiths, S. (2019) 'Let pupils pick their teachers, says head', *Sunday Times*, 6 January).

35 Swain, H. (2012) 'Should students be given the power to decide how universities are run?', *Guardian*, 12 May, https://www.theguardian.com/education/2012/jun/11/universities-giving-students-more-power.

36 Watters, A. O. (2013: 60) 'Recentring pedagogy in an age of narcissism', *Journal of General Education*, 62(1): 52–66.

37 Swain, ibid.

38 Gerrard, S. (2019) 'The rise of the Comfort College', Bloomberg Opinion, 9 September, https://www.bloombergquint.com/gadfly/free-speech-is-no-longer-safe-speech-at-today-s-elite-colleges

39 Fazackerley, A. (2013) 'What to do next if you're too cool for university', *Guardian*, 18 March.

40 Whitbourne, S. K. and Cassidy, E. L. (1994) 'Psychological implications of infantilisation: a class exercise', *Teaching of Psychology*, 31(3): 167–168.

Part II

1 Žižek , S. (2016: 37–39) *Against the Double Blackmail*, London: Allen Lane.

Chapter 7

1 Ellis, B. E. (2019: 139-140) *White*, London: Picador.

2 Calcutt, A. (1998: 236).

3 Ibid., 111, 113.

4 Ibid., 4.

5 Initially, the term 'victim Olympics' had a tongue-in-cheek element to it, but as time has passed, it seems increasingly prophetic. For example, in February 2021, during the run-up to the Amir Khan/Kell Brook Welterweight boxing match, pre-fight media coverage went into overdrive after Khan accused his opponent of racism following Brook's description of Khan's chin as being 'like a poppadom'. However, like any good boxer should, Brook immediately slipped Khan's opening jab, and countered with a hook, claiming that Khan had previously homophobically abused him.

6 Pease, K. (2008: 588) 'Victims and victimisation', in Shoham, S.G., Kett, M. and Beck, O. (Eds.) *International Handbook of Penology and Criminal Justice*, New York: Taylor & Francis.

7 Ley, D.J. (2014) 'The culture of victimhood: hoaxes, trigger-warnings, and trauma-informed care', *Psychology Today*, 28 June.

8 Reilly, W. (2019) *Hate Crime Hoax*, Washington DC: Regnery Publishing.

9 McManus, S. (2021) 'Having dissociative identity disorder looks nothing

like it does on TikTok', medium.com, 27 March, https://medium.com/invisible-illness/having-dissociative-identity-disorder-looks-nothing-like-it-does-on-tiktok-995f266c57c9.

10 Fisher, M. (2013) 'Exiting the Vampire Castle', opendemocracy.net, 24 November, https://www.opendemocracy.net/en/opendemocracyuk/exiting -vampire-castle/

11 Similar tendencies were evident in the cultural response to the Russian invasion of Ukraine in 2022. Within days of the invasion, Anglo-American liberals were cancelling anything they could find that had a link to Russia, including performances of Tchaikovsky and exhibitions by Russian artists. Such gestures illustrate just how easy it is for those who claim to be champions of inclusion and diversity to code switch into meanspirited petty censors.

12 Cottee, S. (2020) 'Incel (E)motives: resentment, shame and revenge', *Studies in Conflict and Terrorism*, 44 (2): 93-1124.

13 See e.g., Heggehammer, T. (2017) *Jihadi Culture: The Arts and Social Practices of Militant Islamists*, Cambridge: Cambridge University Press; Cottee, S. and Hayward, K.J. (2011) 'Terrorist (e)motives: the existential attractions of terrorism', Studies in *Conflict and Terrorism*, 34(12) 963-986.

14 This situation is compounded by the fact many Western countries already view the Islamist terrorist as an infantilised other – 'a marginal person whose outstanding characteristic is vulnerability', and who is increasingly (re)framed, not as a dangerous agent of violence, but a 'victim of "extreme" ideas propagated by manipulative "groomers"' (Cottee, S. (2017) 'Snowflakes are not terrorists', *Foreign Policy*, 27 April).

15 Phibbs, T. (2020) 'Confessions of a student Marxist', unherd.com, 17 September, https://unherd.com/2020/09/confessions-of-a-student-marxist/.

16 Ok, E., Qian, Y., Strejcek, B. and Aquino, K. (2021) 'Signaling virtuous victimhood as indicators of dark triad personalities', *Journal of Personality and Social Psychology: Personality Processes and Individual Differences,*120(6):1634-1661.

17 Calcutt, A. (1998: 233).

18 Peyser, A. (2022) 'Clueless, narcissistic celebrities need to shut up about Ukraine', *New York Post*, 25 February.

19 Lunbeck, E. (2014: 41) *The Americanization of Narcissism*, Cambridge, MA: Harvard University Press.

20 Lasch, C. (1979: 7).

21 Lasch, C. (1984: 191, 12, 58, 185–186, 189, 192, 207).

22 Lasch, C. (1979: 173).

23 Twenge, J. M. and Campbell, W. K (2013: 30-31) *The Narcissistic Epidemic*, New York: Atria.

24 Frawley, A. (2015) *Semiotics of Happiness*, London: Bloomsbury.

25 Lasch, C. (1979: 218–222).

26 Lasch, C. (1984: 33).

27 Saward, J. (2014) 'The American Bro: a portrait of the worst guy ever', *Vice*, 21 March, https://www.vice.com/en/article/bn5jb8/this-american-bro-an-etho-logical-study.

28 Martin, C. (2014) 'How sad young douchebags took over modern Britain', vice.com 14 March, https://www.vice.com/en/article/kwpb43/anatomy-of-a-new-modern-douchebag.

29 Hall, S., Winlow, S. and Ancrum, C. (2008: 201) *Criminal Identities and Consumer Culture,* Cullompton: Willan. Interestingly, Hall and his colleagues also identified that, in a world where 'young people grow up in the market not at home', hyper-consumption has made even family life 'ridiculous', a sentiment that closely echoes Lasch's description of the modern family as 'a charade of togetherness'.

30 Lasch, C. (1979: 232).

31 Although Twenge and Campbell were focused on entitlement and not infantilisation, very late in their book they do acknowledge that one of the side effects of youthful fantasies (based on the will to celebritise) is *perpetual adolescence*: 'Adolescence is the most narcissistic time of life, and adolescence is being extended beyond all previous limits.' Twenge, J. M. and Campbell, W. K. (2013: 234).

32 Ibid., 113–114.

33 Williams, P. (2018: 385, 394–96) 'Jules Feiffer's *Tantrum* at the end of narcissism's decade', *Studies in the Novel*, 50(3): 378–399.

Chapter 8

1 Wilson, A. E. (1934) *Christmas Pantomime*. London: Allen & Unwin.

2 In 2016, several Norwegian politicians, including the prime minister, Erna Solberg, were caught playing *Pokémon GO* in the Storting, and in 2022, UK MP Neil Parish was forced to resign after being reported for watching pornography (twice) on his mobile phone in the House of Commons.

3 Earle, S. (2017) 'The new infantocracy in politics', https://www.opendemo-cracy.net/en/transformation/new-infantocracy-in-politics/.

4 Ibid.

5 When Rishi Sunak announced his campaign to succeed Boris Johnson as prime minister in July 2022, he did so inevitably with a slick promotional video released to Twitter. The video exemplified the mindset of the contemporary infantocrat in that it never mentioned anything substantive about politics or policy, but instead prioritised identity and emotionality. Laughably, it even began with the words 'Let me tell you a story'. The perfect verbal illustration of the late-modern politician as wet nurse.

6 Saul, H. (2016) 'David Cameron: the surprising description of him that he "hated"', *Independent*, 13 July; Buist, E. and Gani, A. (2014) 'David Cameron's top downtime tips', *Guardian*, 24 January.

7 Meyrowitz, J. (1985: 269, 279).

8 Earle, S. (2017) The schoolyard comparison also extends to contemporary UK politics. For example, in recent years the House of Commons and various governmental ministries have been affected by all sorts of (usually unproven) claims of bullying. As Stuart Waiton has observed, such incidents demean the entire notion of a 'grown-up' politics, despite moral claims to the contrary. Even anti-bullying initiatives become embroiled in infantilised discourse. In 2021, Lord Kalms and Lord Willoughby de Broke were banned from using House of Lords bars and restaurants for not undertaking compulsory anti-bullying training. It was later claimed that the two peers were being treated like 'recalcitrant schoolboys' who because they 'didn't do their prep, can't go to the tuck shop' (O'Toole, E. (2021) 'House of Lords: Peers band from 'tuck shop' over anti-bullying course', *The National*, 20 July).

9 https://x.com/potus/status/1752518567239536821?s=46

10 See e.g. Filipovic, J. (2017) 'The infantilization of adult professional women', *Cosmopolitan*, 10 October, https://www.cosmopolitan.com/politics/a12815874/female-politicians-little-girls/.

11 Barekat, H. (2020) 'Jess Phillips is not the answer', *The Tribune*, 3 January, https://tribunemag.co.uk/2020/01/jess-phillips-is-not-the-answer.

12 Carr, N. (2015) 'How social media is ruining politics', *Politico* magazine, 2 September. See also Carr's 2015 book *The Glass Cage*, New York: W.W. Norton.

13 Wright, L. A. (2020) *Star Power*, New York: Routledge; Kapoor, I. (2012) *Celebrity Humanitarianism*: Routledge.

14 Harvey, M. (2018: 27) *Celebrity Influence*, Lawrence, KS: Kansas State University Press.

15 Rosenberg, H. and Feldman, C. S. (2008: 1–2) *No Time to Think*, New York: Continuum.

16 Gold, T. (2020) 'Pretend politicians like Maxine Peake have never been more ill-informed or ineffective', *Guardian,* 26 June.

17 Cited in Nichols, T. (2017) 'How America lost faith in expertise', *Foreign Affairs*, March/April.

18 Hedges, C. (2009: 52) *Empire of Illusion*, New York: Nation Books.

19 For example, no account of the rise of partisanship in North America would be complete without a discussion of the prominent role played by local talk radio and its attendant right-wing blogs, a combination Mike Davis once colourfully referred to as 'the clogged toilets of nativist [US] hysteria' (Davis, M. (2007: 137) *In Praise of Barbarians*, Chicago: Haymarket Books).

20 Sontag, S. (2001) 'Talk of the town', *New Yorker*, 24 September.

21 Brooker, C. (2010) *Newswipe*, BBC Four, 1 April.

22 See Butler, I. and Drakeford, M. (2008: 382) 'Booing or cheering?: ambiguity in the construction of victimhood in the case of Maria Colwell', *Crime, Media, Culture*, 4(3): 367–385.

23 Gregg, A. R. (2012) '1984–2012 – The assault on reason', www.allangreg.com, https://allangregg.com/?p=80.

24 See Bail, C. (2021) *Breaking the Social Media Prism*, Princeton: Princeton University Press.

25 Vosoughi, S., Roy, D. and Aral, S. (2018) 'The spread of true and false news online', *Science*, 359:(6380): 1146–1151.

26 Meyer, R. (2018) 'The Grim Conclusions of the Largest-Ever Study of Fake News', *The Atlantic*, 8 March.

27 Bembenek, C. (2020) 'Conspiracy stand down: how extremist theories like QAnon threaten the military and what to do about it', *War on the Rocks*, 10 March, https://warontherocks.com/2021/03/conspiracy-stand-down-how-extremist-theories-like-qanon-threaten-the-military-and-what-to-do-about-it/.

28 Leslie, I. (2021) 'How to have better arguments online', *Guardian*, 16 May.

29 Dery, M. (2021) 'A Close Reading of the QAnon Shaman's Conspiracy Manifesto', Literary Hub, 15 November, https://lithub.com/a-close-reading-of-the-qanon-shamans-conspiracy-manifesto/.

30 Ballard, J. G. (2007) *Kingdom Come*, London: HarperCollins.

31 'Papering Over the Cracks: J.G. Ballard talks to Sarah O'Reilly' (2007: 6) in Ballard, J. G. *Kingdom Come*, London: HarperCollins.

32 On the unacknowledged roots of CRT in 'Re-evaluation counselling' and other pseudo-spiritual self-abnegation rituals see Parenti, C. (2021) 'The first Privilege Walk', nonsite.org, 21 November, https://nonsite.org/the-first-privilege-walk/.

33 On the long, chequered history of race training see Lasch-Quinn, E. (2002) *Race Experts: How Racial Etiquette, Sensitivity Training, and New Age Therapy Hijacked the Civil Rights Revolution*, W.W. Norton & Company: New York.

34 On this subject, see Hall, S. and Winlow, S. (2022) *The Death of the Left*, Bristol: Policy Press.

35 Bartholomew, J. (2015) 'The awful rise of virtue signalling', *Spectator*, 18 April.

36 Swift, D. (2019: 12) *A Left for Itself*, London: Zero Books.

37 This tendency to conflate political resistance with childlike fantasies is perfectly illustrated in the following quote by Tobias Phipps: 'And so Trump's opponents retreated to a world of fantasy, citing quasi-mythical modern folk tales in which good vs evil is binary and uncomplicated; on the one hand

414

Harry Potter, and on the other *Star Wars*. This fantasy caused people to refer to themselves, without any irony or embarrassment, as "the Resistance", a reference both to the Lucas space opera and to occupied France. But the point about being part of the "resistance" is you can't openly talk about it; otherwise, you're not really resisting, you're indulging yourself' (Phibbs, T. (2020) 'Confessions of a student Marxist', unherd.com. 17 September, https://unherd.com/2020/09/confessions-of-a-student-marxist/.

38 Epstein, B. (1991) *Political Protest and Cultural Revolution*, Berkeley: University of California Press.

39 Echolls, A. (1994: 164) 'Nothing distant about it: Women's Liberation and sixties radicalism', in D. Farber (ed) *The Sixties*, Chapel Hill, NC: University of North Carolina Press.

40 Hayward, K. J. and Schuilenburg, M. (2014) 'To resist=to create?': some thoughts on the concept of resistance in cultural criminology', *Cultur & Criminaliteit*, 4(1): 22–36.

41 Lasch, C. (1979: 82).

42 The political right is also guilty of this type of performative resistance. In 2016, Trump supporters started the #TrumpCup protest which involved ordering a coffee at Starbucks and stating their name is 'Trump'. If the barista refused, 'protesters' were urged to video the exchange as evidence of discrimination against Republicans.

43 The Pussy Hat is interesting in that it also illustrates something else about performative protest. I refer here to the way in which resistance can be easily monetised. Initially, the 'Pussyhat Project' was an open-source knitting pattern released so that women unable to attend a Women's March in person could show their support by crafting a pink hat out of recycled wool. However, it was not long before this symbol of resistance was picked up by the fashion house Missoni, who 'sidestepped the anti-capitalist, craftivist ethos of the project' by sending 'models down the runway in pussy hats' and selling their own version of the pink hat on their online store for £140 ($190) (Judah, H. (2018) 'After the year of the Pussy Hat, can fashion activism effect change?', *Artnet*, 3 January). Indeed, this fusion of consumerism with gestural anti-capitalism has emerged as something of a minor staple of the fashion industry. For example, today's pseudo-rebel can now pad out their wardrobe with such market-endorsed anti-capitalist items as a Vintage faux-blood-splattered Kent State sweatshirt (Urban Outfitters, $129), a sequined Ashish 'Stay Woke' T-shirt, a pre-distressed Crass anarchist/punk biker jacket (Urban Outfitters, $375) and even a polyamide rollneck sweater from the Michel Foucault range ($19.99, available in four colours).

44 Davenport, N. (2020) 'The rise of cutesy radicals', spiked.com, 18 May, https://www.spiked-online.com/2020/05/18/the-rise-of-cutesy-radicals/.

45 A similar mindset was evident in the left's response to the death of Margaret

Thatcher in 2013. Rather than using this moment to reflect on their own electoral shortcomings, left-wing activists instead expressed themselves in the only way they knew how: through popular culture and sending 'Ding-Dong! The Witch is Dead' to number two in the UK charts. It was a similar story a decade later when arguably the UK's biggest man-boy, anti-Brexit campaigner Steve Bray, scrambled to record the 'Bye Bye Boris' song following the resignation of Boris Johnson in 2022. These childish attempts at political humour are so lamentable they don't even qualify as satire.

46 Gray, J. (2020) 'The woke have no vision of the future', unherd.com, 17 June, https://unherd.com/2020/12/the-woke-have-no-vision-of-the-future-2/; Gurri, M. (2020) 'Hyper-moral politics and the flagellants of 2020', available at: https://wesleyyang.substack.com/p/hyper-moral-politics-and-the-flagellants.

47 See Gray, J. (2008) *Black Mass*, London: Penguin; and Applebaum, A. (2021) 'The new puritans', *The Atlantic*, 31 August, for a more contemporary gloss.

48 Codevilla, A. M. (2020) 'Millenarian mobs: an old and dangerous story', *Claremont Review of Books*, summer, https://claremontreviewofbooks.com /millenarian-mobs/.

49 Tourish, D. and Wohlforth, T. (2000: 6–13) *On the Edge: Political Cults Right and Left*, New York: Routledge.

50 @ghostofchristopherlasch (2022) 'Cringe dialectics', 28 February, https:// covidianaesthetics.substack.com/p/cringe-dialectics-ghostofchristo1. The very fact that many academics like CLAG now feel the need to 'go dark' rather than publish under their own name is itself an indictment on the state of public discourse in contemporary society.

51 Gottschalk, S. (2018) 'The infantilization of Western culture', theconversation.com, 1 August, https://theconversation.com/the-infantilization-of-western-culture-99556.

52 '. . . co-dependency is directly caused by the infantilization of the employee in today's workforce. I believe we are doing a disservice to our employees by attempting to cover ALL their needs—and thereby making sure they don't have to be responsible for any decisions other than the few we allow within their narrow job descriptions.' Hebert, P. (2018) 'The infantilization of the American workplace', HRExaminer.com, https://www.hrexaminer.com/the -infantilization-of-the-american-workforce/.

Index

417

INDEX

INDEX